THE PSYCHOLOGY OF SOCIAL CONFLICT AND AGGRESSION

The Sydney Symposium of Social Psychology series

This book is Volume 13 in the *Sydney Symposium of Social Psychology* series. The aim of the Sydney Symposia of Social Psychology is to provide new, integrative insights into key areas of contemporary research. Held every year at the University of New South Wales, Sydney, each symposium deals with an important integrative theme in social psychology, and the invited participants are leading researchers in the field from around the world. Each contribution is extensively discussed during the symposium and is subsequently thoroughly revised into book chapters that are published in the volumes in this series. For further details see the website at www.sydneysymposium.unsw.edu.au

Previous Sydney Symposium of Social Psychology volumes:

SSSP 1. FEELING AND THINKING: THE ROLE OF AFFECT IN SOCIAL COGNITION** ISBN 0-521-64223-X (Edited by J.P. Forgas). *Contributors*: Robert Zajonc, Jim Blascovich, Wendy Berry Mendes, Craig Smith, Leslie Kirby, Eric Eich, Dawn Macauley, Len Berkowitz, Sara Jaffee, EunKyung Jo, Bartholomeu Troccoli, Leonard Martin, Daniel Gilbert, Timothy Wilson, Herbert Bless, Klaus Fiedler, Joseph Forgas, Carolin Showers, Anthony Greenwald, Mahzarin Banaji, Laurie Rudman, Shelly Farnham, Brian Nosek, Marshall Rosier, Mark Leary, Paula Niedenthal, Jamin Halberstadt.

SSSP 2. THE SOCIAL MIND: COGNITIVE AND MOTIVATIONAL ASPECTS OF INTERPERSONAL BEHAVIOR** ISBN 0-521-77092-0 (Edited by J.P. Forgas, K.D. Williams, & L. Wheeler). *Contributors*: William & Claire McGuire, Susan Andersen, Roy Baumeister, Joel Cooper, Bill Crano, Garth Fletcher, Joseph Forgas, Pascal Huguet, Mike Hogg, Martin Kaplan, Norb Kerr, John Nezlek, Fred Rhodewalt, Astrid Schuetz, Constantine Sedikides, Jeffry Simpson, Richard Sorrentino, Dianne Tice, Kip Williams, Ladd Wheeler.

SSSP 3. SOCIAL INFLUENCE: DIRECT AND INDIRECT PROCESSES* ISBN 1-84169-038-4 (Edited by J.P. Forgas & K.D. Williams). *Contributors*: Robert Cialdini, Eric Knowles, Shannon Butler, Jay Linn, Bibb Latane, Martin Bourgeois, Mark Schaller, Ap Dijksterhuis, James Tedeschi, Richard Petty, Joseph Forgas, Herbert Bless, Fritz Strack, Eva Walther, Sik Hung Ng, Thomas Mussweiler, Kipling Williams, Lara Dolnik, Charles Stangor, Gretchen Sechrist, John Jost, Deborah Terry, Michael Hogg, Stephen Harkins, Barbara David, John Turner, Robin Martin, Miles Hewstone, Russell Spears, Tom Postmes, Martin Lea, Susan Watt.

SSSP 4. THE SOCIAL SELF: COGNITIVE, INTERPERSONAL, AND INTERGROUP PERSPECTIVES** ISBN 1-84169-062-7 (Edited by J.P. Forgas & K.D. Williams). *Contributors*: Eliot R. Smith, Thomas Gilovich, Monica Biernat,

Joseph P. Forgas, Stephanie J. Moylan, Edward R. Hirt, Sean M. McCrea, Frederick Rhodewalt, Michael Tragakis, Mark Leary, Roy F. Baumeister, Jean M. Twenge, Natalie Ciarocco, Dianne M. Tice, Jean M. Twenge, Brandon J. Schmeichel, Bertram F. Malle, William Ickes, Marianne LaFrance, Yoshihisa Kashima, Emiko Kashima, Anna Clark, Marilynn B. Brewer, Cynthia L. Pickett, Sabine Otten, Christian S. Crandall, Diane M. Mackie, Joel Cooper, Michael Hogg, Stephen C. Wright, Art Aron, Linda R. Tropp, Constantine Sedikides.

SSSP 5. SOCIAL JUDGMENTS: IMPLICIT AND EXPLICIT PROCESSES* ISBN 0-521-82248-3. (Edited by J.P. Forgas, K.D. Williams, & W. Von Hippel). *Contributors*: Herbert Bless, Marilynn Brewer, David Buss, Tanya Chartrand, Klaus Fiedler, Joseph Forgas, David Funder, Adam Galinsky, Martie Haselton, Denis Hilton, Lucy Johnston, Arie Kruglanski, Matthew Lieberman, John McClure, Mario Mikulincer, Norbert Schwarz, Philip Shaver, Diederik Stapel, Jerry Suls, William von Hippel, Michaela Waenke, Ladd Wheeler, Kipling Williams, Michael Zarate.

SSSP 6. SOCIAL MOTIVATION: CONSCIOUS AND UNCONSCIOUS PROCESSES* ISBN 0-521-83254-3 (Edited by J.P. Forgas, K.D. Williams, & S.M. Laham). *Contributors*: Henk Aarts, Ran Hassin,Trish Devine, Joseph Forgas, Jens Forster, Nira Liberman, Judy Harackiewicz, Leanne Hing, Mark Zanna, Michael Kernis, Paul Lewicki, Steve Neuberg, Doug Kenrick, Mark Schaller, Tom Pyszczynski, Fred Rhodewalt, Jonathan Schooler, Steve Spencer, Fritz Strack, Roland Deutsch, Howard Weiss, Neal Ashkanasy, Kip Williams, Trevor Case, Wayne Warburton, Wendy Wood, Jeffrey Quinn, Rex Wright, Guido Gendolla.

SSSP 7. THE SOCIAL OUTCAST: OSTRACISM, SOCIAL EXCLUSION, REJECTION, AND BULLYING* ISBN 1-84169-424-X (Edited by K.D. Williams, J.P Forgas, & W. Von Hippel). *Contributors*: Kipling D. Williams, Joseph P. Forgas, William von Hippel, Lisa Zadro, Mark R. Leary, Roy F. Baumeister, and C. Nathan DeWall, Geoff MacDonald, Rachell Kingsbury, Stephanie Shaw, John T. Cacioppo, Louise C. Hawkley, Naomi I. Eisenberger Matthew D. Lieberman, Rainer Romero-Canyas, Geraldine Downey, Jaana Juvonen, Elisheva F. Gross, Kristin L. Sommer, Yonata Rubin, Susan T. Fiske, Mariko Yamamoto, Jean M. Twenge, Cynthia L. Pickett, Wendi L. Gardner, Megan Knowles, Michael A. Hogg, Julie Fitness, Jessica L. Lakin, Tanya L. Chartrand, Kathleen R. Catanese and Dianne M. Tice, Lowell Gaertner, Jonathan Iuzzini, Jaap W. Ouwerkerk, Norbert L. Kerr, Marcello Gallucci, Paul A. M. Van Lange, Marilynn B. Brewer.

SSSP 8. AFFECT IN SOCIAL THINKING AND BEHAVIOR* ISBN 1-84169-454-2 (Edited by J.P. Forgas). *Contributors*: Joseph P. Forgas, Carrie Wyland, Simon M. Laham, Martie G. Haselton Timothy Ketelaar, Piotr Winkielman, John T. Cacioppo, Herbert Bless, Klaus Fiedler, Craig A. Smith, Bieke David, Leslie D. Kirby, Eric Eich, Dawn Macaulay, Gerald L. Clore, Justin Storbeck, Roy F. Baumeister, Kathleen D. Vohs, Dianne M. Tice, Dacher Keltner, E.J. Horberg, Christopher Oveis, Elizabeth W. Dunn, Simon M. Laham, Constantine Sedikides, Tim Wildschut, Jamie Arndt, Clay Routledge, Yaacov Trope, Eric R. Igou, Chris Burke, Felicia A. Huppert, Ralph Erber, Susan Markunas, Joseph P. Forgas, Joseph Ciarrochi, John T. Blackledge, Janice R. Kelly, Jennifer R.Spoor, John G. Holmes, Danu B. Anthony.

SSSP 9. EVOLUTION AND THE SOCIAL MIND* ISBN 1-84169-458-0 (Edited by J.P. Forgas, M.G. Haselton, & W. Von Hippel). *Contributors*: William von Hippel, Martie Haselton, Joseph P. Forgas, R.I.M. Dunbar, Steven W. Gangestad, Randy Thornhill, Douglas T. Kenrick, Andrew W. Delton, Theresa E. Robertson, D. Vaughn Becker, Steven L. Neuberg, Phoebe C. Ellsworth, Ross Buck, Joseph P. Forgas, Paul B.T. Badcock, Nicholas B. Allen, Peter M. Todd, Jeffry A. Simpson, Jonathon LaPaglia, Debra Lieberman, Garth J. O. Fletcher, Nickola C. Overall, Abraham P. Buunk, Karlijn Massar, Pieternel Dijkstra, Mark Van Vugt, Rob Kurzban, Jamin Halberstadt, Oscar Ybarra, Matthew C. Keller, Emily Chan, Andrew S. Baron, Jeffrey Hutsler, Stephen Garcia, Jeffrey Sanchez-Burks, Kimberly Rios Morrison, Jennifer R. Spoor, Kipling D. Williams, Mark Schaller, Lesley A. Duncan.

SSSP 10. SOCIAL RELATIONSHIPS: COGNITIVE, AFFECTIVE, AND MOTIVATIONAL PROCESSES* ISBN 978-1-84169-715-4 (Edited by J.P. Forgas & J. Fitness). *Contributors*: Joseph P. Forgas, Julie Fitness, Elaine Hatfield, Richard L. Rapson, Gian C. Gonzaga, Martie G. Haselton, Phillip R. Shaver, Mario Mikulincer, David P. Schmitt, Garth J.O. Fletcher, Alice D. Boyes, Linda K. Acitelli, Margaret S. Clark, Steven M. Graham, Erin Williams, Edward P. Lemay, Christopher R. Agnew, Ximena B. Arriaga, Juan E. Wilson, Marilynn B. Brewer, Jeffry A. Simpson, W. Andrew Collins, SiSi Tran, Katherine C. Haydon, Shelly L. Gable, Patricia Noller, Susan Conway, Anita Blakeley-Smith, Julie Peterson, Eli J. Finkel, Sandra L. Murray, Lisa Zadro, Kipling D. Williams, Rowland S. Miller.

SSSP 11. PSYCHOLOGY OF SELF-REGULATION: COGNITIVE, AFFECTIVE, AND MOTIVATIONAL PROCESSES* ISBN 978-1-84872-842-4 (Edited by J.P. Forgas, R. Baumeister, & D.M. Tice). *Contributors*: Joseph P. Forgas, Roy F. Baumeister, Dianne M. Tice, Jessica L. Alquist, Carol Sansone, Malte Friese, Michaela Wänke, Wilhelm Hofmann, Constantine Sedikides, Christian Unkelbach, Henning Plessner, Daniel Memmert, Charles S. Carver, Michael F. Scheier, Gabriele Oettingen, Peter M. Gollwitzer, Jens Förster, Nira Liberman, Ayelet Fishbach, Gráinne M. Fitzsimons, Justin Friesen, Edward Orehek, Arie W. Kruglanski, Sander L. Koole, Thomas F. Denson, Klaus Fiedler, Matthias Bluemke, Christian Unkelbach, Hart Blanton, Deborah L. Hall, Kathleen D. Vohs, Jannine D. Lasaleta, Bob Fennis, William von Hippel, Richard Ronay, Eli J. Finkel, Daniel C. Molden, Sarah E. Johnson, Paul W. Eastwick.

SSSP 12. PSYCHOLOGY OF ATTITUDES AND ATTITUDE CHANGE* ISBN 978-1-84872-908-7 (Edited by J.P. Forgas, J. Cooper, & W.D. Crano). *Contributors*: William D. Crano, Joel Cooper, Joseph P. Forgas, Blair T. Johnson, Marcella H. Boynton, Alison Ledgerwood, Yaacov Trope, Eva Walther, Tina Langer, Klaus Fiedler, Steven J. Spencer, Jennifer Peach, Emiko Yoshida, Mark P. Zanna, Allyson L. Holbrook, Jon A. Krosnick, Eddie Harmon-Jones, David M. Amodio, Cindy Harmon-Jones, Michaela Wänke, Leonie Reutner, Kipling D. Williams, Zhansheng Chen, Duane Wegener, Radmila Prislin, Brenda Major, Sarah S. M. Townsend, Frederick Rhodewalt, Benjamin Peterson, Jim Blascovich, Cade McCall.

* Published by Psychology Press
** Published by Cambridge University Press

THE PSYCHOLOGY OF
SOCIAL CONFLICT
AND AGGRESSION

Edited by

Joseph P. Forgas
University of New South Wales

Arie W. Kruglanski
University of Maryland

Kipling D. Williams
Purdue University

Ψ Psychology Press
Taylor & Francis Group

New York   London

Psychology Press
Taylor & Francis Group
711 Third Avenue
New York, NY 10017

Psychology Press
Taylor & Francis Group
27 Church Road
Hove, East Sussex BN3 2FA

© 2011 by Taylor and Francis Group, LLC
Psychology Press is an imprint of Taylor & Francis Group, an Informa business

International Standard Book Number: 978-1-84872-932-2 (Hardback)

**Visit the Taylor & Francis Web site at
http://www.taylorandfrancis.com**

**and the Psychology Press Web site at
http://www.psypress.com**

Contents

SECTION III   CONFLICT AND AGGRESSION IN RELATIONSHIPS

SECTION IV   SOCIAL, CULTURAL, AND EVOLUTIONARY FACTORS IN SOCIAL CONFLICT AND AGGRESSION

Preface

The collection of chapters in this book reviews some of the most recent advances in the study of social conflict and aggression, one of the most perennial and puzzling topics in all of psychology. The chapters represent a variety of theoretical orientations, ranging from evolutionary approaches through cognitive, affective, neuropsychological, and clinical theories all the way to social and cultural analyses of the nature and characteristics of conflict and aggression. Few topics are as important yet as poorly understood about human nature as the question of why *Homo sapiens* happens to be such a uniquely conflict-prone and aggressive species.

The book aims to provide an up-to-date integration of some of the most recent developments in social psychological research on this issue, offering an informative, scholarly, yet readable overview of recent advances in research on the nature, antecedents, management, and consequences of interpersonal and intergroup conflict and aggression. The chapters included here share a broad integrative orientation and will argue that human conflict is best understood through the careful analysis of the cognitive, affective, and motivational processes of those involved in conflict situations, supplemented by a broadly based understanding of the evolutionary, biological, as well as social and cultural contexts within which social conflict occurs.

The book is divided into four parts. Section I deals with basic questions such as the following: What role do early attachment experiences play in determining how people manage and deal with interpersonal and intergroup conflict in later life? Why is social exclusion and ostracism—being ignored and rejected by others—such an important source of conflict and aggression, and what determines whether those who are ostracized respond in prosocial rather than antisocial ways to their predicament? What are the psychological characteristics of those very common everyday behaviors (e.g., spitefulness, condescension, derogation) that fall short of serious and intentional harm-doing yet necessarily produce aversive consequences? What determines how hard and how far people will push in getting their way with others—in other words, what determines assertiveness?

The second section addresses the cognitive, affective, and motivational influences on how people perceive and manage social conflicts, seeking answers to questions such as the following: Why do people sometimes react in an adversarial way to the inferred goals and motives of others? What role do affective states and moods play in the way people perceive, manage, and resolve social conflicts? How can one best manage anger to perform optimally in negotiating situations? How can we explain the apparently irrational and self-sacrificial violence of terrorists and suicide bombers—is the quest for positive social identity and personal significance a possible explanation?

Section III looks at the way conflict and aggression occur in social relationships, perhaps the most common everyday setting for real-life conflict experiences. Chapters in this section investigate a number of intriguing questions. For example, why is violence between couples so often explained and treated in terms of feminist explanations that focus on male dominance rather than being based on the best available psychological evidence that does not support feminist ideology? What is the role of the interdependent versus conflicting goals of partners in producing relationship conflict? How do people in relationships cope with the consequences of being ignored and ostracized, one of the most common real-life conflict strategies in relationships? What role does forgiveness play in conflict management and resolution—could it be that forgiveness is sometimes counterproductive and may result in suboptimal outcomes for victims?

Section IV of the book analyzes conflict and aggression in terms of large-scale evolutionary, social, and cultural mechanisms and seeks answers to questions such as the following: How can we best explain the almost universal tendency in all human societies for tribalism and intergroup violence? Are there evolutionary pressures for a distinctive "male warrior" culture to emerge? If the global warming hypothesis is indeed correct, what are the likely implications of the predicted climate change for interpersonal, intergroup, and intercultural conflict in the decades to come? What are the consequences of violence presented in the media and especially on the Internet for the prevalence of conflict and aggression in our societies? What is the role of apparently irrational, supernatural beliefs in fostering in-group cohesion and intergroup conflict? And finally, how does a religious upbringing and practice help to prevent aggression and violence in later life?

One needs to recognize, of course, that no single book could possibly include everything that is interesting and exciting in current research on conflict and aggression. In selecting and inviting our contributors, we aimed to achieve a broad and varied coverage that is nevertheless representative of the major new developments in social psychological research on conflict and aggression. The chapters included here represent some of the best examples of clear theorizing and careful research in this critically important area.

THE ORIGINS OF THIS BOOK: THE SYDNEY SYMPOSIUM OF SOCIAL PSYCHOLOGY SERIES

This book is the thirteenth volume in the Sydney Symposium of Social Psychology series, held every year at the University of New South Wales (UNSW), Sydney. Perhaps a few words are in order about the origins of this volume and the Sydney Symposium of Social Psychology series in general. First, we should emphasize that this is not simply an edited book in the usual sense. The objective of the Sydney Symposia is to provide new, integrative understanding in important areas of social psychology by inviting leading researchers in a particular field to a 3-day residential symposium in Sydney. This symposium has received financial support from the University of New South Wales and the Australian Research Council, allowing the careful selection and funding of a small group of leading researchers as contributors. Draft papers by all contributors are prepared and circulated well in advance of the symposium and are placed on our dedicated website. Thus, participants had an opportunity to review and revise their papers in light of everybody else's draft contribution even before they arrived in Sydney.

A vital part of the preparation of this book has been the intensive 3-day face-to-face meeting among all invited contributors. Sydney Symposia are characterized by open, free-ranging, and critical discussion among all participants, with the objective of exploring points of integration and contrast among the proposed papers. A further revision of each chapter is prepared soon after each symposium, incorporating many of the shared points that emerged in our discussions. Thanks to these collaborative procedures, the book does not simply consist of a set of chapters prepared by researchers in isolation. Rather, this Sydney Symposium volume represents a collaborative effort by a leading group of international researchers intent on producing a wide-ranging and up-to-date review of research on the nature, antecedents, and consequences of social conflict and aggression.

We hope that the published papers will succeed in conveying some of the sense of fun and excitement we all shared during the symposium. For more information on the Sydney Symposium series and details of our past and future projects (as well as photos that show our contributors in more or less flattering situations, and other background information) please see our website (www.sydneysymposium. unsw.edu.au). Twelve previous volumes of the Sydney Symposium series have been published. All Sydney Symposium books feature original contributions from leading international researchers on key issues in social psychology. Detailed information about our earlier volumes can be found on the series page in this book and also on our website.

Given its breadth of coverage, the present book should be useful both as a basic reference book and as an informative textbook to be used in advanced courses dealing with social conflict and aggression. The main target audience for this book comprises researchers, students, and professionals in all areas of the social and behavioral sciences, such as social, cognitive, clinical, counseling, personality, organizational, forensic and applied psychology, and sociology, communication studies, and social work. The book is written in a readable yet scholarly style, and students at the undergraduate and at the graduate level should find it an engaging overview of the field and thus useful as a textbook in courses dealing with social conflict and aggression. The book should also be of particular interest to people working in applied areas where dealing with and understanding the processes involved in preventing, managing, and resolving social conflict and aggression are important, such as organizational, forensic, clinical, counseling, educational, sports, and health psychology.

We want to express our thanks to the people and organizations that helped to make the Sydney Symposium of Social Psychology series, and this thirteenth volume in particular, a reality. Producing a complex, multiauthored book such as this is a lengthy and sometimes challenging task. We have been very fortunate to work with such an excellent and cooperative group of contributors. Our first thanks must go to them. Because of their help and professionalism, we were able to finish this project in record time and ahead of schedule. Past friendships have not been frayed, and we are all still on speaking terms; indeed, we hope that working together on this book has been as positive an experience for them as it has been for us.

The idea of organizing the Sydney Symposia owes much to discussions with and encouragement by Kevin McConkey, Peter Lovibond, and numerous others at the UNSW. Our past and present colleagues at the School of Psychology at UNSW such as Marilynn Brewer, Kip Williams, Bill von Hippel, and Tom Denson and friends and colleagues from further afield have helped with advice, support, and sheer hard work to share the burden of preparing and organizing the symposium and the ensuing book. We are especially grateful to Suellen and Bill Crano, who helped in more ways than we could list here. We also wish to acknowledge financial support from the Australian Research Council and UNSW, support that was of course essential to get this project off the ground. Most of all, we are grateful for the love and support of our families who have put up with us during the many months of work that went into producing this book.

Joseph P. Forgas, Arie W. Kruglanski, and Kipling D. Williams
Sydney, Australia

List of Contributors

Daniel Ames
Columbia University
New York, New York, USA

Craig A. Anderson
Iowa State University
Ames, Iowa, USA

Joanna E. Anderson
University of Waterloo
Waterloo, Ontario, Canada

Paul Boxer
Rutgers University
Newark, New Jersey, USA
and
University of Michigan
Ann Arbor, Michigan, USA

Tanya L. Chartrand
Duke University
Durham, North Carolina, USA

John Christner
University of Pennsylvania
Philadelphia, Pennsylvania, USA

Matt DeLisi
Iowa State University
Ames, Iowa, USA

Thomas F. Denson
University of New South Wales
Sydney, Australia

Ed Donnerstein
University of Arizona
Tucson, Arizona, USA

Eric F. Dubow
Bowling Green State University
Bowling Green, Ohio, USA
and
University of Michigan
Ann Arbor, Michigan, USA

Chris Eckhardt
Purdue University
West Lafayette, Indiana, USA

Emma C. Fabiansson
University of New South Wales
Sydney, Australia

Eli J. Finkel
Northwestern University
Evanston, Illinois, USA

Gráinne M. Fitzsimons
University of Waterloo
Waterloo, Ontario, Canada

Joseph P. Forgas
University of New South Wales
Sydney, Australia

Adam D. Galinsky
Northwestern University
Evanston, Illinois, USA

Debra Gilin
Saint Mary's University
Halifax, Nova Scotia, Canada

Georgina S. Hammock
Augusta State University
Augusta, Georgia, USA

L. Rowell Huesmann
University of Michigan
Ann Arbor, Michigan, USA

Arie W. Kruglanski
University of Maryland
College Park, Maryland, USA

Robert Kurzban
University of Pennsylvania
Philadelphia, Pennsylvania, USA

N. Pontus Leander
Duke University
Durham, North Carolina, USA

Laura B. Luchies
Northwestern University
Evanston, Illinois, USA

William W. Maddux
INSEAD
Fontainebleau, France

Mario Mikulincer
Interdisciplinary Center (IDC),
  Herzlyia
Herzliya, Israel

Edward Orehek
University of Groningen
Groningen, the Netherlands

Deborah South Richardson
Augusta State University
Augusta, Georgia, USA

Phillip R. Shaver
University of California, Davis
Davis, California, USA

Hui Bing Tan
University of New South Wales
Sydney, Australia

Mark Van Vugt
University of Amsterdam
Amsterdam, the Netherlands

Eric D. Wesselmann
Purdue University
West Lafayette, Indiana, USA

Kipling D. Williams
Purdue University
West Lafayette, Indiana, USA

Lisa Zadro
University of Sydney
Sydney, Australia

Section *I*

Introduction and Basic Issues

STUDYING CONFLICT AND AGGRESSION

The study of human aggression, the violence of people against their own kind, is also one of the most time-honored and fundamental topics of psychological research and, before that, of social philosophy. Many of the great thinkers over the centuries have addressed the topic, including Plato, Niccolo Machiavelli, Thomas Hobbes, Georg Spinoza, and Jonathan Swift. In psychology, all the venerated grand theorists of our discipline commented on human aggression including William James, Sigmund Freud, William McDougall, and Konrad Lorenz. Even Albert Einstein was moved to comment on human destructiveness that he explained in terms of the inborn "lust for hatred and destruction."

The centrality of conflict and aggression as a key topic for understanding human nature is evidenced by the fact that it has been studied from an extremely broad variety of psychological perspectives, including motivational theories of instinct, behavioral theories of learning, cognitive approaches to information processing and attribution, evolutionary theories, models of self-regulation and automaticity, and biological and neuroscientific vantage points.

Aggression and conflict are now also foundational topics in social psychology, as they were in sociology and anthropology before. Probably no single topic enjoys as much cross-disciplinary interest as aggression. Major theories and much empirical research on these topics emerged from many fields, including sociology, behavioral genetics, anthropology, ethology, philosophy, literature, and biology. Within psychology, every subdiscipline is represented: developmental, clinical and counseling, cognitive, neuroscience, human and animal learning, motivation, and industrial and organizational psychology. The major grand theories in psychology all weigh in on aggression: Freud's psychoanalytic theory, B. F. Skinner's behaviorism, and Carl Rogers's and Abraham Maslow's humanism have all proposed explanations for and mechanisms to guard against aggression. This all-encompassing interest is undoubtedly because even though aggression and conflict are ubiquitous among nearly all animals they are especially so among humans. As the chapters in this book suggest, conflict and aggression can alternatively be viewed as functional or dysfunctional, can be analyzed at the individual, relational, and societal level, and are often discussed as a constant source of concern as a legal, political, and social problem.

DEFINITIONS OF CONFLICT AND AGGRESSION

Given the ubiquity of conflict and aggression, one may think that at the very least we do know what it is that we are talking about. Alas, this is not the case. A recent international symposium on conflict (Kruk, 2009) representing nearly all of the relevant disciplines resulted in spirited discussion about whether there was even common agreement about the definition of aggression. Whereas intent to harm was a core definitional property used in many of the disciplines, others required additional features such as overt actions, while some denied that intention to harm is even relevant to a definition (see also Chapter 4). Some focused solely on direct aggression, whereas others considered indirect and subtler forms. So, to ask whether conflict and aggression are related presupposes that everyone has a mutually agreed-on definition for aggression and for conflict. Rather than imposing consensus, it is probably best to acknowledge the existing diversity of definitions and foci, as we do here, so that further research can determine the extent to which these concepts are related or operate by different processes.

To determine the extent that conflict and aggression are related, one must ask, "Do factors that increase (or decrease) aggression—however we define it—also similarly increase conflict?" If the same factors have similar effects on our measures of both constructs, then we can claim a degree of functional overlap. If a factor increases aggression but decreases conflict, then we have evidence that we are talking about two very different things. The research represented in this book certainly suggests that conflict and aggression are at least related—conflict often, but not always, leads to aggression, and aggression is as likely as not to perpetuate and exacerbate conflict. We should also note, however, that whereas conflict often has functional, real-world origins and is therefore often resolvable by nonaggressive and rational means, aggression in contrast is often based on deeply seated, universal, and subconscious human characteristics that often defy rational explanation and resolution (see especially Chapters 10, 15, and 18).

PSYCHOLOGICAL APPROACHES TO CONFLICT AND AGGRESSION: A HISTORICAL OVERVIEW

In general, psychological research on conflict and aggression addressed three fundamental questions: (1) Where does conflict and aggression come from? (2) What elicits it? and (3) What modifies it?

Where Do Conflict and Aggression Come From?

Several early theorists stressed the universal and instinctual nature of conflict and aggression. In this vein, James assumed that human "bellicosity" was biologically rooted and that people were the most formidable of all the beasts of prey. Freud (1922), in reacting to the huge atrocities of World War I, assumed that humans have an innate aggressive drive, the death instinct or *thanatos*. In an imaginative, if not poetic (but also rather far-fetched) theoretical move, he assumed that the *thanatos* stems from people's basic drive to escape stimulation and to return to the peace and quiet of the inorganic world. Why, then, do people not just go ahead and kill themselves? Because of the contrary force embodied in the life instinct, or *eros*. As a consequence, the *thanatos* is displaced, and instead of killing themselves people find conflict with and aggress against others; in this way they find an outlet to instinctual pressures that would have otherwise led to their own demise.

In a somewhat similar vein, McDougall (1921) postulated a *pugnacity* instinct in his famous *Introduction to Social Psychology*. For McDougall, an instinct was a general propensity to pay attention to a given class of objects, to experience a given emotion to those objects, and to act toward them in a particular manner. McDougall also believed that the instinctual disposition could be modified by learning, so that initially neutral stimuli repeatedly associated with original instigators could come to excite the instinctive process. Of course, such instinct-based explanations really amount only to a semantic sleight of hand—by calling aggression an instinct we are no closer to understanding its fundamental nature and origins.

Later on, Konrad Lorenz (1966), known as the "father of ethology," also embraced the instinct doctrine in the explanation of aggression. Ethologically minded researchers, basing their theories on the careful observation of other species, thus saw aggression as a species-specific adaptation system, an innate behavioral tendency that is ultimately functional by promoting the survival of the group (as do also some recent evolutionary models of aggression; see Chapters 15 and 18). Aggression is released in response to specific stimuli. Lorenz's model uses a hydraulic system metaphor, where pent-up pressure is released by the right kinds of eliciting stimuli.

Lorenz, an avowed pessimist about the aggressive tendencies of our species, suggested that to reduce the likelihood of major "explosions" of aggression it is beneficial to engage in slow and controlled releases of aggressive energy, for example, in the form of competitive games or sport. Not surprisingly, such grand insights based on generalizations of observations of lower animals, including the Greylag goose, resulted in Lorenz being much vilified and ridiculed. His notion of instinct was much narrower than those of McDougall and Freud; whereas they talked of a general but flexible tendency whose expression can take different forms, Lorenz assumed that instincts involve rigid fixed action patterns that have their own energies and that are released by specific stimuli.

Are instinct notions of aggression dead? Not exactly. McDougall's approach, though heavily criticized in his own day, anticipated Len Berkowitz's contemporary approach in which the tendency to aggress is seen as innate, can be elicited subconsciously, for example through exposure to a weapon, but is also flexible and modifiable by learning. In this model, all members of the species are assumed to possess the innate capacity to aggress, just like they have the innate capacity for language—what Steven Pinker (1994) labeled "the language instinct." The way this innate proclivity for conflict and aggression is expressed may vary depending on a variety of factors. Just like you may express the language instinct by speaking French, Hungarian, or English, one may express one's aggressive instinct by playing hockey or rugby, spreading malicious rumors, writing nasty reviews about the work of others, or engaging in terrorist activities.

What Elicits Conflict and Aggressive Behavior?

The situational cues and circumstances that elicit conflict and aggression represent the second fundamental area of investigation addressed by researchers. Freud, in his early theorizing, before introducing the concept of the *thanatos*, believed that aggression arose when pleasure-seeking or pain-avoidance impulses were thwarted. McDougall argued (contrary to Lorenz) that no specific category of stimuli sets off the aggressive process. According to him, the instigation of aggression has to do with the experience of frustration or interference with activities dictated by other instincts. In this sense, McDougall's view is rather similar to that offered by the early work of Freud.

Intriguingly, the notion that thwarting is at the root of aggression found a powerful and influential reformulation in the well-known frustration–aggression hypothesis by Dollard, Doob, Miller, Mowrer, and Sears (1939). The frustration–aggression link is also central to Berkowitz's (1993) neoassociationist model of aggression in which aggression is assumed to follow from anger (see also Chapter 9), and anger, in turn, is assumed to follow from some unpleasant experience, such as having one's foot stepped on, having someone rear end your car, or finding out that the classy wine you just ordered in a restaurant tastes like vinegar. In this sense, Berkowitz's view is related to the notion of thwarting: thwarting of your wishes to have your foot free of pain, or your taste buds pleasantly stimulated rather than shocked and traumatized.

What Modifies Conflict and Aggression?

In contrast to the rigid model of conflict and aggression predicting inflexible fixed action patterns as described by Lorenz's ethological approach, most contemporary theories recognize that conflict and aggression in humans occur in highly flexible and contextually determined ways and can be modified by a variety of mental and situational factors. Much research attention has been paid to the question of what modifies aggression—indeed, most of the chapters featured here deal with the cognitive (Chapter 7), affective (Chapters 8 and 9), motivational (Chapters 6 and 10), and cultural as well as ideological mediators of conflict and aggression (Chapters 18 and 19). More specifically, a variety of psychological mechanisms have been shown to influence conflict and aggression.

Modeling   Albert Bandura's theoretical work on modeling of aggression has been extensively applied to the question of whether aggression in the media may or may not increase the viewers' tendency to aggress. The scientific consensus on this point seems to be that depiction of violence in the entertainment media legitimizes aggression and increases the tendency to aggress (see also Chapter 17). The U.S. surgeon general came to this conclusion, and so did six professional societies of physicians and psychologists. Despite the impressive scientific consensus and the strength of the evidence on which it is based, the entertainment industry and the news media remain largely skeptical about the suggestion that violence in the media has any adverse social effects. Depictions of ever more ingenious forms of conflict and violence in the media continue unabated.

Catharsis   The question of whether aggression has a cathartic effect has been examined by a great deal of research, and the general answer seems to be in the negative. However, a more nuanced view suggests that aggression against a perpetrator of some offense (whether alone or with others) can be satisfying and may reduce one's tendency to aggress against that person, and in this limited sense aggression is cathartic. On the other hand, such satisfaction may on occasion also act as a reinforcer and may increase the tendency to employ aggressive means in the future.

Norms   In the same way that modeling and media depictions may legitimize aggression, other social norms and regulations may have the opposite effects, reducing and delegitimizing conflict and aggression. For instance, gender differences in physical aggression have been partially explained in terms of social norms, as were cross-cultural differences in the display of aggressive behaviors, in particular the notion that individualistic cultures are more aggressive than collectivistic cultures (see also Chapters 11 and 15).

Hormones   The hormonal basis of aggression has been tied to testosterone, and the tentative conclusion seems to be that a connection exists between the male hormone and assaultive behavior. Intriguingly, the connection seems to be bidirectional—high degrees of testosterone appear to augment aggressive behavior, and situations that elicit aggression in turn increase the level of testosterone.

Evolution   The evolutionary approach to aggression has led to several intriguing recent lines of research and theorizing (see also Chapters 15 and 18). Among others, it has been applied to the finding that blood relatives kill each other rarely as well as to gender differences in aggression and the finding that spouse battering and abuse are more likely to occur among lower (vs. higher) socioeconomic classes (see also Chapter 11).

In an impressively audacious analysis, Koestler (1972) even argued that the human species suffers from a serious evolutionary flaw, in that our brain evolved in a way that is characterized by the poor neural integration between the lower, emotional and the higher, symbolic and rational areas. Koestler, reviewing an impressive range of psychological, neurological, anatomical, as well as historical and sociological evidence, went so far as to suggest that our species is doomed to extinction by our own unchecked aggressive tendencies, unless we first find a way to correct the flawed structural properties of our central nervous system. Koestler wrote at a time when the nuclear annihilation of all humans was a distinct possibility, and his theories received their fair share of criticism; however, the idea that the unparalleled human capacity for intraspecies violence may reflect a serious evolutionarily flaw remains and intriguing possibility (see also Chapter 15).

Self-Regulation   The self-regulation perspective on aggression departs from the notion that the impulse to aggression is automatic or innate. Instead, self-regulation models suggest that conflict and aggression are amenable self-regulatory efforts. However, the successful application of self-regulatory control against aggression requires scarce psychological resources. The self-regulatory framework suggests that depleting one's resources would necessarily reduce one's ability to control aggression.

The chapters in this book offer a broad range of new insights on these issues and focus on how conflict and aggression can be modified, for example, by intraindividual (see Chapters 6, 8, and 12) as well as by interpersonal (see Chapter 14) and social and cultural variables (see Chapters 10, 17, and 19).

MEASURING AND OPERATIONALIZING
CONFLICT AND AGGRESSION

Perhaps more than in other areas of social psychology, conflict and aggression researchers have employed an ingenious variety of measures in an effort to render their operational definitions isomorphic with the concept of intending harm. From the earliest research on aggression, clever methods have abounded that attempt to bridge the gap between measuring aggression on one hand and being ethical on the other. This is a tough requirement that makes aggression measures delightfully clever yet always a bit short of the mark. Thus, in addition to the well-known measures of punching Bobo dolls (Bandura, Ross, & Ross, 1961) and pressing levers to shock another individual (Buss, 1961; Milgram, 1974), researchers have placed participants into a situation in which they are asked to sound painful or unpleasant blasts of noise, to deliver hot sauce to individuals who are on record as disliking hot sauce (Lieberman, Solomon, Greenberg, & McGregor, 1999), to choose a weapon with which to shoot another participant (Russell, Arms, Loof, & Dwyer, 1996), to draw graffiti on classic works of art (Norlander & Gustafson, 1997), or even to kill pill bugs in a grinder (Martens, Kosloff, Greenberg, Landau, & Schmader, 2007). Of course, there are also self-report measures of what participants would like to do to another individual (i.e., aggressive temptations and desires) that list any number of mean acts from insult to severe injury (see Ritter & Eslea, 2005, for a review of these methods; see also Chapter 9).

Yet one issue that remains a concern in all areas that examine aggression and conflict is the external validity of the measures and their relevance to understanding real-world aggression and conflict. In much laboratory work, concern for ethical treatment of participants outweighs desires for externally valid measures. Thus, aggression is measured symbolically, indirectly, and almost always, with the implicit or explicit approval of the experimenters. Presenting participants with the opportunity to shock another person, to deliver loud noise blasts, or to serve mass quantities of hot sauce that another individual must consume all have in common an intent to harm another, but within the context of experimental permission and to that extent these measures lack a key characteristic of real-life aggression: that it is socially undesirable and often sanctioned.

To claim, therefore, that these studies necessarily predict aggression in the real world assumes that the impact of external permission is negligible. But this assumption is questionable. It would be like saying to high school students as they enter the building, "Here are some guns; you may use them if you wish." Clearly, in the real world, people are aware that being aggressive is undesirable, unwanted, and often unlawful. Experimental paradigms should attempt to capture and manipulate "nonpermissible, inappropriate" aggression so that we can accumulate evidence as to whether permission matters for the both patterns and magnitudes of aggression.

Similarly, the use of games in conflict research has had a long history of controversy, yet such simulated and controlled conflict situations are clearly useful in some contexts (see also Chapter 8). However, many conflicts in the real world are not so structured with clear rules and outcomes and are not conducted under the eye of experimenters who have created and supervise the rules. Neighbors argue over property and fences and are free to use a variety of tactics but are also mindful that the tactics they choose might be used against them in a court of law. These types of unstructured, freewheeling, yet nonpermissible forms of conflict are also important to study, and experimental social psychologists should strive to create paradigms that create such an atmosphere within a controlled context (see also Chapters 3, 4, and 13). These contexts are not easy to create; otherwise, we would have seen them by now. But social psychologists are a clever bunch, and undoubtedly someone will devise such a paradigm in the future. We hope the future is soon.

OVERVIEW OF THE VOLUME

Section I: Basic Issues and Theories

The book is organized into four parts. The first part, after this introductory chapter, is devoted to discussing some of the basic issues and recent theories that inform contemporary research on conflict and aggression.

Chapter 2, by Mario Mikulincer and Phillip Shaver, offers a novel, attachment theoretical perspective on interpersonal and intergroup conflict. In particular, they suggest that attachment theory can help us to understand how (1) people experience and cope with interpersonal conflicts, (2) maladaptive forms of resolving relationship conflicts arise, and (3) intergroup hostility and aggression can be understood within an attachment theoretical framework. Attachment theory offers important new insights to help explain individual differences in adaptive and maladaptive forms of conflicts and conflict resolution in relationships. The chapter also suggests that attachment theory can be a useful framework to understand a person's attitudes and behavior toward out-groups and their propensity for intergroup conflict.

In Chapter 3, Kipling Williams and Eric Wesselmann outline a comprehensive theory of ostracism—being ignored and excluded. Ostracism is a painful yet common experience, and humans seem to be equipped with an evolved mechanism for detecting and responding to cues of exclusion. Such an ostracism detection system can be triggered by even the most minimal cues, and responses to ostracism serve to fortify the need satisfaction threatened by ostracism. The chapter reviews research on reactions to ostracism, particularly on when and why individuals choose aggressive responses rather than prosocial options, and suggests that an important factor in ostracized individuals' responses is the likelihood of being reincluded depending on their behavioral responses.

In Chapter 4, Deborah Richardson and Georgina Hammock look at a variety of "everyday" forms of conflict and aggression that are often ignored in aggression research: passive and psychological aggression that is not motivated by the intention to cause harm (e.g., inducing guilt), although the effect is often to harm the target. Whereas direct or physical aggression is relatively rare in day-to-day life, indirect or psychological aggression such as snide remarks or hostile attitudes are very common. Indirect aggression is likely to affect individuals' relationship experience and success as well as their sense of self. Richardson and Hammock's research program brings to the forefront forms of everyday harm-doing and moves the focus of aggression from the intent of the aggressor to the effect on the victim. Such a victim-centered definition is consistent with a simple definition of aggression as any behavior that causes harm.

In Chapter 5, Daniel Ames discusses another common and universal aspect of social conflict and aggression: what determines the extent to which people will seek to be assertive and push hard for their interests? In daily interactions, we must frequently choose between giving in or asserting our wishes over others. When should we push? Can we push too hard? Ames explores peoples' informal theories of assertiveness and their expectancies for success. What are the short-term gains but long-term losses in being assertive? The chapter argues that we all have a general belief as to how assertive we should be and how likely it will lead to success. Further, people will adjust these expectations depending on the other individuals with whom a conflict arises.

Section II: Cognitive and Affective Influences

The second part of the book deals with cognitive and affective influences on the way conflict and aggression occurs. In Chapter 6, Pontus Leander and Tanya Chartrand explore the cognitive and motivational mechanisms involved when an individual's own goals conflict with the goals and preferences held by others. Such goal conflicts often emerge and escalate automatically in social situations. In some circumstances people will automatically accommodate to the goals and preferences of the people around them. However, more recent studies indicate that the mere knowledge about others' goals is often sufficient to elicit adversarial responses, especially when the individual is nonconsciously pursuing goals that are oriented toward social divergence or competition (e.g., achievement, autonomy, self-enhancement). Thus, interpersonal conflicts may often unfold automatically, as individuals are not always conscious of the origins of their interpersonal conflicts or know that such conflicts have even occurred.

Chapter 7 explores the role of perspective taking and empathy in conflict strategies. Adam Galinsky, Debra Gilin, and William Maddux suggest that the cognitive skill and ability to become aware of others' thoughts and the affective capacity for empathy—feeling what the others are feeling—play a very important role in how individuals deal with and resolve conflicts. Their experiments point to the benefits in terms of payoffs of perspective taking over empathy. They also find, however, that in certain circumstances in which shared feelings are important empathy might result in better outcomes and more positive social benefits.

Chapter 8 looks at affective influences on conflict behaviors. Joseph Forgas and Hui Bing Tan argue that mood states have a strong and reliable effect on the way people perceive, interpret, and respond to conflict. They report numerous experiments showing that positive affect produces a more confident, optimistic, and assertive response to conflicts, as happy people negotiate more confidently, make interpersonal demands more assertively, and interpret their own and others' social behaviors more optimistically. Other studies find that negative moods can also produce distinct benefits in conflict situations, when close attention to external information is required. Thus, those in negative mood are better at detecting deception, are less likely to commit judgmental errors, have better eyewitness memories, and produce more effective persuasive messages.

Anger regulation and negotiation is the topic of Chapter 9 by Thomas Denson and Emma Fabiansson. They examine the effectiveness of different emotion regulation strategies such as reappraisal, rumination, and distraction in controlling anger during negotiation. Denson and Fabiansson present the results from two experiments exploring what impact different anger regulation strategies have on behavior in negotiations. Their results suggest that the application of reappraisal in negotiation settings is useful in reducing anger, aggressive behavior, and conflict compared with rumination or distraction. Thus, training in reappraisal skills may be particularly beneficial for individuals who would otherwise use other emotion regulation strategies.

In Chapter 10, Arie Kruglanski and Edward Orehek look at the role of the quest for personal significance and identity in extreme forms of aggression such as terrorism and suicide bombers. What is the psychological explanation for the motivation to become a suicide bomber? They suggest that a quest for personal significance may be an underlying factor. Ironically, the act of carrying out a suicidal mission on behalf of one's group or religion can elevate one's sense of importance and meaning. In other words, death ensures a sense of immortality. In a series of ingenious experiments, Kruglanski and Orehek provide initial support for their provocative theory.

Section III: Conflict and Aggression in Relationships

This section of the book turns to research on conflict and aggression that occur within the framework of established personal relationships.

In a thoughtful Chapter 11, Chris Eckhardt discusses the damaging role that entrenched feminist ideology has played in the way intimate couple violence is defined, understood, and dealt with within the U.S. social and judicial system. Eckhardt reviews the known risk factors that influence interpartner violence such as cognitive processing, emotion regulation, and relational dynamics that effectively discriminate between abusive and nonabusive individuals. He argues that, despite strong and consistent empirical findings that could inform effective etiologic and intervention models of interpartner violence, there remains a strong, dominant, and ideologically based reactionary feminist view that sees interpartner violence as primarily caused by male dominance and male-centered social norms and hierarchies. There is little convincing evidence supporting this ideological position, yet interpartner violence continues to be defined and treated, at least in the United States, by interventions and methods that are informed by feminist ideology rather than the objective evidence. This chapter brings very valuable insights to the issue of how sometimes biased and prejudged ideological positions may thwart the most effective treatment of violence.

In Chapter 12, Grainne Fitzsimons and Joanna Anderson look at the role of incompatible goals in the generation and management of conflict between couples. Couples have to manage coordination and conflict on a daily basis, yet most research on couples' conflict focuses on negotiations and trust games. In their chapter, Fitzsimons and Anderson summarize their innovative program of work examining how couples that share different goals are also more likely to experience conflict. Unlike traditional work on couple conflict, Fitzsimons and Anderson's project examines similar versus dissimilar goal pursuits and argues that goals underlie much of how partners view each other and understand each other and their motivations to cooperate with each other. They find that dissimilar personal goals can lead to increased rates of fighting and increased negativity in response to common disagreements.

In Chapter 13 Lisa Zadro examines the possible psychological, contextual, and emotional factors that may motivate targets of relational ostracism to enact punitive and vengeful behaviors. Factors that potentially moderate the consequences of exclusion are discussed in terms of whether they ameliorate or exacerbate aggressive reactions. The chapter also introduces new experimental research using a novel ostracism paradigm, *O-Cam*, a simulated Web conference that specifically investigates the forms of vengeance that targets of ostracism are willing to impose on sources.

Chapter 14 deals with the potential dangers of unilateral forgiveness in resolving conflicts in relationships. Laura Luchies and Eli Finkel look at questions of forgiveness in conflict management and suggest that unilateral forgiveness, when it helps victims preserve a valuable relationship, is beneficial, but when it preserves a relationship that is unlikely to be valuable it leads to negative outcomes. Given that victims and perpetrators share joint control over victims' postconflict outcomes, the data suggest that conflict resolution strategies promoting victims' forgiveness should also heighten victims' sensitivity to whether forgiveness is of future benefit to them. Further, forgiveness should be supplemented with strategies designed to promote perpetrators' amend making.

Section IV: Social, Cultural, and Evolutionary Factors in Social Conflict and Aggression

The final and fourth part of the book discusses some of the larger evolutionary, cultural, and social influences that influence the way social conflict and aggression occurs.

In Chapter 15, Mark Van Vugt outlines an evolutionary "male warrior hypothesis" to explain the many intriguing forms of evidence for human tribalism: the tendency to categorize individuals on the basis of their group membership and to treat in-group members benevolently and out-group members malevolently. He argues that this tribal inclination is an evolved response to the threat of intergroup aggression and violence that was endemic in ancestral human environments (and is still common today). Van Vugt suggests that intergroup conflict has profoundly affected the psychology of men in particular—the male warrior hypothesis—and discusses the implications of this hypothesis for managing intergroup relations in our society.

In Chapter 16 Craig Anderson and Matt DeLisi present research and theory that speculates about the role of environmental variables associated with global warming on aggression. If experts are correct in their predictions of global warming (and there are many unanswered questions about this issue), Anderson and DeLisi contend that aggression will increase for two reasons: (1) increased temperature has a direct impact on increased aggression; and (2) increased temperature has an indirect impact on societal factors that are related to increased aggression, like displacement, poverty, and physically uncomfortable living conditions. They rely on Anderson's General Aggression Model to derive these intriguing predictions.

In Chapter 17, Ed Donnerstein reviews the literature on various forms of media violence (film, TV, games) as well as violence on the Internet. As nearly all aggressive movies and games can be readily accessed online, exposure to violence is becoming more accessible than ever, including to minors. Further, entirely new and realistic forms of aggression are available on YouTube and other Internet sites, with the attendant implicit suggestion that there exists a social consensus about the appropriateness and frequency of violent acts. It is a whole new world out there, and much of it is violent. What effects should we expect to see? Donnerstein suggests that Internet violence has serious implications for the way human beings will come to conceive and define acceptable and unacceptable forms of aggression.

Chapter 18 by Robert Kurzban and John Christner applies an evolutionary approach to analyzing what role supernatural beliefs play in generating and maintaining intergroup conflict. They propose that shared supernatural beliefs serve an adaptive purpose, in that they signal to both in-group and out-group members alike that an individual cannot easily change groups. Thus, supernatural beliefs function as commitment devices in the same way that bodily marks, scars, and tattoos work as permanent signals of group identification, precluding group switching. Shared supernatural beliefs are thus "mental markers," and the surprising prevalence of otherwise clearly irrational supernatural beliefs may be understood in those terms.

In the final chapter, Chapter 19, Rowell Huesmann, Eric Dubow, and Paul Boxer suggest an intriguing and complementary view: that adherence to some forms of supernatural beliefs, especially traditional religious beliefs, may act to limit and channel social conflict and aggression. In particular, regular exposure to religious activities in childhood has ameliorative effects on antisocial and aggressive behavior. It could be that regular church attendance is a marker of good parenting, that religious organizations provide social support when problems occur, or that religious exposure helps build strong self-regulating internal standards. A 40-year prospective longitudinal study finds that parental religiosity may act as a long-term protective factor against adult aggression. Remarkably, high religiosity seems to exacerbate the tendencies of low-aggressive youth to grow up to be low-aggressive adults but also exacerbates the tendency of high-aggressive youth to grow up to be more aggressive. These results are discussed in terms of the potential social and psychological processes that could explain the effects.

CONCLUSIONS

Understanding the nature and causes of social conflict and aggression is one of the core questions for psychology. As this introductory review shows, despite literally hundreds of years of philosophical and empirical interest in this topic, a complete understanding of the nature, characteristics, and consequences of human conflict and violence remain as elusive as ever. Theories range from pessimistic predictions that see *Homo sapiens* as a fundamentally flawed and violent evolutionary freak doomed to extinction (Koestler, 1972) to optimistic views that see conflict and aggression as necessary and adaptive response systems that can be effectively managed using social and cultural engineering (see also Chapters 15 and 19). The chapters presented here represent some of the best contemporary work on social conflict and aggression by social psychologists. We have learned a great deal about the cognitive, affective, and motivational mechanisms that influence the generation, experience, and management of social conflict. The chapters included here, in their various ways, all confirm that the study of social conflict and aggression is a thriving and productive field today. We hope that readers will find this book an informative and interesting overview of the current status of this fascinating area of inquiry.

REFERENCES

Bandura, A., Ross, D., & Ross, S. A. (1961). Transmission of aggression through imitation of aggressive models. *Journal of Abnormal and Social Psychology, 63*, 575–582.

Berkowitz, L. (1980). The frustration–aggression hypothesis. In R. A. Falk & S. S. Kim, (Eds.), *The war system: An interdisciplinary approach.* (pp. 116–??) Boulder, CO: Westview Press.

Berkowitz, L. (1993). *Aggression: Its causes, consequences, and control.* New York: McGraw-Hill.

Buss, A. H. (1961). *The psychology of aggression.* New York: Wiley.

Dollard, J., Doob, L. W., Miller, N. E., Mowrer, O.H., & Sears, R. R. (1939). *Frustration and aggression.* New Haven, CT: Yale University Press.

Dunbar, R.I.M. (2008). The social brain hypothesis and its relevance to social psychology. In Forgas, J. P., Haselton, M. G., & von Hippel, W. (Eds.) *Evolution and the social mind.* (pp. 21–33). Vol. 9 in the Sydney Symposium of Social Psychology Series. New York: Psychology Press.

Freud, S. (1922). *Beyond the pleasure principle.* London: International Psychoanalytic Press.

Freud, S. (1930/1989). *Civilization and its discontents.* New York: W. W. Norton & Company; Reissue edition.

Fromm, E. (1973). *The anatomy of human destructiveness.* Greenwich, CT: Fawcett Crest.

Koestler, A. (1972). *Janus: A summing up.* London: McMillan.

Kruk, M. R. (2009). Context, causes, and consequences of conflict. Lorentz Center International Center for Workshops in the Sciences. http://www.lorentzcenter.nl/lc/web/2009/343/extra2.php3?wsid=343

Lieberman, J. D., Solomon, S., Greenberg, J., & McGregor, H. A. (1999). A hot new way to measure aggression: Hot sauce allocation. *Aggressive Behavior, 25*, 331–348.

Lorenz, K. (1966). On aggression. (Marjorie Kerr Wilson, Trans.) New York: Harcourt, Brace & World, Inc.

Martens, A., Kosloff, S., Greenberg, J., Landau, M. J., & Schmader, T. (2007). Killing begets killing: Evidence from a bug-killing paradigm that initial killing fuels subsequent killing. *Personality and Social Psychology Bulletin, 33*, 1251–1264.

McDougall, W. (1921). *An introduction to social psychology,* 14th ed. Boston: Luce.

Milgram, S. (1974). *Obedience to authority: An experimental view.* London: Tavistock.

Norlander, T., & Gustafson, R. (1997). Effects of alcohol on picture drawing during the verification phase of the creative process. *Creativity Research Journal, 10,* 355–362.

Pinker, S. (1994). *The language instinct.* New York: Harper.

Ritter, D., & Eslea, M. (2005). Hot sauce, toy guns, and graffiti: A critical account of current laboratory aggression paradigms. *Aggressive Behavior, 31,* 407–419.

Russell, G. W., Arms, R. L., Loof, S. D., & Dwyer, R. S. (1996). Men's aggression toward women in a bungled procedure paradigm. *Journal of Social Behavior and Personality, 11,* 729–738.

2

An Attachment Perspective on Interpersonal and Intergroup Conflict

MARIO MIKULINCER

Interdisciplinary Center (IDC) Herzliya

PHILLIP R. SHAVER

University of California, Davis

*I*n recent years, attachment theory (Bowlby, 1973, 1980, 1982, 1988), which was originally formulated to describe and explain infant–parent emotional bonding, has been applied first to the study of adolescent and adult romantic relationships and then to the study of group dynamics and intergroup relationships. In the present chapter we expand the theory as it applies to adults by discussing attachment-related processes involved in (1) the ways people think, experience, and cope with interpersonal conflicts; (2) maladaptive forms of conflict resolution within romantic and marital relationships; and (3) intergroup hostility and aggression. We will begin by presenting an overview of attachment theory and our theoretical model of the activation and psychodynamics of the adult attachment behavioral system (Mikulincer & Shaver, 2007a), along with an overview of some of the intrapsychic and interpersonal manifestations of the senses of attachment security and insecurity (attachment anxiety and avoidance). We will then focus on attachment theory's characterization of individual differences in adaptive and maladaptive forms of experiencing interpersonal conflicts and coping with them. Next, we will review findings concerning the ways attachment security and the major forms of insecurity affect various forms of conflict resolution in close relationships. Finally, we will review recent findings concerning ways the senses of attachment security and insecurity (anxiety and avoidance) shape a person's attitudes and behavior toward out-groups and reduce or intensify intergroup conflict.

OVERVIEW OF ADULT ATTACHMENT THEORY

According to Bowlby (1982), human beings are born with an innate psychobiological system (the *attachment behavioral system*) that motivates them to seek proximity to supportive others (*attachment figures*) in times of need. This system, which emerged over the course of evolution, accomplishes basic regulatory functions (protection from threats and alleviation of distress) and increases the likelihood of survival of human infants, who are born with immature capacities for locomotion, feeding, and defense. Although the attachment system is most critical during the early years of life, Bowlby (1988) assumed that it is active over the entire life span and is manifested in thoughts and behaviors related to support seeking.

Bowlby (1973) also described important individual differences in the functioning of the attachment system. Interactions with attachment figures who are available in times of need, are sensitive to one's attachment needs, and are responsive to one's bids for proximity facilitate the optimal functioning of the system. According to Bowlby (1988), these kinds of positive interactions promote the formation of a sense of attachment security—a sense that the world is safe, that attachment figures are helpful when called upon, and that it is possible to explore the environment curiously and engage effectively and enjoyably with other people. Moreover, positive expectations about others' availability and positive views of the self as competent and valued (which Bowlby called *internal working models*) are formed, and affect-regulation strategies are organized around these positive beliefs. However, when attachment figures are not reliably available and supportive, a sense of security is not attained, negative internal working models are formed (e.g., worries about others' intentions and doubts about self-worth), and strategies of affect regulation other than appropriate proximity seeking (*secondary attachment strategies*, conceptualized in terms of two dimensions, *avoidance and anxiety*) are adopted.

In studies of adolescents and adults, tests of these theoretical ideas have generally focused on a person's *attachment orientation*—the systematic pattern of relational expectations, emotions, and behavior that results from a particular history of attachment experiences (Fraley & Shaver, 2000; Shaver & Mikulincer, 2002). Initially, research was based on Ainsworth, Blehar, Waters, and Wall's (1978) typology of attachment patterns in infancy—secure, anxious, and avoidant—and Hazan and Shaver's (1987) conceptualization of parallel adult styles in romantic relationships. However, subsequent studies (e.g., Brennan, Clark, & Shaver, 1998; Fraley & Waller, 1998) revealed that attachment orientations are best conceptualized as regions in a two-dimensional space. The first dimension, attachment *anxiety*, reflects the degree to which a person worries that relationship partners will not be available in times of need and is afraid of being rejected or abandoned. The second dimension, attachment-related *avoidance*, reflects the extent to which a person distrusts relationship partners' goodwill and strives to maintain behavioral independence and emotional distance from partners. People who score low on both dimensions are said to be secure, or to have a secure attachment style. The two dimensions can be measured with reliable and valid self-report scales and are associated in theoretically predictable ways with various aspects of personal adjustment and relationship quality (see Mikulincer & Shaver, 2007a, for a review).

Attachment orientations are initially formed in interactions with primary caregivers during early childhood, as a large body of research has shown (Cassidy & Shaver, 2008), but Bowlby (1988) claimed that memorable interactions with others throughout life can alter a person's working models and can move the person from one region of the two-dimensional space to another. Moreover, although a person's attachment orientation is often conceptualized as a single global orientation toward close relationships, it is actually rooted in a complex network of cognitive and affective processes and mental representations, which includes many episodic, context-related, and relationship-specific as well as general attachment representations (Mikulincer & Shaver, 2003). In fact, many studies indicate that a person's attachment orientation can change depending on context and recent experiences (Mikulincer & Shaver, 2007b). This makes it possible to study the effects of experimentally primed security and insecurity.

A MODEL OF ATTACHMENT-SYSTEM FUNCTIONING IN ADULTHOOD

In summarizing the hundreds of empirical studies of adult attachment processes, we (Mikulincer & Shaver, 2003, 2007a) created a flowchart model of the activation and dynamics of the attachment system. The model includes three major components: (1) monitoring and appraising threatening events; (2) monitoring and appraising the availability of external or internalized attachment figures; and (3) monitoring and appraising the viability of seeking proximity to an "attachment figure" as a means of coping with attachment insecurity and distress. It also includes excitatory and inhibitory pathways that result from recurrent use of secondary attachment strategies, and these feedback pathways affect the monitoring of threatening events and attachment figures' availability.

Mikulincer and Shaver (2007a) assumed that the monitoring of unfolding events results in activation of the attachment system when a potential or actual threat is sensed (unconsciously) or perceived (consciously). That is, during encounters with physical or psychological threats—either in the environment or in the flow of internal free associations—the attachment system is activated, and the primary attachment strategy is set in motion. This strategy leads adults to turn to internalized representations of attachment figures or to actual supportive others and to maintain symbolic or actual proximity to these figures. Recent studies have shown that thoughts related to proximity seeking as well as mental representations of internalized attachment figures tend to be activated even in minimally threatening situations (Mikulincer, Birnbaum, Woddis, & Nachmias, 2000; Mikulincer, Gillath, & Shaver, 2002). However, although age and development result in an increased ability to gain comfort from symbolic representations of attachment figures, no one of any age is completely free of reliance on others (Bowlby, 1982, 1988).

Activation of the attachment system forces a decision about the availability of attachment figures (the second module of our model). An affirmative answer to the implicit or explicit question "Is an attachment figure available and likely to be responsive to my needs?" heightens the sense of attachment security and facilitates the use of constructive emotion-regulation strategies. These strategies are aimed at alleviating distress, maintaining supportive intimate relationships, and bolstering a person's sense of love worthiness and self-efficacy. Moreover, they sustain what Shaver and Mikulincer (2002), following Fredrickson (2001), call a "broaden-and-build" cycle of attachment security, which expands a person's resources for maintaining coping flexibility and emotional stability in times of stress, broadens the person's perspectives and capacities, and facilitates the incorporation of mental representations of security-enhancing attachment figures into the self. This broaden-and-build process allows relatively secure individuals to maintain an authentic sense of personal efficacy, resilience, and optimism even when social support is temporarily unavailable (Mikulincer & Shaver, 2007a).

Perceived unavailability of an attachment figure results in attachment insecurity, which compounds the distress aroused by the appraisal of a situation as threatening. This state of insecurity forces a decision about the viability of further (more active) proximity seeking as a protective strategy (the third module of the model). The appraisal of proximity as feasible or essential—because of attachment history, temperamental factors, or contextual cues—results in energetic, insistent attempts to attain proximity, support, and love. These attempts are called *hyperactivating strategies* (Cassidy & Kobak, 1988) because they involve up-regulation of the attachment system, including constant vigilance and intense concern until an attachment figure is perceived to be available and supportive. Hyperactivating strategies include attempts to elicit a partner's involvement, care, and support through clinging and controlling responses (Shaver & Mikulincer, 2002), over-dependence on relationship partners as a source of protection (Shaver & Hazan, 1993), and perception of oneself as relatively helpless with respect to emotion regulation (Mikulincer & Shaver, 2003). Hyperactivating strategies are characteristic of people who score relatively high on the attachment anxiety dimension (Mikulincer & Shaver, 2007a).

The appraisal of proximity seeking as nonviable can result in inhibition of the quest for support and active attempts to handle distress alone (which Bowlby, 1988, labeled *compulsive self-reliance*). These secondary strategies of affect regulation are called *avoidant deactivating strategies* (Cassidy & Kobak, 1988), because their primary goal is to keep the attachment system deactivated to avoid frustration and further distress caused by attachment-figure unavailability. This goal leads to the denial of attachment needs; avoidance of closeness, intimacy, and dependence in close relationships; maximization of cognitive, emotional, and physical distance from others; and strivings for autonomy and independence. With practice and experience, these deactivating strategies often broaden to include literal and symbolic distancing of oneself from distress whether it is directly attachment related. Deactivating strategies are characteristic of people scoring relatively high on avoidant attachment (Mikulincer & Shaver, 2007a).

In short, each attachment strategy has a major regulatory goal (insisting on proximity to an attachment figure or on self-reliance), which goes along with particular cognitive and affective processes that facilitate goal attainment. These strategies affect the formation and maintenance of close relationships as well as the experience, regulation, and expression of negative emotions, such as anxiety, anger, or sadness (Mikulincer & Shaver, 2007a). Moreover, the strategies affect the ways a person experiences and handles conflictual situations with other individuals (including a romantic partner or spouse) or groups. This is the main focus of the following sections of this chapter.

ATTACHMENT ORIENTATIONS AND INTERPERSONAL CONFLICTS

When analyzing the possible links between the functioning of the attachment system and the ways a person experiences and regulates conflicts with other people, it is important to remember that the attachment system was "designed," during evolution, as an interpersonal regulatory device. According to Bowlby (1982), perceived threats and dangers make salient the goal of gaining proximity to and support from an attachment figure, and this encourages people to learn, organize, and implement behavioral plans aimed at attaining safety and security. Importantly, Bowlby also assumed that the attachment system operates in a "goal-corrected" manner. That is, a person evaluates the progress he or she is making toward achieving support and comfort from a partner and corrects intended actions if necessary to attain these goals. Therefore, effective functioning of the attachment system includes the use of partner-tailored proximity-seeking strategies that take into account a partner's needs and preferences (creating what Bowlby, 1973, called a "goal-corrected partnership"). This facilitates satisfying, harmonious interactions that might otherwise devolve into intrusive, coercive, or conflictual exchanges rooted in coordination failures and mismatched needs and goals. Moreover, smooth functioning of the attachment system helps people rapidly and effectively restore relationship harmony whenever they and their partner have incompatible needs and goals that can result in painful interpersonal conflicts.

According to Mikulincer and Shaver (2007a), competent management of interpersonal conflicts is originally learned during interactions between infants and their primary caregivers, mainly when infants search for a caregiver's protection or support. During such episodes, children must not only express their needs for proximity and support to gain a sense of security but also must learn to manage occasional goal conflicts between them and their caregivers, because these may interfere with continued support. Although the foundation of this ability is assumed to be an innate aspect of the attachment system (given the goal-corrected nature of the system's operation), interactions with sensitive and responsive caregivers who can flexibly adapt their goals and responses to children's attempts to deal with goal conflicts allow children to learn effective conflict management skills and practice and refine them. In contrast, interactions with a rejecting figure who rigidly maintains his or her own goals regardless of children's attempts to tailor their bids for proximity to this figure's preferences cast a pall over early efforts to regulate interpersonal conflicts. Unresponsive attachment figures force a child to acquire alternative conflict management skills that may seem adaptive in their original context (e.g., inhibiting expression of one's needs when a parent responds badly to need expression) but can cause trouble later on, when a person encounters new relationship partners with different salient needs and preferences.

Mikulincer and Shaver (2007a) hypothesized that relatively secure adolescents and adults are likely to emphasize the challenging rather than the threatening aspects of interpersonal conflicts and believe they can deal effectively with them. These positive beliefs about conflict and conflict management are rooted in secure individuals' views of others as "well intentioned and kind hearted" (Hazan & Shaver, 1987, pp. 518–519) and their views that they are capable of handling life's problems (e.g., Mikulincer & Florian, 1998). Moreover, their constructive approach to emotion regulation (Shaver & Mikulincer, 2007) may help them communicate openly but not threateningly during conflict, negotiate with others in a collaborative manner, and apply effective conflict-resolution strategies, such as compromising and integrating their own and their partner's needs and behaviors. In so doing, secure individuals are likely to move their relationships back from inevitable conflicts to states of harmony.

Insecure people are likely to appraise interpersonal conflicts in more threatening terms and apply less effective conflict-resolution strategies. For anxious people, conflicts threaten their wish to gain approval, support, and security; they arouse fear of rejection and trigger hyperactivating affect-regulation strategies. The people are likely to appraise conflict in catastrophic terms, display intense negative emotions, ruminate obsessively, and hence fail to attend to and understand what their relationship partner is trying to tell to them. This egocentric, fearful stance is likely to interfere with calm, open communication, negotiation, and the use of compromising and integrating strategies that depend on keeping a partner's needs and perspective in mind. Anxious individuals are likely either to try to dominate the interaction (in an effort to get their own needs met) or accede submissively to a partner's demands to avoid rejection.

Avoidant individuals are likely to view conflicts as aversive primarily because conflicts interfere with autonomy and call for expressions of love and care or need and vulnerability. Avoidant people are likely to downplay the significance of conflict while minimizing the importance of their partner's complaints, to distance themselves cognitively or emotionally from the conflict, or to try to avoid interacting with their partner. When circumstances do not allow escape from conflict, avoidant individuals are likely to attempt to dominate their partner, in line with their need for control, negative models of others, and confidence in their own views. This defensive stance is likely to interfere with negotiation and compromise.

The hypothesized links between attachment orientations and responses to interpersonal conflict have been examined in several correlational studies. In these studies, participants completed self-report scales measuring attachment orientations as well as scales assessing subjective appraisals of conflicts (e.g., Pistole & Arricale, 2003), conflict-management skills (e.g., Taubman-Ben-Ari, Findler, & Mikulincer, 2002), the use of constructive conflict-management tactics (e.g., Carnelley, Pietromonaco, & Jaffe, 1994), or the use of aggression and conflict-escalation tactics (e.g., Creasey & Hesson-McInnis, 2001). Other studies have used Rahim's Organization Conflict Inventory (ROCI; Rahim, 1983) to assess reliance on integrating, compromising, dominating, obliging, and avoiding strategies during interpersonal conflicts (e.g., Corcoran & Mallinckrodt, 2000; Levy & Davis, 1988).

These studies indicate that people who score relatively high on attachment anxiety or avoidance appraise conflicts in more threatening terms and believe they are less capable of dealing with conflicts. Moreover, they report having relatively poor conflict-management skills (e.g., understanding their partner's perspective), being unlikely to rely on compromising and integrative strategies, and being relatively likely to escalate conflicts (using coercion or outright fighting) or to leave a conflict unresolved. Research also indicates that attachment anxiety is associated with concerns about closeness during conflicts (Pistole & Arricale, 2003) and strong conflict-related distress (e.g., Creasey & Hesson-McInnis, 2001). In addition, anxiously attached individuals react to the priming of rejection concerns with less flexibility in conflict-management strategies (Beinstein Miller, 1996), suggesting that their fear of rejection, when heightened experimentally, interferes with constructive approaches to conflict resolution.

There are also many studies documenting the links between self-reports of attachment insecurities and conflict-management problems within dating and marital relationships (e.g., Feeney, 1994; Heene, Buysse, & Van Oost, 2005; Roberts & Noller, 1998). Specifically, attachment insecurities have been associated with reports of less expression of affection and empathy during conflicts, less frequent reliance on compromising strategies, more frequent use of coercive or withdrawal strategies, more frequent engagement in verbal and physical aggression, and higher levels of postconflict distress. At the couple level, Senchak and Leonard (1992) found that couples in which one or both partners were insecurely attached reported more withdrawal and aggression during conflicts than couples in which both partners were secure.

There is also evidence that insecure people's conflict-management difficulties are evident to observers of couple members' behavior during laboratory discussions of unresolved conflicts. For example, Kobak and Hazan (1991) used a Q-sort measure of marital attachment and found that husbands and wives who were less secure in their marriage were more likely to display facial expressions of rejection while discussing a disagreement. In addition, insecure husbands were less likely to provide support during the discussion. Similarly, Simpson, Rholes, and Phillips (1996), Feeney (1998), and Campbell, Simpson, Boldry, and Kashy (2005) found that self-reports of attachment insecurities were associated with expressions of distress during a conflict discussion with a dating partner. Feeney also found that self-reports of attachment insecurities were associated with fewer displays of warmth and affection during conflict discussions.

Relying on the Adult Attachment Interview (AAI; George, Kaplan, & Main, 1985) to assess adult attachment orientations, several studies have provided evidence for the expected association between insecurities and destructive behaviors during conflicts with a romantic partner (e.g., Babcock, Jacobson, Gottman, & Yerington, 2000; Creasey & Ladd, 2005; Crowell et al., 2002). Specifically, individuals categorized as insecure based on the AAI have been coded as displaying less positive affect than their secure counterparts during conflict discussions and more frequent expressions of contempt, withdrawal, and stonewalling.

There is also evidence linking self-reports of attachment insecurities with heightened physiological reactivity to relationship conflicts. Powers, Pietromonaco, Gunlicks, and Sayer (2006) asked couples to spend 15 minutes discussing an unresolved conflict. Salivary cortisol levels (an index of physiological reactivity) were assessed before, during, and after the discussion. Results indicated that attachment insecurities were associated with greater physiological reactivity to the discussion and that gender moderated the effects of the specific kind of attachment insecurity (anxiety or avoidance). Whereas avoidant but not anxious women showed heightened cortisol reactivity, anxious but not avoidant men evinced this kind of response in reaction to the discussion. According to Powers et al., these gender differences can be explained in terms of gender-related norms concerning conflicts. Previous studies have indicated that whereas women are expected to take an active, leading role during conflicts (e.g., to articulate relationship concerns) men are assigned a less active role (e.g., Christensen & Heavey, 1990). As a result, the discussion may be particularly stressful for avoidant women, who prefer to distance themselves from relationship problems, and for anxious men, who tend to express distress and take a controlling position in the discussion.

Studies have also found that self-reports of attachment anxiety are associated with intensification of the negative consequences of conflict discussions. For example, Simpson et al. (1996) found that anxiously attached people reported a stronger decline than secure people in love and commitment after discussing a major relationship problem with a dating partner. Gallo and Smith (2001) also found that anxious wives, compared with secure wives, reacted to a discussion about a relationship disagreement with more negative appraisals of their husbands. In Campbell et al.'s (2005) diary study of daily conflicts between dating partners, more anxious participants reported more conflictual interactions across 14 consecutive days and reacted to days of intense conflict with a sharper decline in relationship satisfaction and a more pessimistic view of the relationship's future.

Insecure people's deficiencies in handling interpersonal conflicts are also evident in studies assessing attachment-related variations in domestic violence. This kind of violence often results from repeated failures to solve interpersonal conflicts and to prevent conflict escalation—deficiencies we expect to be associated with attachment insecurity. However, despite both anxious and avoidant people's problems in handling interpersonal conflicts, studies have revealed that attachment anxiety is more strongly associated with domestic violence than is avoidant attachment (e.g., Dutton, Saunders, Starzomski, & Bartholomew, 1994; Henderson, Bartholomew, Trinke, & Kwong, 2005). For example, Dutton et al. studied 160 court-mandated men convicted of wife assault and found that self-reports of attachment anxiety were associated with more frequent and severe acts of coercion and partner abuse during couple conflicts. Secure attachment was negatively associated with most features of domestic violence even in this self-selected, court-mandated population.

The link between attachment anxiety and domestic violence is evident in two other kinds of studies. First, studies comparing attachment orientations of violent and nonviolent samples have found that partners who engage in domestic violence are more anxiously attached, on average, than partners who do not resort to violence (e.g., Bookwala & Zdaniuk, 1998). Second, studies in unrestricted samples of adolescents and young adults have consistently found that young men and women who score higher on attachment anxiety are likely to report more engagement in couple violence (e.g., Roberts & Noller, 1998). Importantly, these associations cannot be explained by other relationship or personality variables and seem to be mediated by reliance on ineffective conflict-management strategies.

With regard to avoidant attachment, some researchers have suggested that avoidant individuals withdraw from conflict rather than become so emotional that they attack a relationship partner (e.g., Mikulincer & Shaver, 2007a). Bartholomew and Allison (2006) found, however, that avoidant people sometimes became violent when involved in an escalating series of conflicts, especially with an anxiously attached partner who demanded involvement. Similarly, Holtzworth-Munroe, Stuart, and Hutchinson (1997) found that avoidance was associated with wife battering, and Rankin, Saunders, and Williams (2000) found that it was associated with more frequent and severe acts of domestic violence on the part of a sample of African American men arrested for partner abuse. In addition, Collins, Cooper, Albino, and Allard (2002) reported that avoidance measured during adolescence predicted relationship violence 6 years later.

ATTACHMENT ORIENTATIONS AND INTERGROUP CONFLICT

The link between attachment insecurities and destructive responses to conflict is also evident in the field of intergroup relations. In this context, tensions, frictions, and conflicts between groups are a constant and pervasive source of intergroup hostility, which is directly manifested in out-group derogation (i.e., the tendency to perceive members of other cultural or ethnic groups in less favorable terms than members of one's own group; see Brewer & Brown, 1998, for a review), prejudice, and discrimination against out-group members. When intergroup relations become tense and conflictive, these hostilities can result in violence, rape, and killing of out-group members—even genocide (Staub & Bar-Tal, 2003). Although several economic and political factors are involved in the escalation of intergroup violence (e.g., economic instability, totalitarian regimes), the ways individuals experience and handle intergroup tensions and conflicts can explain individual differences in intergroup hostility and aggression. With this in mind, we (Mikulincer & Shaver, 2001) hypothesized that attachment insecurities, which are characterized by conflict-management deficiencies, would be associated with destructive responses to intergroup conflict and thereby with more hostility and aggression toward out-group members.

Social identity theory (Tajfel & Turner, 1986) assumes that out-group derogation serves a self-protective function: maintenance of self-esteem ("We," including I, are better than "them"). This defensive tendency seems likely to be especially characteristic of insecurely attached people. Securely attached individuals can maintain a stable and authentic sense of self-worth by virtue of feeling loved and accepted by others and possessing special and valuable qualities (Mikulincer &

Shaver, 2005). They should have less need to fear and disparage out-group members. In his account of human behavioral systems, Bowlby (1982) stated that activation of the attachment system is closely related to innate fear of strangers and that secure attachments mitigate this innate reaction and foster a more tolerant attitude toward unfamiliarity and novelty.

In a series of five studies, we (Mikulincer & Shaver, 2001) found strong evidence for these theoretical ideas. First, higher scores on a self-report measure of attachment anxiety were associated with more hostile responses to a variety of out-groups (as defined by secular Israeli Jewish students): Israeli Arabs, Ultra-orthodox Jews, Russian immigrants, and homosexuals. Second, experimental heightening of the sense of attachment security (subliminal presentation of security-related words such as *love* and *proximity*, evocation via guided imagery of the components of security-enhancing interpersonal interactions, and visualization of the faces of security-enhancing attachment figures) eliminated negative responses to out-groups. These effects were mediated by threat appraisals and were found even when participants' sense of personal value was threatened or their in-group had been insulted by an out-group member. That is, experimentally augmented attachment security reduced the sense of threat created by encounters with out-group members and seemed to eliminate hostile responses to out-group members.

Building on these studies, Mikulincer and Shaver (2007b) found that increasing people's sense of attachment security reduced actual aggression between contending or warring social groups. Specifically, Israeli Jewish undergraduates participated in a study together with another Israeli Jew or an Israeli Arab (in each case, the same confederate of the experimenter) and were subliminally and repeatedly exposed (for 20 milliseconds on each trial) to the name of their own security-enhancing attachment figure, the name of a familiar person who was not viewed as an attachment figure, or the name of an acquaintance. Following the priming procedure, participants were informed that they would evaluate a food sample and that they had been randomly selected to give the confederate hot sauce to evaluate. They also learned indirectly that the confederate strongly disliked spicy foods. (This procedure has been used in other studies of interpersonal aggression; e.g., McGregor et al., 1998). The dependent variable was the amount of hot sauce allocated to the confederate.

When participants had been subliminally primed with the name of someone who was not an attachment figure, they delivered a larger amount of hot sauce to the Arab confederate than to the Jewish confederate, a sign of intergroup aggression. But security priming eliminated this difference: participants whose sense of security had been enhanced delivered equal (relatively low) amounts of hot sauce to both the Arab and the Jewish confederate. In addition, participants scoring higher on attachment anxiety gave more hot sauce to the out-group member (Israeli Arab) than to the in-group member (Israeli Jew). Thus, it seems that people who are either dispositionally secure or induced to feel more secure in a particular setting are better able than their insecure counterparts to tolerate intergroup differences and to refrain from intergroup aggression.

Although these studies indicate that attachment insecurities are associated with stronger intergroup derogation and aggression, they did not include assessments of the cognitive processes that underlie such conflict-escalation responses. According to Bar-Tal, Kruglanski, and Klar (1989), these destructive responses are driven by what they called conflict schemas or mental sets. In their view, people who hold a cooperation set anticipate constructive interactions with out-group members and cooperative and satisfactory conflict-resolution discussions, which, in turn, moves them away from hostile and aggressive responses to out-groups. In contrast, people who hold a conflict set anticipate hostile and competitive interactions with out-group members and unpleasant and antagonistic conflict resolutions, which, in turn, promote intergroup hostility and aggression. These mental sets may be brought about by either person factors (e.g., prosocial orientation, Carnevale & Probst, 1998) or situational factors (e.g., De Dreu & Nijstad, 2008). Based on findings reviewed earlier, attachment orientations may be one of these factors, with attachment insecurities, either dispositional or contextually enhanced, increasing the likelihood of adopting a conflict mental set and secure attachment increasing endorsement of a cooperation set.

To examine this issue, we followed up a recent series of studies by De Dreu and Nijstad (2008) on mental sets and creative thought. In one of these studies, participants were asked to indicate the extent to which a particular object varying in its degree of prototypicality (e.g., car, elevator) is an example of a particular category (e.g., vehicle). In this task, inclusion rather than exclusion of the weak prototypical objects (e.g., elevator) reflects broad cognitive categories and flexible cognitive processing (Rosch, 1975), which are assumed to foster creative thought (e.g., Amabile, 1983). De Dreu and Nijstad hypothesized that a conflict set leads individuals to focus their attention on conflict-related issues and to dismiss or ignore conflict-irrelevant issues. As a result, a conflict set will involve broader and more inclusive thinking about conflict but will result in narrow-minded, black-and-white thinking about conflict-irrelevant issues. Indeed, the findings indicated that a conflict mental set was associated with more inclusion of weak prototypical exemplars of conflict-related categories but less inclusion of weak prototypical exemplars of neutral categories.

Based on this finding, we conducted an exploratory two-session laboratory study, reported here for the first time, that involved 80 Israeli Jewish university students (53 women and 27 men). We hypothesized that the pattern of category inclusion responses reflecting a conflict mental set would be more characteristic of insecurely than of securely attached people and would be mitigated by security priming (subliminally presenting the name of a security-enhancing attachment figure). The first session was designed to assess participants' attachment orientations and acquire specific names of security-enhancing figures and other close persons to be used later as primes in the second session. In that first session, participants completed the ECR inventory (Brennan et al., 1998), a measure of attachment anxiety and avoidance, plus two computerized measures of the names of attachment figures and other close persons who were not attachment figures. The first of these two computerized measures was a Hebrew version of the WHOTO scale (Fraley & Davis, 1997), in which participants were asked to type in a Microsoft Excel worksheet the names of their security-enhancing attachment figures. The scale included six items (e.g., Who is the person you would count on for advice?

Who is the person you can always count on?), and, for each item, participants wrote the name of the person who best served the targeted attachment-related function. In the second measure, participants were asked to write the names of their father, mother, brothers, sisters, best friend, current romantic partner, grandfathers, and grandmothers without making any reference to the attachment functions they did or did not serve. We assumed that because some of these people's names were not provided as primary attachment figures they probably did not meet the strict requirements for that role.

In the second session, conducted 2 weeks later by a different experimenter, participants (all of them Israeli Jews) were invited to have a conversation with an Israeli Arab student about the Middle East conflict. However, before the conversation, participants were asked to perform two cognitive tasks. In the first task—a 30-trial computerized word-relation task—participants were randomly assigned to one of two conditions: security or neutral priming. In the security priming condition (n = 40), participants were subliminally exposed (for 20 milliseconds) to the name of their most security-enhancing attachment figure (based on the first session of the study). In the neutral priming condition (n = 40), they were subliminally exposed to the name of a familiar person who was not selected as an attachment figure.

Following the priming procedure, participants in both priming conditions performed the second cognitive task: a category inclusion task. This task was identical to the one used by De Dreu and Nijstad (2008). Specifically, participants received four neutral categories and three conflict-related categories (randomly ordered), and for each category they rated three objects in terms of their prototypicality using a 10-point scale ranging from 1 (*not at all*) to 10 (*very prototypical*). The four neutral categories (with strong, intermediate, and weak exemplars) were vehicle (bus, airplane, camel), vegetable (carrot, potato, garlic), clothes (skirt, shoes, handbag), and furniture (couch, lamp, telephone). The three conflict-related categories (with strong, intermediate, and weak exemplars) were weapon (gun, jet fighter, screwdriver), army (Cavalry, Al Qaida, hooligans), and ammunition (bullet, dynamite, paving stones). Statistical analyses were performed on the prototypicality ratings of weak exemplars. No significant effects were found for ratings of strong and intermediate exemplars. For each participant, we computed two total scores: (1) inclusiveness of neutral categories (average of ratings for the weak exemplars of the four neutral categories, Cronbach's alpha = .71); and (2) inclusiveness of conflict categories (average of ratings for the weak exemplars of the three conflict categories, alpha = .74).

To test our predictions, we conducted two-step hierarchical regression analyses with participants' scores on the ECR attachment anxiety and avoidance scales and security priming (a contrast variable contrasting security priming, 1, with neutral priming, –1) as the independent variables. In the first step of these analyses, we entered attachment anxiety and avoidance (Z-scores) and security priming as a block to examine the unique main effects of these predictors. In the second step, the two-way interactions between security priming and each of the ECR scores were entered as additional predictors. These regressions were performed separately for inclusiveness of conflict-related categories and inclusiveness of neutral categories.

For inclusiveness of conflict-related categories, the regression analysis revealed significant main effects of attachment anxiety (β = .35, p < .01), avoidant attachment (β = .24, p < .05), and security priming (β = −.27, p < .05). As expected, the higher the attachment anxiety and avoidance, the higher the prototypicality ratings of weak exemplars of conflict-related categories. Moreover, compared with neutral priming, security priming reduced the prototypicality ratings of weak exemplars of conflict-related categories. The interaction effects were not significant. That is, whereas attachment insecurities seemed to involve broader and more inclusive thinking about conflict, security priming seemed to reduce the inclusiveness of conflict-related categories.

For inclusiveness of neutral categories, the regression analysis revealed significant main effects of attachment anxiety (β = −.28, p < .01) and security priming (β = .36, p < .01). As expected, the higher the attachment anxiety, the lower the prototypicality ratings of weak exemplars of neutral categories. Moreover, compared with neutral priming, security priming increased the prototypicality ratings of weak exemplars of neutral categories. Also, the interaction between security priming and attachment anxiety was significant (β = .31, p < .01). Examination of the significant interactions (using the procedure from Aiken & West, 1991) revealed that attachment anxiety was associated with lower inclusiveness of neutral categories in the neutral priming condition (−1) (β = −.59, p < .01) but not in the security priming condition (+1) (β = .03). These slopes indicate that security priming was able to mitigate anxiously attached participants' tendency to think about neutral categories in less broad and inclusive terms—a tendency Mikulincer and Sheffi (2000) observed previously using other neutral categories and other tasks assessing creative thoughts.

These results provide encouraging preliminary evidence that attachment insecurities are associated with a conflict mental set and that even a temporary sense of attachment security reduces the likelihood of adopting such mental sets during encounters with out-group members. Further research is needed to determine (1) whether insecurely attached individuals' conflict mental sets are activated during encounters with out-group members or tend to be chronically activated during even neutral interpersonal interactions and (2) whether these mental sets underlie insecurely attached individuals' hostile and aggressive reactions to out-group members.

CONCLUDING REMARKS

Attachment theory, which was originally developed to explain infant–caregiver attachment and different attachment patterns in infant–caregiver relationships that seem to result from different kinds of caregiving, has been extended first to the realm of adult couple relationships and now to relationships in organizations (e.g., Shaver & Mikulincer, 2008) and to intergroup relations. Both correlational and experimental studies indicate that interpersonal conflicts are handled worse by people with an insecure attachment style, whether anxious or avoidant, and are handled better by people with a secure style. We consider it highly significant that intergroup conflicts might be reduced by helping conflicting parties to feel more secure, not just in the intergroup relationships where the conflicts are occurring but also in their close relationships, which attachment theory views as the source of security and insecurity. Our experiments, while fairly simple, suggest that this is a causal process—that is, that security enhancement precedes a movement toward more prosocial attitudes and behaviors (Mikulincer & Shaver, 2007b). The effects of such security most likely stem from fairly deep, in some cases not verbally accessible, feelings. They thus add to all of the work in social psychology that focuses more intently on forms of verbal negotiation, rationally induced changes in cognitions, and various forms of exposure to members of out-groups. Our studies suggest that there may be many contributions to constructive conflict resolution, including ones that depend on evolved behavioral systems that may at first seem to have little to do with interpersonal conflicts.

REFERENCES

Aiken, L. S., & West, S. G. (1991). *Multiple regression: Testing and interpreting interactions*. Newbury Park, CA: Sage.

Ainsworth, M. D. S., Blehar, M. C., Waters, E., & Wall, S. (1978). *Patterns of attachment: A psychological study of the strange situation*. Hillsdale, NJ: Erlbaum.

Amabile, T. M. (1983). *The social psychology of creativity*. New York: Springer-Verlag.

Babcock, J. C., Jacobson, N. S., Gottman, J. M., & Yerington, T. P. (2000). Attachment, emotional regulation, and the function of marital violence: Differences between secure, preoccupied, and dismissing violent and nonviolent husbands. *Journal of Family Violence, 15*, 391–409.

Bar-Tal, D., Kruglanski, A. W., & Klar, Y. (1989). Conflict termination: An epistemological analysis of international cases. *Political Psychology, 10*, 233–255.

Bartholomew, K., & Allison, C. J. (2006). An attachment perspective on abusive dynamics in intimate relationships. In M. Mikulincer & G. S. Goodman (Eds.), *Dynamics of romantic love* (pp. 102–127). New York: Guilford Press.

Beinstein Miller, J. (1996). Social flexibility and anxious attachment. *Personal Relationships, 3*, 241–256.

Bookwala, J., & Zdaniuk, B. (1998). Adult attachment styles and aggressive behavior within dating relationships. *Journal of Social and Personal Relationships, 15*, 175–190.

Bowlby, J. (1973). *Attachment and loss: Vol. 2. Separation: Anxiety and anger*. New York: Basic Books.

Bowlby, J. (1980). *Attachment and loss: Vol. 3. Sadness and depression*. New York: Basic Books.

Bowlby, J. (1982). *Attachment and loss: Vol. 1. Attachment* (2nd ed.). New York: Basic Books. (Original ed. 1969)

Bowlby, J. (1988). *A secure base: Clinical applications of attachment theory*. London: Routledge.

Brennan, K. A., Clark, C. L., & Shaver, P. R. (1998). Self-report measurement of adult attachment: An integrative overview. In J. A. Simpson & W. S. Rholes (Eds.), *Attachment theory and close relationships* (pp. 46–76). New York: Guilford Press.

Brewer, M. B., & Brown, R. J. (1998). Intergroup relations. In D. T. Gilbert, S. T. Fiske, & G. Lindzey (Eds.), *The handbook of social psychology* (4th ed., Vol. 2, pp. 554–594). New York: McGraw-Hill.

Campbell, L., Simpson, J. A., Boldry, J., & Kashy, D. A. (2005). Perceptions of conflict and support in romantic relationships: The role of attachment anxiety. *Journal of Personality and Social Psychology, 88*, 510–531.

Carnelley, K. B., Pietromonaco, P. R., & Jaffe, K. (1994). Depression, working models of others, and relationship functioning. *Journal of Personality and Social Psychology, 66,* 127–140.

Carnevale, P. J., & Probst, T. M. (1998). Social values and social conflict in creative problem solving and categorization. *Journal of Personality and Social Psychology, 74,* 1300–1309.

Cassidy, J., & Kobak, R. R. (1988). Avoidance and its relation to other defensive processes. In J. Belsky & T. Nezworski (Eds.), *Clinical implications of attachment* (pp. 300–323). Hillsdale, NJ: Erlbaum.

Cassidy, J., & Shaver, P. R. (Eds.). (2008). *Handbook of attachment: Theory, research, and clinical applications* (2nd ed.). New York: Guilford Press.

Christensen, A., & Heavey, C. L. (1990). Gender and social structure in the demand/withdraw pattern of marital conflict. *Journal of Personality and Social Psychology, 59,* 73–81.

Collins, N. L., Cooper, M., Albino, A., & Allard, L. (2002). Psychosocial vulnerability from adolescence to adulthood: A prospective study of attachment style differences in relationship functioning and partner choice. *Journal of Personality, 70,* 965–1008.

Corcoran, K. O., & Mallinckrodt, B. (2000). Adult attachment, self-efficacy, perspective taking, and conflict resolution. *Journal of Counseling and Development, 78,* 473–483.

Creasey, G., & Hesson-McInnis, M. (2001). Affective responses, cognitive appraisals, and conflict tactics in late adolescent romantic relationships: Associations with attachment orientations. *Journal of Counseling Psychology, 48,* 85–96.

Creasey, G., & Ladd, A. (2005). Generalized and specific attachment representations: Unique and interactive roles in predicting conflict behaviors in close relationships. *Personality and Social Psychology Bulletin, 31,* 1026–1038.

Crowell, J. A., Treboux, D., Gao, Y., Fyffe, C., Pan, H., & Waters, E. (2002). Assessing secure base behavior in adulthood: Development of a measure, links to adult attachment representations, and relations to couples' communication and reports of relationships. *Developmental Psychology, 38,* 679–693.

De Dreu, C. K. W., & Nijstad, B. A. (2008). Mental set and creative thought in social conflict: Threat rigidity versus motivated focus. *Journal of Personality and Social Psychology, 95,* 648–661.

Dutton, D. G., Saunders, K., Starzomski, A., & Bartholomew, K. (1994). Intimacy-anger and insecure attachment as precursors of abuse in intimate relationships. *Journal of Applied Social Psychology, 24,* 1367–1386.

Feeney, J. A. (1994). Attachment style, communication patterns, and satisfaction across the life cycle of marriage. *Personal Relationships, 1,* 333–348.

Feeney, J. A. (1998). Adult attachment and relationship-centered anxiety: Responses to physical and emotional distancing. In J. A. Simpson & W. S. Rholes (Eds.), *Attachment theory and close relationships* (pp. 189–219). New York: Guilford Press.

Fraley, R. C., & Davis, K. E. (1997). Attachment formation and transfer in young adults' close friendships and romantic relationships. *Personal Relationships, 4,* 131–144.

Fraley, R. C., & Shaver, P. R. (2000). Adult romantic attachment: Theoretical developments, emerging controversies, and unanswered questions. *Review of General Psychology, 4,* 132–154.

Fraley, R. C., & Waller, N. G. (1998). Adult attachment patterns: A test of the typological model. In J. A. Simpson & W. S. Rholes (Eds.), *Attachment theory and close relationships* (pp. 77–114). New York: Guilford Press.

Fredrickson, B. L. (2001). The role of positive emotions in positive psychology: The broaden-and-build theory of positive emotions. *American Psychologist, 56,* 218–226.

Gallo, L. C., & Smith, T. W. (2001). Attachment style in marriage: Adjustment and responses to interaction. *Journal of Social and Personal Relationships, 18,* 263–289.

George, C., Kaplan, N., & Main, M. (1985). *The Adult Attachment Interview.* Unpublished protocol, Department of Psychology, University of California, Berkeley.

Hazan, C., & Shaver, P. R. (1987). Romantic love conceptualized as an attachment process. *Journal of Personality and Social Psychology, 52,* 511–524.

Heene, E. L. D., Buysse, A., & Van Oost, P. (2005). Indirect pathways between depressive symptoms and marital distress: The role of conflict communication, attributions, and attachment style. *Family Process, 44,* 413–440.

Henderson, A. J. Z., Bartholomew, K., Trinke, S., & Kwong, M. J. (2005). When loving means hurting: An exploration of attachment and intimate abuse in a community sample. *Journal of Family Violence, 20,* 219–230.

Holtzworth-Munroe, A., Stuart, G. L., & Hutchinson, G. (1997). Violent versus nonviolent husbands: Differences in attachment patterns, dependency, and jealousy. *Journal of Family Psychology, 11,* 314–331.

Kobak, R., & Hazan, C. (1991). Attachment in marriage: Effects of security and accuracy of working models. *Journal of Personality and Social Psychology, 60,* 861–869.

Levy, M. B., & Davis, K. E. (1988). Love styles and attachment styles compared: Their relations to each other and to various relationship characteristics. *Journal of Social and Personal Relationships, 5,* 439–471.

McGregor, H., Leiberman, J., Greenberg, J., Solomon, S., Arndt, J., Simon, L. et al. (1998). Terror management and aggression: Evidence that mortality salience promotes aggression against worldview-threatening individuals. *Journal of Personality and Social Psychology, 74,* 590–605.

Mikulincer, M., Birnbaum, G., Woddis, D., & Nachmias, O. (2000). Stress and accessibility of proximity-related thoughts: Exploring the normative and intraindividual components of attachment theory. *Journal of Personality and Social Psychology, 78,* 509–523.

Mikulincer, M., & Florian, V. (1998). The relationship between adult attachment styles and emotional and cognitive reactions to stressful events. In J. A. Simpson & W. S. Rholes (Eds.), *Attachment theory and close relationships* (pp. 143–165). New York: Guilford Press.

Mikulincer, M., Gillath, O., & Shaver, P. R. (2002). Activation of the attachment system in adulthood: Threat-related primes increase the accessibility of mental representations of attachment figures. *Journal of Personality and Social Psychology, 83,* 881–895.

Mikulincer, M., & Shaver, P. R. (2001). Attachment theory and intergroup bias: Evidence that priming the secure base schema attenuates negative reactions to out-groups. *Journal of Personality and Social Psychology, 81,* 97–115.

Mikulincer, M., & Shaver, P. R. (2003). The attachment behavioral system in adulthood: Activation, psychodynamics, and interpersonal processes. In M. P. Zanna (Ed.), *Advances in experimental social psychology* (Vol. 35, pp. 53–152). New York: Academic Press.

Mikulincer, M., & Shaver, P. R. (2005). Mental representations of attachment security: Theoretical foundation for a positive social psychology. In M. W. Baldwin (Ed.), *Interpersonal cognition* (pp. 233–266). New York: Guilford Press.

Mikulincer, M., & Shaver, P. R. (2007a). *Attachment in adulthood: Structure, dynamics, and change.* New York: Guilford Press.

Mikulincer, M., & Shaver, P. R. (2007b). Boosting attachment security to promote mental health, prosocial values, and inter-group tolerance. *Psychological Inquiry, 18,* 139–156.

Mikulincer, M., & Sheffi, E. (2000). Adult attachment style and cognitive reactions to positive affect: A test of mental categorization and creative problem solving. *Motivation and Emotion, 24,* 149–174.

Pistole, M., & Arricale, F. (2003). Understanding attachment: Beliefs about conflict. *Journal of Counseling and Development, 81*, 318–328.

Powers, S. I., Pietromonaco, P. R., Gunlicks, M., & Sayer, A. (2006). Dating couples' attachment styles and patterns of cortisol reactivity and recovery in response to a relationship conflict. *Journal of Personality and Social Psychology, 90*, 613–628.

Rahim, M. A. (1983). Measurement of organizational conflict. *Journal of General Psychology, 109*, 189–199.

Rankin, L. B., Saunders, D. G., & Williams, R. A. (2000). Mediators of attachment style, social support, and sense of belonging in predicting woman abuse by African American men. *Journal of Interpersonal Violence, 15*, 1060–1080.

Roberts, N., & Noller, P. (1998). The associations between adult attachment and couple violence: The role of communication patterns and relationship satisfaction. In J. A. Simpson & W. S. Rholes (Eds.), *Attachment theory and close relationships* (pp. 317–350). New York: Guilford Press.

Rosch, E. (1975). Cognitive representations of semantic categories. *Journal of Experimental Psychology: General, 104*, 192–233.

Senchak, M., & Leonard, K. E. (1992). Attachment styles and marital adjustment among newlywed couples. *Journal of Social and Personal Relationships, 9*, 51–64.

Shaver, P. R., & Hazan, C. (1993). Adult romantic attachment: Theory and evidence. In D. Perlman & W. Jones (Eds.), *Advances in personal relationships* (Vol. 4, pp. 29–70). London: Jessica Kingsley.

Shaver, P. R., & Mikulincer, M. (2002). Attachment-related psychodynamics. *Attachment and Human Development, 4*, 133–161.

Shaver, P. R., & Mikulincer, M. (2007). Adult attachment strategies and the regulation of emotion. In J. J. Gross (Ed.), *Handbook of emotion regulation* (pp. 446–465). New York: Guilford Press.

Shaver, P. R., & Mikulincer, M. (2008). Augmenting the sense of security in romantic, leader-follower, therapeutic, and group relationships: A relational model of psychological change. In J. P. Forgas & J. Fitness (Eds.), *Social relationships: Cognitive, affective, and motivational processes* (pp. 55–74). New York: Psychology Press.

Simpson, J. A., Rholes, W. S., & Phillips, D. (1996). Conflict in close relationships: An attachment perspective. *Journal of Personality and Social Psychology, 71*, 899–914.

Staub, E., & Bar-Tal, D. (2003). Genocide, mass killing and intractable conflict: Roots, evolution, prevention and reconciliation. In D. O. Sears, L. Huddy, & R. Jervis (Eds.) *Oxford handbook of political psychology* (pp. 710–751). New York: Oxford University Press.

Tajfel, H., & Turner, J. C. (1986). The social identity theory of intergroup behavior. In S. Worchel & W. Austin (Eds.), *Psychology of intergroup relations* (pp. 7–24). Chicago: Nelson.

Taubman-Ben-Ari, O., Findler, L., & Mikulincer, M. (2002). The effects of mortality salience on relationship strivings and beliefs: The moderating role of attachment style. *British Journal of Social Psychology, 41*, 419–441.

3

The Link Between Ostracism and Aggression

KIPLING D. WILLIAMS and ERIC D. WESSELMANN[1]

Purdue University

"Socially, Mack and the boys were beyond the pale. Sam Malloy didn't speak to them as they went by the boiler. They drew into themselves and no one could foresee how they would come out of the cloud. For there are two possible reactions to social ostracism—either a man emerges determined to be better, purer, and kindlier or he goes bad, challenges the world and does even worse things. This last is by far the commonest reaction…"

John Steinbeck, Cannery Row (1987, pp. 250–251)

*O*stracism[2]—being ignored and excluded—is a painful situation that the majority of individuals have experienced at least once in their lives and sometimes is a daily occurrence (Nezlek, Wheeler, Williams, & Govan, 2004; Williams, 2009). These experiences can be psychologically and emotionally damaging to the target: they can lead to self-defeating behavior (Twenge, Catanese, & Baumeister, 2002), impaired self-regulation (Baumeister, DeWall, Ciarocco, & Twenge, 2005; Oaten, Williams, Jones, & Zadro, 2008), and self-perceptions of dehumanization (Bastian & Haslam, 2010). Furthermore, ostracism has been shown to activate the same regions of the brain associated with physical pain

[1] Both authors contributed equally to the preparation of this manuscript. This material is based on work supported by the National Science Foundation under Grant No. 0519209.

[2] Research is unclear on the specific differences among *ostracism, rejection,* and *social exclusion;* oftentimes these three terms are used interchangeably. We acknowledge there are debates about the relations among these terms (see Leary et al., 2006; Williams, 2009), but for the sake of simplicity we will use the term *ostracism* throughout this chapter.

(Eisenberger, Lieberman, & Williams, 2003) and to lower significantly the targets' perceptions of four basic human needs: belonging, control, meaningful existence, and self-esteem (Williams, 2001, 2009; Williams, Cheung, & Choi, 2000; Zadro, Williams, & Richardson, 2004; see also Chapter 13 in this volume).

WHY OSTRACISM HURTS THE INDIVIDUAL

Social psychologists have theorized that humans are equipped with an evolved mechanism for detecting and responding to cues of ostracism (Kerr & Levine, 2008; Leary, Tambor, Terdal, & Downs, 1995; Spoor & Williams, 2007; see other evolutionary links to conflict in Chapters 15 and 18 in this volume). These systems are adaptive because at one time in our evolutionary history being ostracized from a social group could harm an individual's chances at survival—a form of "social death" (see Williams 2007; also Baumeister & Leary, 1995). Williams (2009) argues that these systems should be quick and crude, reacting at the slightest cue of ostracism, so that the individual can preemptively forestall or avoid permanent expulsion. Williams posits these cues set off the detection system, which elicits the experience of pain in the target individual (see Chen, Williams, Fitness, & Newton, 2008, for a discussion of social and physical pain; also MacDonald & Leary, 2005), and perceptions of threatened basic needs satisfaction.

Recent Evidence for the Ostracism Detection System

Several recent studies have examined the sensitivity of the ostracism detection system by examining the minimal cues and boundary conditions that exist for individuals to feel the sting of ostracism. Previous research had focused on studying ostracism in various types of face-to-face (Williams & Sommer, 1997) or electronic social interactions (Smith & Williams, 2004; Williams et al., 2000; Williams et al., 2002). Wirth and colleagues (Wirth, Sacco, Hugenberg, & Williams, 2010) decided to focus on how simple nonverbal cues of ostracism (e.g., lack of eye contact) influenced the detection system. These researchers found participants who received less eye contact from a virtual confederate were more likely to feel ignored and excluded, exhibiting the typical ostracism effects of threatened need satisfaction and worsened moods.

Kassner, Wirth, Law, and Williams (2010) argue that even the most minimal cues can trigger the detection system as long as social information is inherent in these cues. They used a virtual reality-based paradigm called Minimal World to ostracize participants in a situation where there was no social information present. Minimal World placed participants in a virtual environment where they saw two squares and a sphere in front of them (nonsocial versions of the player avatars and the ball in the Cyberball paradigm; Williams et al., 2000). The sphere moved back and forth between the two squares and occasionally moved toward the participant's point of view and disappeared. Participants were instructed to press one of two buttons when the sphere disappeared—one button sent the sphere back to the left square, and the other button sent the sphere to the right square. Participants were assigned randomly to one of four conditions in a 2 (ostracism–inclusion) × 2 (social information–no information) design. In the *inclusion* conditions, they were given the opportunity to control the sphere 33% of the time (similar to inclusion manipulations in other ostracism paradigms). Participants in the ostracism conditions had control over the sphere only twice at the beginning and then never again for the duration of the study. The researchers manipulated the *social information* by instructing half of the participants to mentally visualize a "coherent story" about the movement of the shapes; the other participants were not given these instructions. Results demonstrated that participants who were ostracized and given the social information experienced distress akin to ostracism in other paradigms, whereas participants who were not given the social information did not have different experiences from the inclusion conditions. These researchers concluded that as long as there is social information present, cues of ostracism should activate the detection system and thwart individuals' need satisfaction.

Other research suggests cues of ostracism do not have to be directed specifically at the individual to activate their detection system. Wesselmann and colleagues (Wesselmann, Bagg, & Williams, 2009) investigated how individuals responded to witnessing a stranger being ostracized (i.e., not thrown to during a virtual ball-toss game). Not only did participants recognize the ostracized individual would feel the effects of ostracism (i.e., thwarted need satisfaction and worsened mood), but these participants demonstrated distress similar to what they would feel as if they were personally experiencing the ostracism. These results, taken with the other research on boundary conditions for ostracism, lend credence to the argument that the ostracism detection system should crudely and quickly react to even the most minimal cues of ostracism (Williams, 2009).

WHY THE OSTRACIZED INDIVIDUAL HURTS OTHERS

Williams (2009) argued that behavioral responses to ostracism serve a fortification function for the need satisfaction threatened by ostracism (see also Leary, Twenge, & Quinlivan, 2006; Warburton, Williams, & Cairns, 2006; Williams & Govan, 2005). A substantial amount of research has been dedicated to examining the effects of ostracism on individuals' subsequent behavior, specifically aggressive behavior. Individuals appear to be more likely to behave aggressively toward another person after being ostracized, regardless of whether the person was involved or uninvolved in the targets' ostracism (Buckley, Winkel, & Leary, 2004; Carter-Sowell, Van Beest, van Dijk, & Williams, 2010; Chow, Tiedens, & Govan, 2008; Twenge, Baumeister, Tice, & Stucke, 2001; Twenge & Campbell, 2003; Warburton et al., 2006; Williams, 2001). Archival research even suggests long-term ostracism was a potential impetus for the violent behavior of many of the school shooters over the last decade (Leary, Kowalski, Smith, & Phillips, 2003). The ostracism→aggression link is not limited to current ostracism experiences—even recalling a previous experience of social pain is enough to increase individuals' temptations for aggressive behavior (Riva, Wirth, & Williams, 2010).

Restored Control Reduces Aggression After Ostracism

Some researchers have begun to explore the potential that aggressive responses to ostracism may serve to fortify control. Preliminary evidence suggests that individuals strive to exert control after being ostracized (Lawson Williams & Williams, 1998). In two studies, they found that ostracized males told a confederate to turn his head (supposedly to better "read" his nonverbal facial expressions) more often than included males and that ostracized females reported higher desire for control than included females. Furthermore, aggression allows the individual to assert control (Tedeschi, 2001). As an example, research has found that individuals who felt no control over their elevation to new majority status (they were previously in the minority) were more likely to exert abusive control over the new minority members compared with individuals whose rise to new majority status appeared to be the result of their own efforts (Prislin, Williams, & Sawiki, 2010). Thus, we reasoned that when control was sufficiently thwarted ostracized individuals might resort to aggression. Warburton, Williams, and Cairns (2006) argued that if aggressive responses to ostracism served to fortify threatened needs (e.g., need for control), aggressive responses should decrease if individuals were given a nonaggressive option to fortify themselves after ostracism. The researchers manipulated this nonaggressive option by having participants listen to a series of aversive noise blasts. Half of the participants were given control over the onset of the blasts; the other half had no control over blast onset. Warburton and colleagues found that ostracized participants who were not given the chance to fortify themselves by having control over the noise task responded most aggressively to ostracism. Ostracized participants given control over the noise task were no more likely to aggress than nonostracized people. The researchers concluded that giving ostracized participants control over an aspect of their environment fortified their threatened needs and reduced their reliance on aggression as a means of fortifying these needs.

Predictive Control, Ostracism, and Increased Aggression

Wesselmann and colleagues (Wesselmann, Butler, Williams, & Pickett, 2010) extended the argument that control needs have an important function in the ostracism→aggression relation. These researchers argued that unpredictable ostracism (typically the type experienced in laboratory studies; see Twenge et al., 2001) provides a double threat for targets: not only does this type of ostracism threaten need satisfaction, but it also shakes their confidence in their *sociometer*. Sociometer theory (Leary et al., 1995) is one of the social psychological theories that propose the existence of a psychological mechanism (i.e., a sociometer) that enables individuals to detect cues of potential ostracism during social interactions; a properly working sociometer affords an individual predictive control over an interaction.

Wesselmann and colleagues (2010) hypothesized the lack of predictive control inherent in unpredictable ostracism should increase participants' aggressive responses; participants who can predict ostracism should still perceive some predictive control and be less inclined to respond aggressively. They manipulated predictive control by varying confederate behavior toward participants before an ostracism manipulation. Confederates were trained to treat each participant either in a *friendly* or *unfriendly* manner during a group discussion. After the discussion, participants were informed that either everyone (*inclusion*) or no one (*ostracism*) wanted to work with them in an upcoming activity. In either of these conditions, participants were informed that the task would not accommodate that outcome so they would be working with a new participant who arrived late for a different study (thus not part of the participants' group discussion). Participants were instructed to prepare a sample of hot sauce for their partner to consume (the aggression measure). Participants were told that their partner did not like spicy foods and that their partner would have to consume however much the participant allocated. Results indicated that participants who were treated friendly but subsequently ostracized (*unpredictable ostracism*) perceived that they were less capable of predicting others' behavior (i.e., had a broken sociometer) and subsequently allocated more grams of hot sauce than participants who were treated unfriendly before being ostracized (*predictable ostracism*). Wesselmann and colleagues interpreted these findings as further evidence for the importance of control needs in how aggressively individuals may respond to ostracism.

ARE OSTRACIZED INDIVIDUAL ALWAYS ANTISOCIAL?

Antisocial or aggressive reactions are not the only way individuals respond to ostracism. Several studies have found that ostracized individuals may respond to their treatment in prosocial ways, perhaps striving to become reincluded. Ostracized individuals have been found to work harder on a collective group task (Williams & Sommer, 1997), to conform (Williams et al., 2000), to comply (Carter-Sowell, Chen, & Williams, 2008), to obey (Torstrick, 2010), to like or show interest in new groups (Maner, DeWall, Baumeister, & Schaller, 2007; Predmore & Williams, 1983), and to attempt to gain social reassurance by remaining a member of a group (Snoek, 1962) than included individuals. Research also finds these individuals more likely to emulate a cooperative group member (Ouwerkerk, Kerr, Gallucci, & Van Lange, 2005) and to engage in nonconscious mimicry (Lakin & Chartrand, 2005; Lakin, Chartrand, & Arkin, 2008). Finally, ostracized individuals are more socially attentive (Bernstein, Young, Brown, Sacco, & Claypool, 2008; DeWall, Maner, & Rouby, 2009; Gardner, Pickett, & Brewer, 2000; Pickett, Gardner, & Knowles, 2004).

How do we make sense of these seemingly contradictory behavioral response patterns? Recall that Williams (2009) argued that behavioral responses to ostracism are focused on fortifying their basic needs that have been threatened. Williams argued further that specific behavioral responses to ostracism should depend on the types of needs individuals are motivated to fortify. Prosocial responses likely focus on fortifying needs for belonging and self-esteem—we refer to these as the *inclusionary* needs cluster—and aggressive responses likely focus on fortifying needs for meaningful existence and control (the *power–provocation* needs cluster).

This premise has yet to be tested directly in an experimental setting, but there are several studies that could be reinterpreted within this framework. First, Warburton and colleagues (2006) found that ostracized participants who had their control needs restored before the aggression measure were no more likely to aggress than included participants; ostracized participants who were not afforded this restoration replicated the typical ostracism→aggression relation. According to Williams (2009), ostracized participants who were fortified subsequently would not need to respond aggressively because they had already recovered their need satisfaction. The research by Wesselmann and colleagues (2010) also supports this idea—because predicted ostracism is less of a threat to needs than unpredicted ostracism, less aggression would be necessary to recover. Additionally, the Lawson, Williams, and Williams study demonstrated increased or desired control following ostracism was most likely to occur when individuals were ostracized by two others who were friends with each other (but not with the participant). Follow-up research demonstrated that people feel the most control threat when they are strangers among others who are friends, so we once again see increased control exertion as control threat increases (Lawson, Williams, & Williams, 1998).

Other research offers support for Williams's (2009) need-fortification argument from a different perspective. Twenge and colleagues (Twenge et al., 2007) found that ostracized participants who were either reminded of a positive social relationship or had a pleasant interaction with an experimenter before an aggression measure were subsequently less likely to respond aggressively. Finally, Bernstein and colleagues (Bernstein, Sacco, Brown, Young, & Claypool, 2010) demonstrated that participants' needs for belonging and self-esteem had an important impact on their prosocial responses to ostracism. These researchers found that higher need threats to belonging and self-esteem mediated the relation between ostracism and participants' preferences for interacting with potential sources of affiliation.

WHAT FACTORS DETERMINE WHICH NEEDS ARE SALIENT?

Williams (2009) argues that attributions based on situational context and individual differences are likely to to be an important predictor in how individuals choose to fortify their threatened needs behaviorally. These attributions will dictate which cluster of needs (inclusionary or power–provocation) is most salient and thus the primary focus for fortification. For example, if the inclusionary cluster is most salient, ostracized individuals should choose to behave in prosocial ways, which elevate their chance for satisfying belonging and self-esteem. Alternatively, when the power–provocation cluster is most salient, ostracized individuals should choose antisocial (e.g., aggressive) behaviors to elevate their chance for satisfying control and meaningful existence.

Several different situational and individual difference factors can influence attributions for ostracism and ultimately the behavioral reponses from individuals (see Williams, 2009, for discussion). We propose that an important factor in ostracized individuals' attribution processes is their likelihood of being reincluded by the target of their subsequent behavioral responses (see also Twenge, 2005). The potential for reinclusion by another individual or group should make the inclusionary cluster most salient; if there is little chance for reinclusion, then the cluster that is most likely to be focused on is power–provocation. We will now review each of the paradigms used in studying the ostracism→aggression relation and then discuss how the potential for reinclusion (or lack thereof) may have facilitated anti-social responses to ostracism due to making the power–provocation cluster most salient in each of these paradigms.

General Descriptions of the Typical Ostracism Paradigms

Several paradigms are used to investigate the ostracism→aggression relation in experimental settings. We will now describe the general elements of each of these paradigms. One is the *life-alone* paradigm (Twenge et al., 2001), in which participants fill out a personality inventory and are first given accurate feedback about their introversion–extraversion. Following this, they are randomly assigned to receive a prognosis about their future lives: they are told they will have a life characterized by strong close relationships or that they will live a life alone, devoid of strong continuous relationships. For participants in the life-alone condition, the feedback informs them that they are powerless to do anything about their lack of inclusion.

Another paradigm is the *get-acquainted* paradigm (Buckley et al., 2004; Chow et al., 2008; Twenge et al., 2001; Twenge & Campbell, 2003; Wesselmann et al., 2010). Researchers who use this type of paradigm typically ask participants to engage in a group activity designed to allow members of the group to get to know each other. Following this interaction, participants are told that they either had been rejected by members of this group or had been accepted by them.

The third common paradigm in ostracism research is the *ball-tossing* paradigm (Carter-Sowell et al., 2010; Chow et al., 2008; Warburton et al., 2006). Studies using this paradigm engage participants in a ball-tossing game with other con-federates, either in a face-to-face format (originally used in Williams & Sommer, 1997) or via an electronic-based computer program called Cyberball (originally used in Williams et al., 2000; see also the "O-Cam" in Chapter 13 of this volume). Regardless of the format for ball tossing, participants are either included by the confederates (i.e., tossed the ball 33% of the time) or ostracized by confederates (i.e., tossed the ball twice at the beginning of the game and then never again). A typical game lasts between 3 and 5 minutes.

Each of these paradigms has been adapted in various studies, manipulat-ing different situational factors to elucidate the processes and nuances of the ostracism→aggression relation. We will now discuss these studies in detail, focus-ing on how these different situational factors may have influenced participants' perceptions of no potential for reinclusion, making the power–provocation cluster more salient than the inclusionary cluster.

Aggression Toward the Source of Ostracism

The majority of research on the ostracism→aggression link has examined aggres-sive behavior toward the sources of ostracism. These studies have used varia-tions on both the get-acquainted paradigm (Buckley et al., 2004; Chow et al., 2009, Study 2; Twenge & Campbell, 2003, Study 3) and the Cyberball paradigm

(Carter-Sowell et al., 2010; Chow et al., 2008, Study 1). In all of these studies, participants were given the opportunity to aggress against the individuals who were responsible for their previous ostracism. Participants also were not given a reason or explanation for their ostracism. In these situations, the power–provocation cluster should be most salient because participants likely did not expect the opportunity for reinclusion by the sources of ostracism. Chow and colleagues (2009, Study 2) manipulated information about the sources' perceptions of the participant and found that participants who thought they were ostracized due to the sources' misinformation were less likely to aggress because the participants could make an external attribution for the ostracism. These participants knew that they would not have the ability to be reincluded by the sources of ostracism, but they also thought that the ostracism was due to misinformation rather than something inherent about themselves.

Anecdotally, there are also indications that targets of the dyadic and interpersonal form of ostracism, the silent treatment, often resort to aggression toward the source of the silent treatment as a way to provoke a response (Zadro, Arriaga, & Williams, 2008; for other examples of interpersonal assertiveness and violence in this volume, see Chapters 2, 5, 11, 12, and 13).

Aggression Toward a Stranger

There have also been programs of research examining participants' aggressive responses toward strangers. These studies have also used variations on the get-acquainted (Twenge et al., 2007, Studies 4 and 5; Twenge & Campbell, 2003, Study 4) and ball-toss paradigms (Warburton et al., 2006), as well as the life-alone paradigm (Twenge et al., 2001, Studies 1–3). We argue that the power–provocation cluster was most salient in each of these studies, similar to the studies where the targets of aggression were responsible for participants' ostracism. The studies that used the life-alone paradigm (also Twenge et al., 2001, Study 4) gave ostracized participants the opportunity to aggress against a stranger who provoked them. Participants likely did not expect to be included by these strangers, even though they were not the source of participants' ostracism— provocation is not a typical response from a source of inclusion or acceptance (see Leary et al., 1995). The studies using the ball-tossing and get-acquainted paradigms are a bit more perplexing when considering how the power–provocation cluster was most salient. None of these studies offered participants the opportunity to interact with the stranger other than via the aggression measure, effectively removing this stranger as a potential source of reinclusion for participants. Wesselmann and colleagues (2010) offer us an additional explanation for why the get-acquainted paradigm may make the power–provocation cluster more salient than the inclusionary cluster. The traditional get-acquainted paradigm confronts participants with unexpected ostracism, thus threatening their perceptions of their ability to predict and forestall ostracism. These individuals would be less likely to focus on striving for reinclusion (i.e. inclusionary cluster) and instead should focus more on fortifying power–provocation cluster (typically via aggression).

THE INFLUENCE OF ATTRIBUTIONS AND EXPECTATIONS IN THE RESIGNATION STAGE

Williams (2009) argues that if ostracism persists over an extended period of time individuals will progress to a third stage—*resignation*. Extended ostracism can be from the same individual or group or by any number of different sources. If individuals find that their behavioral responses to ostracism fail to restore their need satisfaction, they learn that any attempt to recover from ostracism is likely futile. These individuals should then develop feelings of alienation, depression, helplessness, and unworthiness. It is likely that each of these negative outcomes from chronic ostracism will influence attributions for ostracism and ultimately expectations for reinclusion.

The resignation stage of ostracism has been largely ignored in scientific research, particularly in experimental paradigms due to the ethical and practical concerns of manipulating chronic ostracism in a laboratory. Several studies lend support to a potential link among chronic ostracism, expectations for reinclusion, and aggression. Maner and colleagues (2007) found that individuals who were high in Fear of Negative Evaluation (who expect generally unpleasant social interactions) perceived potential sources for reinclusion as hostile after experiencing ostracism, whereas individuals low in this trait responded favorably to these sources. Zadro (2004; Chapter 13 in this volume; see also Williams, 2001) conducted qualitative interviews with over 50 individuals who reported experiencing chronic ostracism from coworkers, friends, or family members. Several of these individuals reported engaging in aggressive behaviors in an attempt to be noticed, particularly when other attempts at reinclusion proved futile. Finally, research using the life-alone paradigm (Twenge et al., 2001) may also be reinterpreted in this framework. Recall that individuals in the life-alone condition are told that they will face ostracism for the rest of their lives, regardless of how much effort they dedicate to reinclusion. Participants in this condition typically respond to potential sources of reinclusion with aggression. This life-alone condition is the closest experimental manipulation of chronic ostracism currently in the literature, even though it is limited by its prospective nature.

RESIGNATION STAGE, NEED SALIENCE, AND EXTREME AGGRESSION

Perhaps one reason for the current fascination with the ostracism→aggression relation is that we are searching for explanations for a recent surge in seemingly irrational and socially intolerable behaviors that have appeared worldwide: random acts of monstrous violence. In news reports that we consider almost routine now, we are bombarded with stories of countless incidences in which individuals, often students in high school or college, have wielded weapons and, without apparent concern for their own survival, have shot and killed many of their peers and teachers. We have witnessed people's willingness to conduct terrorist acts against countless and unknown others, again with plausible certainty that in carrying out these acts they will perish with the victims.

School Violence

Since 1994, in U.S. schools alone there have been more than 220 separate shoot-ing incidents in which at least one person was killed and 18 episodes that involved multiple killings (Anderson et al., 2001). Mass shootings at schools and other public places are occurring with increasing frequency and in a growing number of other countries. Reasons for this upsurge in violence are still not clear, but a recent line of investigation has linked such incidents with growing social isolation (Twenge, 2000), and further evidence is beginning to emerge that prolonged experiences of ostracism may have played a significant motivating role in the actions of many perpetrators. In their case analysis of 15 post-1995 U.S. school shootings, Leary et al. (2003) suggest that chronic ostracism was a major contributing factor in 87% of cases. Studies of Martin Bryant, who, in 1996, killed 35 people at a popular tour-ist attraction at Port Arthur in Tasmania, suggest that he felt lonely and isolated (Bingham, 2000; Crook, 1997), and Robert Steinhauser, who killed 16 people at his former high school in Erfurt, Germany, in 2002, though not a social outcast (Lemonick, 2002), had been greatly upset by a significant act of ostracism—expul-sion from his school. Very recently, at Valparaiso High School in Indiana, a 15-year-old boy held hostage and slashed with two sharp-edged blades—one described as a machete—seven of his classmates. When peers were asked about this boy, it was reported, "He was so invisible at Valparaiso High School this fall that students who sat next to him in Spanish class didn't know his name" ("7 Valparaiso High Students Hurt in Stabbing Rampage," *Indianapolis Star*, November 25, 2004). The consequences of being ostracized, either intentionally or unintentionally, seem to be a thread that weaves through case after case of school violence.

We propose that these events can be reinterpreted as situations where the power–provocation cluster was likely more salient than inclusionary needs. Individuals who face chronic ostracism should not expect opportunities for reinclusion, having any previous attempts to fortify the inclusionary cluster prove ineffective. If an individ-ual has been continually thwarted in attempts to be reincluded, then he or she has no reason to expect to be included in future interactions. Thus, the power–provoca-tion cluster should be the most salient option for need fortification, and aggressive behavior is an effective method for satisfying this goal (Williams, 2009).

Extremist Groups

Many instances of school violence involve lone perpetrators, or at most a small group of perpetrators (e.g., the perpetrators of the Columbine High School mas-sacre). There are other acts of violence perpetrated by larger groups of disaffected individuals in different social settings that may be relevant to our discussion of how extended exposure to ostracism can facilitate violence. Wesselmann and Williams (2010) argued that individuals who are consistently ostracized by individuals or groups may become potential candidates for recruitment by dubious groups, such as cults, gangs, and even terrorist organizations. In general, ostracized individuals are more likely to comply with social influence tactics (Carter-Sowell et al., 2008) or to conform to group norms and expectations (Ouwerkerk et al., 2005; Williams &

Sommer, 1997). This striving for acceptance extends beyond controlled behaviors; ostracized individuals are more likely to mimic other individuals in a nonconscious manner (Lakin & Chartrand, 2005; Lakin, Chartrand, & Arkin, 2008). What if ostracized individuals strive to be reincluded so much that they do not rationally appraise the motives behind or consequences of being willingly influenced by the potential sources of reinclusion? Chapter 10 in this volume sheds further light on this possibility.

We propose that long-term ostracism can cause such a strong desire to belong, to be liked, by someone—perhaps anyone—that individuals' ability to discriminate good from bad and right from wrong may be impaired to the point that they may become attracted to cults and extremist groups that could ultimately influence them to acts of violence. Political scientists Tom Nairn and Paul James (2005) suggest that the profile of Australian citizens who had recently joined terrorist groups like Al Qaeda is of individuals who feel isolated, marginalized, or ostracized within their society and who are attracted to the intense face-to-face connectedness that these extremist groups have to offer. Joining and following the dictates of extremist groups fulfill needs not only for belonging and self-esteem but also for control and recognition because these groups promise retribution, worldwide attention, and personal significance (see Kruglanski, Chen, Dechesne, Fishman, & Orehek, 2009; see also Chapter 10 in this volume).

CONCLUSIONS AND FUTURE DIRECTIONS FOR RESEARCH

Ostracism is a painful event that many individuals experience, sometimes on a daily basis (Nezlek et al., 2004). Research has demonstrated that aggression is a common response to ostracism and is likely focused on recovering thwarted need satisfaction (Williams, 2009). This chapter reviewed research on individuals' reactions to ostracism over time, particularly on when and why individuals choose aggressive responses rather than prosocial options. We proposed an extension to Williams's need–recovery hypothesis on how to predict whether individuals will respond with pro- or antisocial behaviors in response to ostracism. We argue that an important factor in ostracized individuals' attribution processes is their likelihood of being reincluded by the target of their subsequent behavioral responses. We reviewed the experimental research documenting the ostracism→aggression link, highlighting the elements of those studies that are consistent with this interpretation.

The third stage of ostracism—the resignation stage—is particularly relevant to our discussion of expectations for reinclusion. Individuals who experience chronic ostracism have had their need satisfaction consistently thwarted and likely have resigned themselves to their lack of opportunities for inclusion. These individuals find themselves in a situation where power–provocation needs are their last bastion for fortification. This argument is consistent with the literature documenting the link between chronic ostracism and extreme violence (Leary et al., 2003; Williams, 2001). However, much of this research is correlational and often based on qualitative interviews or anecdotes. Future research needs to focus on investigating the resignation stage in rigorous experimental settings, particularly how perceptions for reinclusion may make aggressive responses more likely than prosocial responses to ostracism. When we achieve a sophisticated understanding of chronic ostracism, we will have better insight into when and why individuals may engage in antisocial and destructive responses.

REFERENCES

"7 Valparaiso High Students Hurt in Stabbing Rampage," *Indianapolis Star*, November 25, 2004.

Anderson, M. A., Kaufman, J., Simon, T. R., Barrios, L., Paulozzi, L., Ryan, G., et al. (2001). School-associated violent deaths in the United States. *Journal of the American Medical Association, 286*, 2695–2700.

Bastian, B., & Haslam, N. (2010). Excluded from humanity: The dehumanizing effects of social ostracism. *Journal of Experimental Social Psychology, 46*, 107–113.

Baumeister, R. F., DeWall, C. N., Ciarocco, N.J., & Twenge, J. M. (2005). Social exclusion impairs self-regulation. *Journal of Personality and Social Psychology, 88*, 589–604.

Baumeister, R. F., & Leary, M. R. (1995). The need to belong: Desire for inter-personal attachments as a fundamental human motivation. *Psychological Bulletin, 117*, 497–529.

Bernstein, M. J., Sacco, D. F., Brown, C. M., Young, S. G., & Claypool, H. M. (2010). A preference for genuine smiles following social exclusion. *Journal of Experimental Social Psychology, 46*, 196–199.

Bernstein, M. J., Young, S. G., Brown, C. M., Sacco, D. F., & Claypool, H. (2008). Adaptive responses to social exclusion: Social rejection improves detection of real and fake smiles. *Psychological Science, 19*, 981–983.

Bingham, M. (2000). *Suddenly one Sunday* (2d ed.) Pymble, New South Wales: Harper Collins.

Buckley, K. E., Winkel, R. E., & Leary, M. R. (2004). Reactions to acceptance and rejection: Effects of level and sequence of relational evaluation. *Journal of Experimental Social Psychology, 40*, 14–28.

Carter-Sowell, A. R., Chen, Z., & Williams, K. D. (2008). Ostracism increases social susceptibility. *Social Influence, 3*. 143–153.

Carter-Sowell, A. R., Van Beest I., van Dijk, E., & Williams, K. D. (2010). Groups being ostracized by groups: Is the pain shared, is recovery quicker, and are groups more likely to be aggressive? Manuscript in preparation.

Chen, Z., Williams, K. D., Fitness, J., & Newton, N. C. (2008).When hurt won't heal: Exploring the capacity to relive social pain. *Psychological Science, 19*, 789–795.

Chow, R. M., Tiedens, L. Z., & Govan, C. L. (2008). Excluded emotions: The role of anger in antisocial responses to ostracism. *Journal of Experimental Social Psychology, 44*, 896–903.

Crook, J. B. (1997). *Port Arthur: Gun tragedy, gun law miracle.* Melbourne: Gun Control Australia.

DeWall, C. N., Maner, J. K., & Rouby, D. A. (2009). Social exclusion and early-stage interpersonal perception: Selective attention to signs of acceptance. *Journal of Personality and Social Psychology, 96*, 729–741.

Eisenberger, N. I., Lieberman, M. D., & Williams, K. D. (2003). Does rejection hurt? An fMRI study of social exclusion. *Science, 302*, 290–292.

Gardner, W., Pickett, C. L., & Brewer, M. B. (2000). Social exclusion and selective memory: How the need to belong influences memory for social events. *Personality and Social Psychology Bulletin, 26,* 486–496.

Kassner, M. P., Wirth, J. H., Law, A. T., & Williams, K. D. (2010). Effects of mental visualization and social cues on detection and influence of ostracism. Manuscript in preparation.

Kerr, N. L., & Levine, J. M. (2008). The detection of social exclusion: Evolution and beyond. *Group Dynamics: Theory, Research, and Practice, 12,* 39–52.

Kruglanski, A. W., Chen, X., Dechesne, M., Fishman, S., & Orehek, E. (2009). Fully committed: Suicide bombers' motivation and the quest for personal significance. *Political Psychology, 30,* 331–357.

Lakin, J. L., & Chartrand, T. L. (2005). Exclusion and nonconscious behavioral mimicry. In K. D. Williams, J. P. Forgas, & W. von Hippel (Eds.), *The social outcast: Ostracism, social exclusion, rejection, and bullying* (pp. 279–295). New York: Psychology Press.

Lakin, J. L., Chartrand, T. L., & Arkin, R. M. (2008). I am too just like you: Nonconscious mimicry as an automatic behavioral response to social exclusion. *Psychological Science, 19,* 816–822.

Lawson Williams, H., & Williams, K. D. (1998, April). *Effects of social ostracism on desire for control.* Presented at Society for Australasian Social Psychology, Christchurch, NZ.

Leary, M. R., Kowalski, R. M., Smith, L., & Phillips, S. (2003). Teasing, rejection, and violence: Case studies of the school shootings. *Aggressive Behavior, 29,* 202–214.

Leary, M. R., Tambor, E. S., Terdal, S. K., & Downs, D. L. (1995). Self-esteem as an interpersonal monitor: The sociometer hypothesis. *Journal of Personality and Social Psychology, 68,* 518–530.

Leary, M. R., Twenge, J. M., & Quinlivan, E. (2006). Interpersonal rejection as a determinant of anger and aggression. *Personality and Social Psychology Review, 10,* 111–132.

Lemonick, M. D. (2002, May 6). Germany's Columbine. *Time Magazine* (New York), *159* (18), 36–39.

MacDonald, G., & Leary M. R. (2005). Why does social exclusion hurt? The relationship between social and physical pain. *Psychological Bulletin, 131,* 202–223.

Maner, J. K., DeWall, C. N., Baumeister, R. F., & Schaller, M. (2007). Does social exclusion motivate interpersonal reconnection? Resolving the "porcupine problem." *Journal of Personality and Social Psychology, 92,* 42–55.

Nairn, T., & James, P. (2005). *Global matrix: Nationalism, globalism, and state-terrorism.* London: Pluto Press.

Nezlek, J., Wheeler, L., Williams, K., & Govan, C. (2004, January). Ostracism in everyday life. Presented at the Society for Personality and Social Psychology, Austin, TX.

Oaten, M., Williams, K. D., Jones, A., & Zadro, L. (2008). The effects of ostracism on self-regulation in the socially anxious. *Journal of Social and Clinical Psychology, 27,* 471–504.

Ouwerkerk, J. W., Kerr, N. L., Gallucci, M., & Van Lange, P. A. M. (2005). Avoiding the social death penalty: Ostracism and cooperation in social dilemmas. In K. D. Williams, J. P. Forgas, & W. von Hippel (Eds.), *The social outcast: Ostracism, social exclusion, rejection, and bullying* (pp. 321–332). New York: Psychology Press.

Pickett, C. L., Gardner, W. L., & Knowles, M. (2004). Getting a cue: The need to belong and enhanced sensitivity to social cues. *Personality and Social Psychology Bulletin, 30,* 1095–1107.

Predmore, S. J., & Williams, K. D. (1983, May). *The effects of social ostracism on affiliation.* Paper presented at the meeting of the Midwestern Psychological Association, Chicago, IL.

Prislin, R., Williams, K. D., & Sawicki, V. (2010). New majorities' abuse of power: Effects of perceived control and social support. Unpublished manuscript, San Diego State University, CA.

Riva, P., Wirth, J. H., & Williams, K. D. (2010, May). The social impact of suffering: Psychical pain thwarts social needs. Paper presented at the meeting of the Midwestern Psychological Association, Chicago, IL.

Smith, A., & Williams, K. D. (2004). R U There? Effects of ostracism by cell phone messages. *Group Dynamics: Theory, Research, and Practice, 8*, 291–301.

Snoek, J. D. (1962). Some effects of rejection upon attraction to a group. *Journal of Abnormal and Social Psychology, 64*, 175–182.

Spoor, J. R., & Williams, K. D. (2007). The evolution of an ostracism detection system. In J. P. Forgas, M. G. Haselton, & W. von Hippel (Eds.), *Evolution and the social mind: Evolutionary psychology and social cognition* (pp. 279–292). New York: Psychology Press.

Steinbeck, J. (1987). *Of mice and men/Cannery row*. New York: Penguin Books. (Original work published 1945.)

Tedeschi, J. T. (2001). Social power, influence, and aggression. In J. P. Forgas & K. D. Williams (Eds.), *Social influence: Direct and indirect processes* (pp. 109–128). New York: Psychology Press.

Twenge, J. M. (2000). The age of anxiety? The birth cohort change in anxiety and neuroticism, 1952–1993. *Journal of Personality and Social Psychology, 79*, 1007–1021.

Twenge, J. M. (2005). When does social rejection lead to aggression? The influences of situations, narcissism, emotion, and replenishing connections. In K. D. Williams, J. P. Forgas, & W. von Hippel (Eds.), *The social outcast: Ostracism, social exclusion, rejection, and bullying* (pp. 201–212). New York: Psychology Press.

Twenge, J. M., Baumeister, R. F., Tice, D. M., & Stucke, T. S. (2001). If you can't join them, beat them: Effects of social exclusion on aggressive behavior. *Journal of Personality and Social Psychology, 81*, 1058–1069.

Twenge, J. M., & Campbell, W. K. (2003). "Isn't it fun to get the respect that we're going to deserve?" Narcissism, social rejection, and aggression. *Personality and Social Psychology Bulletin, 29*, 261–272.

Twenge, J. M., Catanese, K. R., & Baumeister, R. F. (2002). Social exclusion causes self-defeating behavior. *Journal of Personality and Social Psychology, 83*, 606–615.

Twenge, J. M., Zhang, L., Catanese, K. R., Dolan-Pascoe, B., Lyche, L. R., & Baumeister, R. F. (2007). Replenishing connectedness: Reminders of social activity reduce aggression after social exclusion. *British Journal of Social Psychology, 46*, 205–224.

Warburton, W. A., Williams, K. D., & Cairns, D. R. (2006). When ostracism leads to aggression: The moderating effects of control deprivation. *Journal of Experimental Social Psychology, 42*, 213–220.

Wesselmann, E. D., Bagg, D., & Williams, K. D. (2009). "I feel your pain": The effects of observing ostracism on the ostracism detection system. *Journal of Experimental Social Psychology, 45*, 1308–1311.

Wesselmann, E. D., Butler, F. A., Williams, K. D., & Pickett, C. L. (2010). Adding injury to insult: Unexpected rejection leads to more aggressive responses. *Aggressive Behavior, 35*, 232–237.

Wesselmann, E. D., & Williams, K. D. (2010). The potential balm of religion and spirituality for recovering from ostracism. *Journal of Management, Spirituality, and Religion, 7*, 29–45.

Williams, K. D. (2001). *Ostracism: The power of silence*. New York: Guilford Press.

Williams, K. D. (2007). Ostracism: The kiss of social death. *Social and Personality Psychology Compass, 1*, 236–247.

Williams, K. D. (2009). Ostracism: Effects of being excluded and ignored. In M. P. Zanna (Ed.), *Advances in experimental social psychology* (Vol. 41, pp. 275–314). New York: Academic Press.

Williams, K. D., Cheung, C. K. T., & Choi, W. (2000). Cyberostracism: Effects of being ignored over the Internet. *Journal of Personality and Social Psychology, 79,* 748–762.

Williams, K. D., & Govan, C. L. (2005). Reacting to ostracism: Retaliation or reconciliation? In D. Abrams, M. A. Hogg, & J. M. Marques (Eds.), *The social psychology of inclusion and exclusion* (pp. 47–62). New York: Psychology Press.

Williams, K. D., Govan, C. L., Croker, V., Tynan, D., Cruickshank, M., & Lam, A. (2002). Investigations into differences between social and cyberostracism. *Group Dynamics: Theory, Research, and Practice, 6,* 65–77.

Williams, K. D., & Sommer, K. L. (1997). Social ostracism by coworkers: Does rejection lead to social loafing or compensation. *Personality and Social Psychology Bulletin, 23,* 693–706.

Wirth, J. H., Sacco, D. F., Hugenberg, K., & Williams, K. D. (2010). Eye gaze as relational evaluation: Averted eye gaze leads to feelings of ostracism and relational devaluation. *Personality and Social Psychology Bulletin, 36,* 869–882.

Zadro, L. (2004). *Ostracism: Empirical studies inspired by real-world experiences of silence and exclusion.* Unpublished doctoral dissertation. University of New South Wales, Sydney.

Zadro, L., Arriaga, X. B., & Williams, K. D. (2008). Relational ostracism. In J. P. Forgas & J. Fitness (Eds.), *Social relationships: Cognitive, affective, and motivational processes* (pp. 305–320). New York: Psychology Press.

Zadro, L., Williams, K. D., & Richardson, R. (2004). How low can you go? Ostracism by a computer is sufficient to lower self-reported levels of belonging, control, self-esteem, and meaningful existence. *Journal of Experimental Social Psychology, 40,* 560–567.

4

Is It Aggression?
Perceptions of and Motivations for Passive and Psychological Aggression

DEBORAH SOUTH RICHARDSON and
GEORGINA S. HAMMOCK

Augusta State University

*T*his chapter reviews programs of research on correlates and perceptions of "everyday" forms of aggression that often are not considered in traditional aggression research. These studies reveal that everyday passive and psychological aggression are often motivated by intentions other than the intention to cause harm (e.g., inducing guilt), although the effect is to harm the target. Similarly, comparison of perceptions of psychological and physical aggression reveal that psychological aggression, which is defined in terms of harming an individual's self-regard, may be perceived as less damaging than physical aggression, although the potential for long-term harm is greater (e.g., Follingstad, Rutledge, Berg, Hause, & Polek, 1990).

INTRODUCTION

Aggression is typically defined as behavior intended to harm another person (Baron & Richardson, 1994). Although there has been some argument about whether intention should be central to the definition of aggression (i.e., aggression is behavior that harms, regardless of intention of the aggressor), most current definitions of aggression involve the concept of intention to harm. Such definitions thus require that we consider the observer's inference about an actor's goals (Tedeschi & Felson, 1994) and that we consider a variety of types of harm.

The harm of direct aggression is readily apparent, and intention seems to be easily determined. A person who delivers a blow or a face-to-face insult to another person is clearly intending to cause harm. Most theoretical treatments and empirical findings regarding human aggressive behavior have focused on such obvious aggressive acts. However, some types of harm are more elusive, more open to alternative interpretations. For example, I might comment on an acquaintance's unusual form of attire out of curiosity or to make him feel self-conscious; my curiosity would not be harmful, but an attempt to make him self-conscious would be. Similarly, forgetting to pick up the wine on the way home when we are having a dinner party might be an honest mistake, or it might be an attempt to make my partner look bad to company (that I didn't want to have anyway). These less direct forms of aggression do indeed cause harm, but they are easier to deny and more difficult to interpret; in addition, the aggressor can deny the intent to harm. These forms of aggressive behavior may have other goals in addition to or instead of harm to the target. For example, psychological aggression may harm the target by humiliating or demeaning him or her; passive aggression may harm a target by obstructing a goal; indirect aggression may harm a target by disrupting relationships.

We argue that it is important to consider the various forms of aggression because direct or physical aggression is not what people are likely to experience most frequently in their day-to-day lives. They are more likely to be victims of snide remarks or hostile attitudes than they are to be victims of criminal violence. Individuals are more likely to gossip about someone than to slap or kick them. The more subtle, less direct kinds of aggression are likely to affect individuals' relationship experience and success as well as their sense of self. Thus, we have focused on these forms of aggression in an attempt to capture the experience of everyday people experiencing everyday aggression. Of course, a variety of forms of everyday aggression are not addressed in this chapter—experiences such as road rage, racial or sexual discrimination—but in many cases those specific forms of everyday aggression might also be considered expressions of either passive or psychological aggression.

PASSIVE AGGRESSION

Passive aggression is behavior that is intended to harm another living being by not doing something, by obstructing the target's goals. This is in contrast to other forms of aggression such as direct or indirect verbal or physical aggression. Direct aggression involves direct confrontation with the target (e.g., physical blows, verbal insults), whereas indirect aggression is nonconfrontive, delivering harm through another person or object (e.g., spreading rumors, damaging target's property). Indirect aggression (sometimes called relational or social aggression) has received considerable attention from researchers in recent years (Archer & Coyne, 2005; Björkqvist, Osterman, & Lagerspetz, 1994; Crick & Grotpeter, 1995; Richardson & Green, 2006). Chapter 17 in this volume notes that indirect aggression may take a variety of forms, including cyberaggression and using social networking to deliver harm to another. Passive aggression, however, has received little attention.

Passive aggression has been defined, conceptually and operationally, in a wide variety of ways in the research literature. In a study of driver characteristics associated with aggressive driving and road rage, passive aggression was defined as "impeding traffic" (Dukes, Clayton, Jenkins, Miller, & Rodgers, 2001, p. 323). Kingery's (1998) Adolescent Violence Survey includes a passive aggression subscale consisting of items such as "Talked about someone's faults to other people so others wouldn't like them" and "Prevented someone from going where he/she wanted to go by getting in the way." In a study in which participants judged a variety of aggression actions, passive aggression was defined as "withholding available and needed resources" (Berkowitz, Mueller, Schnell, & Padberg, 1986, p. 887).

Although direct reference to passive aggression is relatively rare in the research literature, several lines of research are closely related. For example, Williams and colleagues' work on social ostracism has some clear connections to our concept of passive aggression (Sommer, Williams, Ciarocco, & Baumeister, 2001; Williams, 1997; Williams, Shore, & Grahe, 1998; see also Chapters 3 and 13 in this volume). These researchers define social ostracism as "the silent treatment." Both perpetrators and targets of such social ostracism report that the primary motive is punitive, "to punish or correct the target; to hurt or seek revenge" (Sommer et al., p. 229), and the primary emotion reported in both target and source narratives is anger. Thus, such social ostracism might be reasonably considered a form of passive aggression, behavior that is intended to punish or hurt, that involves anger, and that involves not doing something (i.e., not attending to the target).

Passive aggression is likely to be an especially attractive strategy in some contexts. Like other nondirect forms of aggression (which may include both indirect or social aggression as well as passive aggression), passive aggression may be a desirable alternative when an individual wants to avoid detection or retaliation. It provides the aggressor an easy opportunity for denial (i.e., "I didn't do anything") as if by not doing he or she is blameless. Thus, the passive aggressor denies the harm that may come from such behavior.

We have conducted two lines of research aimed at providing a clearer understanding of the nature of passive aggression. The first was designed to determine whether passive aggression can be considered a unique form of aggression, differentiated from other forms of nondirect aggression (e.g., indirect or relational aggression). The second, which was designed to determine how the different forms of aggression are perceived by aggressors and targets, is most directly relevant to the topic of this chapter; as we consider the question of the extent to which each form of aggression is perceived to be harmful or might be perceived as meeting other goals, we are, in essence, asking, "Is it aggression?"

An understanding of the distinctiveness (or lack thereof) of passive aggression is an important starting point. Thus, we will summarize the results of the first line of research before focusing on the research that examines motivations and effects of the different forms of aggression.

Distinctiveness of Passive Aggression

Three studies examined whether passive aggression could be distinguished from direct and indirect aggression. The Richardson Conflict Response Questionnaire (RCRQ), which has been used in a variety of investigations of direct and indirect aggression (Richardson & Green, 2003), was modified to include items measuring passive aggression (e.g., "Did not do what the other person wanted me to do," "Gave the person the 'silent treatment,'" "Failed to return calls or respond to messages"). In the first study, on conflict in the workplace, participants reported how they responded when angry with a supervisor, a coworker, or a subordinate. The second study examined responses "in general." The third study inquired about responses when angry with romantic partners, siblings, coworkers, or friends.

If passive aggression is a distinct form of aggression it should also be differentially correlated with other measures. The second two studies in this series examined the relationship of the three forms of aggression with other measures of anger and aggression: Spielberger's (1999) State-Trait Anger Expression Inventory–2 (STAXI-2) and the Buss–Perry Aggression Questionnaire (AQ; 1992). The STAXI measures trait (i.e., dispositional) anger as well as anger expression (anger-in, anger-out, anger control). Anger-in involves the frequency with which an individual experiences anger but holds it in (e.g., "I tend to harbor grudges that I don't tell anyone about"). Anger-out involves the frequency with which a person experiences anger and openly expresses it (e.g., "I lose my temper"). Anger control considers the frequency with which an individual experiences anger but controls it (e.g., "I control my temper").

The results of the two studies were consistent. The primary distinction among the forms of aggression was that passive and indirect aggression were more highly correlated with anger-in than was direct aggression and that direct aggression was more highly correlated with trait anger, anger-out, and anger control. Correlations with subscales of the AQ revealed similar findings. RCRQ direct aggression was more highly associated with anger and direct verbal and physical aggression subscales of the AQ than were passive or indirect aggression. Replicating results of previous research (Richardson & Green, 2003), these findings suggest that passive and indirect aggression are likely to be employed by individuals who experience, but may have difficulty directly expressing, their anger. Direct aggression, on the other hand, may be used by individuals who express their anger more (i.e., anger-out), who are generally more angry (i.e., trait anger), and find controlling their anger to be a challenge.

Based on anecdotal evidence from everyday experiences of members of our research team (who could give multiple examples of passive aggressive behavior from their romantic partners) as well as literature on dynamics of different types of relationships, we expected that passive aggression would be a frequent strategy in romantic relationships. For example, Gottman (1994) reports that one common response of individuals in unhappy relationships is "stonewalling," which involves withdrawing from interaction and refusing to address the partner's complaints, a behavior that our model would clearly classify as passive aggression.

We were correct in this prediction. Participants reported using more passive than indirect or direct aggression when angry with a romantic partner. However, we found that respondents reported more passive aggression when angry with *any-one* (i.e., coworkers, friends, and siblings as well as romantic partners). So, is it aggression?

Motivators and Effects of Different Forms of Aggression

The common correlates of passive and indirect aggression suggest that the two forms of aggression may not be clearly distinguishable—that they both belong to a general category of nondirect aggression. On the other hand, we have distinguished them conceptually (i.e., circuitous harm versus harm by not doing), and those conceptual definitions suggest that aggressors might be motivated by different factors when they are using passive aggression than when they are using indirect aggression. For example, passive aggression, which involves harming another person by not doing something, may be intended to annoy the target as much as to harm and may not be perceived by either aggressor or target as particularly aggressive. Thus, we conducted two studies to determine whether people might perceive the aggressor's motives and the effects on the victim to vary as a function of type of aggression.

We asked participants to evaluate a series of behaviors from the perspective either of the aggressor or of the target. Direct aggressive behaviors included "yell or scream," "threaten to hit or throw something," and "push, grab, shove." Indirect aggressive behaviors included "make negative comments about appearance," "call names behind back," and "gather other people to my side." Passive aggressive behaviors included "give silent treatment," "avoid interacting," and "fail to return calls."

Participants responding from the perspective of the aggressor were asked why they would engage in the behavior and to imagine how the target would feel. For example, "Why would you yell or scream at someone?" and "Imagine that you yell or scream at someone. How do you think that person would feel?" Participants responding from the perspective of the target were asked why someone would behave that way toward them and how they would feel in response. For example, "Why would someone yell or scream at you?" and "How would you feel if someone yelled or screamed at you?" The aggressor motivations and target effects were as follows: to harm–felt harmed, to gain power–felt powerless, to control–felt controlled, to cause distress–felt distressed, to humiliate–felt humiliated, to cause guilt–felt guilty.

The first study in this series asked for responses "in general"; the second study asked for responses in specific relationships. In both studies, responses for the specific forms of each type of aggression (e.g., for direct aggression, yelling, pushing, threatening) were highly consistent, so we created summary scores for direct, indirect, and passive aggression.

Because the different motivations and effects were highly correlated in Study 1, we also created indices of general motivation (i.e., average response to all motivations) and general effects (i.e., average response across all effects). Thus, in Study 1 we were actually assessing the extent to which aggressors would be generally motivated to perform the aggressive behaviors and the extent to which targets would be generally affected by the aggressive behaviors.

Participants perceived that the perpetrator of passive aggression would be generally less motivated than the perpetrator of either direct or indirect aggression. Participants also perceived that passive aggression would have less effect on the target than either direct or indirect aggression. Since all of the motivations and effects involved a negative experience for the victim, we can infer that passive aggression was perceived to be intended to produce a less negative experience for the victim, and it was perceived to be less motivated by the desire for negative outcomes for the victim. So is it aggression?

The second study in this series involved the same basic procedures as the first, but participants were asked to respond with reference to either a same-sex friend or a romantic partner. That is, from the perspective of the aggressor, participants were asked the extent to which they would be motivated by the various factors (e.g., control, harm, humiliate) if they were to aim the passive, indirect, and direct aggressive acts toward a same-sex friend or toward a romantic partner and the extent to which the target would experience the different effects. When responding from the perspective of the target, participants were asked the extent to which they would experience the various effects and the extent to which they would perceive the aggressor to be motivated by the various factors.

Participants responding from the perspective of an aggressor perceived harm to be associated more with direct and indirect aggression than with passive aggression. Control was associated with direct aggression; humiliation and low levels of distress with indirect aggression; guilt with passive aggression. Passive aggression was perceived as being less motivated by the desire to cause harm to or to humiliate the victim and more motivated by the desire to induce guilt than direct or indirect aggression. Nevertheless, passive aggression was perceived as being intended to cause as much distress as direct aggression and more distress than indirect aggression.

The perceived effects on victim of each type of aggressive behavior are notably consistent with perceptions of aggressor motivation. From the perspective of the target of the aggressive acts, power was associated with direct aggression; humiliation and distress with indirect aggression; guilt with passive aggression. Passive aggression was perceived to produce less humiliation, distress, or harm than either of the other forms of aggression. Again, harm was associated primarily with direct and indirect aggression.

Passive aggression was the most frequently endorsed anger response in all three studies; in general, participants reported more frequent use of passive aggression than either direct or indirect aggression. Thus, it appears that aggression researchers may be ignoring a form of aggression that people report they engage in quite frequently.

In sum, our examination of aggressor and victim perspectives on the motivations and effects of direct, indirect, and passive aggression provides a further understanding of the distinctiveness (or lack thereof) of passive aggression. Everyday indirect aggression, which is seen as causing harm, humiliation, and distress, is consistent with our definition of aggression. Everyday passive aggression is seen as causing distress and guilt but as causing relatively little harm; so is it aggression?

Conclusion: Is Passive Aggression Aggressive?

Our series of studies on passive aggression reveal that it is an "attractive" response when angry with someone; it is the behavior that respondents indicated they performed most frequently in general and across a variety of relationships when they were angry. The correlations of self-reports of aggression with measures of anger suggest that nondirect forms of aggression, including indirect and passive aggression, are endorsed especially by individuals who report difficulty expressing their anger. The nondirect nature of these forms of aggression allows the individual to respond when angry but to avoid direct confrontation with the victim.

According to current definitions of aggression, a behavior must be intended to cause harm to be considered as aggressive. Our research suggests that the nature of that harm may vary with type of aggression. For example, although passive aggression was perceived to be less harmful than indirect or direct aggression, it was perceived as a mechanism for inducing guilt and for causing distress to the victim. An interesting corollary of this aspect of passive aggression is that the ultimate effect of the behavior on the victim may depend to a considerable extent on the victim's chosen response to the aggression. For example, if I intend to induce guilt by passive aggressively noting how much hard work I have done for you, but you refuse to experience guilt, then my passive aggressive strategy will have failed. When one administers direct verbal or physical blows to a victim—or even indirect verbal or physical blows—it is difficult for the victim to avoid or deny the harm; the victim has little control over the administration of the harm. However, in the case of passive aggression, the victim can, in effect, choose whether to acknowledge or experience the harm. This might be an interesting question for future research that would focus on differential victim response to passive aggressive attempts.

In sum, these examinations of passive aggression suggest that such behavior is deserving of the attention of aggression researchers. It is a behavior that can cause harm; it is a preferred response to anger; the nature and degree of harm is subject to interpretation by the victim.

PSYCHOLOGICAL AGGRESSION

Aggression researchers have paid more attention to everyday harm that is referred to as psychological aggression, especially in the context of research on intimate partner violence. Although the research literature reveals no consistent definition of psychological aggression, the definitions typically refer to emotional harm or the use of tactics such as degradation, ridicule, and social and financial isolation. We conceptualize psychological aggression as harmful behaviors that damage the self-concept of the individual. The "everyday" nature of this type of aggression can be seen in its prevalence in intimate relationships: Capaldi and Crosby (1997) reported that 80% of intimate partners engaged in at least one act of psychological aggression while being observed discussing a problem with a partner; O'Leary and Williams (2006) reported prevalence rates of approximately 90% in a community sample.

Psychological aggression is perceived by targets as more harmful than physical aggression (Follingstad, Rutledge, Berg, Hause, & Polek, 1990; Katz, Arias, & Beach, 2000). Studies of the correlates of psychological and physical aggression reveal common predictors (e.g., Hammock, 2003; Hammock & O'Hearn, 2002), and the two forms of aggression commonly co-occur (e. g., Follingstad et al.; Hamby & Sugarman, 1999; Hammock & O'Hearn; Murphy & O'Leary, 1989). Some researchers (e.g., Murphy & Cascardi, 1999; Stets, 1991) have suggested that the primary motivation for both forms of aggression in the context of intimate partner relationships may be control of the partner and the relationship. As is the case with passive aggression, these "other" motivations do not directly suggest intent to harm, but harm may nevertheless be the effect on the victim.

We conducted two studies to determine how third parties perceive the motivation or intentions behind psychologically and physically aggressive acts in a conflict between a husband and wife. The first study examined the effects of type of aggression (physical vs. psychological) as well as gender of aggressor. The second study also considered the effect of the perceiver's own experience as victim or perpetrator of aggression in intimate relationships.

Participants were asked to imagine that they were observing their married neighbors having a fight. The scenario depicted a couple engaged in a heated discussion about money. Some participants read a scenario about the perpetrator using physically aggressive acts such as throwing books at the victim, slapping the victim, and slamming the victim against the wall; others read about the perpetrator using psychologically aggressive acts such as belittling the victim and the victim's family, ridiculing the victim, threatening to financially isolate the victim, and insulting the victim. We also manipulated gender composition of the perpetrator–victim dyad, with some participants reading about husband-to-wife aggression and others about wife-to-husband aggression.

Participants responded to questions about their judgment of the actions and actors in the scenario, such as whether the behavior displayed would be considered abusive, whether the perpetrator should be punished for his or her actions, and whether the victim suffered any harm. Respondents also reported the extent to which the aggressor was motivated to make the victim feel bad, to control the relationship, to injure the victim, to hurt the victim, to gain power in the relationship, and to control the victim.

Physical aggression was generally perceived to have more negative outcomes than psychological aggression. Participants reported that perpetrators of physical aggression should be punished more and had engaged in more abusive actions than perpetrators of psychological aggression. They also considered the victim of physical aggression to have suffered more harm than the victim of psychological aggression. Nevertheless, the high ratings for both forms of aggression (well above midpoint of scale) suggest that psychologically aggressive actions were considered to be harmful, abusive, and deserving of punishment—just not as much so as physical aggression.

Psychologically aggressive perpetrators were perceived to be more motivated to control the relationship or partner, to gain power in the relationship, and to make the victim feel bad than were physically aggressive perpetrators. However, psychological and physical aggression were not rated as differentially motivated to cause injury or hurt the victim. Thus, it appears that third parties recognize that the intent of the perpetrator of psychological aggression may be negative in a variety of ways, especially with regard to control and power.

In terms of an overall comparison of psychological and physical aggression, participants considered physical aggression to lead to more negative outcomes (e.g., abuse, harm), but they did not see it as being more motivated to hurt or injure the victim. And, as suggested earlier, psychological aggression was considered to be more motivated to control or gain power in the relationships. In terms of defining aggression, perceivers certainly recognize that harm derives from attempts to cause psychological damage to a partner.

As mentioned earlier, those who have experienced psychological and physical aggression report that psychological aggression is more harmful and damaging than physical aggression (Follingstad et al., 1990; Katz et al., 2000). Therefore, we reasoned that individuals who have been victims of psychological aggression may be more likely to recognize the pain and harm of such actions when serving as third-party perceivers. In Study 2 we hypothesized that those who had been victims of physical or psychological aggression would perceive those actions as more damaging than those who had not experienced such victimization. We measured experience with psychological and physical aggression with the Abusive Behavior Inventory (Shepard & Campbell, 1992).

Experience with physical and psychological aggression did not relate to participants' judgments of the outcomes of psychological and physical aggression. Again, participants believed the physically aggressive actions of the perpetrator were more deserving of punishment and more abusive than psychologically aggressive actions. They also perceived the physically aggressive acts as more wrong than the psychologically aggressive acts. Nevertheless, participants consistently judged the psychologically aggressive actions quite negatively—though not as negatively as those associated with physical aggression.

Participant experience as victims of physical aggression did not relate to perceptions of aggressor motivations. However, respondents who had more experience as victims of psychological aggression perceived the psychologically aggressive perpetrator as being more motivated to make the victim feel bad about himself or herself and more motivated to control the victim than those who had less experience as victims of psychological aggression. Experience with psychological aggression was not related to the perception of physical aggression.

These studies taken together suggest that people perceive psychological aggression as harmful to the target of such actions—although there is considerable variability in the nature of the harm they perceive to be inflicted. Rather than harming the physical person, the harm may be in the form of psychological distress (making the victim feel bad about himself or herself) or in terms of manipulation of the victim (controlling the relationship or victim, gaining power in the relationship). These types of harm may not come immediately to mind when considering the impact of aggressive acts. Nevertheless, the distress and powerlessness experienced by the victim of psychological aggression are likely to have a strong negative impact on the recipient and on the relationship between the victim and the aggressor, and these bruises to the psyche are more frequent occurrences than the more salient, more visible bruises to the body.

CONCLUSION

The programs of research reviewed in this chapter bring to the forefront forms of harm-doing behavior that are frequently ignored by aggression researchers. This research suggests a more inclusive definition of aggression that considers aggression to have occurred if a target has been harmed, thus moving the focus from the intent of the aggressor to the effect on the victim and recognizing that a variety of aggressor motivations may lead to a variety of harmful outcomes for the victim. Such a victim-centered definition would move us toward new acceptance of the simple definition of aggression as a behavior that causes harm.

Or we may want to consider a revolutionary social psychological definition of aggression that would incorporate the intention of the aggressor to produce negative outcomes for a target who experiences harm. Such an approach, which would define aggression as an interaction, would be truly social psychological.

REFERENCES

Archer, J., & Coyne, S. M. (2005). An integrated review of indirect, relational, and social aggression. *Personality and Social Psychology Review, 9*, 212–230.

Baron, R. A., & Neuman, J. H. (1996). Workplace violence and workplace aggression: Evidence on their relative frequency and potential causes. *Aggressive Behavior, 22*, 161–173.

Baron, R. A., & Richardson, D. R. (1994). *Human aggression.* New York: Plenum.

Basow, S. A., Cahill, K. F., Phelan, J. E., Longshore, K., & McGillicuddy-DeLisi, A. (2007). Perceptions of relational and physical aggression among college students: Effects of gender of perpetrator, target, and perceiver. *Psychology of Women Quarterly, 31*, 85–95.

Berkowitz, M. W., Mueller, C. W., Schnell, S. V., & Padberg, M. T. (1986). Moral reasoning and judgments of aggression. *Journal of Personality and Social Psychology, 51*, 885–891.

Björkqvist, K., Osterman, K., & Lagerspetz, K. (1994). Sex differences in covert aggression among adults. *Aggressive Behavior, 20*, 27–33.

Buss, A. H. (1961). *The psychology of aggression.* New York: John Wiley and Sons, Inc.

Buss, A., & Perry, M. (1992). The aggression questionnaire. *Journal of Personality and Social Psychology, 63*, 452–459.

Capaldi, D. M., & Crosby, L. (1997). Observed and reported psychological and physical aggression in young, at-risk couples. *Social Development, 6*(2), 184–206.

Crick, N., & Grotpeter, J. (1995). Relational aggression, gender and social-psychological adjustment. *Child Development, 66*, 710–722.

Dukes, R. L., Clayton, S. L., Jenkins, L. T., Miller, T. L., & Rodgers, S. E. (2001). Effects of aggressive driving and driver characteristics on road rage. *Social Science Journal, 38*, 323–331.

Follingstad, D. R., Rutledge, L. L., Berg, B. J., Hause, E. S., & Polek, D. S. (1990). The role of emotional abuse in physically abusive relationships. *Journal of Family Violence, 5*, 107–120.

Gottman, J. M. (1994). *Why marriages succeed or fail.* New York: Simon & Schuster.

Hamby, S. L., & Sugarman, D. B. (1999). Acts of psychological aggression against a partner and their relation to physical assault and gender. *Journal of Marriage and the Family, 61*, 959–970.

Hammock, G. S. (2003). Physical and psychological aggression in dating relationships: Similar or different processes? *International Review of Social Psychology, 16*, 31–51.

Hammock, G. S., & O'Hearn, R. (2002). Psychological aggression in dating relationships: Predictive models for males and females. *Violence and Victims, 17*, 525–540.

Katz, J., Arias, I., & Beach, S. R. H. (2000). Psychological abuse, self-esteem, and women's dating relationship outcomes. *Psychology of Women Quarterly, 24*, 349–357.

Kingery, P. M. (1998). The Adolescent Violence Survey: A psychometric analysis. *School Psychology International, 19*, 43–59.

Murphy, C. M. & Cascardi, M. (1999). Psychological abuse in marriage and dating relationships. In R. L. Hampton (Ed.), *Family violence: Prevention and treatment* (2nd ed.) (pp. 198–220), Thousand Oaks, CA: Sage.

Murphy, C. M., & O'Leary, K. D. (1989). Psychological aggression predicts physical aggression in early marriage. *Journal of Consulting and Clinical Psychology, 57*, 579–582.

O'Leary, K. D., & Williams, M. C. (2006). Agreement about acts of aggression in marriage. *Journal of Family Psychology, 20*, 656–662.

Richardson, D. R., & Green, L. R. (1997). Circuitous harm: Determinants and consequences of nondirect aggression. In Kowalski, R. M. (Ed.), *Aversive interpersonal behaviors.* (pp. 171–188). New York: Plenum Press.

Richardson, D. S., & Green, L. R. (2003). Defining direct and indirect aggression: The Richardson Conflict Response Questionnaire. *International Review of Social Psychology, 16*, 11–30.

Richardson, D. S., & Green, L. R. (2006). Direct and indirect aggression: Relationships as social context. *Journal of Applied Social Psychology, 36*, 2492–2508.

Richardson, D. S., Warren, P., Ferguson, H., & Daniel, S. (2007, January). *Is passive aggression a unique strategy?* Paper presented at International CICA Aggression Symposium, Augusta, GA.

Shepard, M. F., & Campbell, J. A. (1992). The Abusive Behavior Inventory: A measure of psychological and physical abuse. *Journal of Interpersonal Violence, 7*, 291–305.

Sommer, K. L., Williams, K. D., Ciarocco, N. J., & Baumeister, R. F. (2001). When silence speaks louder than words: Explorations into the intrapsychic and interpersonal consequences of social ostracism. *Basic and Applied Social Psychology, 23*, 225–243.

Spielberger, C. D. (1999). *Manual for the State-Trait Anger Expression Inventory-2.* Odessa, FL: Psychological Assessment Resources.

Stets, J. E. (1991). Psychological aggression in dating relationships: The role of interpersonal control. *Journal of Family Violence, 6*, 97–114.

Tedeschi, J. T., & Felson, R. B. (1994). *Violence, aggression, and coercive actions.* Washington, DC: American Psychological Association.

Williams, K. D. (1997). Social ostracism. In R. Kowalski (Ed.), *Aversive interpersonal behaviors* (pp. 133–170). New York: Plenum.

Williams, K. D., Shore, W. J., & Grahe, J. E. (1998). The silent treatment: Perceptions of its behaviors and associated feelings. *Group Processes and Intergroup Relations, 1*, 117–141.

APPENDIX A. PASSIVE AGGRESSION
ITEMS FOR REVISED RCRQ

1. Did not do what the person wanted me to do.
2. Made mistakes that appeared to be accidental.
3. Seemed uninterested in things that were important to the person.
4. Gave the person the "silent treatment."
5. Ignored the person's contributions.
6. Excluded the person from important activities.
7. Avoided interacting with the person.
8. Failed to deny false rumors about the person.
9. Failed to return calls or respond to messages.
10. Showed up late for planned activities.
11. Slowed down on tasks.

5

Pushing Up to a Point
The Psychology of
Interpersonal Assertiveness

DANIEL AMES

Columbia University

O n most days, it does not take a great deal of social interaction for us to remember that other peoples' goals and interests are not perfectly aligned with our own. We want to sleep in late, and our spouse or child wants to get up early. We want a clean sidewalk, but our neighbor forgets to pick up after his dog. We want our work colleagues to meet the deadlines they have given us, but apparently they have other plans. Wishing it were otherwise—that everyone would want exactly the same things we do—is folly. Besides, it would not make for a very interesting world; variety is the spice of life. So dealing with this "spice" is a significant part of the human condition. How do we cope with the ever-present fact that others surround us whose interests and goals diverge from, and sometimes oppose, our own? Do we press hard for our goals to be satisfied—and, if so, why? Do we yield to others' claims—and, if so, when?

In this chapter, I want to argue that these questions of how hard we push pervade and to some extent define our lives. Accordingly, the matter of when and why people push hard or relent in interpersonal conflicts large and small deserves considerable attention and care. Indeed, for decades it has been a topic of academic scrutiny in the literatures on interpersonal conflict, negotiation, and social dilemmas. There, a well-established theme in the account of who pushes hard and why is that motivations play a central role. Some people care more about winning; others just want to get along. This seems irrefutable. One goal of the present chapter is to describe past and recent work that takes a complimentary approach to motivation-focused accounts, highlighting the role of expectancies in interpersonal assertiveness. Pushing hard is not solely a function of what people want but also of what they believe will happen when they make forceful demands or capitulate to others' requests. I contend that a complete account of interpersonal assertiveness needs both of these pieces—expectancies and motivations. And because our lives have so much spice in them, with the question of "how hard should I push" shaping our behavior from sunrise to sleep, we need a complete account of interpersonal assertiveness.

ASSERTIVENESS DEFINED

I begin by clarifying what I mean by the term *assertiveness*, which comes not so much from an a priori scholarly model but from my interpretation of every-day perceptions of interpersonal behavior. This could be seen as a folk model of interpersonal assertiveness: a continuous dimension characterizing how persons behave or respond in a situation in which their positions or interests are, or could be, in conflict with others' positions or interests. In other words, when goals diverge, how hard do people push for their own interests? In considering the set of an actor's possible responses in any given social conflict, I believe both actors and observers can and often do array behaviors along a rough dimension of assertiveness ranging from passivity and capitulation at one extreme to aggression and hostility at the other. Later in this chapter I discuss how this unidimensional model of folk perceptions fits with past theoretical distinctions (e.g., between assertion and aggression).

Some concrete examples help to illustrate assertiveness as it is approached in this chapter. Imagine that members of a newly formed academic research center meet to discuss a senior hire. One member advocates a particular choice, but another believes this would be a disastrous move. Does the skeptical member unequivocally disparage the proposed choice and champion her own ideas? Does she make a more measured observation about expanding the set of options? Or does she hold back entirely, hoping someone else will break the silence?

Imagine directors of two nonprofit organizations who share a building are planning for much-needed renovations. One director begins by telling the other he expects his organization's space to be entirely refurbished even though he intends to pay only a small share of the cost. Does the other director forcefully reject the proposal and demand greater cost-sharing? Does she probe for flexibility, and propose revisions to the plan? Or does she accept the offer as given?

Last, consider a manager concerned with her subordinate's time management skills. Does she confront him directly, stressing negative repercussions if he fails to improve? Does she raise questions and offer suggestions for change? Or does she avoid the issue altogether, hoping it will correct itself in time?

These cases highlight the kinds of daily choices individuals make in their interpersonal assertiveness toward others. These situations and behaviors may seem disparate, but I believe that they have common underlying psychological processes that shape actors' choices about behavior and observers' interpretations of acts. I define assertiveness as a dimension in everyday perceptions reflecting individuals' interpersonal willingness to stand up and speak out for their own interests and ideas, pursuing their objectives and resisting others' impositions. As shown in Figure 5.1, one end of this folk spectrum entails passivity and yielding, whereas

Avoidance	Initiation	Collaboration	Competition
Withdrawal	Engagement	Resistance	Aggression
Passivity	Accommodation	Assertion	Hostility

Assertiveness

Domain	Illustrative behavior or style		
Conflict	Avoidant, trivializing	Candid, constructive	Belligerent, demanding
Negotiation	Weak opening, ready concessions	Strong opening, integrative solutions	Extreme opening, aggressive tactics
Teamwork	Silent with opinions, conformist	Egalitarian, open, engaged	Confrontational, dominance-seeking
Influence	Supplicant, appeasing	Active, forthright, persuasive	Bullying, cajoling
Decision making	Equivocal, indecisive	Proactive, inclusive	Unilateral, self-serving

Figure 5.1   The everyday perception of assertiveness.

the other end features aggression and hostility. In between are gradations ranging from engagement and initiation to collaboration and resistance.

This unidimensional approach may seem to confound dimensions that deserve to be separated (e.g., how much one asks for vs. how one asks for it) and to make neighbors out of constructs that are qualitatively foreign to one another (e.g., aggression and assertion). A first point to note is that I use the term assertiveness here to describe the wide spectrum that grades possible responses in social conflict (i.e., some acts are seen as more or less assertive than others) rather than a particular point or subrange of responses on the spectrum (i.e., "assertive behaviors" as those that fall between passivity and aggression). A second point to stress is that this spectrum reflects everyday perceptions of possible responses in a social conflict. When people think about how hard they might push in a social conflict, I suggest they often consider gradations of responses ranging from "giving in" to "asking for what I want" to "demanding that I get my way." Scholars have understandably taken pains to distinguish between constructs such as assertiveness, often defined as expressing one's own interests, and aggression, usually seen as involving coercion or an intent to harm (e.g., DeGiovanni & Epstein, 1978; see also Chapter 4 in this volume). My argument does not deny the importance of such scholarly distinctions but rather reflects the fact that these boundaries may be blurred or gradual in folk judgments (which is exactly why scholars have worked so hard to be precise in their own discussions). The present model simply suggests that people may consider the implications of different, perhaps qualitatively disparate, responses in social conflict, deciding that some go too far whereas others don't go far enough. Whether this approach has merit should be judged, I think, by how well it fares in predicting behavior in social conflict.

ASSERTIVENESS AND OUTCOMES

I eventually want to present an account of choices of assertive behaviors (how do people decide how hard to push?), but I first turn to some evidence of how assertiveness relates to actual interpersonal outcomes (what happens when someone pushes hard?). This step lays important groundwork for the nature and role of assertiveness expectancies because it seems entirely likely that peoples' folk theories of assertiveness will at least partly reflect how actual assertiveness plays out. Put another way, people decide how hard to push in part because they predict, flawlessly or not, what happens when they push hard or relent in a particular situation. So what happens when people push hard or give in?

My answer to this question comes from research I've done with Frank Flynn in the domain of organizational leadership (Ames & Flynn, 2007; see Ames, 2008a; Ames, 2009 for reviews). We began by reviewing thousands of open-ended anonymous comments professionals, including working managers and MBA students, gathered from coworkers on their behavioral strengths (e.g., what makes them effective) and weaknesses (e.g., what behaviors could be developed or improved). Assertiveness was not much of a factor in comments about strengths, which tended to revolve around intelligence and conscientiousness. However, references to assertiveness dominated weakness comments. Importantly, they did so in both directions, with some comments referring to too much assertiveness and others referring to too little. What many professionals and leaders struggle with, at least in the eyes of onlookers, is striking the right balance with assertiveness, pushing hard enough to get things done but not so hard that they fail to get along.

This stands in contrast to a long tradition of work on individual differences as linear predictors of leadership effectiveness—though there are important exceptions, such as Fleishman (1995) and Simonton (1985). Past work has tended to hypothesize about and test for qualities that are positively and linearly associated with leadership—that is, more of a given attribute (e.g., intelligence, ambition, extraversion) means more effective leadership. However, our work on qualitative comments from coworkers suggested a curvilinear, inverted-U-shaped relationship between assertiveness and leadership effectiveness. Indeed, several follow-up studies with managers using continuous rating measures have shown that both comparatively low and comparatively high assertive leaders were rated as less effective by coworkers than those in the middle range (Ames & Flynn, 2007).

To unpack why this happens, we decomposed outcomes into two domains: instrumental and relational outcomes. In brief, we found that each domain seemed to account for the effect at one end of the spectrum. Instrumental outcomes (getting one's way, getting things done) seem to improve noticeably as actors move from low to moderate assertiveness, with fewer gains beyond that point. Relational outcomes (getting along with others) seem to improve considerably as actors move from high to moderate assertiveness, with few gains beyond that point. Thus, high assertive leaders tended to be ineffective largely because they failed to get along, whereas low assertive leaders tended to be ineffective largely because they failed to get their way or get things done.

I believe the lessons from this work on organizational leadership hold more generally, characterizing the consequences of interpersonal assertiveness as a curvilinear effect with instrumental and relational components. What happens when people push very hard? They may undermine their relationships without gaining much instrumentally. What happens when people give in? They may lose instrumentally without gaining much relationally. While situational differences surely dictate different appropriate levels of assertiveness in a given situation (see Ames, 2009), it seems that there may be some middle range of assertiveness that tends to optimize outcomes. This idea is the starting point for an expectancy-based account of assertive behavioral choices: what does an individual actor *believe* is the optimal level of assertiveness? Do individuals vary in where they believe this optimal point lies—and does such variance predict their behavioral choices? The notion that expectancies such as these govern behavior is certainly not new and so before zeroing in specifically on assertiveness expectancies, it is worth recognizing this context.

EXPECTANCIES

From its earliest days, psychology has portrayed people as having expectations about others around them and suggested that these beliefs have a function in regulating behavior (see Roese & Sherman, 2007 for a review). Much of the scholarship on interpersonal expectancies has focused on expectations about other people's characteristics and behavior, as in work on stereotyping and self-fulfilling prophecies (e.g., Miller & Turnbull, 1986). Another important and relevant tradition of work, addressed in Chapter 2 in this volume, examines the nature and development of people's internal working models of others and their interpersonal attachment styles (see also Campbell, Simpson, Boldry, & Kashy, 2005; Pietromonaco & Barrett, 2000). Numerous researchers have highlighted the role of competitive expectations about others, linking conflict behaviors to a prediction that one's conflict partner may be aggressive, hostile, or untrustworthy (e.g., Crick & Dodge, 1994; Diekmann, Tenbrunsel, & Galinsky, 2003; Kelley & Stahelski, 1970; Van Lange, 1992).

Such basic expectations about others—whether in the form of a stereotype, an attachment style, or some other kind of representation—are certainly important in shaping behavior. However, the assertiveness expectancy account presented here departs from this tradition by emphasizing expected reactions by another to one's own assertive behavior. Rather than basic or noncontingent expectancies, this account deals with contingent ones: If I do X, this other person will do, think, or feel Y. Building on social cognitive models of behavior (e.g., Bandura, 1986; Mischel & Shoda, 1995), several noteworthy traditions of work have examined such contingent expectancies. One body of research deals with relational schemas or scripts and their impact on relationship behavior and self-construal (see Baldwin & Dandeneau, 2005 for a review). Research in this vein has shown, for instance, that the amount of anger displayed in a close relationship depends on anticipated partner response (Fehr, Baldwin, Collins, Patterson, & Benditt, 1999). A related area of inquiry has examined rejection sensitivity, which revolves around "anxious expectations" of interpersonal rejection and the associated activation of defensive responses that can have negative or even self-fulfilling effects (e.g., Downey & Feldman, 1996). Elsewhere, researchers examining gender dynamics in negotiation have linked women's assertive behaviors to "anticipated backlash," namely, women's expectations of how their behavior will be viewed and derogated by others (Amanatullah & Morris, 2010; Bowles, Babcock, & Lai, 2007).

In all of these programs of work, people are portrayed as having different internal models of how others will react to them or their behavior. Person-to-person variance in these models has been linked to a variety of interpersonal behaviors and outcomes, such as psychological adjustment. Together, this body of work suggests that there is substantial promise in exploring how general assertiveness expectancies might shape behavior—how hard people push—across a variety of contexts. Those who pessimistically expect that high levels of assertiveness will be costly will tend to show lower levels of assertiveness than those who optimistically believe that high levels of assertiveness bring benefits. However, to harness assertiveness expectancies in our conceptual models and to use them in our research, we first need to establish the form these expectancies typically take and how they can best be measured, a matter to which I turn next.

THE NATURE OF ASSERTIVENESS EXPECTANCIES

Based on the prior work showing that interpersonal assertiveness often has a curvilinear, inverted-U-shaped effect on interpersonal relations (Ames & Flynn, 2007), I expect that many people will have curvilinear expectancies, assuming that they can push up to a point but no further without incurring damage to their outcomes or relationships. For instance, in a negotiation, people may feel that making a moderately assertive opening offering could be effective but that at some point of heightened assertiveness an opening could backfire, undermining both results and relationships. While people in general may show this form of expectancy, individuals will vary in what point they think they can push up to. Some may be very optimistic, assuming they can display very high levels of interpersonal assertiveness before incurring costs. Others may be much more pessimistic, assuming that even modest levels of assertiveness could spell trouble. If this characterization is correct, it would invite a research approach that attempts to identify an individual's perceived "optimal" level of assertiveness or some kind of proxy for this expectancy.

I tested this idea by asking research participants to literally draw their expectancies (Ames, 2008, Study 1). Participants received a blank chart, with an x-axis indicating degrees of assertiveness and a y-axis indicating either social or instrumental outcomes; they were then asked to draw a line representing the outcomes they would generally expect for each level of assertiveness. Pilot work showed that people found this task to be an intuitive way of expressing their expectations that

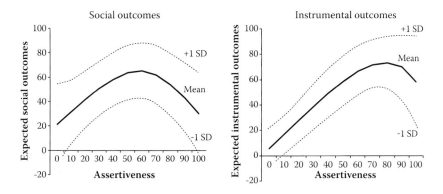

Figure 5.2   Plots of expectancy drawing means and variance.

were sometimes hard to put into words. As expected, the majority of participants (some 60 to 70%) drew lines that had a clear inverted-U shape, with a midpoint and downturned ends, for both social and instrumental outcomes. Responses from undergraduate students and MBA students were nearly identical. This suggests that assertiveness expectancies often take the form of implying an ideal or optimal level of assertiveness that varies from one person to the next and could be taken as a measure of expectancies. The drawing results also showed greatest variance at the extremes: most everyone agreed that some middle level of assertiveness led to good outcomes; people varied more considerably on the outcomes they thought would be associated with extreme levels of assertiveness. This was especially true for expected instrumental outcomes at high assertiveness: some people thought high assertiveness would bring instrumental gains, and others thought it would backfire (see Figure 5.2). This suggests that expected outcomes for very high levels of assertiveness would be another way of measuring expectancies.

ASSERTIVENESS EXPECTANCIES AND BEHAVIOR

Having characterized assertiveness expectancies as often taking a curvilinear form and varying from person to person at extreme levels of assertiveness, I sought evidence linking these expectancies to behavior. Initial evidence comes from the previously noted line-drawing study (Ames, 2008), where measures of both optimal assertiveness (the level of assertiveness for each participant that yielded the greatest social or instrumental outcomes) and extreme assertiveness (the expected social or instrumental outcomes for the lowest or highest levels of assertiveness) were associated with self-reported assertiveness. However, non-self-report measures of assertiveness would arguably make a more compelling case.

In subsequent studies (Ames, 2008, Studies 3 and 4), I pursued and found such evidence. For the independent measure of expectancies, participants predicted social and instrumental outcomes for a range of specific behaviors spanning from low assertiveness to high assertiveness. For instance, participants reviewed a scenario involving a manager's low-ball offer in a salary negotiation. Participants went on to consider a number of responses, ranging from accepting the low-ball offer to responding with an aggressive counteroffer, and then rated the outcomes they expected would result, such as final negotiated salary and liking and trust for the new employee on behalf of the manager. In another scenario, participants imagined they were in a team meeting with a fellow manager who recommended a strategic initiative they knew would not be successful. Participants rated outcomes for responses ranging from saying nothing to vociferously and forcefully objecting. In effect, across these scenarios, participants made a forecast of what they thought would happen if they yielded ground or fought hard. To what extent would they get their way? And what extent would they get along? These expectancies served as an independent variable, tapping into participants' more general views of what happens when they push hard or give in.

As expected, participants' self-reported expectancy measures based on a series of specific but hypothetical situations predicted indices of participants' assertive behavior based on reports from negotiation counterparts and real-life coworkers. Those who expected relatively minimal costs for high levels of interpersonal assertiveness (e.g., they thought a manager would find an aggressive counteroffer in the salary negotiation acceptable) were seen by partners in an unrelated dyadic, fixed-sum negotiation exercise as considerably more assertive. Expectancies also predicted the value claimed in negotiation settlements: those who were more optimistic about the payoffs of highly assertive behavior achieved more favorable deal terms. In another study, participants were rated by work colleagues for their typical level of assertiveness in the actual workplace (e.g., standing their ground in a conflict). As predicted, work colleagues saw those who were more optimistic about the payoffs of highly assertive behavior in the scenarios as considerably more assertive in the workplace.

The evidence I have gathered suggests that individuals' assertiveness expectancies have a place in predicting their behavior. While my work to date has gauged only certain kinds of assertive behavior, I suspect assertiveness expectancies shape other behaviors as well, including those addressed elsewhere in this volume. For instance, Chapter 11 addresses intimate partner violence, noting models (e.g., Holtzworth-Munroe, 1992) that describe how individuals choose behavioral responses, ranging from passivity or acquiescence to violence, based in part on their expectations of the behavior's consequences. Chapters 3 and 13 address aggression in the wake of ostracism. Expectancies about what different behaviors will achieve (e.g., renewed acceptance by the ostracizers, punishing outcomes for the ostracizers, experienced remorse on behalf of the ostracizers) may play a role in responses to being ostracized. Chapter 9 notes work on the display of anger in conflict and negotiations. Some displays are certainly spontaneous and uncontrolled, whereas other displays may be calculated. Behind these calculated displays likely lie expectancies, whether right or wrong, about what displays of anger will achieve (e.g., intimidation). Chapter 10 presents a compelling motivational model of terrorist behavior revolving around the quest for significance. Expectancies may help delineate these processes: charting an individual's expectancies about which acts will lead to what kinds of significance (e.g., "If I die in an attack I will be martyred" vs. "Only if I both die and kill others will I be martyred") could help us better understand and possibly curtail acts of dramatic violence and harm.

In sum, people vary in what they expect happens when they push hard or give in, and these idiosyncratic expectancies are predictive of at least some assertive behaviors. But are these effects distinct from the effects of motivations, such as a desire to win or a concern for maintaining relationships? Are expectancies themselves merely reflections of motivations? The next section takes up these questions.

ASSERTIVENESS EXPECTANCIES AND MOTIVES

Over the last half century, scholars of conflict, negotiation, and social dilemmas have repeatedly linked interpersonal conflict behavior to underlying motivations—variously identified as preferences, concerns, priorities, orientations, and values. While interaction-specific objectives surely matter (e.g., "I want my manager to give me a 10% raise today"), considerable attention has been paid to more general social motives (e.g., "I don't care what happens to others as long as I get what I want"). One of the most active traditions of such work revolves around dual-concern theory (e.g., Carnevale & Pruitt, 1992) and motivational orientations (e.g., Messick & McClintock, 1968), which posit that people vary in their attitudes about their own and their conflict partners' outcomes. Combinations of these dimensions yield different orientations that are often labeled proself or competitive (concerned with maximizing the positive difference between self and other), individualist (concerned solely with one's own outcome), and prosocial or cooperative (concerned with maximizing joint outcomes). An abundance of research has linked these social value orientations to assertive behaviors in social dilemmas and games (e.g., McClintock & Liebrand, 1988; Van Lange, 1999) and in conflict and negotiation (e.g., De Dreu & Van Lange, 1995; De Dreu, Weingart, & Kwon, 2000; Olekalns & Smith, 2003).

While these social orientations seem to account for the bulk of motivational work on conflict behavior, other interpersonal motives have been invoked as well, such as communal values (e.g., Amanatullah, Morris, & Curhan, 2008), agreeableness (e.g., Barry & Friedman, 1998; Graziano, Jensen-Campbell, & Hair, 1996), and need to belong (e.g., Baumeister & Leary, 1995; De Cremer & Leonardelli, 2003). In addition, there is evidence to suggest that identity motivations, such as the need to save face or maintain an image of toughness, can affect conflict behavior (e.g., White, Tynan, Galinsky, & Thompson, 2004). In short, ample evidence shows that what people care about affects their assertiveness in conflict and negotiation. Put simply, motives matter.

The results about expectancies reviewed above raise the question about how motives and expectancies relate. Will the link between expectancies and behavior remain after controlling for motivations, or will it be overshadowed? Are expectancies simply derivatives of motives? I expect that whereas assertiveness expectancies might be related to social motivations, an independent expectancy–behavior link will generally remain after controlling for motivations. The logic can be illustrated by work in the domain of risky choice that distinguishes between risk preferences and risk perceptions (e.g., Weber & Milliman, 1997). Risk preferences, analogous to motivations, concern a person's appetite for risk. Risk perceptions, analogous to expectancies in the current account, concern a person's assessment of how risky a given option is. Empirically, these preference and perception constructs have proven to be distinct and both appear to exhibit independent effects on risky choice (e.g., Weber & Hsee, 1998). Two people could have identical risk preferences but differ in their choices because one perceives the option as risky and the other does not. In the domain of conflict, two people could have identical motives—the same concerns for maintaining relationships, for instance—but differ in their assertiveness simply because one expects a behavior would damage a relationship and the other does not.

In brief, the recent work I have done on assertiveness expectancies is consistent with this idea. Across the studies (Ames, 2008), I found weak or nonsignificant links between expectancies and measures of motivations, including social value orientations, conflict styles, unmitigated communion, and basic questions about concerns for winning and maintaining relationships. In other words, expectancies are not mere reflections of motivations. Further, across the studies, both expectancies and motivations appeared to be simultaneously and separately predictive of behavior, suggesting that they each have a distinct role to play. Assertive behavior appears to be a product of both what people care about and what they believe will happen when they give in or push hard.

I have not yet found evidence for an interaction between expectancies and motivations. However, the logic for such interactions seems clear. Imagine a team leader advocating on her team's behalf to an organizational leader. She might expect that the harder she pushes the more costly it will be in terms of her relationship with her leader but the better she will do in terms of resources for her team. Along with these two expectancies would be two motivations: concern for her relationship with the leader and concern with the resources for her team. It stands to reason that if she cares vastly more about, say, her team's resources, the resource expectancy would be more predictive of her behavior than the relationship expectancy. Alternately, if she cares very little about the team's resources, it seems unlikely that the resource expectancy would be a powerful predictor of her behavior. In short, the expectancies that matter most in predicting our behavior are likely those about outcomes that mean the most to us. A full account of interpersonal assertiveness and behavioral choice would likely need to have roles for both motivations and expectancies as well as an interaction between the two.

SOURCES OF EXPECTANCIES

Evidence that expectancies are an important predictor of assertive behavior naturally raises another question: where do expectancies come from? The fact that expectancies seem to carry across domains implies an underlying core, such as basic working models for the self, others, and relationships that are built up over the course of a lifetime (Chapter 2 in this volume). Self-esteem may be part of this core. Baldwin and Keelan (1999) argued that individuals higher in trait self-esteem had more positive interpersonal expectancies about their own ability to secure affiliation from others. Indeed, there was some evidence of a modest positive link between self-esteem and optimal assertiveness in the line drawing study discussed earlier (Ames, 2008, Study 1). Those lower in self-esteem were more pessimistic about their ability to pursue their interests without suffering relational costs. Future work might further explore the links between assertiveness expectancies and relevant working models or schema, such as self-esteem, rejection sensitivity, and attachment styles.

While expectancies may be partly rooted in long-held models that accumulate over a lifetime, they may also be shaped and reinforced—validly or not—by more immediate evidence. Part of the process no doubt reflects the fact that people only experience the outcomes of behaviors they choose, not of behaviors they forego. Such is the case with anxiety disorders, where someone afraid of driving over bridges for fear of collapse, for example, never does so and thus does not experience the outcome of driving safely over a bridge, left instead to imagine that the worst might have happened if she had done so. Someone who is pessimistic about asserting his own opinion in a group setting systematically holds back, never experiencing the positive effects of speaking up and thus never overturning his overly pessimistic expectancy. Confirmation biases and selective interpretation no doubt also play a role. Someone who is optimistic about her ability to push hard without damaging relationships may see what she expects to see in the wake of a conflict. She may take superficial signs of acceptance as a signal of her counterpart's contentment even though the counterpart's ample resentment is lingering below the surface.

Another type of evidence for expectancies is "vicarious experience" through various media sources. People of all ages are frequently exposed to media portraits of assertion–outcome contingencies, as when characters in movies or television show aggression and experience positive or negative outcomes (e.g., Huesmann, Moise-Titus, Podolski, & Eron, 2003). As Chapter 17 in this volume notes, the Internet is increasingly ubiquitous as a source of information, giving viewers new ways to watch actual acts of aggression (e.g., videos of "happy slapping" aggression) or to assert themselves or watch others assert themselves in novel ways (e.g., flaming in a chat room or posting disparaging remarks to a Facebook page). Elsewhere, work on video game violence examines the impact of game playing and exposure on behavior (e.g., Anderson et al., 2004). Together, these traditions of work highlight that the development of assertiveness expectancies is likely not simply a product of one's own direct experience with assertion and outcomes but partly a product of the contingencies presented in the media environment. To the extent that people are chronically exposed to overly optimistic assertiveness contingencies in the media (e.g., that aggression reliably brings desirable outcomes), they may come to hold expectancies that reflect such contingencies and behave accordingly. One implication is that the link between media exposure or consumption and aggressive behavior may be partially mediated by expectancies.

Situational influences could also affect expectancies in "nonevidentiary" ways (i.e., through processes other than apparent evidence what happens when one pushes hard or gives in). For instance, while attachment styles may reflect a somewhat stable interpersonal schema, evidence suggests that attachment motivations can also be primed and manipulated, such as through focusing individuals on various attachment figures (see Chapter 2 in this volume). Research on mood also suggests that those in happy compared with sad moods are less polite in their interpersonal requests from others (Forgas, 1999). It could be that happy moods engender more optimistic assertiveness expectancies whereas sad moods engender more pessimistic ones. Situations that promote or inhibit empathic or cognitive perspective taking could also affect expectations about how others will react to one's own assertive or acquiescent behavior (see Chapter 7 in this volume).

For a variety of reasons—such as developmental history, distorted or misinterpreted evidence, and situational factors—people may often have misguided expectancies and may not effectively bring them in line with reality. The implication may seem disconcerting: left to their own devices, people with misguided expectancies might persist in behaving on the basis of distorted forecasts. However, I believe the facts that expectancies shape behavior and that expectancies can be revised in the face of evidence and feedback is a rather hopeful one. Although people may not naturally or spontaneously confront the right kinds of evidence, individuals, organizations, and trainers can find ways to help them do so, potentially leading to more effective assertiveness and constructive interpersonal conflict. Within organizations, multirater feedback has the potential to deliver useful information; in business schools, negotiations training with role-play exercises and debriefing often helps individual calibrate their sense of what happens when they push hard or give in.

EXPECTANCIES AND OTHER EXPERIENCES

Other contributions in this volume have encouraged me to think beyond the focal question of this chapter (when and why do people push more or less in interpersonal conflicts?) and to consider how expectancies might relate to other experiences. Chapter 12 in this volume describes a research program charting how goal similarity predicts conflict in romantic relationships: partners who have less goal similarity report more conflict in their relationships. It is possible that similarity and divergence between instrumental and relational expectancies could shed light on conflict in romantic relationships. While I have generally focused on instrumental and relational expectancies having a common core (e.g., people who are optimistic about instrumental outcomes for pushing hard tend to be more optimistic about relational outcomes, too), they can also diverge. Take the case of a person with very optimistic instrumental expectancies about her personal goals (e.g., "If I resist my spouse's demands on my time, I can devote more to my work and achieve greater professional success") but very pessimistic relational expectancies (e.g., "If I resist my spouse's demands on my time, he will resent me and our relationship will suffer"). Such a pattern could be a stressful one, regardless of the actor's behavioral choices. Contrast this with a person who has optimistic relational expectancies in addition to instrumental ones (e.g., "If I resist my spouse's demands on my time, he will understand and our relationship will remain secure"). This person may not feel a bind or trade-off, though it is possible that these optimistic expectancies could lead to behavioral choices that would create relationship stress.

Chapter 14 in this volume describes how the impact of a victim's forgiveness in the wake of a transgression depends on the extent and quality of the harm-doer's amend making. Victims who showed forgiveness toward a harm-doer who failed to make amends had lower subsequent self-respect than those who forgave a harm-doer who made amends. It seems likely that some people are simply habitual "for-givers" who may suffer when their forgiveness is unrequited. In other cases, this effect may represent a failed prediction such that the forgiver had a contingent expectancy about what would happen (e.g., "If I forgive him, he will apologize, make amends, and change his ways") that was not borne out. To the extent that some cases entail such prediction failures, it could be useful to explore what leads to this kind of misplaced optimism. The opposite effect would be interesting as well: when an overly pessimistic expectancy (e.g., "If I forgive him, it won't mat-ter because he'll never change his ways") leads someone to avoid forgiveness that could have been beneficial to both parties involved (cf. Kammrath & Dweck, 2006).

CONCLUSION

Our lives are, in many ways, enriched by interacting with others who aspire to things that we do not. But the fact that we are surrounded by people with different objectives and interests means that we are in a constant series of conflicts, mostly low-grade ones, throughout our days, confronting again and again the same ques-tions: How hard should I push? Should I resist my spouse or child? Should I defy my neighbor or boss? Should I give in? All of us who interact with other people answer an ongoing barrage of such questions, often arriving at our answers seam-lessly, perhaps even unconsciously. As scholars, we already know some about how people answer these questions, but we can, should, and no doubt will know more. I believe assertiveness expectancies have the potential to help us better under-stand how people choose how hard to push and that complete models of assertive behavior should afford a place for expectancies. Yet variety is the spice of life, and I would be disappointed if other scholars did not see the matter differently. I look forward to them pushing back, but maybe not too hard.

REFERENCES

Amanatullah, E. T., & Morris, M. W. (2010). Negotiating gender roles: Gender differences in assertive negotiating are mediated by women's fear of backlash and attenuated when negotiating on behalf of others. *Journal of Personality and Social Psychology*, 98, 256–267.

Amanatullah, E. T., Morris, M. W., & Curhan, J. R. (2008). Negotiators who give too much: Unmitigated communion, relational anxieties, and economic costs in distributive and integrative bargaining. *Journal of Personality and Social Psychology*, 95, 723–738.

Ames, D. R. (2008a). In search of the right touch: Interpersonal assertiveness in organiza-tional life. *Current Directions in Psychological Science, 17*, 381–385.

Ames, D. R. (2008b). Assertiveness expectancies: How hard people push depends on the consequences they predict. *Journal of Personality and Social Psychology*, 95, 1541–1557.

Ames, D. R. (2009). Pushing up to a point: Assertiveness and effectiveness in leadership and interpersonal dynamics. In A. Brief and B. Staw (Eds.), *Research in Organizational Behavior, 29*, 111–133.

Ames, D. R., & Flynn, F. J. (2007). What breaks a leader: The curvilinear relation between assertiveness and leadership. *Journal of Personality and Social Psychology, 92*, 307–324.

Anderson, C. A., Carnagey, N. L., Flanagan, M., Benjamin, A. J., Eubanks, J., & Valentine, J. C. (2004). Violent video games: Specific effects of violent content on aggressive thoughts and behavior. *Advances in Experimental Social Psychology, 36*, 199–249.

Baldwin, M. W., & Dandeneau, S. D. (2005). Understanding and modifying the relational schemas underlying insecurity. In M. Baldwin (Ed.), *Interpersonal cognition* (pp. 33–61). New York: Guilford Press.

Baldwin, M. W., & Keelan, J. P. R. (1999). Interpersonal expectations as a function of self-esteem and sex. *Journal of Social and Personal Relationships, 16*, 822–833.

Bandura, A. (1986). *Social foundations of thought and action: A social cognitive theory.* Englewood Cliffs, NJ: Prentice Hall.

Barry, B., & Friedman, R. A. (1998). Bargainer characteristics in distributive and integrative negotiation. *Journal of Personality and Social Psychology, 74*, 345–359.

Baumeister, R.F., & Leary, M.R. (1995). The need to belong: Desire for interpersonal attachments as a fundamental human motivation. *Psychological Bulletin, 117*, 497–529.

Bowles, H. R., Babcock, L., & Lai, L. (2007). Social incentives for gender differences in the propensity to initiate negotiations: Sometimes it does hurt to ask. *Organizational Behavior and Human Decision Processes, 103*, 84–103.

Campbell, L., Simpson, J. A., Boldry, J. G., & Kashy, D. (2005). Perceptions of conflict and support in romantic relationships: The role of attachment anxiety. *Journal of Personality and Social Psychology, 88*, 510–531.

Carnevale, P. J., & Pruitt, D. G. (1992). Negotiation and mediation. *Annual Review of Psychology, 43*, 531–582.

Crick, N. R., & Dodge, K. A. (1994). A review and reformulation of social information-processing mechanisms in children's social adjustment. *Psychological Bulletin, 115*, 74–101.

De Cremer, D., & Leonardelli, G. J. (2003). Cooperation in social dilemmas and the need to belong: The moderating effect of group size. *Group Dynamics: Theory, Research, and Practice, 7*, 168–174.

De Dreu, C. K., & Van Lange, P. A. (1995). Impact of social value orientation on negotiator cognition and behavior. *Personality and Social Psychology Bulletin, 21*, 1178–1188.

De Dreu, C. K., Weingart, L. R., & Kwon, S. (2000). Influence of social motives on integrative negotiation: A meta-analytic review and test of two theories. *Journal of Personality and Social Psychology, 78*, 889–905.

DeGiovanni, I. S., & Epstein, N. (1978). Unbinding assertion and aggression in research and clinical practice. *Behavior Modification, 2*, 173–192.

Diekmann, K. A., Tenbrunsel, A. E., & Galinsky, A. D. (2003). From self-prediction to self-defeat: Behavioral forecasting, self-fulfilling prophecies, and the effect of competitive expectations. *Journal of Personality and Social Psychology, 85*, 672–683.

Downey, G., & Feldman, S. I. (1996). Implications of rejection sensitivity for intimate relationships. *Journal of Personality and Social Psychology, 70*, 1327–1343.

Fehr, B., Baldwin, M., Collins, L., Patterson, S., & Benditt, R. (1999). Anger in close relationships: An interpersonal script analysis. *Personality and Social Psychology Bulletin, 25*, 299–312.

Fleishman, E. A. (1995). Consideration and structure: Another look at their role in leadership research. In F. Dansereau & F. J. Yammarino (Eds.), *Leadership: The multiple-level approaches* (pp. 51–60). Stamford, CT: JAI Press.

Forgas, J. P. (1999). On feeling good and being rude: Affective influences on language use and request formulations. *Journal of Personality and Social Psychology, 76,* 928–939.

Graziano, W. G., Jensen-Campbell, L. A., & Hair, E. C. (1996). Perceiving interpersonal conflict and reacting to it: The case for agreeableness. *Journal of Personality and Social Psychology, 70,* 820–835.

Huesmann, L. R., Moise-Titus, J., Podolski, C., & Eron, L. D. (2003). Longitudinal relations between children's exposure to TV violence and their aggressive and violent behavior in young adulthood: 1977–1992. *Developmental Psychology, 39,* 201–221.

Kammrath, L. K., & Dweck, C. (2006). Voicing conflict: Preferred conflict strategies among incremental and entity theorists. *Personality and Social Psychology Bulletin, 32,* 1497–1508.

Kelley, H. H., & Stahelski, A. J. (1970). Social interaction basis of cooperators' and competitors' beliefs about others. *Journal of Personality and Social Psychology, 16,* 66–91.

McClintock, C. G., & Liebrand, W. B. (1988). Role of interdependence structure, individual value orientation, and another's strategy in social decision making: A transformational analysis. *Journal of Personality and Social Psychology, 55,* 396–409.

Messick, D. M., & McClintock, C.G. (1968). Motivational basis of choice in experimental games. *Journal of Experimental Social Psychology, 4,* 1–25.

Miller, D. T., & Turnbull, W. (1986). Expectancies and interpersonal processes. In M.R. Rosenzweig & L. W. Porter (Eds.), *Annual review of psychology* (Vol. 37, pp. 233–256). Palo Alto, CA: Annual Reviews, Inc.

Mischel, W., & Shoda, Y. (1995). A cognitive-affective system theory of personality: Reconceptualizing situations, dispositions, dynamics, and invariance in personality structure. *Psychological Review, 102,* 246–268.

Olekalns, M., & Smith, P.L. (2003). Testing the relationships among negotiators' motivational orientations, strategy choices and outcomes. *Journal of Experimental Social Psychology, 39,* 101–117.

Pietromonaco, P. R., & Barrett, L. F. (2000). Internal working models: What do we really know about the self in relation to others? *Review of General Psychology, 4,* 155–175.

Roese, N. J., & Sherman, J. W. (2007). Expectancy. In A. W. Kruglanski & E. T. Higgins (Eds.), *Social psychology: Handbook of basic principles* (pp. 91–115). New York: Guilford Press.

Simonton, D. K. (1985). Intelligence and personal influence in groups: Four nonlinear models. *Psychological Review, 92,* 532–547.

Van Lange, P. A. M. (1992). Confidence in expectations: A test of the triangle hypothesis. *European Journal of Personality, 6,* 371–379.

Van Lange, P. A. M. (1999). The pursuit of joint outcomes and equality in outcomes: An integrative model of social value orientation. *Journal of Personality and Social Psychology, 77,* 337–349.

Weber, E. U., & Hsee, C. K. (1998). Cross-cultural differences in risk perception but cross-cultural similarities in attitudes towards perceived risk. *Management Science, 44,* 1205–1217.

Weber, E. U., & Milliman, R. (1997). Perceived risk attitudes: Relating risk perception to risky choice. *Management Science, 43,* 123–144.

White, J. B., Tynan, R., Galinsky, A. D., & Thompson, L. (2004). Face threat sensitivity in negotiation: Roadblock to agreement and joint gain. *Organizational Behavior and Human Decision Processes, 94,* 102–124.

Section *II*

Cognitive and Affective Influences on Conflict and Aggression

6

Nonconscious Battles of Will
Implicit Reactions Against the Goals and Motives of Others

N. PONTUS LEANDER and TANYA L. CHARTRAND

Duke University

S ome of the most complex and consuming relationships we experience involve people with whom we do not always agree—relationship partners whose wants, demands, and needs are incompatible with our own. When in the real or imagined presence of those relationships, we may not be so readily inclined to acquiesce to their interests, and research in recent years suggests that—much in contrast to our apparent assimilative tendencies (e.g., Aarts, Gollwitzer, & Hassin, 2004; Shah, 2003)—we will often automatically react against others and their goals. Although it may be important for people to get along with and be accepted by others (Baumeister & Leary, 1995), so, too, is it important for them to regulate their affiliative tendencies and needs vis-à-vis their other desires—for personal autonomy, achievement, and positive-self regard—needs that may often be well served by ignoring or even opposing the wills and wants of others. Managing such conflicting motivations is a fundamental issue in self-regulation (Cantor & Blanton, 1996), and although psychology has examined several ways such conflicts play out within the individuals' own minds (Shah, Friedman, & Kruglanski, 2002; Shah & Kruglanski, 2002), it is not entirely clear how those conflicts play out in their interactions with others. Nevertheless, research in recent years suggests that reacting against others' goals can often facilitate self-regulation in subtle but important ways—even if it ends up pushing people apart and undermining their relationships.

In the present chapter we consider three basic routes through which active goals can nonconsciously foment interpersonal conflicts and, to at least some extent, socially aggressive behavior. First, individuals' nonconscious and chronic goals can influence their social perceptions in ways that put a negative or hostile tinge on their evaluations of others and their goals. Second, individuals may often react against the perceived goals and motives of others by either moving to counteract their influence or by adopting contrasting goals instead. Third, nonconscious goals often act as behavioral juggernauts in that they can operate and trigger aggressiveness toward others over the natural course of their pursuit. Taken together, we intend to demonstrate that active goals can nonconsciously encourage conflict and aggression by influencing how their pursuers perceive, react to, and generally behave toward others.

NONCONSCIOUS, GOAL-DIRECTED SOCIAL BEHAVIOR

Research in the last few decades has increasingly found that much of human behavior and goal pursuit is automatic, in that it occurs spontaneously, uncontrollably, and with little to no conscious intent or awareness (Bargh, 1994; see Bargh & Chartrand, 1999, for review). This means that many of the goals that individuals pursue may not be as subject to the types of conscious, deliberative processing that helps individuals behave in socially appropriate or acceptable ways (see also Chapter 4 in this volume on other kinds of passive and unconscious forms of aggression). Indeed, whereas pursuers of a consciously held goal might attend to interpersonal conflicts that arise by carefully reappraising their own goal and adjusting their goal-directed behavior, pursuers of a nonconsciously held goal may not. If one were consciously pursuing a highly competitive goal—say, to win a marathon—one might pursue it only as far as it isn't hurting others or disrupting one's relationships to those others. As negative feedback from others increased, particularly regarding one's behavioral pursuit of the goal, one might respond by scaling back that pursuit or by finding other ways to ameliorate any rifts that were created (Carver & Scheier, 1998). With nonconscious goal-directed behavior, however, individuals may not be as sensitive to such feedback because their goal-directed actions are occurring largely outside their conscious awareness or control; therefore, any negative feedback they receive from their environment may not be as easily attributed to the goal (Chartrand, Cheng, Dalton, & Tesser, in press). Indeed, obnoxious people often do not believe that they are being obnoxious (Cunningham, Barbee, & Druen, 1997; Davis & Schmidt, 1977), and this may be in part because they do not consciously realize how their behavior is influencing and affecting others.

The automaticity of socially aggressive behavior has been examined in past work by considering the associations that may form in memory between particular situations and certain behavioral responses (Todorov & Bargh, 2002), such that mere exposure to such situations in the future automatically invokes (or "primes") a hostile or aversive behavioral reaction (Anderson & Carnagey, 2004; Ratelle, Baldwin, & Vallerand, 2005). In this chapter we will examine recent work suggesting that goals, too, may become linked in memory to situational cues to be triggered to activation automatically (Bargh, 1990). In some cases this could involve the direct activation of a socially aggressive goal (e.g., competition), while at other times this could involve the activation of concepts in memory that indirectly increase the aggressiveness of one's behavioral pursuit of a given goal. As a classic example of this latter form of indirect influence, participants in one study who were subtly exposed to a series of rudeness-related words were later more likely to interrupt the experimenter to move on to the next part of the study (Bargh, Chen, & Burrows, 1996). Similarly, study participants have also been found to play more greedily in an "ultimatum game" by keeping more money for themselves when a corporate-style briefcase was subtly present in the room (Kay, Wheeler, Bargh, & Ross, 2004). Even subliminal exposure to images of guns and other weapons—stimuli that represent physically violent means of attaining one's goals—can increase the aggressiveness of individuals' thoughts (Anderson, Benjamin, & Bartholow, 1998). Exposure to cues representing other people whom individuals regard as threatening may automatically invoke corresponding goals in memory (Gillath et al., 2006), even if those cues are only incidentally related to their interaction partners.

Nonconscious, socially aggressive behavior may also have self-reinforcing qualities to them that might make it difficult for individuals to justify behaving in other ways. As classically demonstrated by Chen and Bargh (1997), participants who had been subliminally primed with Black faces subsequently demonstrated more hostility toward another White participant than participants who had been primed with White faces. Interestingly, the other participant responded more aggressively in turn, effectively confirming the Black-primed participants' initially hostile expectancies. This suggests that individuals store hostile scripts in memory that may be triggered incidentally by social cues to affect not just their own behavior but also the corresponding behaviors of those with whom they interact. It is perhaps not surprising, then, that individuals who behave in aggressive or confrontational ways often regard their own actions as more justified than when they see others behaving in the same way (Baumeister, Stillwell, & Wotman, 1990; Gilbert & Malone, 1995).

In effect, mere exposure to certain social cues—be they objects or people, behaviors or situations—can suffice to activate concepts in memory that set individuals against others and engender conflict with them (see also Chapter 8 in this volume on mood effects on spontaneous aggression toward Muslims). In the next several sections, we will examine research that considers how individuals' nonconscious goals both instigate and are instigated by interpersonal conflict and aggression. We will examine how nonconsciously activated goals and chronic motives tinge and distort individuals' perceptions of others in ways that lead them to "see" those others in more hostile ways. We will then consider how cues to others' goals seem to inherently pressure individuals to respond in kind, sometimes leading them to emulate the aggressive pursuits of those around them and at other times leading them to react against others and their goals. In a third section we will examine how goals may, on their own, nonconsciously facilitate behavioral aggression over the natural course of their pursuit. The larger body of this work will focus on the ways nonconscious goals may engender conflicts of interest and interpersonal aggression, but we will conclude by reviewing important evidence suggesting that nonconscious goals also often serve to attenuate conflicts as well.

PART 1: COMING INTO CONFLICT: THE POLARIZING NATURE OF GOALS

Research in the last decade has identified at least two broad ways active goals can nonconsciously influence social perception: via evaluation and inference. Evaluations are the subjective assessments perceivers make of a target's favorableness or unfavorableness, and inferences are the assumptions that perceivers make regarding the traits, preferences, and goals that others possess. Evaluations and inferences can be highly automatic processes (Duckworth, Bargh, Garcia, & Chaiken, 2002; Hassin, Aarts, & Ferguson, 2005), and both have been found to operate in service of (and be skewed by) the perceivers' active goals (Ferguson, 2005; Kawada, Oettingen, Gollwitzer, & Bargh, 2004).

We examine in this section research suggesting that active goals may nonconsciously influence how individuals evaluate their relationships to others and interpret the actions of those around them. In particular, we focus on the ways active goals can facilitate devaluation of relationships and disliking for people who do not facilitate goal pursuit. We will present evidence suggesting that active goals can nonconsciously lead individuals to regard others in more negative and hostile ways, potentially setting those individuals against others in ways that create discord and undermine the social relationship. Indeed, the hostility that individuals nonconsciously bring into their social interactions can be self-reinforcing, for interaction partners who feel that they are being devalued and rejected tend to respond with greater anger and hostility themselves (Leary, Twenge, & Quinlivan, 2006). At the earliest stages of perception, then, active goals may be operating to nonconsciously polarize individuals against others and, thus, set the stage for interpersonal conflict.

Goal-Tinged Interpersonal Evaluations

Goals have long been regarded as a filter for perceiving the world, leading individuals to evaluate stimuli as either positive or negative based on the relevance of those stimuli to the individuals' current needs and goals (Lewin, 1935). Importantly, such goal-tinged evaluations occur spontaneously and without much conscious intent, awareness, or control (Ferguson & Bargh, 2004). This means that individuals might automatically dismiss or devalue stimuli that are seen as irrelevant or interfering with their goals (Brendl, Markman, & Messner, 2003), even when such "stimuli" are other people. Indeed, recent work by Fitzsimons and Shah (2008) found that participants who were primed in advance with a nonconscious achievement goal (as opposed to not being primed with any goal in particular) reported lower relationship closeness and placed less importance on their relationships to others who were not instrumental to their pursuit of achievement. These goal-primed study participants were also more motivated to avoid noninstrumental others—indicating an implicit aversion to those relationships—while in active pursuit of their nonconscious goal.

Such goal dependency in relationship evaluation occurs not just within close relationships where such evaluations may be targeted toward a specific other but may also extend to their evaluations of others whom they only see peripherally or incidentally. In one recent study by Bargh and colleagues (Bargh, Green, & Fitzsimons, 2008), participants were given the goal to evaluate a videotaped person for what they thought was either a reporter job (one where rudeness and assertiveness is a positive attribute) or a waiter job (where rudeness is a negative attribute). As such, the goal participants were given in advance would favor either rudeness or politeness—treating one as positive and one as negative depending on which job the videotaped interview was presumably for. Partway through the videotaped interview, a "colleague" of the interviewer entered the room and interrupted the interview, doing so either very politely (apologizing profusely) or very rudely (acting annoyed and aggressive). Importantly, although participants initially expected to evaluate the interviewee, they were actually tasked with rating the "colleague" who interrupted—an incidental other who was not the focal target of the participant's goal. Nevertheless, consistent with the perspective that active goals can affect even one's evaluations of incidental others, results indicated that participants who had the focal goal of evaluating for the waiter position tended to show less liking for the rude interrupter than the polite one; in contrast, participants who had the focal goal of evaluating for the reporter position tended to show less liking for the polite interrupter than the rude one. Subsequent debriefing found that participants were not consciously aware of the influence that their focal goal had on their subsequent, unrelated evaluation, which suggests that active goals may often nonconsciously set people against not just the focal target of their evaluations but also anyone who enters the pursuer's field of perception along the way.

Thus, individuals may often nonconsciously devalue relationships and dislike others who do not meet the criteria for their active goals, even if those others are not the focal targets of their evaluations. This might promote interpersonal conflicts in a couple ways. First, individuals may withdraw from or react with aversion to noninstrumental others, which may in turn elicit more anger and hostility from those others (Leary et al., 2006). Second, and intriguingly, it also suggests that individuals who are themselves pursuing more socially aggressive goals may actually draw closer to others who possess appropriately aggressive traits—attributes that may be desirable in the moment but may quickly lose their appeal and become toxic to their relationship once their focal goal is satiated and they are now entangled with this aggressive other (Bargh et al., 2008; Forster, Liberman, & Higgins, 2005). Indeed, past work on "fatal attractions" has shown that the very features that initially draw individuals toward others can often be the same features that end up fomenting relationship conflict and negativity later on (Felmlee, 1995). Goal-dependent evaluations, then, may nonconsciously polarize individuals and set them against others by either pushing them away from those who are not useful in the moment or drawing them toward those who are useful in the moment but may be difficult to put up with later on.

Goal-Biased Inferences

The broad influence of active goals—such as their tendency to distort and bias social perception—can affect not just individuals' evaluations of others but also how those individuals interpret the actions of others. Indeed, perceivers tend to rather automatically assume that the actions of others operate in service of some corresponding goal (Hassin et al., 2005), meaning that they infer goals in others automatically and based on whatever behavioral cues are readily perceptible. However, individuals typically rely on very little information to make their automatic inferences (Winter & Uleman, 1984): not only are social situations often highly ambiguous, but also perceivers' own active goals and chronic motives tend to influence what behavioral cues they are sensitive to and what goals they are most likely to "see" in others. As perhaps best described by Kelly (1955), perceivers' own motivational orientations (e.g., aggressiveness vs. gentleness) seem to operate as personal scanning patterns projected onto the environment to detect blips of meaning. For example, chronically aggressive individuals tend to rather automatically interpret the actions of others in more aggressive terms, something not observed among nonaggressive individuals (Zelli, Huesmann, & Cervone, 1995). Relatedly, activating a self-protection goal led one sample of White study participants to report "seeing" greater anger in the photographed faces of Black men—more anger than they reported seeing in the photographed faces of White men (or women of any race; Maner et al., 2005). This suggests that individuals' own active goals nonconsciously influence how much aggression and hostility they infer in others.

The tendency for individuals to project their own motivations onto the environment also extends to goals that are activated nonconsciously. In a study by Kawada and colleagues (2004), participants were first primed either with a nonconscious goal to compete with others or with no goal in particular. Participants then read a fictional scenario in which two men were about to engage in a prisoner's dilemma game in which cooperation by both parties would yield mildly positive outcomes for both men but competition by one of them would yield greater gains for him at the expense of his partner. Although participants were not given any concrete cues regarding how the two men would behave, it was made clear that if either partner decided to play this game aggressively he would handily beat his partner in terms of total gains. To assess the kind of inference participants made as a function of their nonconscious goal priming condition, participants were instructed to guess how aggressively they thought the men would play. Results indicated that participants primed with a nonconscious goal to compete guessed that the two men would play more aggressively against each other than participants not primed with a goal, suggesting that their own nonconscious competitiveness goal had biased them to infer greater competitiveness in others.

It may also be the case that individuals' goal-tinged evaluations of others interact with their goal-biased inferences, resulting in perceptions of others that are both negatively tinged and hostilely interpreted. For instance, individuals' own motivational orientations can interact in important ways to influence the kinds of motivations brought to mind by others. In one recent study (Brazy, Shah, & Devine, 2005), White participants initially completed an implicit measure of their own chronic prevention and promotion motivational orientations and also a measure of their prejudicial attitudes toward Blacks. Participants were then subliminally primed with concept words relating to African Americans, during which their response latencies to motivational words linked to either promotion (e.g., *lazy, outgoing*) or prevention (e.g., *threatening, considerate*) were assessed. The researchers found that highly prejudiced participants who possessed strong promotion-related motivational orientations demonstrated greater cognitive accessibility of the stereotyped promotion-related words (e.g., *lazy*), whereas highly prejudiced participants who possessed strong prevention-related motivational orientations demonstrated greater cognitive accessibility of the stereotyped prevention words (e.g., *threatening*). In effect, these participants' own motivational orientations interacted with their prejudices to show different types of negatively tinged motivational inferences. This study indicates that individuals' own motivations may nonconsciously influence both their evaluations and inferences to be more negative and hostile.

In this section we reviewed two routes through which goals can nonconsciously set people against others: by devaluing them due to their lack of goal instrumentality or by nonconsciously projecting their own goals onto them. Thus, even at the earliest moment of exposure to certain others, individuals may already be evaluating them negatively or perceiving them as potential threats, obstacles, or competitors to goal pursuit. Importantly, these initial and immediate impressions of others might inform the perceivers' later behavior; if those initial impressions are aversive or hostile, then the perceivers may react by taking on oppositional goals or by pursuing their goals more aggressively in those situations. Whereas this section was about the ways active goals might nonconsciously influence social perception, we now move on to the ways that individuals react to others and their perceived goals and motives.

PART 2: COUNTERACTING AND CONTRASTING AGAINST OTHERS' GOALS

A growing part of the work on implicit motivational influences has examined how individuals automatically adopt and pursue the goals they perceive in others (Aarts et al., 2004); some goals are even linked in memory to certain relationship partners, such that subliminal exposure to cues reminding individuals of those relationships (e.g., priming concept words related to *father*) can suffice to trigger activation of a goal associated with that relationship (e.g., to achieve academically; Shah, 2003). Indeed, mere exposure to certain cues can nonconsciously trigger the pursuit of goals that others hold for us, that we typically pursue in those others' company, or even that those others pursue for themselves (Fitzsimons & Bargh, 2003; Leander, Shah, & Chartrand, 2009; Shah). Moreover, such influences are frequently enhanced when the triggering cue represents a close relationship partner or in-group member, suggesting that implicit motivational influences are felt more strongly when they come from others with whom we may be entangled in other ways (Leander et al.; Loersch, Aarts, Payne, & Jefferis, 2008; Shah). However, not all motivational influences are desired, and, as is often the case, the perceived influence of others and their goals can be experienced as aversive or unwanted, often triggering an implicit reaction against such influence.

This may be especially true in one's close relationships, where the influence of others may be more frequent, harder to escape, and potentially recurring if the individual allows it to happen (Brehm, 1989). Research on social allergens, for example, has found that individuals' relationship partners often unintentionally exhibit a range of odious personal habits that grate on the individuals over time and foment increasingly hostile reactions (Cunningham et al., 1997; Cunningham, Shamblen, Barbee, & Ault, 2005). We propose that a similar process may occur for the perceived goals of others: people may automatically react against the goals held or pursued by others when such influences are, in some way, perceived as intrusive, aversive, or unwanted.

The lure exerted by goal-triggering environmental cues can be very difficult to ignore; such cues pull at individuals' attentional and self-regulatory resources rather automatically (Shah & Kruglanski, 2002). This potentially suggests that, when the motivational influence of another person is perceived as interfering with one's own pursuits or ongoing sense of self, individuals will feel compelled to react in oppositional ways without knowing why, or even realizing that they are reacting against anything at all. Such reactions against others' goals could lead people to nonconsciously counteract others by moving to oppose or compete with those others' goals or to simply contrast themselves against those others' goals. Either way, despite the influence of others often only occurring within the individuals' own minds, they may nevertheless react to such perceived influence by engaging in proverbial battles of will before they or their interaction partners consciously realize that a conflict of interests exists between them. In the present section, then, we examine how goal counteraction and contrast might occur nonconsciously in everyday social situations to foment interpersonal conflict and aggression in subtle but important ways.

Counteraction

Sometimes the perceived influence of others' goals and the potential impact of their pursuits can be regarded as imposing, interfering, or violating individuals' self-regulatory priorities. When this occurs, individuals might respond by moving to counteract the impact of the other person's motivational influence. Such goal counteraction—reacting against the implicit motivational influence of others— has been observed most readily in research in which others' goals are perceived to interfere with individuals' fundamental self-related needs—for autonomy and self-directedness, positive self-regard, and optimal distinctiveness (Brehm, 1966; Brewer, 1991; Tesser, 1988). Counteraction might involve adopting an opposing goal—that is, one that is incompatible with the other person's goal (a motivational "counterforce"; Brehm)—to supersede the impact of the other person's influence; however, it may also often involve adopting a very similar goal to effectively compete with the offending other.

Perhaps the best well-known form of counteraction is reactance against the perceived controlling influence of others. Indeed, a long history of psychological research indicates that when individuals feel like their behavioral freedom is being threatened by someone or by some social institution those individuals will often react by directly opposing the perceived motives of the target other (Brehm, 1966). In recent years, studies have demonstrated that such reactance against the goals held by others might often play out nonconsciously and automatically. In one such study (Chartrand, Dalton, & Fitzsimons, 2007), chronically reactant participants (and their chronically nonreactant counterparts) first provided the names of others who had a goal for them to either work hard or relax. Participants were then subliminally primed with one of those names (or with a nonsense word in the control condition), after which their performance on an anagram task was assessed. Results indicated that nonreactant individuals primed with the "work hard" significant other performed better on the anagram test than those primed with the "relax" significant other. However, chronically reactant individuals showed the opposite pattern—they performed worse (better) on the anagram task when subliminally primed with the name of someone who wanted them to work hard (relax). This suggests nonconscious reactance against the goals held by others.

Beyond reacting against the goals that others want individuals to pursue, there is also evidence to suggest that reactant individuals will implicitly counteract the goals that others are pursuing for themselves. Although past research suggests that individuals automatically "catch" the goals they see others pursuing ("goal contagion"; Aarts et al., 2004), so too might they counteract the goals they see others pursuing. In a study conducted shortly after the 2005 hurricane Katrina (Leander, Shah, & Chartrand, 2010), participants imagined that their roommate was planning a trip to the Southern Coast and were shown one of two sets of images implying what their friend had packed for it (and, therefore, their goal for the trip). In the "volunteer" goal-inference condition, the friend had packed materials implying a goal to work for hurricane relief (images showing, e.g., work boots, cleaning supplies), and in the other condition the roommate had packed materials suggesting a goal unrelated to work. Similar to results observed by Chartrand et al. (2007), chronically reactant participants were less motivated to volunteer after inferring that their roommate possessed a goal to volunteer, suggesting counteraction against the roommate's goal.

Other research suggests that, rather than adopting an oppositional motivational state, individuals may move to counteract others by nonconsciously adopting and pursuing a related goal themselves, which effectively suggests a move to compete with those others. One recent series of studies demonstrated that seeing others engaging in blame attributions to protect their self-images often led participants to nonconsciously adopt a similar self-image protection goal and subsequently to engage in more blame behaviors themselves (Fast & Tiedens, 2010). This indicates that individuals will often nonconsciously adopt the same goals they see others pursuing in order to counteract those others.

Taken together, the previously described studies suggest that mere exposure to others and their goals can elicit counteractive responses. In all of these studies, debriefing procedures were used to ensure that participants were not aware of the influence that their exposure to the goals of others had on their own subsequent motivations, supporting the notion that counteraction may occur with little to no conscious intent or awareness and that people may often set their own goals against the goals of others after merely assuming that those others are acting against their interests in some way.

Contrast

Sometimes the impact of others' goals and motives does not elicit a counteractive reaction so much as a differentiating one. When individuals regard themselves or their values as different from others, they might automatically infer from cues to those others' goals that they should be doing the opposite. Whereas counteraction implies a motivational counteroffensive, contrast is more about differentiation— distinguishing their own motivational state from a target other that they regard as "unlike" themselves.

The implicit nature of individuals' tendencies toward contrasting themselves away from "different" others was first demonstrated in Dijksterhuis et al.'s (1998) work on assimilation and contrast to social stereotypes. In their research, participants were first primed with either an intellectually stereotyped group ("professors" vs. "supermodels") or with an exemplar from one of those intellectually stereotyped groups ("Albert Einstein" vs. "Claudia Schiffer"). Participants then completed an intellectual task, and demonstrated opposing effects: Whereas the stereotyped group prime (e.g., "professors") facilitated assimilation to the stereotype (better performance on the intellectual task), the exemplar primes (e.g., "Einstein") facilitated contrast against the stereotype (worse performance on the intellectual task). Similar contrast effects have been observed following subtle exposure to members of out-groups when one's antagonism toward them is high (Spears, Gordijn, Dijksterhuis, & Stapel, 2004), against others when one's motivation to affiliate with them is low (Sinclair, Huntsinger, Skorinko, & Hardin, 2005), and against others when one's competitiveness motivation or control motivation is high (Stapel & Koomen, 2005; Tiedens & Jimenez, 2003). As we review in this section, such contrast effects may also apply to the ways that individuals react to others' goals and motivational states. For instance, individuals will implicitly devalue goals that they regard as being too ordinary or typical to pursue—a direct result of their tendencies to contrast themselves motivationally from others when seeking to differentiate themselves (Leander, Shah, & Chartrand, 2010).

A classic example of motivational contrast involves individuals distancing themselves from goal domains in which they are being outperformed. Although the successes of close others can often be inspiring, so too can they be deflating when they remind individuals of their own shortcomings (Lockwood & Kunda, 1997). Such influences can lead individuals to adopt contrasting goals and motivational states when in the company of close others who are outperforming them (Tesser, 1988). Recent work has examined the implicit nature of this contrast effect (Leander, Shah, & Chartrand, 2010). Participants in one study first imagined that they were either being outperformed academically by a friend or not, after which they were led to infer that the friend was either still actively pursuing an achievement goal or not. Participants who had first imagined being outperformed academically and were then led to infer that their friend was currently in pursuit of an achievement goal subsequently showed reduced salience of an academic achievement goal themselves on a word judgment task, suggesting that they contrasted themselves against the achievement goal of their outperforming friend. Importantly, participants indicated no conscious awareness of how the imagined scenario might have affected their subsequent behavior on the goal salience task, suggesting the implicit nature of their contrast.

Individuals may also contrast themselves to the goals of others when those goals conflict with their own values or chronic tendencies. For instance, Aarts and colleagues (2004) demonstrated that exposure to cues suggesting that a target other was in pursuit of a goal to have casual sex actually reduced the desirability of a sex goal in participants who also learned that the target other was in a committed relationship already (and was thus cheating). In another study involving subliminal priming, we assessed participants' history of marijuana use and also obtained the first names of relationship partners whom they assumed intended to either use marijuana or not in the upcoming month. Participants were then subliminally primed with one of those two names (the prodrug tempter or someone else), after which they were given a drug prevention manual to read and the amount of time they spent reading it was recorded. Interestingly, those participants who tended to abstain from marijuana use who were subliminally primed with the name of a prodrug tempter spent relatively more time reading the drug prevention manual (Leander et al., 2009), suggesting implicit contrast against the tempter's goal to use drugs.

Sometimes individuals may contrast themselves to others simply because they see those others as unmotivated toward a goal to which they are themselves highly committed. In one recent set of experiments examining the impact that others' indifference has on individuals' own motivation and behavior (Leander & Shah, 2010), participants were either subliminally primed with images of others expressing apathy and a lack of motivation toward academic achievement or primed with other images before they worked on an anagram task assessing their own pursuit of academic achievement. Prior to this, however, half the participants in each subliminal priming condition were primed in advance with a nonconscious achievement goal, with the other half not primed with any goal. The results that followed support nonconscious motivational contrast: participants who had been primed in advance with a nonconscious achievement goal subsequently demonstrated heightened anagram task performance when primed with the indifference of others. That is, individuals with an activated achievement goal contrasted themselves to the absence of motivation they saw in others by working harder toward their nonconsciously held academic achievement goal.

Individuals might also contrast to the goals of interaction partners whose nonverbal mannerisms subtly indicate social asynchrony. Recent work on behavioral mimicry has found that individuals tend to assimilate to the goals perceived to be held by those who mimic them, but they might ignore or even contrast to the goals of those who do not mimic them. In two recent studies (Leander & Chartrand, 2010), participants who indicated high sensitivity to behavioral cues to others' internal states—a form of empathy—showed a significant loss of achievement motivation themselves when interacting with a confederate who expressed high achievement motivation over the course of the interaction but did not mimic them. Importantly, participants indicated no conscious awareness of the confederate's nonverbal behavior or how it might have influenced them, suggesting that individuals who are highly sensitive to behavioral cues to others' internal states might use such cues to determine whether to assimilate to or contrast against those others' goals. This suggests that the subtlest behavioral cues may nonconsciously trigger contrast against the goals assumed to be held by an interaction partner, even at zero acquaintance with that person.

It may also be that individuals nonconsciously assimilate to others' goals to contrast to the goals assumed of broader social institutions—assimilating to a friend's goal to rebel against a broader societal law or norm. As discussed earlier, many individuals can be implicitly tempted to indulge in illegal substances (Leander et al., 2009), but recent studies go as far as to suggest that reactance motivation—which is usually associated with reacting against the goals of others—can actually facilitate assimilation to others' pursuits of such things as underage alcohol consumption (Leander, Shah, Chartrand, & Fitzsimons, 2010). Thus, even when individuals are not contrasting against the goals of others, they may often assimilate to others to contrast against broader social influences, which may foment other forms of conflict that extend beyond the immediate interpersonal situation.

Whether by counteracting the impositions of others' goals or by contrasting to dissimilar or disliked others, individuals readily and nonconsciously adopt and pursue goals that go against the perceived will and preferences of those around them. Importantly, such goal conflict between individuals may be a basic source of relationship strife and dissatisfaction—history is certainly rife with examples of how competing or incompatible goals can preclude the opportunity to establish functional relationships. What's interesting about these studies is that these conflicts of interest occur not just nonconsciously but also wholly within the minds of study participants who are simply being presented with social cues in a laboratory setting. This suggests that individuals are quite susceptible to cues that trigger their oppositional tendencies, cues that lead them to spontaneously react against and oppose the perceived goals of others before they or any potential interaction partner is consciously aware that such a conflict exists.

PART 3: GOAL-DIRECTED AGGRESSION

In the previous sections we considered ways interpersonal conflict and aggression may stem from responding to or reacting against others and their goals. Yet to be examined, however, is how active goals might foment aggressive behavior on their own, over the natural course of their pursuit. Given the relatively reflexive nature and uncontrollability of nonconscious goals, they may not be as burdened by the rules of polite society in the same way that consciously held goals are. In this third and final section, then, we examine evidence suggesting that dispositional and situational factors might often lead individuals to nonconsciously pursue their goals with greater impunity and heightened behavioral aggression. Examples of this from past work have considered how individuals' own chronic predispositions might lead them to nonconsciously pursue their goals with greater aggression when the situation warrants. Children with more aggressive tendencies, for instance, rather automatically generate more hostile solutions to social problems compared with children with less aggressive tendencies (Bloomquist, August, Cohen, Doyle, & Everhart, 1997), suggesting an implicit tendency toward aggression in pursuing their social goals.

Research on nonconsciously cued social power also supports the notion that individuals with certain chronic tendencies may automatically respond to such cues by pursuing their goals in more aggressive or self-centered ways. For instance, participants in one study who had a relatively strong exchange orientation to their social relationships (tit-for-tat, as opposed to a more communal orientation) who were nonconsciously primed with social power subsequently behaved more selfishly on a task-sharing exercise by overloading their partner with the more onerous tasks and assigning the easier tasks to themselves (Chen, Lee-Chai, & Bargh, 2001). The effects of priming social power can also nonconsciously enhance the pursuit of sex goals among men with high power–sex associations in memory and among men with stronger predispositions toward sexual harassment (Bargh, Raymond, Pryor, & Strack, 1995). Thus, situational cues that implicitly invoke concepts of social power can often enhance individuals' own behaviorally aggressive tendencies.

Recent work suggests that failing at a nonconscious goal may also instigate socially aggressive behavior. Psychology has long acknowledged that failing at a goal can sometimes trigger more hostile and aggressive responses in individuals (Berkowitz, 1989; Dill & Anderson, 1995), and one recent series of studies demonstrates that such aggression can occur among individuals who fail at nonconscious goals (Jefferis & Chartrand, 2010). In these studies, participants were first primed with an impression formation goal and then led to fail at that goal prior to completing various tasks meant to assess their subsequent aggressiveness. In one of these studies, participants who were led to fail at their nonconsciously activated impression–formation goal subsequently poured more hot sauce into a container that was going to be consumed by someone whom they knew hated spicy foods.

Thus, individuals' chronic tendencies and goal outcomes may nonconsciously influence the aggressiveness of their social behaviors, suggesting that goals may often instigate conflicts and interpersonal aggression on their own and over the natural course of their pursuit.

CONCLUSION

In this work we examined three broad ways goals can nonconsciously foment interpersonal conflict and aggression. First, active goals can shape social perceptions in ways that promote devaluing of relationships and set individuals against others whom they assume are potential competitors for their goals. Second, individuals might often counteract or contrast themselves against others' goals, either in reaction to the perceived imposition of others' influence or to simply differentiate themselves from those others. Third, nonconscious goals may often employ socially aggressive behavioral strategies to facilitate goal pursuit or cope with a failed pursuit. Evidence from these three routes suggests that interpersonal conflict and aggression may often be inherent in the pursuit of goals and be a contributor to the goals that individuals take on, value, and oppose. Given that many of these influences are occurring entirely within the minds of the individuals themselves, their "reactions" to the perceived affronts of others may actually be what initiates conflict in an interaction or relationship. Indeed, in the research we examined, it was always the participants' own goals, needs, and chronic tendencies that shaped their perceptions and reactions to others. This potentially suggests that it is through their own subsequent behavior that they elicit the very kinds of hostility that they automatically expected from their interaction partners, effectively reinforcing their initial reactions (Chen & Bargh, 1997).

One may generally conclude that individuals are most likely to oppose or aggress against others' goals and preferences when their own needs are not being met. Some goals that individuals bring into a situation are inherently aggressive (see Parts 1 and 3), and some people inherently elicit motivationally aggressive reactions (Part 2). However, such reactions do not necessarily imply a failed interaction. Whether goals—even competitive or aggressive ones—interfere with one's relationships likely depends on how those goals interact with the goals of one's interaction partner. In any social situation—be it a competitive sport or communal get-together—both interaction partners bring with them certain goals and expectations that, if met, could result in an overall positive experience for that interaction. If both interaction partners want and expect competition, then some level of opposition and aggression will only facilitate the interaction and thus enable the goal's pursuit (to compete you have to have someone to compete with). We suggest that interaction partners likely begin to perceive aggression and interpersonal conflict when there is a mismatch of goals and expectations, such as when one person wishes to be competitive and the other does not—or even when one person wants to pursue (or is overzealously pursuing) an affiliative goal (e.g., helping, romance) that the other does not want to be a part of. Indeed, the motivational fit between two individuals may determine how oppositional and aggressive behaviors are subjectively experienced.

Given that the present chapter focused on interpersonal conflict and aggression, it may be easy to conclude that goals operate with a high degree of impunity, if not disdain, for others' needs. This may certainly be true in many cases, but a wealth of evidence also suggests that goals often operate to nonconsciously reduce and minimize such conflicts. The most powerful example of this stems from research on the nonconscious pursuit of prosocial goals: whereas possessing strong prejudicial attitudes can enhance stereotyped motivational attributions, so too does possessing chronic egalitarian goals help automatically inhibit stereotype activation (Moskowitz, Gollwitzer, Wasel, & Schaal, 1999). Furthermore, whereas exchange-oriented individuals who are primed with power may behave more selfishly, communally oriented individuals primed with power behave more responsibly (Chen et al., 2001). Even when in competition with an interaction partner, individuals who are concurrently pursuing a prosocial goal will often nonconsciously scale back their own efforts when outperforming their competitor (Bargh & Gollwitzer, 1994). Furthermore, research on nonverbal behavior has found a wealth of evidence suggesting that subtle cues in the form of behavioral mimicry readily elicit assimilation to an interaction partner's goals and values (Leander & Chartrand, 2010; Leander, Chartrand, & Wood, 2010; Maddux, Mullen, & Galinsky, 2008). Therefore, despite the many ways goals facilitate conflict and aggression in relationships, so too might individuals nonconsciously move to maintain a relative sense of peace and harmony to protect their relationships.

It is important that we also note that many socially aggressive goals are dependent on others and cannot be effectively pursued in those others' absence (e.g., competition, rebellion, sexuality; Baron & Boudreau, 1987). Despite the potential problems of goal influences on social inferences and reactions, individuals may often be compelled to perceive others as competitors or as viable targets to react against in order to satiate their chronic and recurring needs. After all, rebels need a social institution to rebel against, and partisan politicians need opponents to decry—adopting opposing goals may represent the pursuit of their own unconscious goal to rebel. Thus, active goals might often need to nonconsciously manufacture interpersonal conflicts (real or imagined) to facilitate their own attainment. The very act of aggressing against others and reacting against their goals, then, may have its own functional qualities that have yet to be been fully considered.

REFERENCES

Aarts, H., Gollwitzer, P. M., & Hassin, R. (2004). Goal contagion: Perceiving is for pursuing. *Journal of Personality and Social Psychology, 87*(1), 23–37.

Anderson, C. A., Benjamin, A. J., & Bartholow, B. D. (1998). Does the gun pull the trigger? Automatic priming effects of weapon pictures and weapon names. *Psychological Science, 9*(4), 308–314.

Anderson, C. A., & Carnagey, N. L. (2004). Violent evil and the general aggression model. In A. Miller (Ed.), *The social psychology of good and evil* (pp. 168–192). New York: Guilford Publications.

Bargh, J. A. (1994). The four horsemen of automaticity: Awareness, intention, efficiency, and control in social cognition. In R. S. Wyer, Jr. & T. K. Srull (Eds.), *Handbook of social cognition* (2nd ed.) (pp. 1–40). Hillsdale, NJ: Erlbaum.

Bargh, J. A. & Chartrand, T. L. (1999). The unbearable automaticity of being. *American Psychologist, 54*(7), 462–479.

Bargh, J. A., Chen, M., & Burrows, L. (1996). Automaticity of social behavior: Direct effects of trait construct and stereotype activation on action. *Journal of Personality and Social Psychology, 71*(2), 230–244.

Bargh, J. A., & Gollwitzer, P. M. (1994). Environmental control of goal-directed action: Automatic and strategic contingencies between situations and behavior. In W. D. Spaulding (Ed.), *Integrative views of motivation, cognition, and emotion* (Vol. 41, pp. 71–124). Lincoln: University of Nebraska Press.

Bargh, J. A., Green, M. C., & Fitzsimons, G. M. (2008). The selfish goal: Unintended consequences of intended goal pursuits. *Social Cognition, 26*(5), 534–554.

Bargh, J. A., Raymond, P., Pryor, J. B., & Strack, F. (1995). Attractiveness of the underling: An automatic power-sex association and its consequences for sexual harassment and aggression. *Journal of Personality and Social Psychology, 68*(5), 768–781.

Baron, R. M., & Boudreau, L. A. (1987). An ecological perspective on integrating personality and social psychology. *Journal of Personality and Social Psychology, 53*(6), 1222–1228.

Baumeister, R. F., & Leary, M. R. (1995). The need to belong: Desire for interpersonal attachments as a fundamental human motivation. *Psychological Bulletin, 117*(3), 497–529.

Baumeister, R. F., Stillwell, A., & Wotman, S. R. (1990). Victim and perpetrator accounts of interpersonal conflict: Autobiographical narratives about anger. *Journal of Personality and Social Psychology, 59*(5), 994–1005.

Berkowitz, L. (1989). Frustration-aggression hypothesis: Examination and reformulation. *Psychological Bulletin, 106*(1), 59–73.

Bloomquist, M. L., August, G. J., Cohen, C., Doyle, A., & Everhart, K. (1997). Social problem solving in hyperactive-aggressive children: How and what they think in conditions of automatic and controlled processing. *Journal of Clinical Child Psychology, 26*(2), 172–180.

Brazy, P. C., Shah, J. Y., & Devine, P. G. (2005). *Considering the regulatory focus of implicit associations.* Manuscript under revision, University of Wisconsin–Madison.

Brehm, J. W. (1966). *Social psychology: A series of monographs, treatises, and texts.* New York: Academic Press.

Brehm, J. W. (1989). Psychological reactance: Theory and applications. *Advances in Consumer Research, 16*, 72–75.

Brendl, C. M., Markman, A. B., & Messner, C. (2003). The devaluation effect: Activating a need devalues unrelated objects. *Journal of Consumer Research, 29*(4), 463–473.

Brewer, M. B. (1991). The social self: On being the same and different at the same time. *Personality and Social Psychology Bulletin, 17*(5), 475–478.

Cantor, N., & Blanton, H. (1996). Effortful pursuit of personal goals in daily life. In P. M. Gollwitzer & J. A. Bargh (Eds.), *The psychology of action: Linking cognition and motivation to behavior* (pp. 338–359). New York: Guilford.

Carver, C. S., & Scheier, M. F. (1998). *On the self-regulation of behavior.* Cambridge, UK: Cambridge University Press.

Chartrand, T. L. (2001). *Mystery moods and perplexing performance: Consequences of succeeding and failing at a nonconscious goal.* Unpublished manuscript, The Ohio State University.

Chartrand, T. L., Cheng, C. M., Dalton, A. N., & Tesser, A. (2010). Consequences of failure at nonconscious goals for self-enhancement. *Social Cognition, 28*, 569–588.

Chartrand, T. L., Dalton, A., & Fitzsimons, G. J. (2007). Nonconscious relationship reactance: When significant others prime opposing goals. *Journal of Experimental Social Psychology, 43*, 719–726.

Chen, M., & Bargh, J. A. (1997). Nonconscious behavioral confirmation processes: The self-fulfilling consequences of automatic stereotype activation. *Journal of Experimental Social Psychology, 33*(5), 541–560.

Chen, S., Lee-Chai, A. Y., & Bargh, J. A. (2001). Relationship orientation as a moderator of the effects of social power. *Journal of Personality and Social Psychology, 80*, 173–187.

Cheng, M., & Bargh, J. A. (1997). Nonconscious behavioral confirmation processes: The self-fulfilling consequences of automatic stereotype activation. *Journal of Experimental Social Psychology, 33*, 541–560.

Cunningham, M. R., Barbee, A. P., & Druen, P. B. (1997). Social allergens and the reactions that they produce: Escalation of annoyance and disgust in love and work. In R. M. Kowalski (Ed.), *Aversive Interpersonal Behaviors* (pp. 189–214). New York: Plenum Press.

Cunningham, M. R., Shamblen, S. R., Barbee, A. P., & Ault, L. K. (2005). Social allergies in romantic relationships: Behavioral repetition, emotional sensitization, and dissatisfaction in dating couples. *Personal Relationships, 12*, 273–295.

Davis, M. S., & Schmidt, C. J. (1977). The obnoxious and the nice: Some sociological consequences of two psychological types. *Sociometry, 40*(3), 201–213.

Dijksterhuis, A., Spears, R., Postemes, T., Stapel, D., Koomen, W., Knippenberg, A., et al. (1998). Seeing one thing and doing another: Contrast effects in automatic behavior. *Journal of Personality and Social Psychology, 75*, 862–871.

Dill, J. C., & Anderson, C. A. (1995). Effects of frustration justifaction on hostile aggression. *Aggressive Behavior, 21*, 359–369.

Duckworth, K. L., Bargh, J. A., Garcia, M., & Chaiken, S. (2002). The automatic evaluation of novel stimuli. *Psychological Science, 13*(6), 513–519.

Fast, N. J., & Tiedens, L. Z. (2010). Blame contagion: The automatic transmission of self-serving attributions. *Journal of Experimental Social Psychology, 46*(1), 97–106.

Felmlee, D. H. (1995). Fatal attractions: Affection and disaffection in intimate relationships. *Journal of Social and Personal Relationships, 12*(2), 295–311.

Ferguson, M. J. (2005). Automatic evaluation as an implicit mechanism of goal pursuit. Paper presented at the SPSP Annual Meeting, New Orleans, LA.

Ferguson, M. J., & Bargh, J. A. (2004). Liking is for doing: The effects of goal pursuit on automatic evaluation. *Journal of Personality and Social Psychology, 87*(5), 557–572.

Fitzsimons, G. M., & Bargh, J. A. (2003). Thinking of you: Nonconscious pursuit of interpersonal goals associated with relationship partners. Journal of Personality and Social *Psychology, 84*(1), 148–164.

Fitzsimons, G. M., & Shah, J. Y. (2008). How goal instrumentality shapes relationship evaluations. *Journal of Personality and Social Psychology, 95*(2), 319–337.

Forster, J., Liberman, N., & Higgins, E. T. (2005). Accessibility from active and fulfilled goals. *Journal of Experimental Social Psychology, 41*, 220–239.

Gilbert, D. T., & Malone, P. S. (1995). The correspondence bias. *Psychological Bulletin, 117*(1), 21–38.

Gillath, O., Mikulincer, M., Fitzsimons, G. M., Shaver, P. R., Schachner, D. A., & Bargh, J. A. (2006). Automatic activation of attachment-related goals. *Personality and Social Psychology Bulletin, 32*(10), 1375–1388.

Hassin, R. R., Aarts, H., & Ferguson, M. J. (2005). Automatic goal inferences. *Journal of Experimental Social Psychology, 41*, 129–140.

Jefferis, V. E., & Chartrand, T. L. (2010). *Aggression following failure at nonconscious goals.* Unpublished manuscript, Duke University, Durham, NC.

Kawada, C. L. K., Oettingen, G., Gollwitzer, P. M., & Bargh, J. A. (2004). The projection of implicit and explicit goals. *Journal of Personality and Social Psychology, 86*(4), 545–559.

Kay, A. C., Wheeler, S. C., Bargh, J. A., & Ross, L. (2004). Material priming: The influence of mundane physical objects on situational construal and competitive behavioral choice. *Organizational Behavior and Human Decision Processes, 95*(1), 83–96.

Kelly, G. A. (1955). *A theory of personality: The psychology of personal constructs.* New York: Norton.

Leander, N. P., & Chartrand, T. L. (2010). *On making a lasting impression: When behavioral mimicry elicits motivational conformity.* Manuscript in preparation, Duke University, Durham, NC.

Leander, N. P., Chartrand, T. L., & Wood, W. (2010). *Mind your mannerisms: When mimicry elicits stereotype conformity.* Manuscript submitted for publication, Duke University, Durham, NC.

Leander, N. P., & Shah, J. Y. (2010). *Losing the will: Implicit regulatory reactions to the perceived indifference of others.* Manuscript submitted for publication, Duke University, Durham, NC.

Leander, N. P., Shah, J. Y., & Chartrand, T. L. (2009). Moments of weakness: The implicit context-dependencies of temptations. *Personality and Social Psychology Bulletin, 35*(7), 853–866.

Leander, N. P., Shah, J. Y., & Chartrand, T. L. (2010). *Pushing back pursuits: Regulatory resistance to the implicit motivational influence of others.* Manuscript submitted for publication, Duke University, Durham, NC.

Leander, N. P., Shah, J. Y., Chartrand, T. L., & Fitzsimons, G. J. (2010). *Feeling the pressures: Reactance motivation among peers in underage alcohol consumption.* Manuscript in preparation, Duke University, Durham, NC.

Leary, M. R., Twenge, J. M., & Quinlivan, W. (2006). Interpersonal Rejection as a determinant of anger and aggression. *Personality and Social Psychology Review, 10*(2), 111–132.

Lewin, K. (1935). A dynamic theory of personality: Selected papers (D. E. A. K. E. Zener, Trans.). New York: McGraw Hill.

Lockwood, P., & Kunda, Z. (1997). Superstars and me: Predicting the impact of role models on the self. *Journal of Personality and Social Psychology, 73*, 91–103.

Loersch, C., Aarts, H., Payne, B. K., & Jefferis, V. E. (2008). The influence of social groups on goal contagion. *Journal of Experimental Social Psychology, 44*, 1555–1558.

Maddux, W. W., Mullen, E., & Galinsky, A. D. (2008). Chameleons bake bigger pies and take bigger pieces: Strategic behavioral mimicry facilitates negotiation outcomes. *Journal of Experimental Social Psychology, 44*, 461–468.

Maner, J. K., Kenrick, D. T., Becker, D. V., Robertson, T. E., Hofer, B., Neuberg, S. L., et al. (2005). Functional projection: How fundamental social motives can bias interpersonal perception. *Journal of Personality and Social Psychology, 88*(1), 63–78.

Moskowitz, G. B., Gollwitzer, P. M., Wasel, W., & Schaal, B. (1999). Preconscious control of stereotype activation through chronic egalitarian goals. *Journal of Personality & Social Psychology, 77*(1), 167–184.

Ratelle, C. F., Baldwin, M. W., & Vallerand, R. J. (2005). On the cued activation of situational motivation. *Journal of Experimental Social Psychology, 41*, 482–487.

Shah, J. Y. (2003). Automatic for the people: How representations of significant others implicitly affect goal pursuit. *Journal of Personality and Social Psychology, 84*(4), 661–681.

Shah, J. Y., Friedman, R. S., & Kruglanski, A. W. (2002). Forgetting all else: On the antecedents and consequences of goal shielding. *Journal of Personality and Social Psychology, 83*(6), 1261–1280.

Shah, J. Y., & Kruglanski, A. W. (2002). Priming against your will: How accessible alternatives affect goal pursuit. *Journal of Experimental Social Psychology, 38*, 368–383.

Sinclair, S., Huntsinger, J., Skorinko, J., & Hardin, C. D. (2005). Social tuning of the self: Consequences for the self-evaluations of stereotype targets. *Journal of Personality and Social Psychology, 89*(2), 160–175.

Spears, R., Gordijn, E., Dijksterhuis, A., & Stapel, D. A. (2004). Reaction in action: Intergroup contrast in automatic behavior. *Personality and Social Psychology Bulletin, 30*(5), 605–616.

Stapel, D. A., & Koomen, W. (2005). Competition, cooperation, and the effects of others on me. *Journal of Personality and Social Psychology, 88*(6), 1029–1038.

Tesser, A. (1988). Toward a self-evaluation maintenance model of social behavior. In L. Berkowitz (Ed.), *Advances in Experimental Social Psychology* (Vol. 21, pp. 181–227). San Diego, CA: Academic Press.

Tiedens, L. Z., & Jimenez, M. C. (2003). Assimilation for affiliation and contrast for control: Complementary self-construals. *Journal of Personality and Social Psychology, 85*(6), 1049–1061.

Todorov, A., & Bargh, J. A. (2002). Automatic sources of aggression. *Aggression and Violent Behavior, 7*, 53–68.

Winter, L., & Uleman, J. (1984). When are social judgments made? Evidence for the spon-
taneousness of trait inferences. *Journal of Personality and Social Psychology, 47*(2),
237–252.

Zelli, A., Huesmann, L. R., & Cervone, D. (1995). Social inference and individual differences in aggression: Evidence for spontaneous judgments of hostility. *Aggressive
Behavior, 21*(6), 405–417.

7

Using Both Your Head and Your Heart
The Role of Perspective Taking and Empathy in Resolving Social Conflict

ADAM D. GALINSKY
Northwestern University

DEBRA GILIN
Saint Mary's University

WILLIAM W. MADDUX
INSEAD

If you know the enemy and know yourself, you need not fear the result of a hundred battles. If you know yourself but not the enemy, for every victory gained you will also suffer a defeat.

Sun Tzu

S uccess in strategic conflict situations often necessitates a clear understanding of the underlying motives and likely behaviors of one's opponent. In Tom Clancy's *The Hunt for Red October*, for example, the captain of a Soviet nuclear submarine enters U.S. waters and engages a new technology to avoid detection. Although U.S. military commanders suspect he is preparing to attack the United States, a Central Intelligence Agency (CIA) analyst named Jack Ryan is convinced that the captain is actually trying to defect. The resulting standoff mirrors a classic prisoner's dilemma: Should the United States preventively use force, ensuring a short-term victory, or try the riskier but potentially more rewarding route of mutual cooperation? In the end, Ryan is proved right: the U.S. military delays the attack, the Soviet commander does switch allegiance, and America gains a stalwart ally in the Cold War.

Ryan's deduction came about because he had thoroughly researched his opponent's personal and military background and thus clearly understood the Soviet captain's distaste for the Soviet Union and likely desire to defect. In the real world, the successful resolution of the Cuban missile crisis has been credited to President John F. Kennedy's ability to take the perspective of his Soviet counterpart. By actively appreciating Soviet Premier Nikita Khrushchev's core interests of saving face and retaining power, Kennedy was able to devise a strategic plan that steered the two powers away from the precipice of nuclear war, without sacrificing the long-term interests of the United States. While publicly refusing to remove any of America's missiles placed near the Soviets (i.e., no quid pro quo on missile removal), Kennedy offered that if all nuclear weapons were removed from Cuba the United States would pledge not to invade Cuba in the future, terms that satisfied U.S. interests while also allowing Khrushchev to declare that he had saved Cuba from attack.

These examples, from fiction and fact, illustrate the powerful advantage of having a deep understanding of one's opponent in conflict situations that can sometimes prevent escalation of the conflict to outright aggression. In disparate but related domains such as chess, poker, and business, knowing the motives and likely behaviors of an adversary can illuminate strategies that will bring about personal gain, the downfall of one's nemesis (Findler, 1990; Lopes, 1976; Thagard, 1992), and even long-term peace (Axelrod, 1987). Similarly, in strategic interactions such as negotiations, which involve conflicting interests, negotiators must often understand and satisfy the other party's interests and needs to obtain the best outcome for themselves (Thompson, 1990; Thompson & Hastie, 1990; Fisher, Ury, & Patton, 1991). In contrast, close-mindedness is often the foundation for aggression and impulsive retaliation (Chapter 10 in this volume). By understanding an adversary's explicit and implicit interests, anticipating their words and actions, and thinking through ways to structure solutions that satisfy their own and the other party's interests, individuals can develop creative solutions that reap the rewards—both competitive and cooperative—of strategic social interactions.

Because understanding interests and motives is valuable for competitive success, it seems likely that individual characteristics associated with understanding of and appreciation for other individuals may prove advantageous in strategic, mixed-motives situations, such as negotiations and conflict management. In particular, two related but distinct interpersonal social competences—perspective taking and empathy—have been shown to motivate social understanding across a variety of contexts. Although the terms *perspective taking* and *empathy* are often used interchangeably, there is clear evidence of their differences (Coke, Batson, & McDavis, 1978; Davis, 1980, 1983; Deutsch & Madle, 1975; Hoffman, 1977; Oswald, 1996). On the one hand, perspective taking is a cognitive capacity to consider the world from other viewpoints. It "allows an individual to anticipate the behavior and reactions of others, therefore facilitating smoother and more rewarding interpersonal relationships" (Davis, 1983, p. 115). Empathy, in contrast, is an other-focused emotional response that allows one person to affectively connect with another. Sometimes labeled sympathy or compassion, empathy is a congruent emotion of concern experienced when witnessing another person's suffering (Batson, Fultz, & Schoenrade, 1987).

Davis (1983, p. 113) eloquently described the historical roots of the distinction between perspective-taking and empathy: "Smith (1759) and Spencer (1870), writing centuries ago and a century apart, drew a nearly identical distinction between two broad classes of response: a cognitive, intellectual reaction on the one hand (an ability simply to understand the other person's perspective), and a more visceral, emotional reaction to the other." Although both characteristics are basic building blocks of social competence early in life (Piaget, 1932) and have broad social benefits later in life (Bengtsson & Johnson, 1992; Davis, 1983; Johnson, 1975), we review the extent to which it is more beneficial to get inside the head (perspective taking) versus the heart (empathy) of one's partner in strategic, mixed-motive interactions.

In the current chapter, we examine these two constructs in mixed-motive settings that have explicit implications for our understanding of conflict. We describe research examining the differential effects of perspective taking and empathy in negotiation contexts (Galinsky, Maddux, Gilin, & White, 2008) as well as the effects of perspective taking and empathy in different types of mixed-motive strategic interactions, such as war games and social coalition games (Gilin, Maddux, & Galinsky, 2010). All of these strategic tasks involve an underlying conflict of interest between self and other, creating opportunities for mutual gain on one hand, and for impasse, conflict escalation, or lost opportunities on the other hand. Each therefore mirrors key dynamics of interpersonal and intergroup conflict.

PERSPECTIVE TAKING

Research on perspective taking suggests it is a valuable social skill in three key ways: social coordination, cognitive flexibility, and assertiveness. First, perspective taking increases behavioral matching and facilitates social coordination (Chartrand & Bargh, 1999; Galinsky, Ku, & Wang, 2005; Galinsky, Wang, & Ku, 2008). As early as 1934, George Mead speculated that considering others' viewpoints allows individuals to anticipate others' behavior and reactions, increasing their social maturity. Recent research has directly supported this idea, showing that individuals higher on perspective-taking ability are more likely to mimic others' nonverbal behavior (Chartrand & Bargh, 1999), which in turn engenders liking (Chartrand & Bargh), goodwill (Van Baaren, Holland, Kawakami, & Van Knippenberg, 2004), and assistance (Van Baaren et al.). Thus, a simultaneous give and take of goodwill in social interactions helps perspective takers coordinate with others (Galinsky et al., 2005, 2008).

Second, perspective taking involves cognitive flexibility. Perspective takers are able to step outside the constraints of their own immediate biased frames of reference and step into alternate mindsets. Perspective-taking instructions (compared with control conditions) have reduced a variety of biases, including the myopic tendency to believe one is more hindered by situational constraints than others (Moore, 2005), to actually ignore others' situational constraints (Regan & Totten, 1975; Vescio, Sechrist, & Paolucci, 2003), and to rely on stereotypic and prejudicial assumptions about out-group members (Galinsky & Ku, 2004; Galinsky & Moskowitz, 2000; Galinsky et al., 2006; Vescio et al.). This increase in cognitive flexibility leads to greater problem solving by perspective takers—the ability to cognitively switch between divergent viewpoints, even those with which the perspective taker disagrees (Richardson, Hammock, Smith, Gardner, & Signo, 1994; Tetlock, Skitka, & Boettger, 1989). Perspective taking seems to prompt an external vantage point, allowing an escape from one's own limiting mental sets.

Finally, perspective takers are assertive. The most common lay definition of assertiveness is "standing up for legitimate personal rights" (Wilson & Gallois, 1993, p. 48). Here, we adopt a similar definition of assertiveness espoused by Twenge (2001, p. 134): a targeted use of firmness to protect self-interest in response to others' aggressive tactics (see also Chapter 5 in this volume for a different definition and perspective). Thus, perspective takers strive to satisfy their own and others' interests without being overly concessionary. Overall, dispositionally high perspective takers are lower in their use of dominating conflict behaviors and chronic aggression than others, relying heavily on joint problem solving and discussion in the face of conflict (Richardson et al., 1994). They successfully maintain "mind over matter" when mildly or moderately provoked, resisting retaliation when it is unnecessary and counterproductive (Richardson, Green, & Lago, 1998; see Chapter 4 in this volume). However, when faced with an immediate threat to their interests, perspective takers will aggress and retaliate. In an intergroup competition task, perspective taking, by gaining an understanding that the two sides' positions are truly incompatible, increases appropriately competitive behavior (Johnson, 1967). Similarly, perspective takers retaliate in response to an unambiguous, strong provocation (Richardson et al.). We interpret these results to mean that perspective takers avoid initiating aggressive behavior (Richardson et al.) and strive to satisfy their own and others' interests but will not back down in the face of clear competitive contingencies or a strong attack. This pattern of responses indicates a strategy similar to that of reciprocal altruism (Trivers, 1971), a highly successful strategy in mixed-motive environments (Axelrod, 1984) in which a preference for cooperation is balanced with a mechanism for retaliation following exploitation.

Adaptive flexibility and assertiveness embedded in coordinated social interaction should help perspective takers achieve greater gains at the bargaining table. Perspective taking has been linked to greater use of joint problem solving and discussion during interpersonal conflict (Richardson et al., 1994), behaviors that have independently been shown to be associated with positive negotiations outcomes. Since appreciating different interests is essential for finding win–win solutions in negotiations (Thompson & Hastie, 1990), negotiators' perspective-taking abilities have proven to provide some benefit in crafting integrative deals (Kemp & Smith, 1994).

In addition to joint and integrative gains, perspective taking should enhance distributive gains in negotiation. For example, waitresses who mimic their customers receive bigger tips (Van Baaren, Holland, Steenaert, & Van Knippenberg, 2003). Not surprisingly then, perspective takers elicit greater concessions from an opposing negotiator (Neale & Bazerman, 1982) and can protect themselves from the anchoring effects of an opponent's first offer (Galinsky & Mussweiler, 2001).

Thus, perspective taking allows advantages in adapting to others, and we propose this helps perspective takers discover underlying common interests with an adversary when they are not obvious. Yet perspective takers also seem to protect their own turf, being assertive in defending their own interests and turning aggressive when necessary and improving others' outcomes only so far as their own interests are not sacrificed. We therefore expected that perspective taking would improve individual and joint outcomes in mixed-motive strategic interactions.

EMPATHY

Whereas perspective taking is primarily a cognitive ability, empathy is primarily an affective state of concern for others (Davis, 1983) and includes "feelings that are more other-focused than self-focused" (Batson et al., 1987, p. 2). Empathy does not correlate with the same constellation of personality characteristics as perspective taking. Empathy predicts more intense experience of emotions (Davis; Eisenberg et al., 1994; Okun, Shepard, & Eisenberg, 2000), greater sensitivity to others (Davis), and helping others even at one's own expense (see reviews in Batson, 1991; Batson & Oleson, 1991). Empathy benefits others by prompting prosocial helping (Archer, Diaz-Loving, Gollwitzer, Davis, & Foushee, 1981; Batson, O'Quinn, Fultz, Vanderplas, & Isen, 1983; Batson et al., 1987; Coke et al., 1978). For instance, empathizers volunteer more time to help others compared with perspective takers (Oswald, 1996), and empathy results in participants assigning an unknown partner a more desirable task while accepting a less desirable task for themselves (Batson et al., 2003). As such, empathy is a highly effective means of inducing consideration and helping of others. However, empathy-induced helping is often done at the expense of one's own concerns. Allocation decisions by empathizers can be so other-serving as to harm one's self-interest (Batson et al.).

In strategic interactions, empathy can similarly result in an overconsideration of an adversary. For example, empathizers tend to cooperate in prisoner's dilemma games (Batson & Moran, 1999), even if they know that their opponent has previously defected and therefore cooperation is likely to be to their own detriment (Batson & Ahmad, 2001). Lending support to the idea that empathy may not be an asset but a liability in negotiations is evidence showing that agreeableness is associated with worse distributive outcomes (Barry & Friedman, 1998). Empathy is associated with increased perceived closeness or mental merging with others (Cialdini, Brown, Lewis, Luce, & Neuberg, 1997). Although this "oneness" may expand the boundaries of the self to include the other, a healthy appreciation of different priorities necessary to create win–win outcomes may not result from empathic concern. In addition, close personal relationships increase attention to others' outcomes (Sally, 2000) but reduce concentration on economic gain (Ligthart & Lindenberg, 1994). As a result, romantic partners, compared with strangers, arrive at less integrative outcomes because they set lower aspirations, make fewer offers, and engage in less assertive behavior (Fry, Firestone, & Williams, 1983). Similarly, friends are often less assertive because of a greater concern with maintaining the relationship (Peterson & Thompson, 1997).

Because empathy creates such a strong other-focus, empathizers may be unable to enlarge the negotiation pie or to claim a share of the pie for themselves. Because empathy motivates a low focus on protecting one's own interests and produces a passive stance, we expected empathy to lead to less efficient integration of interests and a failure to claim a fair share of individual gains at the negotiation table.

THE DUAL CONCERN MODEL: PREDICTING THE EFFECTS OF PERSPECTIVE TAKING AND EMPATHY

The Dual Concern Model of negotiations provides a useful framework for making clear predictions about the relative advantages of perspective taking and empathy in strategic, mixed-motive interactions. According to the Dual Concern Model (Pruitt & Rubin, 1986), negotiators can choose to divide their attention between themselves and the other side: Negotiators can be attentive only to their own concerns, only with the concerns of the other side, or have a mix of attention focused on self and other concerns. When attention is focused only on self-interests, negotiators tend to be overly aggressive, displaying obstinate behavior designed to increase individual or distributive gains at the other's expense. However, focusing only on the interests of others encourages self-destructive and spineless concession making. Instead, a balance of attention to both self-interests and the interests of others and concerns facilitates creative problem solving. As such, effective negotiators must find a tenuous balance between facilitating positive and cooperative interactions within a competitive and often distrustful environment; this necessary balancing of competition and cooperation has been dubbed the "negotiator's dilemma" (Lax & Sebenius, 1986).

Extrapolating from this model, empathy could tip the balance of attention too far toward cooperation and the other side's concerns, leading negotiators to sacrifice self-interest and, by not pushing one's own interests, even preventing negotiators from discovering insights that could benefit both sides. In contrast, perspective taking may lead to a more balanced focus on appreciating others' interests without forfeiting one's own claims and therefore produce beneficial outcomes for both the self and other. Indeed, Adam Smith (1759) suggested in his work on moral sentiments that perspective taking was more essential than empathy in achieving efficient outcomes, that looking at things from an outside perspective allows individuals to override passions such as excessive sympathy that can impair insight and creativity. Overall, we predict that perspective taking will enhance both joint and individual outcomes in negotiations, whereas empathy may lead to disadvantages on both these fronts.

However, we believe there are important mixed-motive situations in which empathizers should have a marked advantage, such as coalition building, in which there is a benefit to recognizing subtle emotional reactions that are diagnostic of other's emotional connections with oneself. That is, we expect that empathic individuals will read others' interpersonal cues more accurately. As a result, in tasks where such understanding confers a strategic advantage, affective accuracy might lead to a performance advantage of empathy over perspective taking.

PERSPECTIVE TAKERS ARE BETTER NEGOTIATORS

Galinsky et al. (2008) both measured and manipulated perspective taking and empathy to explore their influence in two negotiation tasks that represent common and challenging barriers to understanding: (1) compatibility of underlying interests in the face of conflicting positions (Studies 1 and 2); and (2) differing preferences and priorities (Study 3). Indeed, perceiving one has dissimilar personal goals is often the foundation of increased rates of fighting in close relationships (Chapter 12 in this volume). These two barriers to mutual understanding are underlying contributors to most interpersonal conflicts. They sought to answer the following question: For individuals involved in such mixed-motive situations, is it more effective to empathize with an opponent (have them inside your heart) or to understand their thoughts and perspective (get inside their head)?

Two of their studies used a negotiation over the sale of the "Texoil" gas station (Goldberg, 2008), where a deal based solely on sale price was impossible. Specifically, the buyer's reservation price (the maximum he or she was authorized to pay) was lower than the seller's reservation price (the minimum he or she was willing to accept), resulting in a negative bargaining zone for sale price. However, both parties' underlying interests were compatible: The buyer wanted to hire managers to run the station, and the seller needed help financing a sailboat trip and to obtain employment after returning. Thus, parties could agree to a sale price below the seller's reservation price, but with a stipulation of future employment. To reach a successful deal, participants had to discover this alternative solution themselves during the course of the negotiation.

In this study, dyadic levels of perspective taking and empathy (controlling for the Big Five traits, and gender) predicted the likelihood of negotiating a deal. However, only dyads' perspective-taking tendencies acted as a significant positive predictor of whether a successful deal was reached. In contrast there was a negative relationship between empathy and deal discovery. Follow-up analyses at the individual level found that only the buyer's chronic perspective taking significantly predicted whether a deal was reached, whereas for sellers only their openness to experience significantly predicted whether a deal was reached.

In other words, perspective-taking tendencies (particularly in the buyer) helped negotiators overcome their apparently conflicting positions and generate a creative resolution to a mutual problem that met both parties' needs. Empathy, in contrast, proved detrimental to discovering a solution. Importantly, the advantages of perspective taking were independent of the Big Five personality variables, providing discriminate validity for its role in negotiations.

In this research only the buyer's perspective-taking tendency made a difference in producing a deal. However, this reasoning is consistent with recent research showing the importance of the buyer's role in soliciting information in this gas station negotiation (Maddux, Mullen, & Galinsky, 2008). Although the seller needs to reveal personal information (not surprisingly, the seller's openness to experience mattered in the current negotiation), a deal cannot be achieved unless the buyer plays an active role in soliciting and appreciating the value of the seller's disclosures in crafting a solution. Thus, only the buyer's perspective-taking ability predicted creative problem resolution.

A second study manipulated the perspective taking and empathy of the buyer in the same Texoil negotiation. Buyers in the empathy condition were given the following instructions: "In preparing for the negotiation and during the negotiation, take the perspective of the service station owner. Try to understand what he or she is feeling, what emotions he or she may be experiencing in selling the station. Try to imagine what you would be feeling in that role." Buyers in the perspective-taking condition were told the following: "In preparing for the negotiation and during the negotiation, take the perspective of the service station owner. Try to understand what he or she is thinking, what his or her interests and purposes are in selling the station. Try to imagine what you would be thinking in that role." The results replicated the overall pattern from the correlational study: perspective takers achieved significantly more deals than empathizers and control participants (who did not differ from each other), overcoming seemingly conflicting interests.

This study also measured another outcome with implications for conflict resolution: the seller's satisfaction with how he or she felt treated during the negotiation. Here empathy proved advantageous; being empathized with led to the highest level of interpersonal satisfaction. Although perspective takers inspired significantly less satisfaction than did empathizers, they still produced significantly more satisfaction than control participants. Thus, although empathy had immediate affective benefits for the other side, empathizers did not have an advantage over control participants in producing more deals, which would provide long-term value for themselves and their opponent and resolve their conflict of interest. In contrast, perspective takers secured the most agreements with sufficient opponent satisfaction.

Galinsky et al. (2008) next examined whether perspective taking and empathy would help negotiators navigate multi-issue negotiations. Whenever a negotiation involves multiple issues, negotiators can have different priorities; negotiators can improve their outcomes by conceding on low-priority issues in exchange for their high-priority ones, a technique called logrolling (Froman & Cohen, 1970). Logrolling is an excellent conflict resolution tool, even in close and ongoing relationships, because it allows the parties to trade off "wins" on issues on which they want opposite things for the sake of the overall deal or relationship (Sheppard, 1999). Mere compromise, or simply "splitting" all issues down the middle, is an impediment to reaching efficient agreements compared with making mutually beneficial trade-offs (Thompson, 1990; 2001; Tripp & Sondak, 1992). Multi-issue negotiations also highlight a dilemma negotiators face: finding a balance between capturing value for oneself (value-claiming) and maximizing the available resources for both parties (value-creating; Lax & Sebenius, 1986). To be most effective, negotiators must both create as large a pie of resources as possible (to produce the most economically efficient agreements) and also claim as much of that pie as possible (to satisfy their self-interest). In the context of ongoing business and personal relationships, sound negotiation deals that create a lot of value and distribute it fairly should also help prevent future disputes (Sheppard, 1999).

In a multi-issue negotiation Galinsky et al. (2008) found that taking the perspective of one's opponent produced both the greatest amount of joint gains and more profitable individual outcomes. Perspective takers achieved the highest level of economic efficiency without sacrificing their own material gains. In contrast, empathizers received the lowest individual outcomes, with increases in joint gains going mostly to the empathizer's opponent (see also Chapter 14 in this volume for when forgiveness can erode self-respect). Interestingly, it appears in their studies that the negotiator who would achieve the best individual outcome is one who takes the perspective of an empathizing opponent, suggesting that negotiation outcomes may be driven by the interaction between these two social competencies.

Overall, the initial studies by Galinsky et al. (2008) suggest that it is better to "think like" rather than to "feel for" one's adversaries. In other words, it is more beneficial to get inside their head than have them inside one's own heart.

PERSPECTIVE TAKERS NAVIGATE MIXED-MOTIVE SITUATIONS BECAUSE THEY ARE MORE ACCURATE IN PREDICTING THEIR OPPONENT'S MOVES

The previous studies focused on negotiations and not conflict per se. However, the results are highly suggestive of performance in conflict-related settings. The Texoil exercise in particular presents a classic dilemma in resolving interpersonal conflicts. When an obvious solution is not possible (in this case, a mutually beneficial price), parties often become angry and frustrated. The key to a solution and to prevent ill will is to discover mutually compatible underlying interests. Indeed, researchers have repeatedly shown that identifying overlapping interests is critical in solving interpersonal conflicts as well as negotiations (Brett, 2007; Ury, Brett, & Goldberg, 1988). Thus, the extent to which perspective taking and empathy predict the ability to identify both parties' underlying interests should likely apply across an array of mixed-motive contexts, including situations involving bargaining as well as those involving interpersonal or strategic disputes.

To see if their findings generalized to settings involving a more explicit degree of conflict, Gilin, Maddux, & Galinsky (2010) followed up these initial studies by exploring the differential effects of perspective taking and empathy in other types of mixed-motive settings. They predicted that perspective taking (but not empathy) would provide an accurate understanding of the opponents' strategy and interests in cognitively based competitive interactions. In contrast, they predicted that empathy would aid performance in competitive tasks requiring an emotional appreciation of and connection with the other side.

Their first study used a simulated "war game" that involved multiple rounds of a potential arms race with an "enemy" country. This task tends to generate realistic emotional conflict responses, such as anger, frustration, and a desire for retaliation in the face of attack, even though it occurs over a relatively brief interaction period. Participants had to make repeated decisions about whether to disarm one's bombs or to use them to bomb the opponent. Games ended as soon as one of two outcomes occurred: either (1) attack: one opponent bombed the other; or (2) peace: 10 bomb-free (peaceful) rounds were concluded. Also, at various points, face-to-face negotiations were mandatory so each player was able to communicate directly with his or her opponent. There are two roads to success in this game. First, one potentially winning strategy is to disarm fewer weapons than one's adversary and then attack. Second, if neither player attacked in the 10 rounds of a game, "peace" was declared, and payments were paid out by a neutral third party, the World Bank. Parties were then rewarded according to the extent to which they met or surpassed the goal of 50% disarmament. Success at this game involves using complex cognitive strategy, anticipating the strategy of the opponent, persuading the opponent to make mutually beneficial moves, and avoiding gratuitous retaliation that will escalate distrust, value destruction, and stalemate with a partner. In other words, the task models real-world strategic conflict situations in which one must keep one's anger and frustration in check to avoid a cycle of increasing provocation and aggression.

Gilin et al. (2010) tested how individual differences in perspective taking and empathy predicted individual profit, joint gain provided by the World Bank, and the percent of total games in which the dyad achieved peace (both parties cooperated through all 10 rounds without attack). With regard to joint gain and attainment of peace, the pattern or results were very similar to those found in the previously described Texoil study. Dyadic-level perspective taking was associated with dyads reaching peace more frequently (i.e., more of their games ended without a "bomb attack"), but dyadic empathy actually predicted a significantly lower percentage of peaceful solutions. In addition, the amount of joint integrative gains resulting from peaceful resolutions (reward money from the "World Bank"), indicating the extent of cooperation in peaceful games, was positively and significantly related to dyadic perspective taking but negatively and significantly related to dyadic empathy.

This pattern of results suggests that, perhaps surprisingly, there was more retaliation when the collective empathy among the adversaries was high. Research shows that regulating anger is a key factor in successfully navigating conflicts (Chapter 9 in this volume). Game-by-game analyses provide some insight into how perspective takers were able to succeed: Those higher on perspective taking not only disarmed their own arsenals to a greater extent but also were able to convince their opponents to do the same and thereby create joint gain. In contrast, high-empathy individuals and dyads had more aggressive attacks and fewer successfully cooperative interactions. High-empathy dyads seemed to get locked in spirals of escalating conflict involving attack and counterattack. We speculate that this may be a function of the greater emotionality of empathic individuals. Perhaps under direct threat and attack, this emotionality can lead to being "carried away" by anger or spite, leading to counterproductive conflict escalation (Pillutla & Murnighan, 1996). With regard to individual gains, higher levels of perspective taking were related to significantly greater profit, whereas empathy predicted fewer individual profits. Thus, perspective takers not only achieved peace but also secured higher profits for themselves.

A second study by Gilin et al. (2010) tested whether perspective taking and empathy would predict performance in a simple ultimatum bargaining game and whether accurate inferences about the opponent's strategy would mediate these effects. An ultimatum bargaining game involves two roles: a "Proposer," whose role is to make a single offer of a pool of resources (e.g., $10) to a Responder, who must simply accept or reject the offer (Pillutla & Murnighan, 1995). Acceptance means parties keep the distribution of money offered by the Proposer; rejection means that neither party receives any amount of the resource.

The ultimatum task therefore models a simple conflict in which one opponent has decision power while the other has the power to respond to and protect against potentially unfair decisions. It provides an ideal context for testing whether cognitive understanding of the partner's perspective drives successful outcomes because the Proposer's outcome largely depends on participants' perceptions of the likely responses of the other person. For example, a Proposer who completely disregards what the opponent might view as a favorable or fair outcome (i.e., by taking most of the money for himself) is likely to have the offer rejected and wind up with no money at all. On the other hand, choosing an offer that the responder perceives as fair will result in an accepted agreement and money for both sides. But this is a classic mixed-motive situation because the sender wants to send as little money as possible that will still be accepted to maximize his or her own gain.

In their study, only the perspective taking but not the empathy of the Proposer predicted both whether a Responder accepted an offer and the amount of money secured. In addition, the Proposers who were higher on perspective taking were more accurate in determining whether their opponent would accept their ultimatum offers and this accuracy mediated their ability to secure acceptances.

EMPATHIZERS ARE MORE EFFECTIVE IN PREDICTING EMOTIONAL CONNECTIONS

All of the studies described in this chapter suggest that perspective taking is superior to empathy in mixed-motive settings: perspective takers can get inside the head of opponents and understand their interests and priorities and can predict and influence their likely behavior. However, in some strategic interactions and coalition–formation situations, the key is determining with whom one has emotionally or affectively connected. To test this hypothesis, Gilin et al. (2010) designed a three-person social coalition game in which participants could win a cash prize but only if they selected as their coalition partner someone who also simultaneously chose them (rather than a third person). However, participants were not told they were playing a strategic coalition game until after an introductory session in which they got to know the two other participants. The game was therefore not primarily a cognitive task, but rather a more intuitive and affective task in which participants needed to retroactively assess their social connections with others during the previous interaction; success depended on having gathered the correct sense of their previous emotional connection with others.

In this game, empathy was a benefit to both winning the game and accuracy about the other players' game choices. In contrast, perspective taking was not associated with either winning or accuracy, although perspective taking was never detrimental to either outcome. In this study, empathic tendencies conferred an advantage, predicting successful coalition building. These results indicate that empathy can be an asset when conflicts are fundamentally based on affective, interpersonal connections, such as interpersonal disputes with spouses, friends, family, and colleagues.

CONCLUSIONS

We have reviewed a number of studies exploring the role of two social competencies—perspective taking and empathy—in predicting success in mixed-motive situations that model key underlying characteristics of conflict. In negotiations, war games, and ultimatum games, where success is typically achieved by understanding the likely strategic moves of one's opponent, perspective taking proves advantageous. Perspective takers are better able to uncover underlying interests to generate creative solutions and to craft more efficient deals in multi-issue negotiations. They are also better able to anticipate and steer likely behavior in war-like clashes, leading them to achieve higher levels of peace. Not only do perspective takers reach agreements and peace while maximizing the size of the bargaining pie, but they also take nice big pieces of that pie, garnering the highest levels of individual profit. They seem to take Sun Tzu's exhortation that to know one's enemy is the road to success on the battlefield.

However, when success in a strategic interaction requires determining if you psychologically connect with another person, empathizers were more likely to win in a coalition-formation game. These results suggest that empathy can promote not just closeness to others but also an accurate assessment of interpersonal connection, leading to success in strategic tasks that require affective understanding.

Overall, these studies suggest that perspective taking and empathy can each promote successful resolution of competitive interactions depending on the type of conflict. In general, the identification of mutually compatible underlying interests, a key conflict resolution strategy, seems to be at the heart of perspective-taking ability, and we found an advantage for perspective takers when interactions (e.g., negotiations, war games) required an appreciation of counterparts' underlying interests. On the other hand, conflicts involving more affective, interpersonal disputes may be best approached with an empathetic mindset.

At the same time, however, we acknowledge that many real-world conflicts involve both affective and cognitive elements, and we believe that having both skills is likely useful: empathy for appreciating and diffusing the affective elements that are defining features of conflict; and perspective taking for deducing compatible interests and possible solutions to achieve an enduring resolution. Indeed, in our opening examples, both Jack Ryan and President Kennedy not only identified key underlying interests of their Soviet counterparts that led to win–win outcomes but were also able to diffuse heated interpersonal tensions among their own decision-making teams (in both cases, government and military officials who pushed for a military response) to get their proposed, peaceful solutions implemented. Thus, although future research is needed for empirical confirmation, we believe there is likely an ideal balance between both mindsets in many conflict situations, suggesting perhaps that the ideal is to strive for something like Aristotle's "golden mean." In deciding when and how best to use one's head and one's heart in conflict situations a little of both may go a long way. Like the famous characters from *The Wizard of Oz*, successful resolution of conflicts requires brains, a heart, and a little courage.

REFERENCES

Archer, R. L., Diaz-Loving, R., Gollwitzer, P. M., Davis, M. H., & Foushee, H. C. (1981). The role of dispositional empathy and social evaluation in the empathic mediation of helping. *Journal of Personality and Social Psychology, 40,* 786–796.

Axelrod, R. (1984). *The evolution of cooperation.* New York: Basic Books.

Axelrod, R. (1987). The evolution of strategies in the iterated prisoners' dilemma. In L. Davis (Ed.), *Genetic algorithms and simulated annealing* (pp. 32–42). Los Altos, CA: Morgan Kaufmann.

Barry, B., & Friedman, R. (1998). Bargainer characteristics in distributive and integrative negotiation: The role of personality and cognitive ability. *Journal of Personality and Social Psychology, 74,* 345–359.

Batson, C. D., & Ahmad, N. (2001). Empathy-induced altruism in a prisoner's dilemma II: What if the target of empathy has defected? *European Journal of Social Psychology, 31,* 25–36.

Batson, C. D., Fultz, J., & Schoenrade, P. A. (1987). Distress and empathy: Two qualitatively distinct vicarious emotions with different motivational consequences. *Journal of Personality, 55*(1), 19–39.

Batson, C. D., & Moran, T. (1999). Empathy-induced altruism in a prisoner's dilemma. *European Journal of Social Psychology, 29,* 909–924.

Batson, C. D., O'Quinn, K., Fultz, J., Vanderplas, M., & Isen, A. (1983). Influence of self-report distress and empathy on egoistic versus altruistic motivation to help. *Journal of Personality and Social Psychology, 45,* 706–718.

Batson, C. D., Lishner, D. A., Carpenter, A., Dulin, L., Harjusola-Webb, S., Stocks, E. L., et al. (2003). As you would have them do unto you: Does imagining yourself in the other's place stimulate moral action? *Personality and Social Psychology Bulletin, 29,* 1190–1201.

Bengtsson, H., & Johnson, L. (1992). Perspective taking, empathy, and prosocial behavior in late childhood. *Child Study Journal, 22,* 11–22.

Brett, J. M. (2007). *Negotiating globally: How to negotiate deals, resolve disputes, and make decisions across cultural boundaries.* San Francisco: Jossey-Bass.

Chartrand, T. L., & Bargh, J. A. (1999). The chameleon effect: The perception-behavior link and social interaction. *Journal of Personality and Social Psychology, 76,* 893–910.

Cialdini, R. B., Brown, S. L., Lewis, B. P., Luce, C., & Neuberg, S. L. (1997). Reinterpreting the empathy-altruism relationship: When one into one equals oneness. *Journal of Personality and Social Psychology, 73,* 481–494.

Coke, J. S., Batson, C. D., & McDavis, K. (1978). Empathic mediation of helping: A two-stage model. *Journal of Personality and Social Psychology, 36,* 752–766.

Davis, M. (1980). A multidimensional approach to individual differences in empathy. *JSAS Catalog of Selected Documents in Psychology, 10,* 85.

Davis, M. (1983). The effects of dispositional empathy on emotional reactions and helping: A multidimensional approach. *Journal of Personality, 51*, 167–184.

Deutsch, F., & Madle, R. A. (1975). Empathy: Historic and current conceptualizations, measurement, and a cognitive theoretical perspective. *Human Development, 18*, 267–287.

Eisenberg, N., Fabes, R. A., Murphy, B., Karbon, M., Maszk, P., Smith, M., et al. (1994). The relations of emotionality and regulation to dispositional and situational empathy-related responding. *Journal of Personality and Social Psychology, 66*, 776–797.

Findler, N. V. (1990). *Contributions to a computer-based theory of strategies*. New York: Springer-Verlag.

Fisher, R., Ury, W., & Patton, B. (1991). *Getting to yes: Negotiating agreement without giving in* (2nd ed.). New York: Penguin.

Froman, L. A., Jr., & Cohen, M. D. (1970). Compromise and logroll: Comparing the efficiency of two bargaining processes. *Behavioral Science, 15*, 180–183.

Fry, W. R., Firestone, I. J., & Williams, D. L. (1983). Negotiation process and outcome of stranger dyads and dating couples: Do lovers lose? *Basic & Applied Social Psychology, 4*, 1–16.

Galinsky, A. D., & Ku, G. (2004). The effects of perspective-taking on prejudice: The moderating role of self-evaluation. *Personality and Social Psychology Bulletin, 30*, 594–604.

Galinsky, A. D., Ku, G., & Wang, C. S. (2005). Perspective-taking and self-other overlap: Fostering social bonds and facilitating social coordination. *Group Processes & Intergroup Relations, 8*, 109–124.

Galinsky, A. D., Magee, J. C., Inesi, M. E., Gruenfeld, D. H. (2006). Power and perspectives not taken. *Psychological Science, 17*, 1068–1074.

Galinsky, A. D., Maddux, W. W., Gilin, D., & White, J. B. (2008). Why it pays to get inside the head of your opponent: The differential effects of perspective taking and empathy in negotiations. *Psychological Science, 19*, 378–384.

Galinsky, A.D., & Moskowitz, G.B. (2000). Perspective-taking: Decreasing stereotype expression, stereotype accessibility, and in-group favoritism. *Journal of Personality and Social Psychology, 78*, 708–724.

Galinsky, A. D., & Mussweiler, T. (2001). First offers as anchors: The role of perspective-taking and negotiator focus. *Journal of Personality and Social Psychology, 81*, 657–669.

Galinsky, A. D., Wang, C. S., & Ku, G. (2008). Perspective-takers behave more stereotypically. *Journal of Personality and Social Psychology, 95*, 404–419.

Gilin, D., & Maddux, W. W., & Galinsky, A. D. (2010). *When to use your head, and when to use your heart: The differential value of perspective taking versus empathy in mixed-motive interactions*. Unpublished manuscript, St. Mary's University.

Goldberg, S. (2000). Texoil. In J. M. Brett (Ed.) *Negotiation and decision making exercises*. Evanston, IL: Dispute Resolution Research Center, Northwestern University CD.

Hoffman, S. (1977). An American social science: International relations. *Daedalus 106*(3), 41–60.

Johnson, D. W. (1967). Use of role reversal in intergroup competition. *Journal of Personality and Social Psychology, 7*, 135–141.

Johnson, D. W. (1975). Affective perspective taking and cooperative predisposition. *Developmental Psychology, 11*, 869–870.

Kemp, K. E., & Smith, W. P. (1994). Information exchange, toughness, and integrative bargaining: The roles of explicit cues and perspective-taking. *The International Journal of Conflict Management, 5*, 5–21.

Lax, D. A. & Sebenius, J. K. (1986). *The manager as negotiator: Bargaining for cooperation and competitive gain*. New York: The Free Press.

Ligthart, P.E.M., & Lindenberg, S. (1994). Ethical regulation of economic transactions: Solidarity frame versus gain-maximization frame. In A. Lewis and K. E. Warneryd (Eds.), *Ethics and economic affairs* (pp. 215–230). London: Routledge.

Lopes, L. L. (1976). Model-based decision and inference in stud poker. *Journal of Experimental Psychology: General, 105*, 217–239.

Maddux, W. W., Mullen, E., & Galinsky, A. D. (2008). Chameleons bake bigger pies and take bigger pieces: Strategic behavioral mimicry facilitates negotiation outcomes. *Journal of Experimental Social Psychology, 44*, 461–468.

Moore, D. A. (2005). Myopic biases in strategic social prediction: Why deadlines put everyone under more pressure than everyone else. *Personality and Social Psychology Bulletin, 31*, 668–679.

Neale, M. A., & Bazerman, M. H. (1982). The role of perspective-taking ability in negotiating under different forms of arbitration. *Industrial and Labor Relations Review, 36*, 378–388.

Okun, M. A., Shepard, S. A., & Eisenberg, N. (2000). The relations of emotionality and regulation to dispositional empathy-related responding among volunteers-in-training. *Personality and Individual Differences, 28*, 367–382.

Oswald, P. A. (1996). The effects of cognitive and affective perspective-taking on empathic concern and altruistic helping. *Journal of Social Psychology, 136*(5), 613–623.

Peterson, E., & Thompson, L. (1997). Negotiation teamwork: The impact of information distribution and accountability on performance depends on the relationship among team members. *Organizational Behavior and Human Decision Processes, 72*, 364–383.

Piaget, J. (1932). *The moral judgment of the child.* Glencoe, IL: Free Press.

Pillutla, M. M., & Murnighan, J. K. (1995). Being fair or appearing fair: Strategic behavior in ultimatum bargaining. *Academy of Management Journal, 38*, 1408–1426.

Pillutla, M. M., & Murnighan, J. K. (1996). Unfairness, anger, and spite: Emotional rejections of ultimatum offers. *Organizational Behavior and Human Decision Processes, 68*, 208–224.

Pruitt, D. G., & Rubin, J. Z. (1986). *Social conflict: Escalation, stalemate, and settlement.* New York: McGraw-Hill.

Regan, D. T., & Totten, J. (1975). Empathy and attribution: Turning observers into actors. *Journal of Personality and Social Psychology, 32*, 850–856.

Richardson, D. R., Green, L. R., & Lago, T. (1998). The relationship between perspective-taking and nonaggressive responding in the face of attack. *Journal of Personality, 66*, 235–256.

Richardson, D. R., Hammock, G. S., Smith, S. M., Gardner, W., & Signo, M. (1994). Empathy as a cognitive inhibitor of interpersonal aggression. *Aggressive Behavior, 20*, 275–289.

Sally, D. (2000). A general theory of sympathy, mind-reading, and social interaction, with an application to the prisoners' dilemma. *Social Science Information, 39*, 567–634.

Sheppard, B. H. (1999). Negotiating in long-term mutually interdependent relationships among relative equals. In R. J. Lewicki, D. M. Saunders, & J. W. Minton (Eds.). *Negotiation: Readings, exercises, and cases* (3rd ed., pp. 278–293). Boston, MA: Irwin/ McGraw-Hill.

Smith, A. (1759). *Theory of moral sentiments.* London: A. Miller.

Spencer, H. (1870). *The principles of psychology.* London: Williams and Norgate.

Tetlock, P. E., Skitka, L., & Boettger, R. (1989). Social and cognitive strategies for coping with accountability: Conformity, complexity, and bolstering. *Journal of Personality and Social Psychology, 57*, 632–640.

Thagard, P. (1992). Adversarial problem solving: Modeling an opponent using explanatory coherence. *Cognitive Science, 16*, 123–149.

Thompson, L. (1990). Negotiation behavior and outcomes: Empirical evidence and theoretical issues. *Psychological Bulletin, 108*, 515–532.

Thompson, L. (2001). *The mind and heart of the negotiator* (2nd ed.). Upper Saddle River, NJ: Prentice Hall.

Thompson, L., & Hastie, R. (1990). Social perception in negotiation. *Organizational Behavior & Human Decision Processes, 47*, 98–123.

Tripp, T., & Sondak, H. (1992). An evaluation of dependent variables in experimental negotiation studies: Impasse rates and Pareto efficiency. *Organizational Behavior and Human Decision Processes, 51*, 273–295.

Trivers, R. L. (1971). The evolution of reciprocal altruism. *Quarterly Review of Biology, 46*, 35–57.

Twenge, J. M. (2001). Changes in women's assertiveness in response to status and roles: A cross-temporal meta-analysis, 1931–1993. *Journal of Personality and Social Psychology, 81*, 133–145.

Ury, W., Brett, J. M., & Goldberg, S. B. (1988). *Getting disputes resolved*. San Francisco: Jossey-Bass.

Van Baaren, R. B., Holland, R. W., Kawakami, K., & Van Knippenberg, A. (2004). Mimicry and prosocial behavior. *Psychological Science, 15*, 71–74.

Van Baaren, R. B., Holland, R. W., Steenaert, B., & Van Knippenberg, A. (2003). Mimicry for money: Behavioral consequences of imitation. *Journal of Experimental Social Psychology, 39*, 393–398.

Vescio, T. K., Sechrist, G. B., & Paolucci, M. P. (2003). Perspective taking and prejudice reduction: The mediational role of empathy arousal and situational attributions. *European Journal of Social Psychology, 33*, 455–472.

Wilson, K., & Gallois, C. (1993). *Assertion and its social context*. Oxford, UK: Pergamon Press Ltd.

8

Affective Influences on the Perception, Management, and Resolution of Social Conflicts[1]

JOSEPH P. FORGAS and HUI BING TAN

University of New South Wales

INTRODUCTION

*I*magine that you are hearing a marching band performing a cheerful, upbeat tune while you are thinking about a serious conflict you need to resolve with your partner. Would the mood induced by the music influence your thoughts, plans, and eventual conflict management strategies? This chapter will explore the psychological mechanisms responsible for such effects, describing a series of experiments demonstrating the influence of mood on various conflict behaviors. It is well known that affect is an integral component of most social conflicts and also plays a crucial role in many aggressive encounters (Forgas, 2002, 2007; Zajonc, 2000; see also Chapter 9 in this volume). Affective states are likely to influence a variety of strategic conflict-related behaviors, such as assertiveness (see Chapter 5 in this volume), forgiveness (see Chapter 14 in this volume), goal setting (Chapters 6 and 12 in this volume), perspective taking (Chapter 7 in this volume), and reactions to ostracism (Chapters 3 and 13 in this volume). Returning to our introductory example, military music has been used ever since antiquity to influence soldiers' mood states, in the hope that upbeat, energetic music creates a more assertive and confident mindset that can influence behavior in conflict situations. In another

[1] This work was supported by a Professorial Fellowship from the Australian Research Council and the Research Prize by the Alexander von Humboldt Foundation to Joseph P. Forgas. For further information on this research project, see also www.psy.unsw.edu.au/users/jforgas.htm.

literary example, Thomas Mann in a short story describes how chess players' decisions whether to use a defensive or aggressive strategy is markedly influenced by the upbeat or downbeat mood of the background music played by an orchestra in the background.

Although the last two decades saw something like an "affective revolution" in psychological research (see also Forgas, 2002, 2006), we are still a long way from fully understanding the age-old puzzle about the links between affect and cognition, feeling and thinking as the two complementary faculties of the human mind (Hilgard, 1980). There is compelling recent evidence from evolutionary social psychology, neuropsychology, and psychophysiology suggesting that affect is an essential component of motivated social thinking and behavior (Adolphs & Damasio, 2001; Blascovich & Mendes, 2000). However, we do not yet fully understand when, how, and why these effects occur. This chapter will describe a series of recent studies showing how positive and negative mood states can influence both the content and the process of how people think about conflict situations, resulting in significant consequences for conflict behaviors and conflict resolution strategies.

We will begin with a brief overview of early research on affect and social conflict and will survey recent cognitive theories relevant to understanding this link. Next, two converging lines of research will be described demonstrating affective influences on the content and process of thinking and behavior in conflict situations. First, experiments demonstrating affect congruence will be described, showing that affective states may color the way people interpret and evaluate conflict situations, influencing their negotiating strategies and the way interpersonal demands are formulated and responded to. A second line of experiments explores affective influences in information-processing strategies, showing that affect impacts on how people process conflict-relevant information. In particular, mild negative moods often trigger a more systematic, accommodative information processing style that results in more effective and more successful judgments and behaviors in conflict situations and greater sensitivity to social norms.

AFFECT, MOOD, AND EMOTION

There is as yet little general agreement in the literature about how best to define terms such as *affect, feelings, emotions,* or *mood* (Fiedler & Forgas, 1988; Forgas, 1992, 1995, 2002). We have argued elsewhere that affect may be used as a generic label to refer to both moods and emotions. Moods in turn could be described as "low-intensity, diffuse and relatively enduring affective states without a salient antecedent cause and therefore little cognitive content (e.g., feeling good or feeling bad)," whereas emotions "are more intense, short-lived and usually have a definite cause and clear cognitive content" (e.g., anger or fear) (Forgas, 1992, p. 230). This distinction is highly relevant to understanding the functions of affect in conflict behaviors. There is much evidence for the influence of specific emotions such as anger, shame, guilt, and pride in conflict behaviors (see Chapter 9 in this volume). In addition, subtle, nonspecific moods may often have a potentially more enduring and insidious motivational influence on social cognition and behaviors in conflict situations (Fiedler, 1991; Forgas, 1992, 1995, 2002; Sedikides, 1992, 1995). Accordingly, our primary concern here is with the effects of low-intensity moods rather than distinct emotions.

AFFECT AND SOCIAL CONFLICTS

The key role of affect in the way people think about and respond to social conflicts has been suggested in a number of early studies. Psychoanalytic theories assumed that affect has a dynamic, invasive quality and can "take over" judgments unless adequate psychological resources are deployed to control these impulses (Feshbach & Singer, 1957). Conditioning and associationist theories provided an alternative account, suggesting that previously "neutral" concepts can become affectively loaded as a result of incidental associations with affect-eliciting stimuli. According to radical behaviorists such as John Watson, all affective reactions acquired throughout life are the product of such a cumulative pattern of associations.

More recent work showed that implicit representations of common social encounters, including conflict situations, are largely determined by the feelings aroused by these events, rather than their objective features (Forgas, 1979, 1982). Feelings of anxiety, confidence, intimacy, pleasure, or discomfort are critical in defining implicit representations of social encounters. Several decades ago, Pervin (1976) noted that what is striking is the extent to which interpersonal situations are "described in terms of affects (e.g., threatening, warm, interesting, dull, tense, calm, rejecting) and organized in terms of similarity of affects aroused by them" (p. 471). More recently, Niedenthal and Halberstadt (2000) showed that such emotional categorization is extremely common. Many social stimuli and events are perceived, categorized, and responded to not based on their objective characteristics but in terms of the emotional reactions they elicit.

Affect also has a dynamic influence on how social information—including information about conflict situations—is interpreted, processed, and remembered (Bower, 1981; Forgas, 1995a, 2001, 2002). Contemporary cognitive theories focus on the information-processing mechanisms that allow affective states to influence both the content and the processes of thinking and judgments.

COGNITIVE MECHANISMS OF AFFECT CONGRUENCE

Affective states can have two kinds of effects on social thinking and behavior. They may influence (1) the content of thinking by selectively priming affect-congruent thoughts and responses, and they may also influence (2) the process of thinking, that is, the way people process social information. We shall consider these two kinds of effects in turn.

Content Effects

The associative network model by Bower (1981) proposed that affect and cognition are integrally linked within an associative network of mental representations.

Selectively primed affect-congruent constructs are more likely to be used in constructive cognitive tasks—for example, when perceiving, interpreting, and constructing responses to a conflict situation. In several experiments, Bower found that happy or sad people were likely to selectively remember positive (or negative) details of their childhood and of their social activities during the preceding weeks, consistent with the predicted selective recall of affect-congruent information. Better access to affect-congruent information should also bias perceptions and behaviors in conflict situations, and such mood effects are most reliably found when the situation is complex and demanding as is typically the case with conflict scenarios (Forgas, 1994, 1999a, 1999b, 2002; Sedikides, 1995).

An alternative theory of content effects was proposed by Schwarz and Clore (1983) who argued that "instead of computing a judgment on the basis of recalled features of a target, individuals may simply just ask themselves: "How do I feel about it?" and when doing so, they may mistake feelings due to a pre-existing mood state as indicative of their reaction to the target" (Schwarz, 1990, p. 529). This simplistic "how-do-I-feel-about-it" heuristic suggests that people often misread their mood as informative of their reactions to an unrelated situation. As earlier conditioning theories by Clore and Byrne (1974), this model also posits an incidental and subconscious link between affect and unrelated stimuli and responses. Research now suggests that people seem to rely on affect as a heuristic cue only when they are unfamiliar with the task, when they have no prior evaluations to fall back on, when their personal involvement is low, and when they have insufficient cognitive resources or motivation to compute a more thorough response (Forgas, 2006). Although affect-as-information may influence quick, superficial judgments (Forgas & Moylan, 1987; Schwarz & Clore), it is unlikely that more complex and demanding reactions in conflict situations would be based on such a superficial and truncated strategy.

Processing Effects

Affect can also influence the process of cognition, that is, how people think (Clark & Isen, 1982; Schwarz, 1990). According to the mood-maintenance hypothesis (Clark & Isen), people in a positive mood should try to avoid effortful thinking to maintain this pleasant state. In contrast, those in negative mood might engage in vigilant, effortful processing as an adaptive response to improve an aversive state. Others such as Schwarz, and Wegener and Petty (1994), offered a functionalist "cognitive tuning" account, suggesting that positive and negative affect have a signaling–tuning function, informing the person of whether a relaxed, effort-minimizing (in positive affect) or a vigilant, effortful (negative affect) processing style is appropriate.

More recent integrative theories suggest a more subtle pattern (Bless, 2001; Bless & Fiedler, 2006; Fiedler, 2001), arguing that the evolutionary significance of affective states is not simply to influence processing effort but to trigger qualitatively different processing styles as well. Thus, positive affect recruits a more assimilative, schema-based, top-down processing style, when preexisting knowledge guides information processing. In contrast, negative affect produces a more accommodative, bottom-up, and externally focused processing strategy where attention to situational information drives thinking (Bless; Fiedler). These processing styles can be equally effortful yet produce qualitatively different outcomes in conflict situations (Tan & Forgas, 2010). Interestingly, the more vigilant processing mood promoted by negative affect can produce some surprising processing advantages, improving performance on tasks that require detailed attention to new information and leading to more successful and adaptive conflict behaviors.

Toward an Integration: The Affect Infusion Model

An integrative theory, the Affect Infusion Model (AIM; Forgas, 1995a, 2002) predicts that affect infusion should occur only in circumstances that promote an open, constructive processing style (Fiedler, 1991; Forgas, 1995b). The AIM thus assumes that (1) affect infusion should depend on the kind of processing strategy people use, and (2) all things being equal, people should use the least effortful and simplest processing strategy. The model identifies four alternative processing strategies: (1) direct access; (2) motivated; (3) heuristic; and (4) substantive processing. These strategies differ in terms of two basic dimensions: (1) the degree of effort; and (2) the degree of openness and constructiveness of the information-search strategy.

The combination of these two processing features—quantity (effort) and quality (openness)—produces four distinct processing styles (Fiedler, 2001): (1) substantive processing (high effort/open, constructive); (2) motivated processing (high effort/closed); (3) heuristic processing (low effort/open, constructive); and (4) direct-access processing (low effort/closed). Direct-access and motivated processing involve highly targeted and predetermined patterns of information search and selection, strategies that limit the scope for incidental affect infusion. Mood congruence and affect infusion are likely only when constructive processing is used, such as substantive or heuristic processing (see also Fiedler, 1991, 2001). The AIM also specifies a range of contextual variables related to the task, the person, and the situation that jointly influence processing choices. An important feature of the AIM is that it recognizes that affect itself can also influence processing choices. The implications of this model have now been supported in a number of studies.

AFFECT CONGRUENCE IN DEALING WITH CONFLICTS

According to the AIM, affective states should have a mood-congruent influence on dealing with conflict situations that recruit constructive, substantive processing (Forgas, 1995a, 2001; Sedikides, 1995). On the most basic level, there may be affect-congruent distortions on the way people interpret observed social behaviors (Forgas, Bower, & Krantz, 1984). Happy subjects tend to see more positive skilled behaviors, whereas sad mood produces more critical, negative behavior interpretations even when objective, videotaped evidence is readily available with obvious implications for conflict situations.

Affective Bias in Explaining Relationship Conflicts

Affect may also influence the way people evaluate their partners and real-life social conflicts (Forgas, 2002; Forgas, Levinger, & Moylan, 1994). Mood effects on dealing with relationship conflicts can have particularly important consequences for the success and longevity of the relationship. In a series of experiments, we asked happy or sad participants to make causal attributions for recent happy and sad conflicts in their current relationships (Forgas, 1994, Experiment 1). There was significant mood congruence, with more self-blaming and pessimistic attributions by sad subjects than by happy subjects. In a further study explanations for simple versus complex relationship conflicts were compared (Experiment 2). Again, sad mood produced more negative, pessimistic attributions. Mood effects were greater when explanations were given for serious rather than simple conflicts as serious conflicts required more substantive processing, and were associated with longer processing latencies (Experiment 3). Consistent with the AIM, these results confirm that paradoxically, extended processing recruited by serious conflicts increased mood effects (Forgas).

Affective Influences on Negotiating Strategies

One of the most common methods for dealing with conflict is negotiation. Effective negotiation is a critical skill in resolving personal and relationship problems and is also routinely used in organizations. In several experiments (Forgas, 1998a), positive, control, or negative mood was induced by giving participants positive, negative, or neutral feedback about their performance on a prior verbal test. Next, they engaged in either (a) an informal interpersonal, or (b) a formal, intergroup negotiating task. Participants in a positive mood set themselves more ambitious goals, formulated more optimistic action plans, and engaged in more cooperative and integrative negotiation than did control, or negative mood participants. They were also more willing to make and reciprocate deals (Figure 8.1) and actually achieved better outcomes. These results provide clear evidence that even slight changes in

Figure 8.1   Mood-congruent influences on negotiation: happy persons plan, use more cooperative and less competitive bargaining strategies, and are more likely to make and honor deals than do negotiators experiencing negative affect. (Data based on Forgas, J.P., *Journal of Personality and Social Psychology, 74*, 565–577, 1998. With permission.)

mood can significantly influence people's perceptions, plans, and behaviors in a negotiating task.

In terms of the AIM, these mood effects on conflict resolution can be explained in terms of affect priming mechanisms. Positive mood should selectively prime more positive thoughts and associations, leading to the formulation and use of more optimistic, cooperative, and integrative bargaining strategies. In contrast, negative mood should prime more pessimistic, negative thoughts and associations, leading to less ambitious goals and less cooperative, more competitive, and ultimately less successful bargaining strategies.

Interestingly, further experiments in this series showed that mood effects were reduced for individuals who scored high on measures such as Machiavellism and the need for approval. These individuals may have approached the bargaining task from a strongly predetermined, motivated perspective, reducing open, constructive processing and thus limiting the extent of affect infusion. Individual differences in tendency to use open, constructive versus guided, motivated processing may significantly mediate affect infusion into behavior in conflict situations (Rusting, 2001).

Mood Effects on Making Requests and Demands

In several experiments we explored the effects of mood on the way people formulate and respond to demands and requests. Requesting is an intrinsically complex behavior characterized by potential interpersonal conflict and psychological ambiguity. Requests must be formulated with just the right degree of assertiveness versus politeness to maximize compliance without risking giving offense. We expected happy people to adopt a more confident, assertive requesting style, due to the greater availability of positively valenced thoughts and associations (Forgas, 1998b, 1999a, 1999b). Further, in terms of the AIM, these mood effects should be particularly strong when the conflict situation is more complex and demanding and requires more substantive and elaborate processing. Mood was induced by asking people to recall and think about happy or sad autobiographical episodes (Forgas, 1999a, Experiment 1). Next, participants selected a more or less polite request formulation that they would use in an easy and a difficult request situation.

Happy participants preferred more direct, assertive requests, whereas sad persons used indirect, polite requests, and these effects were greatest in the more difficult, demanding request situation. In a follow-up experiment, similar effects were found when participants produced their own open-ended requests, which were subsequently rated for politeness and elaboration by two independent raters (Forgas, 1999a, Experiment 2). This pattern was confirmed in a third study, where participants were asked to produce more or less polite versus assertive request alternatives in a variety of different realistic situations (Forgas, 1999b, Experiment 1) following an audiovisual mood induction (watching happy or sad films).

A further unobtrusive field experiment looked at naturally produced requests (Forgas, 1999b, Experiment 2). After an audiovisual mood induction, the

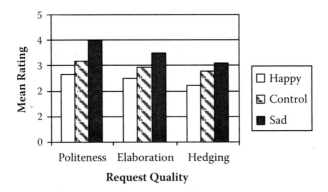

Figure 8.2   Mood effects on naturally produced requests: positive mood increases and negative mood decreases the degree of politeness, elaboration, and hedging in strategic communications. (After Forgas, J.P., *Personality and Social Psychology Bulletin, 25*, 850–863, 1999. With permission.)

experimenter casually asked participants to get a file from a neighboring office. The actual words in requesting the file were recorded by a concealed tape recorder and were subsequently analyzed for politeness and assertiveness. Sad people used more polite, friendly, and more elaborate request forms, whereas happy people used more assertive and less polite forms (Figure 8.2). An analysis of recall data confirmed that unconventional requests were also recalled significantly better, indicating their more elaborate, constructive processing.

Mood Effects on Responding to Interpersonal Demands

We have so far seen that mood states can have a profound influence on how people approach complex conflict situations. Moods may also influence responding to more or less assertive demands, such as being confronted by an unexpected request from a stranger (Forgas, 1998b). Students entering a library found pictures or text placed on their desks designed to induce good or bad moods. A few minutes later, they were approached by another student (in fact, a confederate) and received an unexpected polite or assertive, impolite demand for several sheets of paper. A short time after the incident a second confederate asked them to complete a brief questionnaire evaluating their perceptions, recall, and reactions to the demand and the requester.

People in a negative mood reacted more negatively, formed more critical, negative views of requests, and were less inclined to comply than were positive mood participants. In a particularly interesting result (Figure 8.3), mood effects were greater when the request was assertive and impolite and so required more substantive processing, as also confirmed by better recall memory for these messages later on. It seems that assertive, unconventional demands were processed more substantively and resulted in stronger mood effects. As implied by the AIM, affect infusion into conflict behaviors seem enhanced when complex, unusual tasks require more elaborate processing.

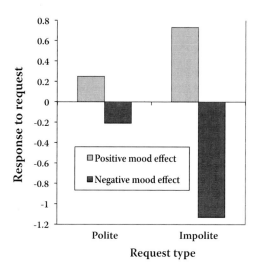

Figure 8.3   Mood effects on reactions to an unexpected demand in a public place (the library): those in a positive mood respond more positively and those in a negative mood respond more negatively (higher values indicate more positive reactions). These mood effects were greater when the request was impolite and atypical and thus required more substantive processing. (Data based on Forgas, J.P., *Personality and Social Psychology Bulletin, 24,* 173–185, 1998. With permission.)

THE INFORMATION-PROCESSING CONSEQUENCES OF AFFECT IN CONFLICT SITUATIONS

In addition to producing affect congruence, affect can also influence the way information is processed. Although it is commonly claimed that feeling good promotes better thinking in terms of creativity, flexibility, and integrative thinking (Ciarrochi, Forgas, & Mayer, 2006; Forgas, 1994, 2002), this is only part of the story. In this section we present several experiments showing that negative affect may also produce desirable and beneficial cognitive consequences. In functional terms, negative affect may operate as an adaptive signal recruiting more attentive and accommodative thinking that may help people to cope with the requirements of demanding social situations (Forgas, 2007). For example, negative affect produces a thinking style that helps reduce certain judgmental biases (Forgas, 1998c) and promotes more successful social influence strategies (Forgas, 2007).

Negative Affect Reduces the Fundamental Attribution Error

Interpreting the behavior of partners and adversaries in a conflict is often subject to the fundamental attribution error (FAE) when people see intentionality and internal causation despite evidence for the influence of situational forces (Gilbert & Malone, 1995). The FAE occurs because people focus on salient and conspicuous information—the actor—and fail to process information about situational constraints (Gilbert, 1991). If negative mood promotes the more detailed process-ing of situational information, the incidence of the FAE and other judgmental biases may be reduced (Forgas, 1998c). In one experiment, happy or sad partici-pants read and made attributions about the writer of an essay advocating a popu-lar or unpopular position (for or against nuclear testing), which they were told was either assigned or freely chosen, using the procedure pioneered by Jones and Harris (1967). Happy mood increased and sad mood reduced the incidence of the FAE, consistent with the more attentive thinking style recruited by negative affect. Similar effects can also occur in real life.

In a field study, happy or sad participants made attributions about the writ-ers of popular and unpopular essays arguing for or against recycling (cf. Forgas & Moylan, 1987). Once again, negative mood reduced the FAE. Recall memory data confirmed that these effects were due to the more attentive processing of situational information in negative mood (Forgas, 1998c, Experiment 3). These effects are consistent with the suggested evolutionary benefits of negative affect in recruiting more accommodative processing styles.

Negative Affect Increases Skepticism and Interpersonal Accuracy

Believing or not believing a partner or an adversary is another crucial decision people often face in conflict situations. How do we know if the information we receive from others is accurate? Accepting invalid information as true (false posi-tives, excessive gullibility) can be just as dangerous as rejecting information that is valid (false negatives, excessive skepticism). Negative moods might produce more critical and skeptical judgments, whereas happy people may accept interpersonal messages at "face value," as genuine and trustworthy due to the information-pro-cessing consequences of affect we discussed previously. To explore this, we asked happy and sad participants to judge the genuineness of people displaying positive, neutral, and negative facial expressions.

As predicted, those in a negative mood were significantly less likely to accept facial expressions as genuine than were those in the neutral or happy condition. Curiously, happy participants were also more confident in their judgments than were other groups. In another study negative mood reduced and positive mood increased people's tendency to accept others' facial displays as genuine, consistent with the more attentive and accommodative processing style associated with nega-tive moods.

Negative mood may also improve perception accuracy and the detection of deception. In one study happy or sad participants had to determine the truthful-ness of videotaped statements by people who were interrogated after a staged theft and were either guilty or not guilty (East & Forgas, 2008). Those in a positive mood were more likely to accept deceptive statements as truthful. Sad participants in turn formed significantly more guilty judgments and were significantly better at correctly detecting deception (Figure 8.4). A signal detection analysis confirmed that sad judges were more accurate in detecting deception (identifying guilty tar-gets as guilty) than were neutral or happy judges, consistent with the predicted mood-induced processing differences.

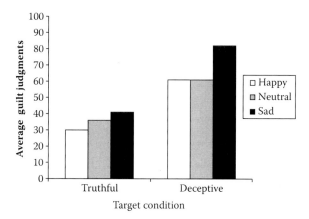

Figure 8.4   The effects of mood and the target's veracity (truthful, deceptive) on judgments of guilt of targets accused of committing a theft (average percentage of targets judged guilty in each condition). (After East, R. & Forgas, J.P., Manuscript, University of New South Wales, 2008. With permission.)

Negative Affect Improves the Efficacy of Persuasive Messages

Accommodative processing promoted by negative affect may also result in more concrete and factual thinking and result in the production of more effective power strategies and persuasive messages. We explored this (Forgas, 2007, Experiment 1) by asking happy or sad participants to produce persuasive arguments for or against an increase in student fees and for or against Aboriginal land rights. Negative mood resulted in arguments that were of significantly higher quality, were more concrete, and were more persuasive than those produced by happy participants. A mediational analysis established that mood-induced variations in argument concreteness improved argument quality. In a further experiment, happy or sad participants produced persuasive arguments for or against Australia becoming a republic and for or against a radical right-wing party. Sad mood again resulted in higher quality and more persuasive arguments, consistent with the prediction that negative mood should promote a more careful, systematic, bottom-up processing style (Bless, 2001; Bless & Fiedler, 2006; Fiedler, 2001; Forgas, 2002; Figure 8.5).

To further test the actual effectiveness of negative mood arguments, in Experiment 3 the arguments produced by happy or sad participants were presented to a naïve audience of undergraduate students. Arguments written by negative mood participants in Experiments 1 and 2 were actually significantly more successful in producing a real change in attitudes than were arguments produced by happy participants. Finally, in Experiment 4 persuasive attempts by happy and sad people were directed at a "partner" to volunteer for a boring experiment using email exchanges (Forgas, 2007). The motivation to be persuasive was also manipulated by offering some of them a significant reward if successful (movie passes). People in a negative mood produced higher-quality persuasive arguments. However, the offer of a reward reduced mood effects, confirming a key prediction of the Affect Infusion Model (Forgas, 1995a, 2002): that mood effects on

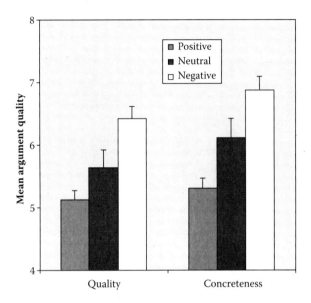

Figure 8.5 Mood effects on the quality and concreteness of the persuasive messages produced: negative affect improves the quality and the degree of concreteness of persuasive arguments. (After Forgas, J.P., *Journal of Experimental Social Psychology, 43,* 513–528, 2007, Experiment 2. With permission.)

information processing—and subsequent social influence strategies—are reduced by motivated processing. Mediational analyses confirmed that negative mood induced longer and more accommodative thinking and more concrete and specific arguments.

These experiments confirm that persuasive arguments produced in negative mood are not only of higher quality as judged by raters but are also significantly more effective in producing genuine attitude change in people. However, when motivation is already high, mood effects tend to diminish, as predicted by the Affect Infusion Model (Forgas, 2002). This finding may have interesting applied implications for managing personal and organizational conflicts that also involve a great deal of persuasive communication. It is an intriguing possibility that mild negative affect may actually promote a more concrete, accommodative, and ultimately more successful communication style in some conflict situations.

When Positive Affect Increases Aggressive Tendencies

After the London bomb attacks, in a tragic mistake British police shot dead a Brazilian man who looked like a Muslim. Could it be that merely appearing Muslim may function as a subliminal cue facilitating aggressive responses? In a recent experiment we investigated the influence of positive and negative moods on aggressive responses in the shoot–don't shoot paradigm with targets who did or did not appear to be Muslim. Using this technique (Correll, Park, Judd, & Wittenbrink, 2002), U.S. participants revealed a strong bias to shoot more at Black rather than

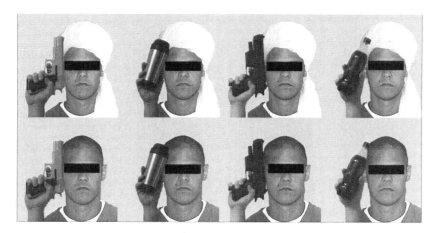

Figure 8.6   The turban effect: stimulus figures used to assess the effects of mood and wearing or not wearing a turban on automatic aggressive responses. Participants had to make rapid shoot–don't shoot decisions in response to targets who did or did not hold a gun and did or did not wear a Muslim headdress (a turban).

White targets. In our study, we expected Muslim targets to elicit a similar bias. In essence, the shooter's bias task is an unobtrusive behavioral measure assessing aggressive reactions to negative stereotypes (Forgas, 1976, 2003).

Partipants were instructed to shoot at targets on a computer screen only when they were carrying a gun. We used morphing software to create targets that did or did not appear Muslim by wearing a turban or the hijab (see Figure 8.6). We expected and found that people tended to shoot more at targets with Muslim headgear, and this effect was greater after a positive mood induction (Figure 8.7). This result confirms that positive affect facilitated an aggressive behavioral response to a negative stereotype, even in a group of otherwise liberal and tolerant Australian undergraduates. As Australia has not been subject to Muslim terrorist attacks on its territory, other countries in the forefront of Muslim terrorism such as the United States and Britain may show an even stronger "turban effect" than the one we demonstrated here. The most intriguing finding here is that positive affect triggered a significant selective bias against Muslims, consistent with recent theories suggesting that positive affect promotes top-down, assimilative processing that facilitates the influence of stereotypes on automatic responses (Bless & Fiedler, 2006; Forgas, 1998, 2007).

Affective Influences on Interpersonal Strategies in the Dictator Game

If somebody gave you $50 to divide between yourself and another person any way you like, how much would you keep for yourself? Does being in a good or a bad mood influence such conflict decisions? People face a conflict between being selfish and being fair in many everyday situations, and the dilemma inherent in these choices has been a major topic for philosophers and writers for decades. Recent research in evolutionary psychology suggests that humans and other primates

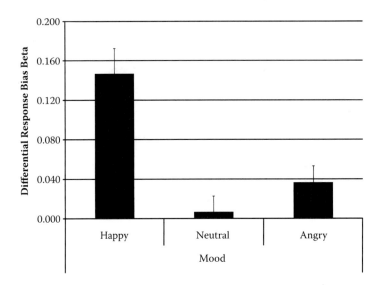

Figure 8.7 The effects of positive and negative mood on people's reliance on stereotypes in the shooters' bias task: those in a positive mood were more likely and those in a negative mood were less likely to selectively shoot at targets wearing a turban. (After Unkelbach, Forgas & Denson, 2008. With permission.)

evolved a sense of justice and fairness as an adaptive strategy to constrain self-ishness and to maintain social cohesion and harmony (Forgas, Haselton, & von Hippel, 2007). Does mood influence how assertive and selfish we are in interpersonal situations? We explored the possibility that a positive mood may increase assertiveness and selfishness whereas a sad mood may produce greater fairness in the dictator game. This question had not been investigated previously. Unlike prior research on altruism, the dictator game allows the exploration of mood effects on pure selfishness in a simple allocation task.

Traditional economic theories predict that a rational allocator in the dictator game should maximize earnings and keep most of the resources. Actual research suggests a far more complex pattern. In fact, allocators often give 30%, and even 50%, to others (Bolton, Katok, & Zwick, 1998; Forsythe, Horowitz, Savin, & Sefton, 1994), suggesting that behavior is governed by a subtle combination of the conflicting demands of self-interest and the norm of fairness (Haselhuhn & Mellers, 2005; Pillutla and Murninghan, 1995). In this situation, moods may influence behavior by subtly shifting the way allocators focus on and interpret internal (selfish) and external (fairness norm) information. As we have seen, positive moods may promote a more internally oriented, selfish processing style (Bless & Fiedler, 2006). In contrast, negative mood seems to promote a more externally focused, accommodative processing style, with greater attention to the external norms of fairness.

In the first experiment, volunteer students approached on campus received a false-feedback mood induction, and then they played the dictator game and made allocations either to an in-group member (student in their own faculty) or an unknown person. Mood was induced by giving participants a bogus six-item "test

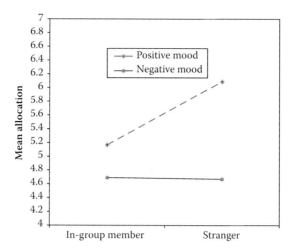

Figure 8.8   The effects of mood (good, bad) and relationship (in-group member vs. stranger) on the fairness of allocations in a dictator game, showing the mean number of tickets, out of 10, individuals kept to themselves in each condition.

of cognitive-spatial abilities," estimating the surface area of randomly sized geometric figures and providing positive or negative manipulated feedback describing their performance as "outstanding" or "poor" to induce good or bad mood (e.g., Forgas, 2007). They were then asked to allocate 10 raffle tickets between themselves and another person, with a $20 voucher as the ultimate prize. Results showed that happy students kept more raffle tickets than did sad students, and there was also a nonsignificant trend for greater selfishness toward a stranger when in a positive mood (Figure 8.8). These results confirm that transient mood had a significantly influence on assertiveness and selfishness.

Experiment 2 replicated this effect using a different mood induction (affect-inducing films) and a more realistic allocation task in the laboratory, with the names and photos of partners also displayed for each task to increase realism. After viewing films designed to induce happy or sad moods, participants performed a series of allocation tasks described as an "interpersonal game" with eight randomly assigned others, each involving the allocation of 10 points. Happy individuals were again more selfish and kept more points to themselves than did sad individuals, and there was also a significant interaction between mood and the eight trials. As the trials progressed, happy individuals became more selfish, and sad individuals became more fair (Figure 8.9).

In a further experiment we explicitly manipulated fairness norms by providing allocators with information about the fair or unfair behaviors of previous players to reinforce or undermine the social norm of fairness. Information about unfair allocations should weaken the social norm and should increase the latitude for individual deliberations, thus increasing the scope for mood effects to occur. After viewing affect-inducing films, participants played the allocation task, after being exposed to information about fair or unfair offers of "past proposers" to emphasize

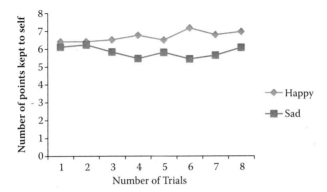

Figure 8.9   The effects of mood on selfishness versus fairness: happy persons keep more points to themselves than do sad people, and these effects are more pronounced as allocation trials progress.

or deemphasize the fairness norm. Happy allocators were significantly more selfish than the sad group, and mood effects on selfishness are greatest when fairness norm was undermined, allowing greater scope for allocators to engage in open, constructive processing about their choices.

These experiments consistently show that happy mood increased assertiveness and selfishness when allocating resources in the dictator game, an almost pure measure of selfishness. Mood effects were greater when the norm of fairness was deemphasized, as allocators were more likely to process the task in an open, constructive manner. These findings are conceptually consistent with prior evidence showing that positive affect produces more assertive, confident, and optimistic interpersonal strategies, whereas negative mood triggers more pessimistic, cautious responses sensitive to external demands (Bless & Fiedler, 2006; Fiedler, 2001; Forgas, 1999, 2002).

This account is also broadly consistent with functionalist evolutionary theories suggesting that affect has a signaling function about situational requirements (Clore & Storbeck, 2006; Forgas et al., 2007; Schwarz, 1990), with negative affect recruiting a more externally focused, accommodative orientation (Bless & Fiedler, 2006). Positive affect in turn promotes more assimilative, internally focused strategies, further enhancing the tendency for selfishness (Bless, 2001; Bless & Fiedler; Fiedler, 2001). Many conflict situations in our private as well as working lives involve decisions between acting assertively and selfishly and acting fairly. The kind of mood effects on assertiveness and selfishness demonstrated here may have important implications for real-life conflict behaviors in personal relationships, organizational decisions, and many other everyday situations where decisions by one person have incontestable consequences for others.

SUMMARY AND CONCLUSIONS

There is little doubt that affective states play an important role in influencing how people perceive, interpret, and respond to conflict situations—a connection that has been intuitively recognized since time immemorial. Theories such as AIM (Forgas, 1992, 1995) offer a simple and parsimonious explanation of when and how affective states may infuse conflict-related thoughts and behaviors such as negotiation and making and responding to demands (Forgas, 1998a, 1998b, 1999a, 1999b). Dealing with social conflict requires complex and elaborate information processing strategies. It is the very richness and elaborateness of conflict situations that makes mood effects particularly likely, as even a minor selective priming of positive and negative memory-based information may have large consequences for what is perceived, how it is interpreted, and the kind of responses that are constructed. Critical decisions and judgments about conflict episodes are more likely to be assertive, confident, and optimistic when a person is in a positive mood state and are more likely to be accommodating, negative, or critical when the person is in a dysphoric mood.

In addition, more recent research also shows that affective states also influence how people deal with social information. It turns out that mild negative moods can have a beneficial effect by recruiting more accommodative processing styles, by reducing judgmental errors, by improving the quality of persuasive arguments, by providing the ability to detect deception, and also by leading to more sensitive and fairer allocation strategies. The processing effects of negative mood described here seem particularly intriguing, since these studies suggest that mild dysphoria could actually improve cognitive strategies and even result in superior outcomes (Forgas, 2007).

Interestingly, these results also challenge the common assumption in much of applied, organizational, clinical, and health psychology that positive affect has universally desirable social and cognitive consequences. Together with other recent experimental studies, our findings confirm that negative affect often produces adaptive and more socially sensitive outcomes. For example, negative moods can reduce judgmental errors (Forgas, 1988c), can improve eyewitness accuracy (Forgas, Vargas, & Laham, 2005), and can improve interpersonal communication strategies (Forgas, 2007), and it seems, as the present experiments show, also can increase fairness and sensitivity to the needs of others. There is much scope in future work to explore mood effects on other kinds of strategic conflict-related behaviors, such as forgiveness (Chapter 14 in this volume), assertiveness (Chapter 5 in this volume), goal preferences (Chapter 6 in this volume), perspective taking (Chapter 7 in this volume), and reactions to ostracism (Chapters 3 and 13 in this volume).

Although much has been discovered about the information-processing and representational functions of affective states, not enough of this evidence has so far come from research directly concerned with studying social conflicts. This is all the more surprising as affect and conflict are closely intertwined, and conflict behaviors present a particularly promising and ecologically valid research domain to study affective influences on thought and behavior. Given the growing sophistication of the theories and methods now employed in research looking at the interface of affect and cognition, the time seems ripe to apply these strategies to the investigation of the role of affect in the way real-life conflict is perceived, managed, and resolved.

REFERENCES

Adolphs, R., & Damasio, A. (2001). The interaction of affect and cognition: A neurobiological perspective. In J. P. Forgas (Ed.), *The handbook of affect and social cognition* (pp. 27–49). Mahwah, NJ: Erlbaum.

Blascovich, J., & Mendes, W. B. (2000). Challenge and threat appraisals: The role of affective cues. In J. Forgas (Ed.), *Feeling and thinking: The role of affect in social cognition* (pp. 59–82). Cambridge UK: Cambridge University Press.

Bless, H. (2001). Mood and the use of general knowledge structures. In L. L. Martin & G. L. Clore (Eds.), *Theories of mood and cognition: A user's guidebook* (pp. 9–26). Mahwah, NJ: Lawrence Erlbaum Associates.

Bless, H., & Fiedler, K. (2006). Mood and the regulation of information processing and behavior. In J. P. Forgas (Ed.), *Affect in social thinking and behavior* (pp. 65–84). New York: Psychology Press.

Bolton, G. E., Katok, E., & Zwick, R. (1998). Dictator game giving: Rules of fairness versus acts of kindness. *International Journal of Game Theory, 27*(2), 269–299.

Bower, G. H. (1981). Mood and memory. *American Psychologist, 36,* 129–148.

Ciarrochi, J., Forgas, J., & Mayer, J. (Eds.) (2006). *Emotional intelligence in everyday life.* (2nd ed.). New York: Psychology Press/Taylor & Francis.

Clark, M. S., & Isen, A. M. (1982). Toward understanding the relationship between feeling states and social behavior. In A. H. Hastorf & A. M. Isen (Eds.), *Cognitive social psychology* (pp. 73–108). New York: Elsevier-North Holland.

Clore, G. L., & Byrne, D. (1974). A reinforcement-affect model of attraction. In T. L. Huston (Ed.), *Foundations of interpersonal attraction* (pp. 143–170). New York: Academic Press.

Clore, G. L., & Storbeck, J. (2006). Affect as information for social judgment, behavior, and memory. In J. P. Forgas (Ed.), *Affect in social cognition and behavior* (pp. 154–178). New York: Psychology Press.

Correll, J., Park, B., Judd, C. M., & Wittenbrink, B. (2002). The police officer's dilemma: Using ethnicity to disambiguate potentially threatening individuals. *Journal of Personality and Social Psychology, 83,* 1314–1329.

East, R., & Forgas, J.P. (2008). *Mood effects on scepticism and the detection of deception.* Manuscript, University of New South Wales.

Feshbach, S., & Singer, R. D. (1957). The effects of fear arousal and suppression of fear upon social perception. *Journal of Abnormal and Social Psychology, 55,* 283–288.

Fiedler, K. (1991). On the task, the measures and the mood in research on affect and social cognition. In J. P. Forgas (Ed.), *Emotion and social judgments* (pp. 83–104). Oxford, UK: Pergamon.

Fiedler, K. (2001). Affective influences on social information processing. In J. P. Forgas (Ed.), *The handbook of affect and social cognition* (pp. 163–185). Mahwah, NJ: Erlbaum.

Fiedler, K., & Bless, H. (2001). The formation of beliefs in the interface of affective and cognitive processes. In N. Frijda, A. Manstead, & S. Bem (Eds.), *Emotions and beliefs* (pp. 144–170). New York: Cambridge University Press.

Fiedler, K., & Forgas, J. P. (1988). *Affect, cognition, and social behavior: New evidence and integrative attempts.* Toronto: Hogrefe.

Forgas, J. P. (1976). An unobtrusive study of reactions to national stereotypes in four European countries. *Journal of Social Psychology, 99,* 37–42.

Forgas, J. P. (1979). *Social episodes: The study of interaction routines.* London: Academic Press.

Forgas, J. P. (1982). Episode cognition: Internal representations of interaction routines. In L. Berkowitz (Ed.), *Advances in experimental social psychology* (Vol. 15, pp. 59–100). New York: Academic Press.

Forgas, J. P. (1992). On bad mood and peculiar people: Affect and person typicality in impression formation. *Journal of Personality and Social Psychology*, *62*, 863-875.

Forgas, J. P. (1994). Sad and guilty? Affective influences on the explanation of conflict episodes. *Journal of Personality and Social Psychology*, *66*, 56–68.

Forgas, J. P. (1995a). Mood and judgment: The affect infusion model (AIM). *Psychological Bulletin*, *117*(1), 39–66.

Forgas, J. P. (1995b). Strange couples: Mood effects on judgments and memory about prototypical and atypical targets. *Personality and Social Psychology Bulletin*, *21*, 747–765.

Forgas, J. P. (1998a). On feeling good and getting your way: Mood effects on negotiator cognition and bargaining strategies. *Journal of Personality and Social Psychology*, *74*, 565–577.

Forgas, J. P. (1998b). Asking nicely? The effects of mood on responding to more or less polite requests. *Personality and Social Psychology Bulletin*, *24*, 173–185.

Forgas, J. P. (1998c). On being happy and mistaken: Mood effects on the fundamental attribution error. *Journal of Personality and Social Psychology*, *75*, 318–331.

Forgas, J. P. (1999a). On feeling good and being rude: Affective influences on language use and request formulations. *Journal of Personality and Social Psychology*, *76*, 928–939.

Forgas, J. P. (1999b). Feeling and speaking: Mood effects on verbal communication strategies. *Personality and Social Psychology Bulletin*, *25*, 850–863.

Forgas, J. P. (Ed.). (2001). *Handbook of affect and social cognition.* Mahwah, NJ: Erlbaum.

Forgas, J. P. (2002). Feeling and doing: Affective influences on interpersonal behavior. *Psychological Inquiry*, *13*, 1–28.

Forgas, J. P. (2003). Why don't we do it in the road...? Stereotyping and prejudice in mundane situations. *Psychological Inquiry*, *14*, 251–257.

Forgas, J. P. (Ed.). (2006). *Affect in social thinking and behavior.* New York: Psychology Press.

Forgas, J. P. (2007). When sad is better than happy: Negative affect can improve the quality and effectiveness of persuasive messages and social influence strategies. *Journal of Experimental Social Psychology*, *43*, 513–528.

Forgas, J. P., Bower, G. H., & Krantz, S. (1984). The influence of mood on perceptions of social interactions. *Journal of Experimental Social Psychology*, *20*, 497–513.

Forgas, J. P., Haselton, M. G., & von Hippel, W. (Eds.) (2007). *Evolutionary psychology and social cognition.* New York: Psychology Press.

Forgas, J. P., Levinger, G., & Moylan, S. (1994). Feeling good and feeling close: Affective influences on the perception of intimate relationships. *Personal Relationships*, *1*, 165–184.

Forgas, J. P., & Moylan, S. J. (1987). After the movies: The effects of transient mood states on social judgments. *Personality and Social Psychology Bulletin*, *13*, 478–489.

Forgas, J. P., Vargas, P., & Laham, S. (2005). Mood effects on eyewitness memory: Affective influences on susceptibility to misinformation. *Journal of Experimental Social Psychology*, *41*, 574–588.

Forsythe, R., Horowitz, J. L., Savin, N. E., & Sefton, M. (1994). Fairness in simple bargaining experiments. *Games and Economic Behavior*, *6*(3), 347–369.

Gilbert, D. T. (1991). How mental systems believe. *American Psychologist*, *46*, 107–119.

Gilbert, D. T., & Malone, P. S. (1995). The correspondence bias. *Psychological Bulletin*, 117, 21–38.

Haselhuhn, M. P., & Mellers, B. A. (2005). Emotions and cooperation in economic games. *Cognitive Brain Research*, *23*, 24–33.

Hilgard, E. R. (1980). The trilogy of mind: Cognition, affection, and conation. *Journal of the History of the Behavioral Sciences*, *16*, 107–117.

Jones, E. E., & Harris, V.A. (1967). The attribution of attitudes. *Journal of Experimental Social Psychology*, *3*, 1–24.

Niedenthal, P., & Halberstadt, J. (2000). Grounding categories in emotional response. In J. P. Forgas (Ed.), *Feeling and thinking: The role of affect in social cognition* (pp. 357–386). New York: Cambridge University Press.

Pervin, L. A. (1976). A free-response description approach to the analysis of person-situation interaction. *Journal of Personality and Social Psychology, 34*, 465–474.

Pillutla, M. M., & Murnighan, J. K. (1995). Being fair or appearing fair: Strategic behavior in ultimatum bargaining. *Academy of Management Journal, 38*, 1408–1426.

Rusting, C. (2001). Personality as a moderator of affective influences on cognition. In J. P. Forgas (Ed.), *The handbook of affect and social cognition* (pp. 371–391). Mahwah, NJ: Erlbaum.

Schwarz, N. (1990). Feelings as information: Informational and motivational functions of affective states. In E. T. Higgins & R. Sorrentino (Eds.), *Handbook of motivation and cognition: Foundations of social behavior* (Vol. 2, pp. 527–561). New York: Guilford Press.

Schwarz, N., & Clore, G. L. (1983). Mood, misattribution and judgments of well being: Informative and directive functions of affective states. *Journal of Personality and Social Psychology, 45*, 513–523.

Sedikides C. (1992). Mood as a determinant of attentional focus. *Cognition and Emotion, 6*, 129–148.

Sedikides,C. (1995). Central and peripheral self-conceptions are differentially influenced by mood: Tests of the differential sensitivity hypothesis. *Journal of Personality and Social Psychology, 69*(4), 759–777.

Tan, H. B., & Forgas, J. P. (2010). When happiness makes us selfish, but sadness makes us fair: Affective influences on interpersonal strategies in the dictator game. *Journal of Experimental Social Psychology, 46*(3), 571–576.

Unkelbach, C., Forgas, J. P., & Denson, T. F. (2008). The turban effect: The influence of Muslim headgear and induced affect on aggressive responses in the shooter bias paradigm. *Journal of Experimental Social Psychology, 44*, 1409–1413.

Wegener, D. T., & Petty, R. E. (1997). The flexible correction model: The role of naïve theories of bias in bias correction. In M. P. Zanna (Ed.), *Advances in experimental social psychology* (Vol. 29, pp. 141–208). New York: Academic Press.

Zajonc, R. B. (2000). Feeling and thinking: Closing the debate over the independence of affect. In J. P. Forgas (Ed.), *Feeling and thinking: The role of affect in social cognition* (pp. 31–58). New York: Cambridge University Press.

9

The Effects of Anger and Anger Regulation on Negotiation

THOMAS F. DENSON and EMMA C. FABIANSSON

University of New South Wales

*N*egotiation is a means of resolving social and economic conflict, which sometimes evokes negative emotions. Recent theoretical approaches acknowledge the consequences that emotions and mood can have on negotiations (Bazerman, Curhan, Moore, & Valley, 2000; Morris & Keltner, 2000; Shapiro, 2002; see also Chapter 8 in this volume). This review focuses on the role that anger plays in negotiations. Anger is important to regulate because it can lead to an escalation of conflict (Allred, Mallozzi, Matsui, & Raia, 1997). We first explore why anger regulation is important despite the sometimes positive effects of expressing anger during negotiation. Next we examine the effectiveness of different emotion regulation strategies such as reappraisal, rumination, and distraction and discuss how these can be applied to the negotiation context. We then present the results from two experiments using emotion regulation to explore what impact these anger regulation strategies have on self-reported emotion and on aggressive behavior in negotiations.

EXPRESSING ANGER IS A LIMITED BUT AT TIMES EFFECTIVE STRATEGY

Whether a negotiator simply expresses or experiences anger can result in very different negotiation outcomes. Anger can be examined from an intrapersonal perspective (i.e., felt anger) or an interpersonal perspective (i.e., the effects of anger expression on others; Van Kleef, Van Dijk, Steinel, Harinck, & Van Beest, 2008). Generally, intrapersonal anger in negotiations is thought to result in poorer negotiation outcomes than interpersonal anger (Van Kleef et al.). For example, intrapersonal anger can produce stalemates, conflict, and economically irrational behavior

(Allred et al., 1997; Liu, 2009; Pillutla & Murnighan, 1996). By contrast, expressing anger can result in financial gain by encouraging opponents to make concessions. For example, a salesperson may be likely to give in to an angry customer demanding a discount to avoid further escalation of conflict and to minimize disruption to other customers.

Despite these sometimes positive benefits, strategically using anger to obtain demands is a limited short-term strategy. For example, anger can negatively impact relationship quality and make people less willing to negotiate again in the future (Allred et al., 1997). Over time negotiating counterparts may habituate to anger expressions and they may no longer be effective (Tiedens, 2001). For example, an angry outburst may be effective the first time; however, the second time one tries this strategy, the other negotiator may resist the demands. Furthermore, over time an angry negotiator may develop an argumentative reputation that could negatively influence subsequent negotiations. Therefore, expressing anger is doubtful as an effective long-term strategy and may be effective only in single instances of negotiation. Moreover, even during one-time negotiations among strangers, research suggests that expressing anger requires very specific conditions to be effective. These variables include how, when, who, and where the anger is expressed. To quote Aristotle, "Anyone can become angry. That is easy. But to be angry with the right person, to the right degree, at the right time, for the right purpose and in the right way—that is not easy."

How Anger Is Expressed

Anger can be expressed in a number of different ways. Gibson, Schweitzer, Callister, and Gray (2009) examined which characteristics are needed for expressing anger to result in constructive negotiation outcomes in organizational settings. Anger episodes from a variety of organizations were analyzed, and the consequences of these episodes were examined by analyzing the respondent's perceived impact of the episode on outcomes at the individual and organizational level. The authors also examined the effect of anger expression on the relationship between the parties involved in the event. Positive outcomes were more likely if the anger episodes were low in intensity, were expressed verbally rather than physically, and were displayed in organizations where expressing anger is considered the norm. However, expressing low-intensity anger is difficult, requires control, and if displayed incorrectly may result in conflict escalation or stalemate (Gibson et al.). Therefore, both how anger is expressed and the context in which it is expressed are important determinants of its effectiveness.

When Anger Is Expressed

The effectiveness of expressing anger may also depend on when in the negotiation anger is expressed (e.g., at the beginning of the negotiation, during the positioning phase, during problem solving, or at the end of the negotiation; Morris & Keltner, 2000). The positioning stage is when one or both negotiators express their negotiation stance to their partner—for example, what points they would be willing to concede and refuse to compromise. Anger expressed during the positioning stage may result in gaining an upper hand through coercive pressure. Anger expressed during the bargaining stage may signal dissatisfaction with the offer and encourage their counterpart to offer a more satisfactory offer. However, negative effects may occur when anger is expressed during other stages. For example, anger expressed during the initial stages of the negotiation may produce a stalemate or unwillingness to negotiate in the first place.

Who Expresses Anger

Whether anger is an effective strategy for claiming value also depends on who expresses the anger and their bargaining position. The moderating effects of gender, status, and the number of alternative offers have been investigated in this regard. Individuals in a high-power position (operationalized as the number of available alternatives) are more likely to gain from expressing anger when they are paired with a low-power opponent who possesses limited alternatives (Friedman et al., 2004; Sinaceur & Tiedens, 2006; Van Kleef & Côté, 2007). For example, participants with few or many clients to choose from read vignettes and rated how much they would concede to a client that expressed anger or did not express anger. Whereas participants with good alternatives conceded similar amounts to nonangry and angry clients, when participants had poor alternatives they were more likely to concede to an angry client than a nonangry client (Sinaceur & Tiedens).

Similarly, Van Kleef and Côté (2007) observed that when participants had few alternatives to choose from and their fictitious opponent expressed anger using written statements such as "This offer makes me really angry; I expect a better offer," participants demanded less from angry opponents than a nonemotional negotiator. Participants tend to concede more to angry opponents because the expressed anger is thought to signal that opponents have higher demands (Van Kleef, De Dreu, & Manstead, 2004; Van Dijk, Van Kleef, Steinel, & Van Beest, 2008).

Expressing anger can also be used to exert an illusion of power and competence. In a series of experiments, Tiedens (2001) illustrated that anger expressions influence the extent to which people confer or bestow status to others. Coworkers who rated their colleagues as highly likely to display anger also tended to confer these colleagues with higher status (i.e., higher salaries and greater likelihood of promotion). However, additional research reveals that the association between anger and status is different for men and women (Brescoll & Uhlmann, 2008). In contrast to an angry professional man, professional women who expressed anger were conferred lower status regardless of their occupational status (chief executive officer or assistant trainee). Women who expressed anger were allocated lower wages, status, and perceived as less competent than unemotional women or angry men. In addition, the extent to which women were conferred lower status depended on whether the anger was attributed as due to internal characteristics (e.g., personality) or external characteristics (e.g., the situation). When external attributions were provided for expressions of anger in professional women they were awarded higher status than women without an external attribution but not higher status than non-emotional women. Therefore, the advantages associated with expressing anger do not extend to everyone, and the effectiveness of expressing anger is constrained by variables including gender and power.

Where Anger Is Expressed

The effectiveness of expressing anger also depends on where it is expressed. Display rules dictate how acceptable expressing anger in the workplace is, and organizational culture partially determines which emotions are considered desirable to display (Barsade & Gibson, 2007; Gibson et al., 2009; Morris & Feldman, 1996). For example, in customer service–based occupations such as airlines, telephone services, and health care, expressing anger is discouraged (Barsade & Gibson; Morris & Feldman), suggesting that individuals in these occupations are typically effective at regulating anger displays. By contrast, some occupations encourage the expression of anger (e.g., ice hockey player, lobbyist, opposition politician, radio shock jock). Thus, organizational norms for expressing anger can determine whether expressing anger has beneficial or detrimental consequences (Gibson et al.). Collectively, the limitations associated with expressing anger illustrate that expressing anger to create gains is constrained by numerous boundary conditions, suggesting that more often than not expressing anger is likely to be ineffective or even detrimental in many contexts.

HOW CAN ANGER BE REGULATED?

Studies examining the expression of anger have typically investigated the phenomenon from the perspective of the receiver rather than examining the bidirectional effects of the sender and receiver on anger experience. Computer simulations of negotiations are often used to examine these variables, which manipulate anger through the use of written comments used to communicate anger to the participant during the deal-making stages of the negotiation (Van Kleef & Côté, 2007; Van Dijk et al., 2008). Although many of these studies illustrate that expressing anger results in better individual negotiation outcomes, they do not take into consideration the impact that expressing anger may have on the sender. For example, the peripheral feedback effect (also known as the facial feedback hypothesis) suggests that expressing emotions can lead to experiencing those emotions (Laird, 1984). If expressing anger results in experiencing anger, then the impact of expressing anger may have the same detrimental consequences associated with studies of intrapersonal anger in negotiations. Experiencing anger may interfere in negotiations because anger can lead to greater competitiveness and desire for retaliation (Allred et al., 1997; Pillutla & Murnighan, 1996). Negotiators who seek retaliation tend to be narrow-minded and more focused on their own interests while being less aware of alternative solutions or joint gains (Liu, 2009; see also Chapter 10 in this volume).

Together, the literature reviewed herein suggests that regulating anger during negotiations might prove efficacious. Previous recommendations for reducing anger have included strategies such as removing oneself from the conflict or venting anger (Fisher & Ury, 1991). However, avoiding or leaving the situation may be impractical and does nothing to resolve the issue. Methods such as venting anger tend to increase rather than decrease aggression (Brown, Westbrook, & Challagalla, 2005; Bushman, 2002; Bushman, Baumeister, & Stack, 1999). Instead, a number of emotion regulation strategies are available, and these differ in terms of their effectiveness. Emotion regulation can be defined as "the processes by which individuals influence which emotions they have, when they have them, and how they experience and express these emotions" (Gross, 1998b, p. 275). There are two general classes of emotion regulation strategies: antecedent focused and response focused.

Cognitive reappraisal is a widely studied example of an antecedent-focused strategy. Reappraisal involves interpreting an anger-eliciting event by adopting a neutral or objective perspective to reduce the emotional impact of the event (Ray, Wilhelm, & Gross, 2008). For example, instead of fixating on what went wrong in a negotiation, reappraisal may involve focusing on future changes that can be made to improve subsequent negotiations. As reappraisal is effortful and involves cognitive change, reappraisal has also been labeled a "deep acting strategy" (Grandey, 2000). Reappraisal works best when it is applied before the full onset of the emotional response (Gross, 1998a) and should therefore be most effective when engaged in prior to negotiation.

One response-focused strategy that has been investigated within the context of anger is rumination. Rumination involves focusing on one's emotions and feelings without constructive problem solving (Nolen-Hoeksema, 1991). For instance, this may include dwelling on the inflexibility of one's negotiation partner and their reluctance to yield in a negotiation rather than focusing on alternative ways of creating value. Rumination also maintains anger and increases aggression (Bushman, Bonacci, Pedersen, Vasquez, & Miller, 2005; Rusting & Nolen-Hoeksema, 1998). There are several different types of rumination. Analytical rumination involves thinking about why an anger provocation occurred and the consequences of this event (Wimalaweera & Moulds, 2008). Experiential rumination is a type of processing that focuses on current and concrete experiences, for example, how you currently feel (Watkins & Teasdale, 2008).

Other examples of response-focused strategies include faking and suppressing emotions. These strategies tend not to produce cognitive change but instead focus on masking felt emotions (Grandey, 2000). Using a call center simulation with a hostile customer, Goldberg and Grandey (2007) found that more errors occurred when placing orders when response-focused strategies were used than when antecedent-focused strategies were used. Emotion regulation not only influences how we experience emotions but can also negatively impact job performance. Response-focused strategies such as rumination tend to be less effective in reducing anger and aggressive behavior because they are often associated with the depletion of self-regulatory resources whereas antecedent-focused strategies such as reappraisal tend not to result in depletion when initiated prior to the full emotional response (Denson, 2009; Goldberg & Grandey; Grandey, Fisk, & Steiner, 2005).

In emotion regulation studies, mental distraction is often used as a control condition. However, distraction can be conceptualized as an emotion regulation strategy in its own right. Instead of focusing on feelings, distraction involves drawing attention to neutral or positive stimuli unrelated to the anger-inducing event (Nolen-Hoeksema, 1991). Distraction is more effective than rumination in reducing anger and aggression (Bushman, 2002; Bushman et al., 2005; Denson, White, & Warburton, 2009; Rusting & Nolen-Hoeksema, 1998). For instance, Rusting and Nolen-Hoeksema experimentally manipulated rumination and distraction and found that compared with rumination distraction decreased anger (Experiment 3) or had no impact on self-reported anger (Experiment 1). Furthermore, participants who engaged in distraction wrote less angry stories in contrast to participants in the rumination condition.

A number of additional variables influence what emotion regulation strategy is used. For example, how stress is appraised can impact whether one engages in adaptive or maladaptive emotion regulation strategies (Grandey, Dickter, & Sin, 2004). Grandey et al. examined how call center employees appraised angry customers and what emotion regulation strategies individuals used. Employees recalled a recent event in which a customer was aggressive and rated the level of stress and the emotion regulation strategy they used. Venting or surface acting strategies were more likely to be used when employees appraised the customer as threatening. Engaging in cognitive reframing or deep acting strategies such as perspective taking was more likely when the customer was interpreted as not threatening (see Chapter 7 in this volume). Another factor that influences the type of emotion regulation strategy used is the level of control individuals possess within their occupation (Grandey et al.).

Only a few studies have specifically examined the effectiveness of reappraisal as an anger regulation strategy (Denson, Moulds, & Grisham, 2009; Mauss, Cook, Cheng, & Gross, 2007; Ray et al., 2008). Mauss et al. examined whether individual differences in reappraisal were related to self-reported anger and cardiovascular responses. The Emotion Regulation Questionnaire (Gross & John, 2003) was used to classify high and low reappraisers. Participants were provoked using a backward counting task with false feedback. High reappraisers displayed more adaptive cardiovascular responses and less self-reported anger in contrast to low reappraisers. However, this experiment relied on preexisting differences in reappraisal and could not determine if generally inducing reappraisal would be associated with the same benefits or whether reappraisal training would be effective for individuals who tend not to naturally reappraise.

By contrast, Ray et al. (2008) induced reappraisal and rumination by using guided instructions. For example, when participants in the reappraisal condition recalled an angry episode they were instructed to think about the event as if they were an objective observer. Reappraisal was associated with less anger and decreased physiological responding compared with rumination (Ray et al.). Collectively these results illustrate the benefits of reappraisal compared with other emotion regulation strategies.

Denson et al. (2009) examined the effectiveness of different anger regulation strategies in response to recalling an angry memory. Participants were allocated to one of four conditions: (1) cognitive reappraisal; (2) analytical rumination; (3) distraction; and (4) a no-instruction control condition in which they wrote about an anger-inducing autobiographical event for 20 minutes. As predicted, rumination was associated with maintenance of self-reported anger, whereas the other conditions decreased anger. Reappraisal was the most effective of the four strategies for reducing anger among individuals high in anger-related traits. To further examine the cognitive processes underlying the emotion regulation strategies, a quantitative content analysis of the written responses from the writing task were analyzed using the Linguistic Inquiry Word Count program (Pennebaker, Chung, Ireland, Gonzales, & Booth, 2007). Participants who reappraised used increased future tense and positive words, whereas participants in the rumination condition used increased past tense and greater negative emotion words. These results converge with other studies examining anger regulation (Mauss et al., 2007; Ray et al., 2008).

NEURAL EVIDENCE FOR EMOTION REGULATION DURING NEGOTIATION

There is evidence to suggest that anger regulation may be especially beneficial in situations where accepting a poor offer is objectively better than rejecting a poor offer. However, accepting a poor offer is particularly difficult to do when angry as anger produces a desire to punish unfair negotiation partners (Pillutla & Murnighan, 1996). Pillutla and Murnighan found that the rejection of low offers in an economic bargaining game was not strictly due to unfairness of the offer but rather to the insulting connotations associated with accepting the poor offer such as the threat to participants' self-worth. Effective anger regulation might help reduce the negative emotional experience and behavioral consequences associated with experiencing anger when negotiating. To our knowledge emotion regulation strategies have not yet been systematically investigated within the context of negotiations.

Evidence for the economic benefit of regulating anger comes from two recent functional magnetic resonance imaging (fMRI) studies using the Ultimatum Game (Sanfey, Rilling, Aronson, Nystrom, & Cohen, 2003; Tabibnia, Satpute, & Lieberman, 2008). In the Ultimatum Game, one player chooses how to divide a monetary amount (typically $10) between himself or herself and another player. The second player chooses whether to accept or reject the offer. If the offer is accepted, the money is divided between the two participants. However, if the proposal is rejected then both participants receive nothing (Güth, Schmittberger, & Schwarze, 1982). Therefore, the latter player has the possibility of punishing his or her opponent for choosing to divide the money unfairly but at the same time suffers a cost. This type of behavior is known as *altruistic punishment* because one chooses to punish at a personal cost (Fehr & Gächter, 2002). In the context of the Ultimatum Game, it is more economically rational to accept an offer regardless of how low the offer is. This is because accepting a small amount is objectively better than rejecting the offer and receiving nothing.

Sanfey et al. (2003) and Tabibnia et al. (2008) illustrate that receiving unfair offers such as $1 and $2 (out of a possible $10) is associated with increased activity in the anterior insula, a region implicated in negative emotional experiences including anger and rumination (Denson, Pedersen, Ronquillo, & Nandy, 2009). Accepting unfair offers requires the ability to regulate negative emotions. The ventrolateral prefrontal cortex (VLPFC) has been implicated in emotion regulation (Lieberman, 2007). Accordingly, accepting more unfair offers was associated with increased activity in the right VLPFC and decreased activity in the anterior insula. Similarly, adults with damage to the ventromedial prefrontal cortex (VMPFC), which is associated with emotion regulation and social functioning, are more likely to reject unfair offers in the Ultimatum Game than matched controls without VMPFC damage (Koenigs & Tranel, 2007). These findings converge on the notion that emotion regulation is important in promoting rational thinking and the avoidance of aggressive retaliation during bargaining.

EMOTION REGULATION IN NEGOTIATIONS

Fabiansson and Denson (2010) examined whether regulating anger using reappraisal would not only decrease self-reported anger but also improve negotiation performance. Participants in the reappraisal condition were told prior to the speech task that their partner was in a bit of a bad mood and not to take it personally if they do appear to be in a bad mood. This timing was important as theoretically reappraisal should occur before the full onset of an emotional response to change the experience of the emotion (Gross, 1998a). Indeed, late reappraisal is more effortful than early reappraisal, and late reappraisal was less effective in reducing a sad mood induced by a film than late distraction (Sheppes & Meiran, 2007).

Participants engaged in a speech task called "unilink" with a confederate via webcam and spoke about personal topics such as their life goals. Following this, participants were provoked with insulting feedback stating that their speech was of poor quality for a university student and that listening to their speech was a waste of time. Participants were led to believe that this was sent from their speech partner. Following this, participants reappraised, ruminated, or engaged in distraction for 20 minutes. Participants who reappraised were given the following instructions: "Describe your experience of the unilink task in a way that makes you adopt a neutral attitude." Participants in the rumination condition were asked to "write about the feelings you have about the other people you have encountered in the study." Instructions in the distraction condition consisted of emotionally neutral items similar to Rusting and Nolen-Hoeksema (1998; e.g., "Write about the layout of the aisles at your local supermarket").

Following the emotion regulation induction, participants played the Ultimatum Game with three bogus participants. These negotiation counterparts consisted of the provocative participant from the prior speech task and two other participants not previously encountered. First, participants proposed an offer to all three counterparts prior to beginning the game. Second, participants played the role of the responder and received multiple offers from these participants. Half of the offers were fair (e.g., $5, $4), and the other half were unfair (e.g., $1, $2). Participants decided whether to accept or reject these offers. On each trial participants saw a picture of their counterpart (as in Sanfey et al., 2003). The two players not encountered before and the insulting opponent gave exactly the same offers in random orders so that these could be compared. Next participants rated their mood at the beginning of the study, postfeedback, during the writing and negotiation task, and at the conclusion of the experiment. Participants also rated their opponents on a variety of negotiation-relevant traits (e.g., trustworthy, competitive).

As expected, there were no significant differences in self-reported anger at baseline among the three conditions. Manipulation checks showed that participants in the rumination condition felt emotional more often and more strongly during the writing task than participants in the other conditions. In addition, participants in the reappraisal condition reported reflecting more on the positive features of the speech task and thinking about it from an objective perspective compared with the remaining conditions.

Importantly, reappraisal was associated with the most adaptive emotional response. Early reappraisal was used in this experiment, and the results showed that participants who reappraised were less impacted by the initial insult and sustained lower levels of anger throughout the experiment. Specifically, following the insulting feedback, all conditions reported increased anger; however, reappraisal was associated with the smallest increase in anger. During the writing task, both reappraisal and distraction were associated with a decrease in anger. Interestingly, during the negotiation task, participants in the distraction condition reported increased anger to a level equivalent to those in the rumination condition. Reappraisal was associated with less anger compared with the distraction and rumination conditions during the negotiation phase. Similarly, at the conclusion of the experiment, reappraisal was associated with significantly less anger compared with the distraction and rumination conditions.

These findings illustrate the effectiveness of reappraisal and distraction for reducing anger within a negotiation context. Furthermore, our results suggest that distraction might serve as a "quick fix" for reducing anger, but its effects do not last. Once the negotiation began, participants in the distraction condition became angry again. This is presumably because distraction does not facilitate effective processing of the anger-inducing event as reappraisal is presumed to do. Presumably, participants in the reappraisal and rumination conditions thought about their speech task opponent and the provocation during the writing task in adaptive and maladaptive manners, respectively. By contrast, participants in the distraction condition were asked to think about topics entirely unrelated to the speech task. Thus, when participants in the distraction condition encountered their speech counterpart again in the negotiation task, this may have reminded them of the initial provocation and thereby resulted in an increased sense of anger at seeing their counterpart's picture.

Participants proposed offers before playing the role of the responder. As expected, participants who reappraised proposed more generous offers to the person that insulted them than either the rumination or distraction conditions. The rumination condition proposed offers that were in between the reappraisal and distraction conditions. When participants played the role of the responder, the emotion regulation strategy that participants engaged in did not significantly influence the number of offers accepted. As can be expected, participants proposed fairer offers and accepted a greater number of offers from the two opponents not encountered before regardless of emotion regulation condition. This is not surprising given that these two opponents did not insult the participant previously. For the positive negotiation relevant traits (e.g., cooperative), participants in the distraction condition rated their speech task opponent more negatively than both the rumination and reappraisal conditions. Collectively these findings suggest which forms of emotion regulation may be most beneficial in negotiations; however, the effect of different emotion regulation strategies on the number of offers accepted remains less clear.

CONCLUDING REMARKS

Research suggests that expressing anger as a negotiation strategy has limited effectiveness. The primary purpose of this chapter was to present emotion regulation strategies as a means to manage the detrimental effects of anger on negotiation outcomes. Specifically, work by ourselves and others suggests that the application of reappraisal to negotiation settings might prove useful in reducing anger, aggressive behavior, and conflict in negotiations. The first two studies we conducted converged with prior work in that reappraisal was associated with decreased anger relative to rumination or distraction (Fabiansson & Denson, 2010; Mauss et al., 2007; Ray et al., 2008).

Although these studies illustrated that reappraisal is effective in reducing experienced anger, further research is necessary to investigate the ability of reappraisal to curb retaliatory negotiation behavior. For example, we found that different forms of emotion regulation influenced how much participants proposed; however, participants accepted a similar number of offers regardless of the emotion regulation strategy they engaged in (Fabiansson & Denson, 2010). Applying emotion regulation strategies such as reappraisal does have benefits; however, the full extent of these strategies in improving negotiation behavior remains to be further investigated. Reappraisal is an effortful emotion regulation strategy and may be difficult to use for individuals who do not naturally tend to reappraise. It might be possible to train negotiators in effective reappraisal over several sessions. Such training could make reappraisal less effortful and may be particularly beneficial for individuals who tend to use other emotion regulation strategies. By improving the ability to reappraise, this not only may change self-reported emotion but also may influence negotiation behavior.

Another way reappraisal may influence negotiation behavior is by using involved negotiation tasks similar to that commonly encountered in real life. For instance, in the Ultimatum Game it is clear what is considered an unfair and fair offer and participants can automatically choose whether to accept or reject offers based on fairness rather than allowing for emotion regulation strategies to influence their decision making. Using more effortful negotiation tasks such as negotiation scenarios that require problem solving may be more amenable to emotion regulation strategies. Using problems that are more abstract and less concrete may mean that participants are less likely to simply apply a fairness-based decision rule when negotiating. Future research might also further investigate the psychological mechanisms responsible for anger's adverse effects in negotiation settings. Topics discussed in this volume such as close-mindedness and lack of perspective-taking ability suggest promising avenues to explore (see Chapters 7 and 10 in this volume).

The ability to effectively regulate emotions in negotiations has several important practical implications. Regulating anger is important for health. Anger is associated with decreased well-being and problems including hypertension (Diamond, 1982). Regulating anger can reduce conflict and prevent aggression and may reduce workplace violence. Effectively regulating anger can help improve relationships between negotiators and facilitate future negotiations and may reduce the likelihood of stalemates.

REFERENCES

Allred, K. G., Mallozzi, J. S., Matsui, F., & Raia, C. P. (1997). The influence of anger and compassion on negotiation performance. *Organizational Behavior and Human Decision Processes, 70*, 175–187.

Axelrod, R. (1984). *The evolution of cooperation.* New York: Basic Books.

Barsade, S. G., & Gibson, D. E. (2007). Why does affect matter in organizations? *Academy of Management Perspectives, 21*, 36–59.

Bazerman, M. H., Curhan, J. R., Moore, D. A., & Valley, K. L. (2000). Negotiation. *Annual Review of Psychology, 51*, 279–314.

Brescoll, V. L., & Uhlmann, E. L. (2008). Can an angry woman get ahead? Status conferral, gender, and expression of emotion in the workplace. *Psychological Science, 19*, 268–275.

Brown, S. P., Westbrook, R. A., & Challagalla, G. (2005). Good cope, bad cope: Adaptive and maladaptive coping strategies following a critical negative work event. *Journal of Applied Psychology, 90*, 792–798.

Bushman, B. J. (2002). Does venting anger feed or extinguish the flame? Catharsis, rumination, distraction, anger, and aggressive responding. *Personality and Social Psychology Bulletin, 28*, 724–731.

Bushman, B. J., Baumeister, R. F., & Stack, A. D. (1999). Catharsis, aggression, and persuasive influence: Self-fulfilling or self-defeating prophecies? *Journal of Personality and Social Psychology, 76*, 367–376.

Bushman, B. J., Bonacci, A. M., Pedersen, W. C., Vasquez, E. A., & Miller, N. (2005). Chewing on it can chew you up: Effects of rumination on triggered displaced aggression. *Journal of Personality and Social Psychology, 88*, 969–983.

Denson, T. F. (2009). Angry rumination and the self-regulation of aggression. In J. P. Forgas, R. F. Baumeister, & D. M. Tice (Eds.), *The psychology of self-regulation.* (pp. 233–248). New York: Psychology Press.

Denson, T. F., Moulds, M. L., & Grisham, J. R. (2009). *The effects of rumination, reappraisal, and distraction on anger experience.* Manuscript submitted for publication.

Denson, T. F., Pedersen, W. C., Ronquillo, J. D., & Nandy, A. S. (2009). The angry brain: Neural correlates of anger, angry rumination, and aggressive personality. *Journal of Cognitive Neuroscience, 21*, 734–744.

Denson, T. F., White, A. J., & Warburton, W. A. (2009). Trait displaced aggression and psychopathy differentially moderate the effects of acute alcohol intoxication and rumination on triggered displaced aggression. *Journal of Research in Personality, 43*, 673–681.

Diamond, E. L. (1982). The role of anger and hostility in essential hypertension and coronary heart disease. *Psychological Bulletin*, 92, 410–433.

Fabiansson, E. C., & Denson, T. F. (2010). *Regulating anger in negotiations*. Unpublished manuscript.

Fehr, E., & Gächter, S. (2002). Altruistic punishment in humans. *Nature*, 415, 137–140.

Fisher, R., & Ury, W. (1991). *Getting to yes: Negotiating agreement without giving in* (2nd ed.). London: Century Business.

Friedman, R., Anderson, C., Brett, J., Olekalns, M., Goates, N., & Lisco, C. C. (2004). The positive and negative effects of anger on dispute resolution: Evidence from electronically mediated disputes. *Journal of Applied Psychology*, 89, 369–376.

Gibson, D. E., Schweitzer, M. E., Callister, R. R., & Gray, B. (2009). The influence of anger expressions on outcomes in organizations. *Negotiation and Conflict Management Research*, 2, 236–262.

Goldberg, L. S., & Grandey, A. A. (2007). Display rules versus display autonomy: Emotion regulation, emotional exhaustion, and task performance in a call center simulation. *Journal of Occupational Health Psychology*, 12, 301–318.

Gouldner, A. W. (1960). The norm of reciprocity. *American Sociological Review*, 25, 161–178.

Grandey, A. A. (2000). Emotion regulation in the workplace: A new way to conceptualize emotional labor. *Journal of Occupational Health Psychology*, 5, 95–110.

Grandey, A. A., Dickter, D. N., & Sin, H.-P. (2004). The customer is not always right: Customer aggression and emotion regulation of service employees. *Journal of Organizational Behavior*, 25, 397–418.

Grandey, A., Fisk, G., & Steiner, D. (2005). Must "service with a smile" be stressful? The moderating role of personal control for American and French employees. *Journal of Applied Psychology*, 90, 893–904.

Gross, J. J. (1998a). Antecedent- and response-focused emotion regulation: Divergent consequences for experience, expression, and physiology. *Journal of Personality and Social Psychology*, 74, 224–237.

Gross, J. J. (1998b). The emerging field of emotion regulation: An integrative review. *Review of General Psychology*, 2, 271–299.

Gross, J.J., & John, O.P. (2003). Individual differences in two emotion regulation processes: Implications for affect, relationships, and well-being. *Journal of Personality and Social Psychology*, 85, 348–362.

Güth, W., Schmittberger, R., & Schwarze, B. (1982). An experimental analysis of ultimatum bargaining. *Journal of Economic Behavior and Organization*, 3, 367–388.

Koenigs, M., & Tranel, D. (2007). Irrational economic decision-making after ventromedial prefrontal damage: Evidence from the ultimatum game. *Journal of Neuroscience*, 27, 951–956.

Laird, J. D. (1984). The real role of facial response in the experience of emotion: A reply to Tourangeau and Ellsworth, and others. *Journal of Personality and Social Psychology*, 47, 909–917.

Lieberman, M. D. (2007). Social cognitive neuroscience: A review of core processes. *Annual Review of Psychology*, 58, 259–289.

Liu, M. (2009). The intrapersonal and interpersonal effects of anger on negotiation strategies: A cross-cultural investigation. *Human Communication Research*, 35, 148–169.

Mauss, I. B., Cook, C. L., Cheng, J. Y. J., & Gross, J. J. (2007). Individual differences in cognitive reappraisal: Experiential and physiological responses to an anger provocation. *International Journal of Psychophysiology*, 66, 116–124.

Morris, J. A., & Feldman, D. C. (1996). The dimensions, antecedents, and consequences of emotional labor. *Academy of Management Review*, 21, 986–1010.

Morris, M., & Keltner, D. (2000). How emotions work: The social functions of emotional expression in negotiations. *Research in Organizational Behavior, 22*, 1–50.

Nolen-Hoeksema, S. (1991). Responses to depression and their effects on the duration of depressive episodes. *Journal of Abnormal Psychology, 100*, 569–582.

Pennebaker, J. W., Chung, C. K., Ireland, M., Gonzales, A., & Booth, R. J. (2007). *The LIWC manual: The development and psychometric properties of LIWC2007.* Austin, TX: LIWC.net.

Pennebaker, J. W., Colder, M., & Sharp, L. K. (1990). Accelerating the coping process. *Journal of Personality and Social Psychology, 58*, 528–537.

Pillutla, M. M., & Murnighan, J. K. (1996). Unfairness, anger, and spite: Emotional rejections of ultimatum offers. *Organizational Behavior & Human Decision Processes, 68*, 208–224.

Ray, R. D., Wilhelm, F. H., & Gross, J. J. (2008). All in the mind's eye? Anger rumination and reappraisal. *Journal of Personality and Social Psychology, 94*, 133–145.

Rusting, C. L., & Nolen-Hoeksema, S. (1998). Regulating responses to anger: Effects of rumination and distraction on angry mood. *Journal of Personality and Social Psychology, 74*, 790–803.

Sanfey, A. G., Rilling, J. K., Aronson, J. A., Nystrom, L. E., & Cohen, J. D. (2003). The neural basis of economic decision-making in the ultimatum game. *Science, 300*, 1755–1758.

Shapiro, D. L. (2002). Negotiating emotions. *Conflict Resolution Quarterly, 20*, 67–82.

Sheppes, G., & Meiran, N. (2007). Better late than never? On the dynamics of online regulation of sadness using distraction and cognitive reappraisal. *Personality and Social Psychology Bulletin, 33*, 1518–1532.

Sinaceur, M., & Tiedens, L. Z. (2006). Get mad and get more than even: When and why anger expression is effective in negotiations. *Journal of Experimental Social Psychology, 42*, 314–322.

Tabibnia, G., Satpute, A. B., & Lieberman, M. D. (2008). The sunny side of fairness: Preference for fairness activates reward circuitry (and disregarding unfairness activates self-control circuitry). *Psychological Science, 19*, 339–347.

Tiedens, L. Z. (2001). Anger and advancement versus sadness and subjugation: The effect of negative emotion expressions on social status conferral. *Journal of Personality and Social Psychology, 80*, 86–94.

Van Dijk, E., Van Kleef, G. A., Steinel, W., & Van Beest, I. (2008). A social functional approach to emotions in bargaining: When communicating anger pays and when it backfires. *Journal of Personality and Social Psychology, 94*, 600–614.

Van Kleef, G. A., & Côté, S. (2007). Expressing anger in conflict: When it helps and when it hurts. *Journal of Applied Psychology, 92*, 1557–1569.

Van Kleef, G. A., De Dreu, C. K. W., & Manstead, A. S. R. (2004). The interpersonal effects of anger and happiness in negotiations. *Journal of Personality and Social Psychology, 86*, 57–76.

Van Kleef, G. A., Van Dijk, E., Steinel, W., Harinck, F., & Van Beest, I. (2008). Anger in social conflict: Cross-situational comparisons and suggestions for the future. *Group Decision and Negotiation, 17*, 13–30.

Watkins, E., & Teasdale, J. D. (2004). Adaptive and maladaptive self-focus in depression. *Journal of Affective Disorders, 82*, 1–8.

Wimalaweera, S. W., & Moulds, M. L. (2008). Processing memories of anger-eliciting events: The effect of asking 'why' from a distance. *Behaviour Research and Therapy, 46*, 402–409.

10

The Role of the Quest for Personal Significance in Motivating Terrorism

ARIE W. KRUGLANSKI

University of Maryland

EDWARD OREHEK

University of Groningen

The secret of happiness is: find something more important than you are and dedicate your life to it.

Daniel Dennett, Philosopher

*O*ne particularly striking form of aggression is the attacking of civilians to reach political objectives, labeled *terrorism*. The use of terrorism is an extreme form of aggression because it targets individuals traditionally viewed as innocent bystanders. Thus, psychologists studying terrorism have focused their aim at understanding the reasons a person becomes a terrorist or supports terrorist activity. In short, researchers and theorists have been concerned with the factors that drive a person to attack civilians. Three general categories of explanations have been offered: (1) ideological reasons; (2) personal causes; and (3) social pressures.

Ideologies constitute belief systems in which some ideal is envisioned and compared with the current status. When a discrepancy between the ideal and the actual status of affairs is perceived, the individual is motivated to reduce it. Terrorist ideologies must identify a culprit believed to be responsible for the discrepancy. In addition to identifying a culprit, the ideology must believe that engaging in violence against the culprit would reduce the discrepancy between the actual and ideal conditions. Finally, to carry out terrorism, the ideology must provide a justification for the attacking of civilians. One example of such an ideology was outlined by Pape (2005), who noted that terrorists often view foreign occupation of their land as the state of affairs to be corrected, the occupier as the culprit, and terrorist action as the means of remedying the situation, ultimately hoping to force the occupier to leave the land.

Personal causes include any experiences that may motivate a person to accept the previously outlined type of ideology. Researchers have proposed a plethora of such experiences, including social rejection and exclusion (Sageman, 2004; Stern, 2003; Chapter 3 in this volume), personal loss and trauma (Speckhard and Akhmedova, 2005), humiliation and injustice (Bloom, 2005; Stern), and poverty (Stern). Each of these, along with many other personal experiences, may predispose and motivate a person to perceive an injustice and to justify the use of violence against civilians as an appropriate means of retaliation.

Social pressures in the form of duty and obligation to the group as well as the acceptance of terrorism as a social norm motivate and allow the violence to be carried out. These social pressures can be internalized or induced by peer pressure. Evidence for such a role of such social pressures can be found in data on Japanese Kamikaze pilots (e.g., Ohnuki-Tierney, 2006) and also applies to present-day terrorism (Bloom, 2005; Gambetta, 2005; Stern, 2003). Consistent with this, Tom Friedman (2010) argued that the lack of outrage among Muslim populations regarding the use of terrorism by members of their community has played a critical role in allowing terrorist activity to continue. For terrorism to be used, it must be viewed as normatively acceptable among a population of people for whom the terrorists believe they are fighting. Without such acceptance, the terrorist activity would be at odds with those whom they claim to be helping.

Although these three components of terrorist motivations neatly organize the abundance of explanations for terrorism, they fall short of explicating the psychological mechanisms for violence. The Quest for Significance Theory attempts to do just that by outlining a fundamental human motivation that leads one to attach oneself to a group and to fight on its behalf. In this chapter, we will review the Quest for Significance Theory and present recent data in support of the theory that was not available at the time it was originally proposed.

THE QUEST FOR SIGNIFICANCE AS THE UNDERLYING MOTIVATION FOR TERRORISM

The quest for significance has been identified as a fundamental human motivation by many psychological theorists (Becker, 1962; Frankl, 2000; Maslow, 1943, 1967). Maslow placed self-actualization concerns at the apex of his motivational hierarchy. According to Frankl, such self-actualization is encapsulated in and attained through attempts to serve a cause higher than the self. Such self-transcendence can be attained only through attachment to the social group. The recent burgeoning field of positive psychology has also argued that the quest for meaning is central to authentic happiness and can be attained by attaching oneself to a larger cause (Seligman, 2002). As noted by Becker (1973) and Terror Management theorists (Greenberg, Koole, & Pyszczynski, 2004), the ultimate threat to personal significance is one's own imminent mortality. To ward off the threat of personal insignificance, individuals are motivated to attach themselves to social groups, to defend the group's worldview, and to work in service to the group.

One important principle of the current framework is that perceptions of injustice and personal significance are based on relative deprivation. According to this view, the injustice or lack of personal significance is not necessarily real or objective. Indeed, poverty, poor education, and political oppression do not constitute root causes of terrorism (Atran, 2003; Berrebi, 2003; Krueger & Maleckova, 2002). Moreover, known perpetrators of terrorism such as Muhammad Atta and his 9/11 coconspirators were neither living in poverty nor lacking education. Yet it seems likely that they perceived that they had less than they deserved, perhaps because they were lacking the financial, religious, or social opportunities granted to their peers. Such a perceived discrepancy should threaten one's sense of personal significance, motivating significance restoration.

Because group memberships function as an important aspect of individuals' social identity, a perceived loss of significance to the groups to which a person belongs may motivate a similar quest for significance restoration. The perceived relative deprivation of a social class, sector, or group has been identified as an underlying factor in large-scale social movements, including those that use violence such as riots and terrorism (Gurr, 1970). We would expect, based on this account, that individuals who define themselves according to their group memberships would be more supportive of aggression against out-groups, including the use of terrorism.

Collectivism and Support for Terrorism

The foregoing analysis suggests that individuals identify strongly with groups, value group memberships, and act on behalf of the group to gain personal significance. Individuals for whom group identifications are central to their worldview are more likely to perceive the boundaries between groups as rigid and clearly defined. When lines are drawn between groups, members of the out-group are derogated, and aggression against out-groups is more likely to be viewed as justifiable (Staub, 2002). As such, a collectivist orientation can lead to aggression and violence toward out-groups perceived to be in conflict with the in-group (Triandis, 2003).

If collectivism is generally related to support for violence against out-groups, then it should also be related to support for terrorism. To test this notion, two survey studies were conducted in Muslim nations (Orehek, Fishman, Kruglanski, Dechesne, & Chen, 2010). The first survey was conducted in 12 Arab countries, Pakistan, and Indonesia via the Internet. Respondents were asked whether they primarily identify as being (1) a member of their religion, (2) a member of their nation, or (3) an individual. Participants who identify primarily with their nation or religion have collective goals, whereas participants who identify as an individual have personal goals. Hence, we expected those who identified with their nation or religion would be more supportive of terrorism against the West than those who identified primarily as an individual. To assess their support for terrorism, they were asked four questions tapping their support for violence against civilian citizens from the United States and Europe. Participants who primarily identified with their nation or religion were significantly more supportive of terrorism than were participants who primarily identified as an individual. These differences were found even when controlling for age, gender, and level of education. There were no significant differences between those who identified with their nation and those who identified with their religion.

While the first study was supportive of the hypothesis that collectivistic identifications would be associated with greater support for terrorism, we collected data as part of a second survey to replicate the findings using a slightly different methodology. Because the first survey sample was limited to individuals with Internet access, the second study used representative samples from Egypt, Indonesia, and Pakistan to ensure that the results would generalize to the rest of the population. Second, we measured collective identifications using a different question, more directly tapping the goals of the respondents. In this survey, respondents were asked to choose which of three statements they agreed with most: (1) "a parent's major goal should be ensuring that their children have a good education and a chance to succeed in life"; (2) "a parent's major goal should be ensuring that their children serve their nation"; or (3) "a parent's major goal should be ensuring that their children serve their religion." Replicating the findings from the first study, we found that those who identified primarily with their nation or religion were more supportive of terrorism against the West than were respondents who identified primarily with their nation. Again, we found these differences even when controlling for age, gender, and level of education. There was no difference between those who identified with their nation and those who identified with their religion.

We can see then that collectivism is associated with greater support for terrorism. There does not seem to be any difference between the collective of a nation and the collective of a religion in supporting violence. Both groups represent potential sources of social identity. When individuals view themselves according to such group memberships, it increases the likelihood that they will be supportive of the use of violence, including when the violence is aimed at civilian targets.

Suicidal Terrorism and the Quest for Significance

Perhaps an even more striking form of terrorism involves the intentional taking of one's own life in the process. Because suicidal terrorism is an extreme means and the perpetrators are hailed as giving the ultimate sacrifice, it has the potential of bestowing greater significance upon the actor. One important implication of the importance placed on the social group in gaining personal significance is that "the willingness to die in an act of suicidal terrorism may be motivated by the desire to live forever" (Kruglanski et al., 2009, p. 335). That is, the significance gained by killing oneself for the sake of the group may lead the person to acquire more personal significance through gaining prestige, and the potential to be remembered by the group members for a long time may make it possible for the individual to gain more personal significance in death than he or she could during an extended life. Consistent with this idea is the proposition offered by the philosopher Daniel Dennett (2002), who states that humans are willing to engage in "the subordination of our genetic interests to other interests. No other species does anything like it." One possible implication of these observations is that humans are not acting in their own genetic interest and instead that ideas and culture are evolving rather than genetic material (see Chapter 15 in this volume).

Yet an alternative account could suggest that ideas are the fabric of a shared social reality that defines the group. This notion is posited by the Quest for Significance Theory and is accepted in psychological theory more generally (Hardin & Higgins, 1996; Kruglanski, Pierro, Mannetti, & De Grada, 2006). According to such an account, evolution then can occur at the group level, meaning that an act of suicide terrorism may in fact bestow an evolutionary advantage onto the close genetic relatives of the martyr. Indeed, recent advances in evolutionary theory have suggested that evolution can occur at the group level, and specific mechanisms for such evolution have been proposed (Wilson & Wilson, 2008; see also Chapter 15 in this volume). This specific theoretical advancement has been applied to the study of suicide terrorism, suggesting that it may bestow an evolutionary advantage on their kin (Victoroff, 2009). According to such an account, suicidal terrorism may be one example of altruistic suicide (Durkheim, 2007; Pedahzur, Perliger, & Weinberg, 2003). Early research suggests that Palestinian suicide bombers did indeed produce evolutionary benefits for their kin (Blackwell, 2005). Future research could profitably explore such claims, investigating whether the genetic relatives of suicide terrorists are really better off than they would have been had the person remained alive.

TESTABLE TENETS OF THE QUEST FOR SIGNIFICANCE THEORY

The original formulation of the Quest for Significance Theory posited several testable tenets that have since motivated research in an attempt to test the claims. Here we will review evidence in support of three primary implications derived from the quest for significance argument. The first such implication has been thoroughly tested in research on the effects of mortality salience. The second and third implications have only recently been empirically tested, and the data in support of them were not available when the original theory was presented.

Mortality Salience as a Threat to Personal Significance

The first testable tenet of the Quest for Significance Theory states that "if reminders of one's own mortality convey one's potential insignificance then such reminders should *augment* the quest for significance as defined by one's cultural norms and accepted ideological frames" (Kruglanski et al., 2009, p. 338). Indeed, research in support of Terror Management Theory has consistently found that reminders of one's mortality lead to defense of one's worldview, including more favorable attitudes toward those who follow group norms (Greenberg, Porteus, Simon, & Pyszczynski, 1995), and support for harsher treatment of deviants (e.g.,

Greenberg et al., 1990; Rosenblatt, Greenberg, Soloman, Pyszczynski, & Lyon, 1989). Particularly relevant to the study of terrorism, Iranians reminded of their own mortality rated a person who supported martyrdom attacks against the United States more favorably than a person who did not support such attacks (Pyszczynski et al., 2006). Yet participants who were not reminded of their own mortality rated the person who did not support martyrdom attacks more favorably than the person who did. We can see, then, that the threat to personal significance in the form of reminding people that their existence is temporary leads them to attempt to regain significance through defense of their social group, including the use of terrorism.

The Collectivistic Shift Hypothesis

The second testable implication of the Quest for Significance Theory, as stated by Kruglanski et al. (2009, p. 338) is that a "perceived loss of significance through events other than mortality reminders should fuel efforts at significance *restoration.*" Specifically, the theory proposed a novel "collectivistic shift hypothesis" in which a loss of personal significance would lead to a shift toward a more collectivistic orientation. When individuals are faced with negative feedback threatening their personal significance, they can restore their lost significance by viewing the self as interdependent with others.

Four studies have been conducted that directly test this hypothesis. In the first study, representative samples from Egypt, Indonesia, and Pakistan completed a survey in which they were asked the extent to which they had experienced personal success and were asked to select whether they identified primarily as a member of their nation, a member of their religion, or as an individual (Orehek, Kruglanski, et al., 2010). These items were embedded in a larger, unrelated survey. As predicted by the collectivistic shift hypothesis, participants who identified with their nation or religion (each representing collective identities) reported lower personal success than participants who identified primarily as an individual.

Although the previous study is consistent with the collectivistic shift hypothesis, the results are subject to a number of alternative interpretations because of the correlational nature of the study, including the direction of causality issue. To address this specifically, we designed three laboratory experiments to further test the hypothesis (Orehek, Belcher, Fishman, Goldman, & Kruglanski, 2010). In the first study, participants completed a language test, which they were told was a good predictor of their future academic and career success. Participants were randomly assigned to receive false feedback indicating that they either succeeded or failed the test. Participants then completed a self-report measure of interdependent self-construal (Singelis, 1995). Participants in the failure condition scored significantly higher on the interdependence scale than did participants in the success condition. It seems that the threat to personal significance engendered by the failure on an important life skills domain led participants to increase their interdependent orientation.

A second study was designed to test the additional prediction that participants who experience failure would not only increase their level of interdependence but would also show decreased independence. Participants in this study were randomly assigned to either write about a time in the past that they succeeded on an important personal goal or a time in the past when they failed at an important personal goal. Participants then completed self-report measures of independent and interdependent self-construal (Singelis, 1995). Consistent with the results of the first study, participants in the failure condition scored significantly higher on the interdependence scale and significantly lower on the independence scale than participants in the success condition. These results suggest a true shifting away from an independent orientation toward an interdependent orientation in the face of failure.

To extend the results from the first two studies, our third study investigated the possibility that after failure participants would elect to work in a group rather than alone. To test this prediction, participants first engaged in a video game on the computer. Participants were told that their performance on this task has been demonstrated to be a reliable predictor of their intelligence and future life success. The video game was rigged so that participants were randomly assigned to either succeed or fail at the task. Following this task, participants were told that they would engage in another task with the chance to win a reward (a chocolate bar). They were told that they had the option of working alone on this task or working in a group. Participants in the success condition were significantly less likely to elect to work in a group than were participants in the failure condition. This study demonstrates that failure not only shifts the individuals' mindset from an independent way of thinking to an interdependent way of thinking but also leads to efforts to engage in collective action.

The results from these four studies provide the empirical evidence for the collectivistic shift hypothesis. Individuals who experience a decline in their personal significance as a result of personal failure seem to attempt to restore their personal significance by shifting to a collectivistic orientation and by engaging in collective action. In this way, individuals are attaching themselves to a social group to attempt significance restoration.

This initial set of data on the collectivistic shift is promising. Yet many questions remain to be answered. For example, data are needed measuring the decline in personal significance following the failure and subsequent restoration in personal significance following the shift. We could also test whether the collectivistic shift is especially likely when one's group membership is made salient. In addition, it is possible that the type of group to which one belongs moderates the tendency to shift to collectivistic goals. For instance, it might be the case that groups characterized by cohesion might be more likely to prompt a collectivistic shift than groups characterized by internal conflict. Finally, one could inquire whether the collectivistic shift may be more likely for individuals under a heightened need for cognitive closure, known for their proclivity for group centrism (Kruglanski et al., 2006).

Extending the Self Through Time: Interdependent Self-Construals

The third testable implication of the Quest for Significance Theory, as stated by Kruglanski et al. (2009, p. 338), is that the "adoption of cultural causes that lend one a sense of personal significance should reduce death-anxiety." In other words, a person who views the self as interdependent with others in the social group should experience less death anxiety than should a person who views the self independently. By viewing the self interdependently, the person is able to extend the self through time (Castano & Dechesne, 2005). Thinking about oneself as part of a group reduces the threat of death because, although the individual's life may be temporary, the group can live on. The more important the interdependence gleaned from group membership becomes relative to the independent self, the more important the group's existence should become and the less important the individual's existence should become. Therefore, priming an interdependent (vs. independent) way of thinking should reduce the aversion toward death of the individual. We tested this prediction in three laboratory experiments (Orehek, Sasota, Ridgeway, Dechesne, & Kruglanski, 2010).

In our first experiment, participants were randomly assigned to one of two experimental conditions, designed to manipulate independent versus interdependent self-construal. In both conditions, participants were instructed to circle all the pronouns in an essay. Participants in the independent condition circled personal pronouns (e.g., *I, me, my*), and participants in the interdependent condition circled interpersonal pronouns (e.g., *we, us, our*). This manipulation has been shown to increase independent versus interdependent self-construals in the appropriate condition (Brewer & Gardner, 1996). Participants then completed a self-report scale of death anxiety (Templer, 1970). Participants in the interdependent condition scored significantly lower on the death anxiety scale than participants in the independent condition. This finding supports our prediction regarding the link between self-construal and death anxiety.

In our second study, we measured death anxiety using a measure designed to tap implicit behavioral dispositions (Fishbach & Shah, 2006) following the same experimental manipulation of self-construal as in the first study. In one condition, participants were asked to push meaningful words (e.g., *pint*) away from them and to pull meaningless words (e.g., *pind*) toward them. In another condition, participants were asked to pull meaningful words toward them and to push meaningless words away from them. In both conditions, words related to death (e.g., *coffin*) were embedded into the task. Based on previous research (Fishbach & Shah), we assumed that faster pulling of death-related words toward the participant reflected greater willingness to approach death, and faster pushing of death-related words away from the participant reflected greater avoidance of death. We found that participants in the interdependent condition pulled death-related words toward themselves faster and pushed death-related words away slower (controlling for speed on neutral trials) than did participants in the independent condition. Thus, it seems that when people are in an interdependent mindset they avoid death to a lesser extent and approach death to a greater extent than do people with an independent mindset.

Our third study was designed to extend these findings to an additional manipulation of self-construal. In this study, participants in the independent self-construal condition were asked to think about the ways they were different from their friends and family. In the interdependent self-construal condition, they were asked to think about the things that they had in common with their friends and family. As in the second study, participants in the interdependent condition were faster to pull death-related words toward themselves and slower to push them away (controlling for speed of responding to neutral words).

Across four studies, we found a consistent pattern of results attesting to the ability of an interdependent self-construal to mitigate the fear toward death. Future research could further extend these results in important ways. For example, we do not have data demonstrating that an interdependent self-construal shifts the focus to the group's life over the individual's life. In addition, our analysis would suggest the reverse pattern for anxiety regarding the group's existence, yet these data have not yet been collected.

Summary of Empirical Support

We have outlined three research programs in support of the major tenets of the Quest for Significance Theory. It has been shown that (1) collectivists support terrorism to a greater extent than do individualists, (2) reminders of one's own mortality augment the adherence to one's cultural norms and accepted ideological frames, (3) threats to personal significance in the form of personal failure leads to a collectivistic shift, and (4) a collectivist orientation reduces death anxiety compared with an individualist orientation. Taken together, these data provide initial support for the Quest for Significance Theory. Threats to one's significance, whether from impending death or personal failure, lead to attempts to restore personal significance. Individuals who attach themselves to a social group are more willing to attack out-group civilians. Finally, construing the self in interdependent ways leads to decreased anxiety about death, which may serve as a critical way of overcoming inhibitions related to martyrdom action.

CONCLUSION

We have summarized the theory related to the quest for personal significance to terrorist activity and the empirical support for its major implications. In short, we have argued that individuals who experience a threat to their personal significance attempt to restore lost significance through their attachment to a social group and defense of that group. The significance motive improved on previous theorizing on terrorist motivations by tying the categories of *ideological reasons, personal causes*, and *social pressures* together and explicating the underlying psychological motivation for terrorist activity. In this chapter we have also outlined how this theory fits more generally with evolutionary theory and may explain suicidal terrorism as a form of aggressive altruism.

The quest for significance has been postulated as a fundamental human motivation, present in all people and universal across cultures. Yet only a minority of people in the world support terrorism, even in regions from which terrorism more commonly originates. Personal significance can be gained from a variety of accomplishments and group memberships. Yet when personal goals and group identities are perceived as relatively deprived, efforts to restore personal significance should be enacted. When the deprivation is perceived to be unjust, a culprit can be identified, and violence can be justified; only then are we likely to see terrorism pursued as a means of restoring significance.

This framework suggests potential ways to reduce the incidence of terrorism in the world. If terrorism is motivated by the quest for significance, then opening alternative opportunities for significance restoration that do not include violence should reduce the use of terrorism-justifying ideologies. This can occur on both the individual and group levels. On an individual level, providing support for an individual's personal aspirations and social mobility should provide alternative avenues for the gaining of personal significance. On a group level, reducing perceived injustices through diplomacy and negotiation should reduce the need for violence as a means of achieving one's objectives.

While the early results of studies in support of the Quest for Significance Theory are consistent with its tenets, future research is needed. We have already outlined multiple ways the claims could be further tested. One important limitation of the data so far is that much of them have been collected on college student samples in laboratories located in the United States. Future tests of the predictions will need to test the claims in other cultures among diverse samples. Because the theory is purported to explain terrorist behavior, testing each tenet among terrorist samples would significantly bolster the credibility of the claims. For the theory to be confidently applied to counterterrorism efforts, empirical tests of interventions relevant to the theory are needed.

REFERENCES

Atran, S. (2003). Genesis of suicide terrorism. *Science, 299,* 1534–1539.

Becker, E. (1973). *The denial of death.* New York: The Free Press.

Becker, W. C. (1962). Developmental psychology. *Annual Review of Psychology,* 13, 1–34.

Berrebi, C. (2003). *Evidence about the link between education, poverty, and terrorism among Palestinians.* Princeton University Industrial Relations Section Working Paper 477.

Blackwell, A. D. (2005). *Terrorism, heroism, and altruism: Kin selection and socio-religious cost benefit scaling in Palestinian suicide attack.* Presented at the 2005 Human Behavior and Evolution Society Meeting.

Bloom, M. (2005). *Dying to kill: The allure of suicide terror.* New York: Columbia University Press.

Brewer, M. B., & Gardner, W. (1996). Who is this "we"? Levels of collective identity and self representations. *Journal of Personality and Social Psychology,* 71, 83–93.

Castano, E., & Dechesne, M. (2005). On defeating death: Group reification and social identification as immortality strategies. *European Review of Social Psychology,* 16, 221–255.

Dennett, D. *On dangerous memes.* TED Talk, February 2002.

Durkheim, E. (2007). *On suicide (Le suicide)* (R. Sennett, Contrib., A. Riley, Ed., R. Buss, Trans.). New York: Penguin Classics. (Original work published 1897)

Fishbach, A., & Shah, J. (2006). Self-control in action: Implicit dispositions toward goals and away from temptations. *Journal of Personality and Social Psychology,* 90, 820–832.

Frankl, V. E. (2000). *Man's search for ultimate meaning.* New York: Basic Books.

Friedman, T. L. (2010, January 6). Father knows best. *New York Times,* p. A23.

Gambetta, D. (2005). *Making sense of suicide missions.* Oxford, UK: Oxford University Press.

Greenberg, J., Koole, S. L., & Pyszczynski, T. (2004). *Handbook of experimental existential psychology.* New York: Guilford Press.

Greenberg, J., Porteus, J., Simon, L., Pyszczynski, T., & Solomon, S. (1995). Evidence of a terror management function of cultural icons: The effects of mortality salience on the inappropriate use of cherished cultural symbols. *Personality and Social Psychology Bulletin, 21*, 1221–1228.

Greenberg, J., Pyszczynski, T., Solomon, S., Rosenblatt, A., Veeder, M., Kirkland, S., et al. (1990). Evidence for terror management theory II: The effects of mortality salience on reactions to those who threaten or bolster the cultural worldview. *Journal of Personality and Social Psychology, 58*, 308–318.

Gurr, T.R. (1970). *Why men rebel.* Princeton, NJ: Princeton University Press.

Hardin, C. D., & Higgins, E. T. (1996). Shared reality: How social verification makes the subjective objective. In R. M. Sorrentino & E. T. Higgins (Eds.), *Handbook of motivation and cognition* (Vol. 3, pp. 28–84). New York: Guilford Press.

Krueger. A. B., & Maleckova, J. (2002, June). Does poverty cause terrorism? *New Republic, 226*, 27–33.

Kruglanski, A., Chen, X., Dechesne, M., Fishman, S., & Orehek, E. (2009). Fully committed: Suicide bombers motivation and the quest for personal significance. *Political Psychology, 30*(3), 331–357.

Kruglanski, A., Pierro, A., Mannetti, L., & De Grada, E. (2006). Groups as epistemic providers: Need for closure and the unfolding of group-centrism. *Psychological Review, 113*(1), 84–100.

Maslow, A. H. (1943). A theory of human motivation. *Psychological Review, 50*, 370–396.

Maslow, A. H. (1967). A theory of metamotivation: The biological rooting of the value-life. *Journal of Humanistic Psychology, 7*, 93–127.

Ohnuki-Tierney, E. (2006). *Kamikaze diaries: Reflections of Japanese student soldiers.* Chicago: University of Chicago Press.

Orehek, E., Belcher, J., Fishman, S., Goldman, L., & Kruglanski, A. W. (2010). *The collectivistic shift hypothesis.* Unpublished data.

Orehek, E., Fishman, S., Kruglanski, A. W., Dechesne, M., & Chen, X. (2010). *The role of individualistic and collectivistic goals in support for terrorist attacks.* Unpublished data.

Orehek, E., Kruglanski, A. W., Fishman, S., Dechesne, M., & Chen, X. (2010). *The link between perceptions of personal success and collective identification.* Unpublished data.

Orehek, E., Sasota, J., Ridgeway, L., Dechesne, M., & Kruglanski, A. W. (2010). *Extending the self through time: The effects of self construal on death anxiety.* Unpublished data.

Pape, R. A. (2005). *Dying to win: The strategic logic of suicide terrorism.* New York: Random House.

Pedahzur, A., Perliger, A., & Weinberg, L. (2003). Altruism and fatalism: The characteristics of Palestinian suicide terrorists. *Deviant Behavior, 24*, 405–423.

Pyszczynski, T., Abdollahi, A., Solomon, S., Greenberg, J., Cohen, F., & Weise, D. (2006). Mortality salience, martyrdom, and military might: The great Satan versus the axis of evil. *Personality and Social Psychology Bulletin, 32*, 525–537.

Rosenblatt, A., Greenberg, J., Solomon, S., Pyszczynski, T., & Lyon, D. (1989). Evidence for terror management theory: I. The effects of mortality salience on reactions to those who violate or uphold cultural values. *Journal of Personality and Social Psychology, 57*, 681–690.

Sageman, M. (2004). *Understanding terror networks.* Philadelphia: University of Pennsylvania Press.

Seligman, M. E.P. (2002). *Authentic happiness: Using the new positive psychology to realize your potential for lasting fulfillment.* New York: Simon and Schuster.

Singelis, T. M. (1994). The measurement of independent and interdependent self-construals. *Personality and Social Psychology Bulletin, 20*, 580–591.

Speckhard, A., & Akhmedova, K. (2005). Talking to terrorists. *Journal of Psychohistory, 33,* 125–156.

Staub, E. (2002). Notes on terrorism: Origins and prevention. *Peace and Conflict: Journal of Peace Psychology, 8,* 207–214.

Stern, J. (2003). *Terror in the name of God: Why religious militants kill.* New York: Ecco/ Harper Collins.

Templer, D. (1970). The construction and validation of a death anxiety scale. *Journal of General Psychology, 82*(2), 165–177.

Triandis, H. C. (2000). Culture and conflict. *International Journal of Psychology, Special issue: Diplomacy and Psychology, 35,* 145–152.

Victoroff, J. (2009). Suicide terrorism and the biology of significance. *Political Psychology, 30,* 397–400.

Wilson, D. S., & Wilson, E. O. (2008). Evolution "for the good of the group." *American Scientist, 96,* 380–389.

Section *III*

Conflict and Aggression in Relationships

11

Intimate Partner Violence
Cognitive, Affective, and Relational Factors

CHRIS ECKHARDT

Purdue University

*I*ntimate partner violence (IPV) is a critical public health problem, as recent research has documented alarmingly high prevalence and incidence rates. In the United States, population-based surveys indicate that as many as 20% of women are physically assaulted by their intimate partner in a given year (Schafer, Caetano, & Clark, 1998; Straus & Gelles, 1990; Tjaden & Thoennes, 1998). Relative to women who have not been victimized, abused women are at substantially higher risk for depression, suicide, posttraumatic stress disorder, alcohol or drug abuse or dependence, and poor physical health (Golding, 1999), and the financial costs of intimate partner violence exceed $5.8 billion each year (Centers for Disease Control and Prevention, 2003). These data strongly indicate the need to develop clear and testable models of IPV etiology and maintenance and to elucidate all possible mechanisms through which IPV perpetrators can be identified, prosecuted, and rehabilitated.

Researchers from a variety of professional backgrounds, including social psychology (Finkel, 2007; see also Chapter 4 in this volume), have explored the individual and relational risk factors that distinguish IPV perpetrators from nonperpetrators (Hotaling & Sugarman, 1986) and established theoretical contexts that have fostered the development of causal models of IPV (O'Leary, Slep, & O'Leary, 2007) and approaches for IPV perpetrators (e.g., Murphy & Eckhardt, 2005). Together, these research efforts have provided critical information that could potentially be put to great use by criminal justice professionals, treatment providers, advocates at the grass-roots level working on behalf of IPV victims, and legislators seeking to set empirically informed policies designed to reduce rates of

IPV. In this chapter, I will review research findings, primarily relying on North American samples, regarding three broad IPV perpetration risk factors of relevance to these outcomes: (1) distortions in social information processing; (2) affective dysregulation; and (3) disturbances in relational dynamics. I will suggest that because of long-standing ideological biases among advocacy groups against the role of individual and relational variables as risk factors for IPV, research findings regarding predictors of IPV are not actually having any substantive influence in the field as a whole, especially those that run counter to traditional IPV ideologies. As a result, these research finding have failed to influence those on the "front lines," including victims' advocacy groups, counselors working in agencies that deal with IPV perpetrators, criminal justice professionals (e.g., police, judges, attorneys) who work with IPV offenders daily, and legislators tasked with setting IPV-focused social policies. Because of this divide, I will argue that IPV victims are being put at greater risk in part by the very organizations dedicated to assist them.

IPV: THE IDEOLOGICAL BACKDROP

Researchers have investigated a diverse range of determinants of aggression and violence; indeed, it is the very diversity of perspectives that makes the field of aggression research so dynamic and broadly influential (Anderson & Bushman, 2002; Baron & Richardson, 1994; Daly & Wilson, 1988; see also Chapter 16 in this volume). However, unlike other areas of aggression research, the IPV field is unusually influenced by ideological factors concerning the presumed "appropriate" causes of spousal abuse. The dominant perspective that guides current IPV policy and intervention programming is based on early profeminist theories of domestic violence that arose following the creation of shelters for abused women in the early 1970s in Duluth, Minnesota, and from resulting programs for male IPV perpetrators developed as offshoots of shelters to rehabilitate male abusers in early 1980s (Pence & Paymar, 1993).

This "Duluth Model" posits that Western society is built on patriarchy, defined as "a system of social organization that creates and maintains male domination over women" (Sugarman & Frankel, 1996, p. 14). Males are therefore socialized from an early age by other powerful males to hold attitudes that justify or support the patriarchal system (see also Chapter 15 in this volume on the "male warrior" hypothesis). These attitudes result in overt and covert desires for men to dominate and control women and, when combined with patriarchal practices in the legal system, religious institutions, and other social systems, result in the collective maintenance of male power structures to dominate women across social domains, including close relationships. This notion is similar to feminist analyses of rape, which also view such violence as power- or control-based enforcement of male privilege (for a review, see Baumeister, Catanese, & Wallace, 2002). Not surprisingly given this gender-focused analysis, proponents of this model maintain that this power and control pattern is exclusive to males and that females' use of violence in relationships is restricted to self-defensive pre-emptive strikes (Walker, 1984). This claim persists despite meta-analytic findings showing that rates of IPV perpetration are higher among females relative to males, even when taking into account violence initiation (Archer, 2000, 2002). Mental health providers and proponents of psychological or interactional models of IPV, in turn, have been criticized by feminist scholars and victims' advocates for their theories and interventions disempower women and blame victims for their experiences of abuse (Adams, 1988; Bograd, 1984; Gondolf, 2007).

As an intellectual starting point, the patriarchal ideology perspective follows logically given historically relevant cultural shifts regarding the role of gender socialization in understanding various cultural phenomena (e.g., Dobash & Dobash, 1979), and, from a more practical perspective, illustrates the fact that sociologists and social workers were the driving forces behind the earliest efforts to understand IPV and intervene with victims of abuse. However, it is problematic that some 35 years later this "power and control model" has remained the dominant perspective in many, if not most, areas of the IPV field, despite vast amounts of disconfirming data (for reviews, see Dutton & Corvo, 2006; Dutton & Nicholls, 2005).

This model has expanded from a useful theory that provided some early structure to a nascent field of study to an overarching ideology that wields enormous political influence in terms of social policy and criminal justice practice (Stuart, 2005). Interventions associated with the Duluth Model (Pence & Paymar, 1993) focus exclusively on male power and control dynamics caused by faulty gender role socialization; little to no focus is directed toward psychological factors, negative emotions, or relational processes that researchers have empirically linked with IPV perpetration (for a review, see Stith, Smith, Penn, Ward, & Tritt, 2004). In their meta-analytic review of intervention programs for abusers, Babcock, Green, and Robie (2004) noted that the Duluth Model is the "unchallenged treatment of choice for most communities" (p. 1026). Of the 45 states that currently have standards outlining the structure of intervention programs for IPV offenders, the majority include statements of etiology or principles of practice that reference the patriarchal ideology model (Dutton & Corvo, 2006). Such assumptions serve not only to guide intervention programming but also to restrict the narrative of what might be considered allowable etiologic factors. However, it is also worth noting that despite these pronouncements, comprehensive meta-analytic reviews indicate that Duluth Model programs are associated with only negligible success in reducing IPV (Babcock et al., 2004; Feder & Wilson, 2006), with effect sizes inversely related to the level of methodological rigor of each study.

With this brief, and somewhat distressing, backdrop, the remainder of this chapter will review selected areas associated with IPV perpetration that highlight the cognitive, affective, and relational risk factors for IPV.

COGNITIVE, AFFECTIVE, AND RELATIONAL RISK FACTORS FOR IPV

Cognitive Factors

Diverse models of IPV etiology have consistently suggested that certain attitudes, beliefs, and cognitive distortions are implicated at some level in the onset and maintenance of abusive behavior. As a result, many theoretical models and intervention programs that focus on IPV-related cognitive factors claim to be "cognitive" or "cognitive-behavioral" in their orientation (Gondolf, 2004). As noted already, initial research on the role of cognitive factors in IPV grew out of profeminist theories of domestic violence (e.g., Dobash & Dobash, 1979), suggesting that long-term exposure to patriarchal communities instilled a deeply held belief in male privilege and superiority that covertly and overtly condones any means necessary to maintain this unequal power arrangement, including the use of coercion and aggressive force (Pence, 1983). Early findings using interviews with female IPV victims supported the notion that abuse was driven by power and control dynamics (Straus, 1976).

An alternative to the patriarchal ideology model as a starting point for establishing cognitive variables as risk factors for IPV emerged from the application of social learning theory to interpersonal violence, which focuses on process-level interactions of the individual with the broader social and interpersonal context (Bandura, 1973). The social learning approach suggests that aggressive behaviors are acquired through basic principles of learning, and as a result of these direct and vicarious learning experiences violent individuals' processing of social information is systematically biased toward negative assumptions of others' behavior and positive associations regarding the acceptability and value of aggressive behaviors (Dodge, 1991). Long-standing cognitive distortions further degrade individuals' ability to self-regulate their emotional responses to interpersonal conflict and impair the development of secure attachments with romantic partners (Dutton, Saunders, Starzomski, & Bartholomew, 1994; see also Chapter 9 in this volume, on a self-regulatory approach to aggression). Together these deficits result in a deficient set of basic relationship skills that favor the use of controlling and abusive behaviors, including belligerent and coercive communication patterns (Jacobson, Gottman, Waltz, Rushe, Babcock, & Holtzworth-Monroe, 1994). Thus, a central difference between the social learning and feminist accounts of how cognitive variables relate to IPV is that the social learning model addresses both cognitive content and cognitive processes presumed to be related to IPV, whereas the feminist account focuses almost entirely on biased cognitive content.

Evidence   The profeminist patriarchal ideology model's conceptualization of gender-focused cognitive–attitudinal disturbances as they relate to IPV is incomplete for a number of reasons. First, there is little evidence to support the notion that patriarchal attitudes and power-related beliefs represent *specific proximal contributors* to the enactment of IPV (Malik & Lindahl, 1998; Stith et al., 2004; Sugarman & Frankel, 1996). Second, partner abuse is quite prevalent in lesbian and gay relationships (e.g., Lie, Schilit, Bush, Montague, & Reyes, 1991), a fact that is difficult to explain if abuse is a purely gender-based system of oppression (Burke & Follingstad, 1999). Third, literature reviews indicate that men in treatment for domestic abuse are no more likely than nonabusive men to endorse sexist beliefs in male privilege or regarding women's roles and rights, as indicated by over a dozen case control studies (Dutton & Corvo, 2006; Eckhardt & Dye, 2000; Sugarman & Frankel). Thus, while misogynistic beliefs are characteristic of a great many men across many societies, they do not appear to be consistent or specific risk factors for IPV perpetration.

Over the last 20 years, researchers have refined the social learning approach in terms of understanding and assessing cognitive mechanisms that may be involved in IPV, again with an eye toward a broader understanding of both cognitive content and process that may translate into intervention advancements. Researchers have developed social information processing models of IPV that have hypothesized decoding, decision making, and enactment deficiencies associated with IPV perpetration (e.g., Holtzworth-Munroe, 1992). Ample evidence supports predictions from this model (Eckhardt & Dye, 2000; Holtzworth-Munroe, 2000; Murphy & Eckhardt, 2005; Stith et al., 2004). Relative to nonviolent males, IPV perpetrators exhibit (1) decoding, interpretation, and hostile attribution biases on questionnaire measures (Fincham, Bradbury, Arias, Byrne, & Karney, 1997) and during imagined conflict scenarios (Eckhardt, Barbour, & Davison, 1998; Eckhardt & Jamison, 2002; Holtzworth-Munroe & Hutchinson, 1993); (2) less competent decision making (i.e., greater generation of aggressive response options) on questionnaires (Field, Caetano, & Nelson, 2004; Sugarman & Frankel, 1996) and during conflict simulations (Anglin & Holtzworth-Munroe, 1997; Barbour, Eckhardt, Davison, & Kassinove, 1998; Jacobson et al., 1994) ; and (3) positive evaluations of violence in close relationships (Kaufman-Kantor & Straus, 1990).

Importantly, these findings involve the use of methods that go beyond mere self-reports of cognitive variables and have used methods of cognitive assessment informed by developments in general social cognition theory and research (e.g., Abelson, 1981; Nisbett & Wilson, 1977) as well as in other areas of interpersonal violence (Baumeister, Catanese, & Wallace, 2002; Huesmann, 1988). For example, our own work has suggested that cognitions related to IPV are "hot" cognitions that tend to accompany intense affective states such as anger rather than "cold" cognitions that can be calmly discussed during a face-to-face interview or endorsed on a paper-and-pencil measure. We have used a unique cognitive assessment method to assess abuse-related cognitive processing, the articulated thoughts in simulated situations paradigm (ATSS; Davison, Robins, & Johnson, 1983). In the ATSS paradigm, participants are asked to imagine a series of audiorecorded interpersonal scenarios involving their wives or girlfriends, to imagine that the scenes they are hearing are happening "right now," that they are involved in each, and to "talk out loud" about their thoughts, feelings, and anything they'd like to do when prompted by a tone every 30 seconds. We have used several different scenarios to serve as contexts for thought articulation, including a jealousy-themed script in which the subject imagines that he has come home early to find his wife having a rather romantic dinner and movie with a male acquaintance and an insult script in which the subject imagines that he is overhearing a conversation between his wife or girlfriend and her female friend wherein the two women proceed to denigrate his professional aspirations, intelligence, and sexual prowess. Articulations are later coded by trained raters for the presence of cognitive distortions linked to anger arousal and aggression (Beck, 1999).

Our results (e.g., Eckhardt et al., 1998; Eckhardt & Jamison, 2002; Eckhardt & Kassinove, 1998) have consistently found that while abusive men did not typically differ from nonabusive men on paper-and-pencil, self-report measures of cognitive distortions, IPV perpetrators articulated more cognitive distortions during

ATSS than nonviolent men. Specifically, IPV perpetrators exhibited cognitions that demeaned their partners' worth, placed absolutistic demands that people act appropriately (demandingness), magnified the importance of situations, categorized the imagined scenarios into polar extremes (dichotomous thinking), and established conclusions in the absence of confirming evidence (arbitrary inference). In addition, severely violent men were more likely than mildly violent men to articulate cognitions reflective of demandingness and awfulizing (characterizing an event as the worst possible outcome).

Other research from our lab suggests that decoding-related biases favoring an angry and aggressive response may occur quite early in social information processing. Using a paradigm borrowed from social psychological researchers (Nisbett, 1993), we have shown that high-trait-anger college students performing an emotional Stroop-like task exhibit automatic attentional biases favoring anger-related stimuli but only during concurrent mood induction (Eckhardt & Cohen, 1997). In a subsequent study using a visual search task, we found that this bias among high-anger individuals diminished with repeated exposure to anger stimuli, suggesting a sensitization–habituation process unique to dispositionally angry individuals (Cohen, Eckhardt, & Schagat, 1998). More recently, we examined automatic processing biases among IPV perpetrators using three implicit association tests (IATs) designed to examine preferences for gender, violence, and the link between violence and gender (Eckhardt, Samper, Holtzworth-Munroe, & Suhr, 2010). Results indicated that IPV perpetrators were faster than nonabusive men to categorize word pairs involving positive words with violence words, and violence words with female names. No group differences were found on the IAT assessing preferences for male or female gender. These findings indicate that individuals who positively endorse the use of aggressive conflict resolution strategies in close relationships may be more likely to use such strategies to manage their own relationship conflicts (Archer & Graham-Kevan, 2003) and to automatically link the presence of a female (but not a male) with aggression-related behavioral intentions.

Nevertheless, these data have had little influence on how counselors on the front lines of IPV treatment conceptualize the offenders in their programs or design treatments to reduce the IPV that brought them there in the first place. Why? They do not lend themselves well to a gender-themed approach to understanding IPV (Dutton & Corvo, 2006). Traditionally, Duluth Model proponents have focused on the notion of accountability and personal responsibility as causes of violence (Adams, 1988) and have been ideologically opposed to the notion that affective, personality, or psychopathological variables can also be proximal causes of IPV perpetration (Gondolf, 2004; Healey, Smith, & O'Sullivan, 1998). Thus, our assertion that cognitive factors relate only to violence in the context of anger arousal is not particularly compelling from the standpoint of the patriarchal ideology model, given the apparent involvement of anger (see the next section for reasons underlying antianger sentiments among Duluth Model proponents). Likewise, suggesting that certain biases may operate at an automatic level to affect IPV is not likely to be a warmly received finding, since it suggests a tacit or implicit process that is not under the conscious control of the perpetrator. Promoting blame accountability and personal responsibility is the most common theme among state standards for

IPV intervention programs (Maiuro, Hagar, Lin, & Olson, 2001), and IPV perpetrators are commonly assumed to engage in a high level of denial and minimization of their actions (Pence & Paymar, 1993); offenders could presumably blame their abuse on processes outside their control rather than acknowledge that their violence is the product of male privilege (i.e., "accountability"). However, these largely automatic and overlearned associations are exactly the kinds of processes known to underlie propensity toward general aggression (e.g., Berkowitz, 1993) and thus have enormous potential to inform etiologic conceptualizations of IPV and influence the development of IPV interventions.

Regulation of Negative Emotions

While decades of theoretical (Ellis, 1962) and empirical (Haaga et al., 1991) work support the general proposition that cognitive disturbances intensify the experience of negative emotions and disrupt how these emotions are expressed interpersonally (see also Chapter 9 in this volume), much controversy exists within elements of the IPV field concerning the relevance of emotional variables in explaining and treating IPV (e.g., Gondolf, 2002). Indeed, while giving a recent talk to a group of battered women's advocates and intervention program workers about risk factors for male-to-female IPV, I was met with a chorus of boos and rather nasty comments from the audience the moment I concluded that the data supported anger disturbances and psychopathology as important risk factors for IPV. Why the negative reaction? Generally, there appears to be a concern among many battered women's advocates and program staff that invoking internal constructs such as psychopathology or emotional problems will lead to a "medical model" approach to IPV that may lead to a focus away from what traditionally have been viewed as the root causes of violence (e.g., community supports that overtly or covertly condone abusive behavior and men's lack of accountability and responsibility). While it would indeed be counterproductive to see the causes of IPV as resting solely with the psychological disturbances of the male perpetrator, it seems similarly unproductive to blithely dismiss such factors when ample empirical evidence exists to substantiate these variables as legitimate risk factors.

In the context of IPV, the negative emotion that has garnered the most attention (favorable and not) is anger. The role of anger arousal in intimate partner violence seems obvious, for it is often assumed that anger and aggression are "inextricably, biologically linked" (Tavris, 1989, p. 24), and one can easily imagine a scenario wherein an abusive male becomes intensely angry and assaults his female partner. Indeed, data are largely supportive of the association between anger problems and IPV perpetration (Norlander & Eckhardt, 2005). However, there are few areas more controversial within areas of domestic violence research and advocacy areas than the issue of anger and IPV. Part of this resistance reflects concerns about the extension of a medical model approach into intervention programs and what this may imply about etiology. That is, if anger control interventions work for IPV perpetrators, then this might suggest that anger-related factors may indeed be involved in the etiology of IPV; as noted already, such a conclusion is unpopular among a large sector of the grass-roots, feminist-advocacy community.

Echoing these suspicions, Gondolf (Gondolf, 2002; Gondolf & Russell, 1986) suggested that "anger management" interventions (1) imply that the victim is to blame, (2) do not account for abuse meant to exert power and control, (3) perpetuate the batterer's denial, (4) may put the female partner at further risk for violence, (5) give communities a reason to shun collective responsibility for IPV, and (6) give perpetrators new tools to coerce and control women. These sentiments are reflected by many advocates for battered women and state domestic violence coalitions (see Healey et al., 1998), which have lobbied effectively against the use of anger control treatments for men mandated to attend batterer intervention programs (BIPs). However, as noted by Maiuro et al. (2001), state standards governing BIP content typically lack any empirical justification, calling into question the basis for the ban on anger control interventions. The net result of these assumptions has not only been a resistance toward anger-based interventions but also a steadfast dismissal of anger as a potential risk factor for IPV. Ultimately, however, all of these concerns must be answered empirically rather than ideologically. So, is there a relationship between anger arousal and IPV?

Evidence   The answer is yes, although the relationship is moderate in strength. From an empirical standpoint, recent quantitative reviews (Norlander & Eckhardt, 2005; Schumacher, Feldbau-Kohn, Slep, & Heyman, 2001) have indicated that disturbances in anger experience and expression distinguish between partner violent and nonviolent men (effect size: $d = .50$). Studies using self-report questionnaires consistently indicate that partner-violent males show elevated trait anger, hostility, increased tendency to express anger outwardly, and decreased anger control (Eckhardt, Barbour, & Stuart, 1997; Norlander & Eckhardt). In addition, anger problems are directly related to more severe and frequent perpetration of IPV (Holtzworth et al., 2000). In observational research examining sequential patterns of couple interaction, violent couples demonstrate increased usage of "destructive" forms of anger, involving expressions of contempt, disgust, and belligerence (e.g., Jacobson et al., 1994). Prior research on anger in subtypes of partner-violent men suggests that some, although not all, partner-abusive men exhibit symptoms of excessive and dysregulated anger (e.g., Chase, O'Leary, & Heyman, 2001; Dutton, 1988; Hershorn & Rosenbaum, 1991; Saunders, 1992; Holtzworth-Munroe & Stuart, 1994; Waltz, Babcock, Jacobson, & Gottman, 2000). Holtzworth-Munroe and colleagues (2000) found that the two most severe subtypes of partner-violent men (labeled Generally Violent and Borderline/Dysregulated) had significantly higher anger levels than less severe subtypes. Other research suggests that anger interacts with alcohol intoxication to increase the likelihood of IPV during relationship conflicts (Eckhardt, 2007). Finally, recent findings using forensic samples of IPV perpetrators suggest that approximately 20–25% of partner-abusive men judicially mandated to attend batterer intervention programs have clinically significant problems with anger experience and expression (Eckhardt, Samper, & Murphy, 2008) and that abusers with problematic anger are less likely to complete such programs and more likely to reassault female partners (Murphy, Taft, & Eckhardt, 2007).

But there are inconsistencies as well. Several studies using self-report question-naires of anger and hostility have not found differences between partner-violent and nonviolent males (see Norlander & Eckhardt, 2005). In addition, researchers using observational methods have typically found that direct statements of anger (e.g., "I'm really mad at you") do not reliably differentiate violent from nonviolent couples (Barbour et al., 1998; Gottman et al., 1995). Thus, while the accumulated data indicate that IPV perpetrators show dysfunctional levels of trait anger and anger control relative to nonviolent males, even after controlling for relationship distress, and that anger problems portend risk for treatment attrition and crimi-nal recidivism, it is unlikely that partner-violent males can be differentiated from their nonviolent counterparts solely on the basis of anger problems; indeed, IPV perpetrators constitute a heterogeneous group of individuals (e.g., Holtzworth-Munroe & Stuart, 1994) who act abusively as a function of a diverse array of causes and situations. Thus, rather than assuming that anger is "always" or "never" involved in IPV, it is more important to consider whether and for whom specific patterns of anger problems may be factors deserving of clinical attention (Murphy et al., 2007).

However, once again, these findings have seen only very limited acceptance in the IPV field. One of the more distressing aspects of how the patriarchal ideology model has limited scientific inquiry is that currently there is no evidence regarding whether changing perpetrators' negative emotions (e.g., anger) in IPV interven-tion programs specifically predict nonviolent outcomes. Such a study would face intense ideological resistance from criminal justice funding agencies and would be practically impossible to conduct using criminal justice samples given prevailing ideologically based opinions that oppose anger-themed research and treatment in those settings. Given that no relevant studies exist concerning whether anger- or emotion-focused techniques specifically reduce IPV risk, it is surprising and disap-pointing to see such vehement pronouncements against the usage of anger-focused interventions for IPV perpetrators (Adams, 1988; Gondolf, 2002), for one would assume that such strongly negative evaluations would be based on actual evidence. Important research needs to be conducted to investigate whether interventions that have an emotion regulation component are more effective relative to standard interventions without such a component or whether interventions with an anger focus could become the intervention of choice for perpetrators with specific emo-tion regulation difficulties (Eckhardt et al., 2008; Murphy et al., 2007).

Relational Factors

One of the hallmark assumptions of feminist-informed models of IPV etiology and intervention is that relationship disturbances are a consequence, rather than a cause, of IPV (Gondolf, 2002). As noted previously, the central theme of these models is that the patriarchal society in which we live provides an enormously influential and reinforcing context for men to use power and control tactics to subjugate their female partners and promote male privilege. Thus, popular mod-els of IPV suggest that aggressive manifestations of abuse are but one example of power and control tactics, as men may also use psychological or emotional abuse, economic coercion, and restriction of social contacts to intimidate, isolate, and control their partners.

Is there evidence that relationship power dynamics are related to IPV? Surveys suggest that couples wherein both partners acknowledge that the male is the dominant partner comprise a very small number (9.6%) of U.S. couples (Coleman & Straus, 1985). In addition, research has not been consistently supportive of the specific links between relationship power and IPV (Malik & Lindahl, 1998). For example, Babcock et al. (1993) found no relationships between power bases (i.e., education, income, socioeconomic status [SES]) and IPV and only a modest relation among power-related outcomes (i.e., control over decision making) and IPV. However, violent husbands reported greater pursuit and demand tactics during conflict discussions, whereas wives reported withdrawing or shutting down (see also Holtzworth-Munroe, Smutzler, & Stuart, 1998). Thus, while the power-and-control model provides an important distal context from which to explore partner abuse, the proximal motivations underlying violent acts are usually complex and multidetermined rather than straightforward expressions of dominance and control.

Prior reviews of the literature regarding risk factors for IPV have concluded that the context of IPV is indeed the relationship—violent couples also tend to be distressed and unhappy couples (Dobash & Dobash, 1979; Schumacher et al., 2001). Overall, the data suggest that problematic couple communication patterns are strong determinants of relationship distress and that lower levels of relationship satisfaction differentiate violent from nonviolent couples (O'Leary et al., 1989; Rogge & Bradbury, 1999). IPV tends to accompany relational distress and verbal arguments (O'Leary, 1999) and is itself a strong predictor of relationship termination. It follows, then, that the many existing strategies for the treatment of relationship dysfunction can be usefully applied to this population.

Research on the mutual nature of IPV further illustrates the importance of contextual factors in relationship conflict and abusive behavior (see also Chapter 12 in this volume). When one partner has been physically aggressive in a relationship, it is highly likely that the other partner has been physically aggressive as well (Archer, 2000). Therefore, it becomes critical to understand the usual ways that couples with a violent partner interact about matters both mundane and serious and to integrate this information into effective clinical interventions. An important area of research in this regard is based on the analysis of the sequential behavioral interaction patterns of violent couples. Researchers have found that, relative to nonviolent couples, violent couples exhibit more offensive negative behaviors during conflict discussions as well as more reciprocal patterns of negative communication (Berns, Jacobson, & Gottman, 1999; Burman et al., 1993; Cordova, Jacobson, Gottman, Rushe, & Cox, 1993; Jacobson et al., 1994; Margolin, John, & Gleberman, 1988). In particular, violent couples seem to be locked in a pattern of reciprocated belligerence, contempt, disgust, and overt hostility, with both partners responding to the other's negative behavior with similarly negative reactions (Gottman, 1994). In contrast to Duluth Model assumptions, few differences have been observed on these variables between husbands and wives within violent couples. These data suggest what has long been observed in clinical settings: among violent couples, both partners are likely to be negative, reactive, and locked in a competitive battle to defeat the other. This contextual reality neither absolves the perpetrator from his or her decision to act abusively nor blames the victim for his or her victimization. But it seems reasonable to suggest that a complete understanding of IPV requires knowledge of the context in which it occurs and that this context also includes the behavior of both partners (Jacobson, 1994; Murphy & Eckhardt, 2005).

There is no topic more contentious among proponents of the Duluth Model than the notion of relational risk factors for IPV. Given that the model emerged as a consequence of intensive advocacy efforts to improve the lives of abused women, it follows that there would be little interest among Duluth Model proponents to examine how behaviors from both partners, including female victims, provide the context for IPV. Advocacy groups that create and enforce standards for abuse intervention programs do not include relational risk factors in lists of variables that predict IPV, since doing so, from the standpoint of the Duluth Model, is tantamount to blaming the victim. Indeed, almost all states with such standards caution against or explicitly prohibit intervention strategies that involve couples' based treatment.

But is there evidence that modifying interpersonal and communication skills in partner violence interventions is associated with nonviolent change? Yes. Recent research indicates that interventions based on improving couple communication and relationship skills are at least as effective at preventing new IPV episodes as standard intervention programs or other comparison interventions (for a more detailed review see Murphy & Eckhardt, 2005). For example, Dunford (2000) examined the effects of a 26-week cognitive-behavioral group BIP, a 26-week couples' therapy group, a rigorous monitoring group, or a no-treatment control group for IPV perpetrators in the military. Follow-up reports from female partners of male participants gathered 6 and 12 months post-treatment indicated that individuals assigned to all treatments exhibited reductions in IPV; no differences in recidivism were found in male-to-female physical aggression across the four groups. In addition, using couples volunteering for treatment at a university marital distress clinic, O'Leary, Heyman, and Neidig (1999) found no difference in recidivism between men assigned to either couples' treatment versus a group Duluth Model intervention. Similar results using a court-referred sample were reported by Brannen and Rubin (1996). Thus, one can either conclude that treatment that focuses on improving relationship skills is unwarranted since it does no better than more traditional group treatments, or one can perhaps see couples' treatment as a useful alternative for some violent couples (especially those who are clearly planning on staying together) since it appears to work just as well as traditional interventions. However, the clinician interested in implementing couples' treatment must take extreme care to make sure the couple is indeed appropriate for the intervention and that the intervention does not exacerbate existing problems in ways that increase risks of future IPV victimization (for more, see LaTaillade, Epstein, & Werlinich, 2006; Murphy & Eckhardt, 2005).

CONCLUSIONS

Substantial progress has been made in the development of etiologic models of IPV and interventions for individuals who assault their relationship partners. Despite the dominating presence of the patriarchal socialization ("Duluth") model, researchers have developed theories of IPV that have broadened the factors that account for abusive behavior in couples, with less ideologically based and more empirically based findings concerning risk factors for IPV (e.g., Finkel, 2007; O'Leary et al., 2007), with an eye toward translating this work into more focused interventions for perpetrators (e.g., Murphy & Eckhardt, 2005). Using methods heavily influenced by social psychological researchers, the current state of IPV research is robust and informative. Relative to nonperpetrators, partner-violent individuals exhibit a variety of social information processing disturbances and show more favorable attitudes toward violence as an acceptable conflict resolution strategy. In terms of emotion regulation, the limited research available indicates that IPV perpetrators show more disturbances in anger experience and expression relative to nonviolent comparison samples and that problems relating to anger control are linearly related to the severity and frequency of IPV perpetration. Laboratory studies indicate that relative to nonviolent males IPV perpetrators induced to feel angry are more likely to respond to relationship conflict situations with expressions of verbal aggression, belligerence, and hostile conflict strategies. Data also clearly indicate the relational nature of violent conflict tactics: abusive behavior, while always the responsibility of the individual perpetrator, emerges in particular relationship contexts and follows a sometimes predictable pattern of reciprocated and escalating interpersonal processes.

Together, these findings make for a compelling framework around which to structure intervention programs for nonviolent change and to inform policymakers tasked with preventing the occurrence of such violence. However, despite the productivity of IPV researchers and the increasing sophistication of the methods used to examine IPV dynamics, the gulf between researchers and practitioners–policymakers remains enormous. As discussed in this review, a central reason for the ever-widening nature of this divide is the ideological resistance on the part of profeminist groups adopting the Duluth "power and control" Model of IPV toward the types of variables and the specific conclusions offered by behavioral science research concerning the etiology of IPV. As noted in a critique of this model by Dutton and Corvo (2006), research that could otherwise improve our understanding of the causes of partner abuse and inform treatment efforts is derided, reinterpreted, or ignored:

> Against a national movement toward evidence-based and best-practice criteria for assessing program continuance, interventions with perpetrators of domestic violence remain immune to those evaluative criteria. The stranglehold on theory and policy development that the Duluth model exerts confounds efforts to improve treatment. There is no rational reason for domestic violence to be viewed outside of the broad theoretical and professional frameworks used to analyze and respond to most contemporary behavioral and psychological problems. On the contrary, this isolation of domestic violence has resulted in a backwater of tautological pseudo-theory and failed intervention programs.

No other area of established social welfare, criminal justice, public health, or behavioral intervention has such weak evidence in support of mandated practice. (p. 478)

Thus, there is still quite a distance left to travel if the social and behavioral sciences are to make the paradigm shift toward an approach to understanding IPV that takes advantage of the most that our science has to offer. One advantage of an approach informed by science, as opposed to ideology, is an openness to novel findings, to new constructs, and to new collaborations that may eventually prove useful (or not) to our understanding of a given phenomenon. "Given our awareness of the limitations of current approaches ..., it is our obligation to apply what we know about the complexity of partner abuse to improve the programs intended to end it" (Stuart, 2005, p. 262). For at the end of the day, no matter how much ideological resistance one experiences, our allegiance to an open, scientifically driven approach to knowledge discovery provides the best hope to solve the one goal that everyone associated with the IPV field can agree on: to reduce the likelihood that involvement in a romantic relationship means an increased risk for violent victimization.

REFERENCES

Abelson, R. P. (1981). Psychological status of the script concept. *American Psychologist, 36*, 715–729.

Adams, D. (1988). Treatment models of men who batter: A profeminist analysis. In K. Yllö & M. Bograd (Eds.), *National conference for family violence researchers* (pp. 176–199). Thousand Oaks, CA: Sage.

Anderson, C. A., & Bushman, B. J. (2002). Human aggression. *Annual Review of Psychology, 53*, 27–51.

Anglin, K., & Holtzworth-Munroe, A. (1997). Comparing the responses of maritally violent and nonviolent spouses to problematic marital and nonmarital situations: Are the skill deficits of physically aggressive husbands and wives global? *Journal of Family Psychology, 11*, 301–313.

Archer, J. (2000). Sex differences in aggression between heterosexual partners: A meta-analytic review. *Psychological Bulletin, 126*, 651–680.

Archer, J. (2002). Sex differences in physically aggressive acts between heterosexual partners. A meta-analytic review. *Aggression and Violent Behavior, 7*(4), 313–351.

Archer, J., & Graham-Kevan, N. (2003). Do beliefs about aggression predict physical aggression to partners? *Aggressive Behavior, 29*, 41–54.

Babcock, J. C., Green, C. E., & Robie, C. (2004). Does batterers' treatment work? A meta-analytic review of domestic violence treatment. *Clinical Psychology Review, 23*, 1023–1053.

Babcock, J. C., Waltz, J., Jacobson, N. S., & Gottman, J. M. (1993). Power and violence: The relation between communication patterns, power discrepancies, and domestic violence. *Journal of Consulting and Clinical Psychology, 61*, 40–50.

Bandura, A. (1973). *Aggression: A social learning analysis.* Oxford, England: Prentice-Hall.

Barbour, K. A., Eckhardt, C. I., Davison, G. C., & Kassinove, H. (1998). The experience and expression of anger in maritally violent and maritally discordant-nonviolent men. *Behavior Therapy, 29*, 173–191.

Baron, R. A., & Richardson, D. R. (1994). *Human aggression* (2nd ed.). New York: Plenum.

Baumeister, R., Catanese, K., & Wallace, H. (2002). Conquest by force: A narcissistic reactance theory of rape and sexual coercion. *Review of General Psychology, 6,* 92–135.

Beck, A. T. (1999). *Prisoners of hate: The cognitive basis of anger, hostility, and violence.* New York: HarperCollins.

Berkowitz, L. (1993). *Aggression: Its causes, consequences, and control.* New York: McGraw-Hill.

Berns, S. B., Jacobson, N. S., & Gottman, J. M. (1999). Demand-withdraw interaction in couples with a violent husband. *Journal of Consulting and Clinical Psychology, 67,* 666–674.

Bograd, M. (1984). Family systems approaches to wife battering: A feminist critique. *American Journal of Orthopsychiatry, 54,* 558–568.

Brannen, S. J., & Rubin, A. (1996). Comparing the effectiveness of gender specific and couples groups in court-mandated spouse abuse treatment programs. *Research on Social Work Practice, 6,* 405–424.

Burke, L. K., & Follingstad, D. R. (1999). Violence in lesbian and gay relationships: Theory, prevalence, and correlational factors. *Clinical Psychology Review, 19,* 487–512.

Burman, B., Margolin, G., & John, R. S. (1993). America's angriest home videos: Behavioral contingencies observed in home reenactments of marital conflict. *Journal of Consulting and Clinical Psychology, 61,* 28–39.

Centers for Disease Control and Prevention. (2003). *Costs of intimate partner violence against women in the United States.* Atlanta, GA: Author.

Chase, K. A., O'Leary, K. D., & Heyman, R. E. (2001). Categorizing partner-violent men within the reactive-proactive typology model. *Journal of Consulting and Clinical Psychology, 69,* 567–572.

Cohen, D. J., Eckhardt, C. I., & Schagat, K. D. (1998). Attention allocation and habituation to anger-related stimuli during a visual search task. *Aggressive Behavior, 24,* 399–409.

Coleman, D., & Straus, M. A. (1985). Marital power, conflict and violence in a nationally representative sample of American couples. *Violence and Victims, 1*(2), 141–157.

Cordova, J. V., Jacobson, N. S., Gottman, J. M., Rushe, R., & Cox, G. (1993). Negative reciprocity and communication in couples with a violent husband. *Journal of Abnormal Psychology, 102,* 559–564.

Daly, M., & Wilson, M. (1988). *Homicide.* New York: Aldine de Gruyter.

Davison, G. C., Robins, C., & Johnson, M.K. (1983). Articulated thoughts during simulated situations: A paradigm for studying cognition in emotion and behavior. *Cognitive Therapy and Research, 7,* 17–40.

Dobash, R. E., & Dobash, R. (1979). *Violence against wives: A case against the patriarchy.* New York: Free Press.

Dodge, K. A. (1991). The structure and function of reactive and proactive aggression. In D. J. Pepler & K. H. Rubin (Eds.), *Earlscourt symposium on childhood aggression* (pp. 201–218). Hillsdale, NJ: Erlbaum.

Dunford, F.W. (2000). The San Diego Navy experiment: An assessment of interventions for men who assault their wives. *Journal of Consulting and Clinical Psychology, 68,* 468–476.

Dutton, D. G. (1988). Profiling of wife assaulters: Preliminary evidence for a trimodal analysis. *Violence and Victims, 3,* 5–29.

Dutton, D. G., & Corvo, K. (2006). Transforming a flawed policy: A call to revive psychology and science in domestic violence research and practice. *Aggression and Violent Behavior, 11,* 457–483.

Dutton, D. G., & Nicholls, T. L. (2005). The gender paradigm in domestic violence research and theory: Part 1—The conflict of theory and data. *Aggression and Violent Behavior, 10,* 680–714.

Dutton, D. G., Saunders, K., Starzomski, A., & Bartholomew, K. (1994). Intimacy-anger and insecure attachment as precursors of abuse in intimate relationships. *Journal of Applied Social Psychology, 24,* 1367–1386.

Eckhardt, C. I. (2007). Effects of alcohol intoxication on anger experience and expression among partner assaultive men. *Journal of Consulting and Clinical Psychology, 75,* 61–71.

Eckhardt, C. I., Barbour, K. A., & Davison, G. C. (1998). Articulated thoughts of maritally violent and nonviolent men during anger arousal. *Journal of Consulting and Clinical Psychology, 66,* 259–269.

Eckhardt, C. I., Barbour, K. A., & Stuart, G. L. (1997). Anger and hostility in maritally violent men: Conceptual distinctions, measurement issues, and literature review. *Clinical Psychology Review, 17,* 333–358.

Eckhardt, C. I., & Cohen, D. J. (1997). Attention to anger-relevant and irrelevant stimuli following naturalistic insult. *Personality and Individual Differences, 23,* 619–629.

Eckhardt, C. I., & Dye, M. L. (2000). The cognitive characteristics of maritally violent men: Theory and evidence. *Cognitive Therapy and Research, 24,* 139–158.

Eckhardt, C. I., Holtzworth-Munroe, A., Norlander, B., Sibley, A., & Cahill, M. (2008). Readiness to change, partner violence subtypes, and treatment outcomes among men in treatment for partner assault. *Violence and Victims, 23,* 446–475.

Eckhardt, C. I., & Jamison, T. R. (2002). Articulated thoughts of male dating violence perpetrator during anger arousal. *Cognitive Therapy and Research, 26,* 289–308.

Eckhardt, C. I., & Kassinove, H. (1998). Articulated cognitive distortions and cognitive deficiencies in maritally violent men. *Journal of Cognitive Psychotherapy, 12,* 231–250.

Eckhardt, C., Samper, R., Holtzworth-Munroe, A., & Suhr, L. (2010). *Implicit associations towards violence among intimate partner violence perpetrators.* Manuscript submitted for publication.

Eckhardt, C. I., Samper, R., & Murphy, C. (2008). Anger disturbances among perpetrators of intimate partner violence: Clinical characteristics and outcomes of court-mandated treatment. *Journal of Interpersonal Violence, 23,* 1600–1617.

Ellis, A. (1962). *Reason and emotion in psychotherapy.* New York: Citadel Press.

Ellis, A. (1994). *Reason and emotion in psychotherapy* (2nd ed.). New York: Citadel Press.

Feder, L., & Wilson, D. (2005). A meta-analytic review of court-mandated batterer intervention programs: Can courts affect abusers' behavior? *Journal of Experimental Criminology, 1,* 239–262.

Field, C. A., Caetano, R., & Nelson, S. (2004). Alcohol and violence related cognitive risk factors associated with the perpetration of intimate partner violence. *Journal of Family Violence, 19,* 249–253.

Fincham, F. D., Bradbury, T. N., Arias, I., Byrne, C. A., & Karney, B. R. (1997). Marital violence, marital distress, and attributions. *Journal of Family Psychology, 11,* 367–372.

Finkel, E. J. (2007). Impelling and inhibiting forces in the perpetration of intimate partner violence. *Review of General Psychology, 11,* 193–207.

Golding, J. M. (1999). Intimate partner violence as a risk factor for mental disorders: A meta-analysis. *Journal of Family Violence, 14,* 99–132.

Gondolf, E. W. (2002). *Batterer intervention systems.* Thousand Oaks, CA: Sage Publications.

Gondolf, E. W. (2004). Evaluating batterer counseling programs: A difficult task showing some effects and implications. *Aggression and Violent Behavior, 9,* 605–631.

Gondolf, E. W. (2007). Theoretical and research support for the Duluth model: A reply to Dutton and Corvo. *Aggression and Violent Behavior, 12,* 644–657.

Gondolf, E. W., & Russell, D. (1986). The case against anger control treatment programs for batterers. *Response to the Victimization of Women & Children, 9,* 2–5.

Gottman, J. M., Jacobson, N. S., Rushe, R. H., Shortt, J. W., Babcock, J. C., LaTaillade, J. J., et al. (1995). The relationship between heart rate reactivity, emotionally aggressive behavior, and general violence in batterers. *Journal of Family Psychology, 9,* 227–248.

Haaga, D. A., Dyck, M. J., & Ernst, D. (1991). Empirical status of cognitive theory of depression. *Psychological Bulletin, 110,* 215–236.

Healey, K., Smith, C., & O'Sullivan, C. (1998). *Batterer intervention: Program approaches and criminal justice strategies.* Washington, DC: National Institute of Justice.

Hershorn, M., & Rosenbaum, A. (1991). Over- vs. undercontrolled hostility: Application of the construct to the classification of maritally violent men. *Violence and Victims, 6,* 151–58.

Holtzworth-Munroe, A. (1992). Social skill deficits in maritally violent men: Interpreting the data using a social information processing model. *Clinical Psychology Review, 12,* 605–617.

Holtzworth-Munroe, A. (2000). Social information processing skills deficits in maritally violent men: Summary of a research program. In J. P. Vincent & E. N. Jouriles (Eds.), *Domestic violence: Guidelines for research-informed practice* (pp. 13–36). London: Jessica Kingsley Publishers.

Holtzworth-Munroe, A., & Hutchinson, G. (1993). Attributing negative intent to wife behavior: The attributions of maritally violent versus nonviolent men. *Journal of Abnormal Psychology, 102,* 206–211.

Holtzworth-Munroe, A. Rehman, U., & Herron, K. (2000). General and spouse specific anger and hostility in subtypes of maritally violent men and nonviolent men. *Behavior Therapy, 31,* 603–630.

Holtzworth-Munroe, A., & Smutzler, N. (1996). Comparing the emotional reactions and behavioral intentions of violent and nonviolent husbands to aggressive, distressed, and other wife behaviors. *Violence and Victims, 11,* 319–339.

Holtzworth-Munroe, A., Smutzler, N., & Stuart, G.L. (1998). Demand and withdraw communication among couples experiencing husband violence. *Journal of Consulting and Clinical Psychology, 66,* 731–743.

Holtzworth-Munroe, A., & Stuart, G. L. (1994). Typologies of male batterers: Three subtypes and the differences among them. *Psychological Bulletin, 116,* 476–497.

Hotaling G., & Sugarman, D. (1986). An analysis of risk markers in husband to wife violence: The current state of knowledge. *Violence and Victims, 2,* 101–124.

Huesmann, L. R. (1988). An information processing model for the development of aggression. *Aggressive Behavior, 14,* 13–24.

Jacobson, N. (1994). Rewards and dangers in researching domestic violence. *Family Process, 33,* 81–85.

Jacobson, N.S., Gottman, J.M., Waltz, J., Rushe, R., Babcock, J., & Holtzworth-Munroe, A. (1994). Affect, verbal content, and psychophysiology in the arguments of couples with a violent husband. *Journal of Consulting and Clinical Psychology, 62,* 982–988.

Kaufman-Kantor, G., & Straus, M. A. (1990). The "drunken bum" theory of wife beating. In M. Straus & R. Gelles (Eds.), *Physical violence in American families* (pp. 203–224). New Brunswick, NJ: Transaction.

LaTaillade, J. J., Epstein, N.B., & Werlinich, C.A. (2006). Conjoint treatment of intimate partner violence: A cognitive behavioral approach. *Journal of Cognitive Psychotherapy, 20,* 393–410.

Leonard, K. (2001). Alcohol and substance abuse in marital violence and child maltreatment. In C. Wekerle & A. Wall (Eds.), *The violence and addiction equation* (pp. 194–219). New York: Brunner-Routledge.

Leonard, K. E., & Roberts, L. J. (1998). The effects of alcohol on the marital interactions of aggressive and nonaggressive husbands and their wives. *Journal of Abnormal Psychology, 107,* 602–615.

Lie, G., Schilit, R., Bush, J., Montague, M., & Reyes, L. (1991). Lesbians in currently aggressive relationships: How frequently do they report aggressive past relationships? *Violence and Victims, 6,* 121–135.

Maiuro, R. D., Hagar, T. S., Lin, H., & Olson, N. (2001). Are current state standards for domestic violence perpetrator treatment adequately informed by research? A question of questions. *Journal of Aggression, Maltreatment & Trauma, 5,* 21–44.

Malik, N. M., & Lindahl, K. M. (1998). Aggression and dominance: The roles of power and culture in domestic violence. *Clinical Psychology: Science and Practice, 5,* 409–423.

Margolin, G., John, R. S., & Gleberman, L. (1988). Affective responses to conflictual discussions in violent and nonviolent couples. *Journal of Consulting and Clinical Psychology, 56,* 24–33.

McMurran, M., & Gilchrist, E. (2008). Anger control and alcohol use: Appropriate interventions for perpetrators of domestic violence? *Psychology, Crime, & Law, 14,* 107–116.

Murphy, C. M., & Eckhardt, C. I. (2005). *Treating the abusive partner: An individualized cognitive-behavioral approach.* New York: Guilford.

Murphy, C. M., Taft, C. T., & Eckhardt, C. I. (2007). Anger problem profiles among partner violent men: Differences in clinical presentation and treatment outcome. *Journal of Counseling Psychology, 54,* 189–200.

Nisbett, R. (1993). Violence and U.S. regional culture. *American Psychologist, 48,* 441–449.

Nisbett, R., & Wilson, T. D. (1977). Telling more than we can know: Verbal reports on mental processes. *Psychological Review, 84,* 231–259.

Norlander, B., & Eckhardt, C. (2005). Anger, hostility, and male perpetrators of intimate partner violence: A meta-analytic review. *Clinical Psychology Review, 25,* 119–152.

O'Leary, K. D. (1988). Physical aggression between spouses: A social learning theory perspective. In V. B. Van Hasselt, R. Morrison, A. Bellack, & M. Hersen (Eds.), *Handbook of family violence* (pp. 31–55). New York: Plenum.

O'Leary, K. D. (1999). Psychological abuse: A variable deserving critical attention in domestic violence. *Violence and Victims, 14,* 3–23.

O'Leary, K. D., Barling, J., Arias, I., Rosenbaum, A., Malone, J., & Tyree, A. (1989). Prevalence and stability of physical aggression between spouses: A longitudinal analysis. *Journal of Consulting and Clinical Psychology, 57,* 263–268.

O'Leary, K. D., Heyman, R. E., & Neidig, P. H. (1999). Treatment of wife abuse: A comparison of gender-specific and conjoint approaches. *Behavior Therapy, 30,* 475–505.

O'Leary, K., Smith-Slep, A., & O'Leary, S. (2007). Multivariate models of men's and women's partner aggression. *Journal of Consulting and Clinical Psychology, 75,* 752–764.

Pence, E. (1983). The Duluth domestic abuse intervention project. *Hamline Law Review, 6,* 247–275.

Pence, E., & Paymar, M. (1993). *Education groups for men who batter: The Duluth model.* New York: Springer.

Rogge, R. D., & Bradbury, T. N. (1999). Till violence does us part: The differing roles of communication and aggression in predicting adverse marital outcomes. *Journal of Consulting and Clinical Psychology, 67,* 340–351.

Saunders, D. (1984). Helping husbands who batter. *Social Casework, 65,* 347–353.

Saunders, D. G. (1992). A typology of men who batter: Three types derived from cluster analysis. *American Journal of Orthopsychiatry, 62,* 264–275.

Schafer, J., Caetano, R., & Clark C. L. (1998). Rates of intimate partner violence in the United States. *American Journal of Public Health, 88,* 1702–1704.

Schumacher, J. A., Feldbau-Kohn, S., Slep, A. M. S., & Heyman, R. E. (2001). Risk factors for male-to-female partner physical abuse. *Aggression and Violent Behavior, 6,* 281–352.

Stith, S. M., Smith, D. B., Penn, C. E., Ward, D. B., & Tritt, D. (2004). Intimate partner physical abuse perpetration and victimization risk factors: A meta-analytic review. *Aggression and Violent Behavior, 10,* 65–98.

Straus, M. A. (1976). Sexual inequality, cultural norms, and wife-beating. *Victimology: An International Journal, 1,* 54–76.

Straus, M. A., & Gelles, R. J. (1990). How violent are American families? In M. A. Straus & R. J. Gelles (Eds.), *Physical violence in American families* (pp. 95–108). New Brunswick, NJ: Transaction Publishers.

Stuart, R. B. (2005). Treatment for partner abuse: Time for a paradigm shift. *Professional Psychology: Research and Practice, 36,* 254–263.

Sugarman, D. B., & Frankel, S. L. (1996). Patriarchal ideology and wife-assault: A meta-analytic review. *Journal of Family Violence, 11,* 13–40.

Tavris, C. (1989). *Anger: The misunderstood emotion* (rev. ed.). New York: Touchstone.

Tjaden, P., & Thoennes, N. (1998). Prevalence, incidence and consequences of violence against women: Findings from the National Violence Against Women Survey. Washington, DC: U.S. Department of Justice.

Walker, L. (1984). *The battered woman syndrome.* New York: Springer.

Waltz, J., Babcock, J. C., Jacobson, N. S., & Gottman, J. M. (2000). Testing a typology of batterers. *Journal of Consulting and Clinical Psychology, 68,* 658–669.

Wathen, C. N., & MacMillan, H. L. (2003). Interventions for violence against women: Scientific review. *Journal of the American Medical Association, 289,* 589–600.

12

Interdependent Goals and Relationship Conflict

GRÁINNE M. FITZSIMONS and JOANNA E. ANDERSON

University of Waterloo

*I*n close relationships, partners' outcomes are mutually dependent. This extensive everyday interdependence is what brings much of what people desire from relationships (e.g., intimacy, understanding, support, and stability) but is also what brings much of what people fear (e.g., hurt, pain, obstruction, and strife; see Chapters 3, 11, 13, and 14 in this volume). From its very inception, Interdependence Theory has explicitly connected interdependence and the likely occurrence of interpersonal conflict (Braiker & Kelley, 1979; Kelley & Thibaut, 1978), noting that with greater interdependence comes greater opportunities for partners to both facilitate and obstruct each other's goals. Because goal obstruction is a common trigger of conflict and aggression (see Chapter 10 in this volume), the greater opportunities for obstruction that accompany interdependence can in turn generate more occurrences of strife in relationships.

If individual goal pursuits are enmeshed in the everyday interdependence of romantic relationships (see Chapters 2 and 6 in this volume), then it may be fruitful for the understanding of both self-regulatory and relationship processes to elucidate the relations of one partner's goals to the other's. In the current research, we suggest that the similarity of the partners' personal goals such as career goals, financial goals, and health and fitness goals may be an important factor in predicting both individuals' progress on their goals as well as relationship coordination, compatibility, and conflict.

In this chapter, we present recent findings examining the links between goal similarity and relationship conflict, testing the hypothesis that romantic partners who pursue dissimilar personal goals experience more conflict in their relationship. Dissimilar personal goals are likelier to be incompatible goals, interfering with each other's progress, and we thus suggest that dissimilar personal pursuits will lead to more conflict in the relationship overall, via a direct effect of goal obstruction on conflict. Dissimilar goals are also likely to create conflict via more indirect routes, such as perceptions that one's partner is not responsive to one's needs (Reis, Clark, & Holmes, 2004) and feelings of being unsupported (Brunstein, Dangelmayer, & Schultheiss, 1996).

BACKGROUND: SIMILARITY AND LIKING

According to the similarity–attraction hypothesis, individuals evaluate others who share their attitudes more positively than they evaluate others who possess dissimilar attitudes (Byrne, 1971; Byrne, Clore, & Worchel, 1966). In a classic program of research, Byrne demonstrated that individuals evaluated a bogus stranger more positively after reading that the stranger possessed attitudes (about issues such as God and premarital sex) that were similar to those reported by the participants themselves (Byrne, 1961). Byrne theorized that similarity produced its positive effects by validating individuals' own views and attitudes about the world, which is inherently rewarding. Because individuals associate the reward of validation with the stranger, they like him or her more (Byrne, 1961). This finding and its interpretation have been challenged (e.g., Rosenbaum, 1986), but the positive link between attraction and similarity is largely viewed as a basic principle underlying initial attraction (e.g., Berscheid & Walster, 1978).

Although the link between similarity and initial attraction among strangers is widely accepted, the link between similarity and satisfaction with existing relationship partners is less clear. Findings have been mixed (Buunk & Bosman, 1986; Montoya, Horton, & Kirchner, 2008; Morry, 2005, 2007), and many studies have suffered from data-analytic weaknesses that limit their interpretability (Griffin, Murray, & Gonzalez, 1999; see also the review in Karney & Bradbury, 1995). Despite these concerns, the most often reported finding is still that similar partners are more satisfied partners (e.g., Gaunt, 2006; Luo & Klohnen, 2005). Less work has directly examined conflict as an outcome; however, some findings have suggested that similarity also reduces the occurrence of everyday conflict (Surra & Longstreth, 1990), and many authors have posited that reduced conflict is one route through which the similarity–satisfaction effect may occur (e.g., Esterberg, Moen, & Dempster-McCain, 1994).

Most of the research to date on similarity has examined personality traits and attitudes, with no studies on similar personal goal pursuits per se. However, several studies have examined similarity in characteristics related to personal goals, finding that similar activity preferences, at least in some domains, predict reduced conflict and increased relationship satisfaction (Surra & Longstreth, 1990) and that similar needs for autonomy and affiliation predict higher reports of marital adjustment (Meyer & Pepper, 1977).

CURRENT RESEARCH

Thus, building on prior work, we explored the influence of similar personal goals on the frequency and intensity of relationship conflict. Because this chapter is inspired by Interdependence Theory and the ideas are driven by our interest in linking interdependence theorizing about relationships with work on self-regulation, our emphasis differs from prior work on similarity. Whereas past work has focused on links between similarity of personality traits, attitudes, values, and demographic characteristics, this chapter focuses on similarity in personal goal pursuits. Personal goals have nothing to do with relationships—they are the individual's own quests—and thus are the ideal characteristic to study to test interdependence theory's predictions about similarity and conflict. In one of our studies, we test the role of other kinds of similarity within relationships to determine if these interdependent goals produce any unique effects on conflict.

Similarly, whereas past work has examined the impact of similarity on attraction, liking, or satisfaction, we emphasize the more direct outcome that should stem from interdependence costs—conflict. Finally, while the most well-known findings on similarity have studied attraction to strangers, we focus on similarity within established long-term romantic relationships. Because of the inherent interdependence in close relationships, we speculate that the processes that promote any positive effects of similarity on reduced conflict are probably not the same simple positive reinforcement principles thought to drive the effects of similarity on initial attraction among strangers. It surely feels good to know that one's romantic partner agrees with one's opinions but that sense of self-validation is only one of many possible processes that could explain a similarity–conflict link within this more complicated interpersonal context.

For example, Holmes and Murray (1996), in their review of research on conflict in relationships, suggest that one major cause of relationship conflict is that partners lack understanding of each other's "untransformed" preferences—that is, the preferences they would possess in the absence of external influence. Before partners can decide how to act in a given situation, they must understand their partner's preferences in the situation (Kelley, 1979; Messick & Brewer, 1983). Indeed, accurate perspective taking has been shown to be crucial to negotiating and resolving conflicts (see Chapter 7 in this volume). Unfortunately, partners are known to be quite inaccurate when it comes to perspective taking—they often misread each other's preferences (Kenny, 1994). Inaccuracies are thought to stem both from people's tendencies to project their own preferences onto their partners (a tendency that is even likelier to happen with close relationships because people assume more similarity) and from people's overreliance on partners' past overt behaviors as cues for their preferences. Overt behaviors can often be misleading reflections of people's real motivations, both because people behave in line with "transformed" motivations (i.e., they alter their preferences to better suit their partner's; Holmes & Murray, 1996) and because people often fail to behave in line with their goals, due to self-control failures (Baumeister, 1998). If partners base their beliefs about each other's preferences on what they see in their partner's behaviors, then they may well miss the mark when it comes to understanding what their partners really want.

We suggest that both of these types of misunderstandings are likelier to happen when partners hold dissimilar personal goals. Partners who pursue similar goals may have no better knowledge of their partner's preferences; however, their assumption of similarity will be well founded, and thus they will project accurate preferences onto their partners. Similarly, when partners have similar goals, past behavior is less likely to reflect transformed motivations and more likely to reflect each partner's actual untransformed interests, simply because there is less need for transformation when both partners share the same goals. In contrast, partners with dissimilar personal goals will be likelier to make particularly inaccurate projections and to have behaved in ways that don't reflect their untransformed interests, out of desire to compromise or get along with each other.

These perspective-taking issues are one possible route through which dissimilar personal goals could generate relationship conflict. It is also possible that partners who hold dissimilar personal goals may obstruct each other's goal progress, which may directly lead to negative emotions and conflict (Berscheid, 1983, 1991; Berscheid & Ammazzalorso, 2001; Fehr & Harasymchuk, 2005; Fitzsimons & Shah, 2008). When goals are obstructed, people tend to feel frustrated with each other (Berscheid & Ammazzalorso, 2001), and may avoid each other and seek more independence (Fitzsimons & Shah, 2008), all of which would promote conflict. In contrast, partners who hold similar personal goals may (whether intentionally or incidentally) facilitate each other's goal progress, which in turn may directly lead to positive emotions, closeness, and cooperation (Berscheid & Ammazzalorso; Fehr & Harasymchuk; Fitzsimons & Shah). Finally, another route through which goal similarity may impact conflict is through the nature of everyday interactions within relationships. If partners are pursuing similar goals, their interactions may be smoother and more efficient than interactions between partners who are pursuing dissimilar goals. If so, they may experience more harmony and synchrony, which again may promote positive, cooperative responses (Dalton, Chartrand, & Finkel, 2010; Wiltermuth & Heath, 2008). In contrast, if partners are pursuing dissimilar goals, their interactions may be discordant and inefficient, which may lead to more conflict.

In this chapter, we describe several studies—correlational, longitudinal, and experimental—that provide preliminary support for the importance of personal goal similarity for the experience of effortless, harmonious interactions within interpersonal interactions and for reduced conflict. The first two studies look at perceptions of goal similarity and compatibility, and the remaining studies compare responses from both partners to get a more "objective" measure of goal similarity.

HOW DOES GOAL SIMILARITY AFFECT CONFLICT AND GOAL PROGRESS OVER TIME?

In an initial exploration of the role of similar personal goals in conflict, we conducted a longitudinal survey study among New York University undergraduate students. We sought to examine whether participants who perceived they cared about an important goal to the same degree as their partners reported lower frequency of conflicts over the next month. Because our participants were college students, we examined perceived similarity in the goal of academic achievement, which is the most commonly noted goal in this sample.

At Time 1, as part of a broader survey, participants answered questions about the extent to which they and their best friend or romantic partner valued academic achievement to the same degree. Specifically, they rated their agreement with three direct statements like, "My partner/friend and I care equally about academic achievement." Participants also rated their agreement with the item, "Academic achievement is very important to me right now," which we used as a measure of their own goal commitment. As a measure of conflict, participants reported how many fights, arguments, or conflicts they had had with their partner or friend over the past month. They also rated their relationship satisfaction using the item, "I am fully satisfied with my relationship/friendship," and their goal progress using the item, "I feel I made good progress on my academic achievement goals this month." At Time 2, 1 month later, participants once again indicated how many fights, arguments, or conflicts they and their partner or friend had had over the past month, rated their relationship satisfaction and goal progress using the same items, and provided the grades they had received on their midterm examinations.

As predicted, perceived goal similarity predicted lower reports of conflict over the following month, a relation that held when controlling for initial ratings of conflict and relationship satisfaction and participants' own ratings of goal importance. Ideally, we would also have assessed participants' perceptions of the other's goal commitment as an additional control: it is conceivable that conflict is not necessarily related to dyads' similarity on this goal but to something about the other's own goal pursuit. Because of the way the goal similarity items were worded, it is unclear whether the rated similarity results from the partner or friend valuing the goal more or less than the participant. That is, the items may have unintentionally captured dissatisfaction with a particularly ambitious or unambitious partner. In subsequent studies, we were careful to include all such variables, which allows us to be more confident about the precise role that dissimilar goals may play in generating conflict within relationships.

Nonetheless, because of the longitudinal nature of the current study, in which perceived similarity predicted change in conflict from Time 1 to Time 2, we can tentatively report evidence that (the perception of) similarity reduces conflict. That is, although the available data cannot rule out third variable influences with this study, they do suggest the directionality of the link between similar goals and conflict. Findings were identical for the friend dyads and romantic partner dyads; according to Interdependence Theory, the processes should work in the same way for all established, long-term, close relationships. That is, there is nothing qualitatively different about romantic relationships. However, if romantic relationships were higher in interdependence, as they would be in most adult samples, we would expect to see stronger effects of similarity on conflict. Because of the heightened opportunity for obstructed goals that emerges in closer relationships with greater interdependence, similarity should be more predictive. Within a college sample, though, close same-sex friendships are not necessarily less close or interdependent than romantic relationships, with many students living with their best friends.

Turning to examine goal progress, we found that perceived goal similarity positively predicted perceptions of progress 1 month later as well as better performance on midterm examinations, effects that held while controlling for initial goal progress. There are many reasons goal similarity could lead to better goal progress. For example, if both partners share the same goals, this could promote the construction of a goal-encouraging environment. As another example, friends and partners who also value academic achievement may actually be more instrumental to goal pursuit, through providing either practical help or emotional support.

However, it is also possible that goal similarity could affect progress by decreasing conflict or increasing coordination. Indeed, these results also indicate that the relationship between goal similarity and goal progress is significantly (partially) mediated by conflict. We have suggested that when partners are pursuing similar personal goals their everyday interactions should be smoother and more harmonious. For example, they should understand each other's perspectives better, should have similar expectations about those interactions, and should be more respectful of each other's goal pursuits. If their everyday interactions are indeed smoother, they are likely also more efficient or less depleting. In contrast, when partners are pursuing dissimilar personal goals, they may have misunderstandings, different expectations, and less respect for each other's goals, which may make their interactions less efficient and more resource consuming (Finkel et al., 2006). If so, these subtle clashes could drain self-regulatory resources, leaving less energy and focus for goal pursuit, and thus negatively affecting goal progress. The next study we describe includes additional measures that allow us to examine this link between high maintenance interactions (Finkel et al.) and goal similarity.

WHAT MECHANISMS DRIVE THE GOAL SIMILARITY–CONFLICT LINK?

In this next study, we sought to replicate the link between perceived goal similarity and conflict while including some additional measures to increase clarity about how goal similarity may affect the frequency and intensity of relational conflict. In particular, we examined the potential role of (1) high-maintenance interactions and (2) partner instrumentality. First, as explained already, partner interactions that are rife with misunderstandings and inefficiencies may be one result of having dissimilar personal goals; if so, these draining interactions may produce more conflict. Second, past research has demonstrated that people feel closer to partners who are helpful or instrumental for ongoing goals (Fitzsimons & Shah, 2008), and we wondered whether instrumentality could play a mediating role in the effects of similarity on relationship satisfaction and conflict. That is, it may be the case that goal similarity produces positive outcomes because of a strong link between goal similarity and instrumentality. Partners with similar goals may be more likely to be helpful to each other than partners with dissimilar goals. However, it is also possible that instrumentality may reduce conflict—people may be more agreeable and accommodating to helpful others—but that it may not act as a mediating mechanism for the relation between goal similarity and conflict.

Married and dating couples at the University of Waterloo took part in a larger investigation consisting of multiple sessions and spanning a 4-month period. In the session relevant to the current study, all participants completed an hour-long series of online questionnaires during which they answered questions about their personal goal pursuits, individual differences in motivational and self-regulatory variables, and features of their relationships, including quality and outcomes.

One of the measures was a new scale created to assess perceptions of personal goal similarity. This scale, modified from an earlier measure (Bohns et al., 2010), consisted of 14 items designed to be face-valid measures of goal similarity. Participants rated their agreement with items like, "My partner and I have very similar personal goals" and, "We have a lot in common when it comes to what personal goals we care about right now." This new scale was positively correlated with measures of closeness and satisfaction; all effects we describe here control for the potential effects of those variables on conflict.

Participants also scored the amount of conflict in their relationship, rating their agreement with a one-item measure that read, "My partner and I disagree about a lot of things day to day." Among the other measures, participants completed commitment and satisfaction subscales of the Investment Model Scale (Rusbult, Martz, & Agnew, 1998).

In addition, we wanted to examine the extent to which everyday interactions within the relationship were depleting or inefficient in nature, to determine if having high-maintenance interactions may be one route through which dissimilar goals are related to conflict. To do so, we included a four-item measure taken from Finkel et al. (2006) that asks participants to rate their agreement with statements like, "Maintaining efficient, well-coordinated interaction with my partner requires a lot of energy" and, "Interactions with my partner generally go smoothly."

Finally, we were interested in the role of perceived partner instrumentality, or the perception that one's partner is helpful or useful for one's goal progress (Fitzsimons & Shah, 2008, 2009). We measured instrumentality with a 13-item scale asking participants to rate their agreement with statements like, "In general, I find my partner to be very helpful with my goal pursuits" and, "In general, my partner is a real source of strength for me in pursuing my goals."

Replicating the pattern established in the longitudinal study, the new measure of perceived goal similarity was negatively related to conflict ratings, a relation that held when we controlled for relationship satisfaction and commitment.

Next, we looked at the role of instrumentality. We found that perceptions of partner instrumentality did predict conflict, even controlling for satisfaction, such that individuals who saw their partners as more helpful for their personal goal pursuits reported fewer incidences of conflict. The directionality of this effect remains unclear: it is conceivable either that partners who have lower rates of conflict may see their partners as more instrumental for their goals or that individuals fight less often with instrumental partners. Instrumentality was also related to goal similarity, as we predicted, such that similar partners were seen as more instrumental for goal progress. When both instrumentality and similarity were entered into a regression predicting conflict, however, we found no evidence of a mediating role for instrumentality. Instead, both variables significantly predicted conflict, even when controlling for relationship satisfaction. Thus, it seems that instrumentality, though related to both goal similarity and to conflict, does not account for the link between these two variables.

However, this study also found significant (albeit partial) mediation of the link between goal similarity and conflict by the high-maintenance interaction measure. This pattern supports the possibility that partners who pursue dissimilar personal goals may find their everyday interactions draining and difficult, which may cause conflict to arise. Because the reverse mediational pathway is also significant (i.e., similarity negatively predicts depletion, with conflict as a significant partial mediator), it may also be the case that partners who pursue dissimilar personal goals may have more frequent conflicts, which may lead them to find their everyday interactions more draining and difficult.

DOES OBJECTIVE GOAL SIMILARITY AFFECT CONFLICT?

Thus, the first two studies found evidence that partners who believe they share similar personal goals report less conflict. Of course, given the correlational nature of these studies, it would be premature to draw conclusions about the directionality of the relationship. Indeed, it seems quite plausible that participants who are engaged in frequent conflict with their partners may infer from that conflict that they must have different or incompatible goals than their partners. Although the next two studies we describe are also correlational (the last study we describe is experimental), we believe we minimize the plausibility of this alternative account by measuring actual goal similarity rather than perceived goal similarity. That is, we look at both target and partner ratings of their own goals and use comparisons of those goals as predictors of target ratings of conflict. Because participants are not privy to the responses of their partners to these goal questionnaires, the reverse causal direction—that conflict leads to goal dissimilarity—is unlikely. It remains possible that frequent conflict could cause partners to begin to pursue different personal goals, but we believe that such an explanation is less parsimonious than our suggestion that pursuing different personal goals generates frequent conflict.

Dal Cin, Anderson, Holmes, and Young (2010) collected self-report data from both partners of dating couples at the University of Waterloo. Participants rated the importance of a series of goals, which ranged from specific and concrete to general and abstract and were diverse in content, including personal goals (academic achievement, finances, health, leisure) and relational goals (communication, sex). Goal similarity was measured by computing an average of the absolute difference between partner goal importance ratings and self goal importance ratings. Participants also rated the degree of conflict in their relationships using items taken from Braiker and Kelley (1979). The scale measured participants' perceptions of the frequency and seriousness of conflicts in their relationship as well as the frequency and intensity of negative affect (anger, frustration) in everyday interactions. Items included, "My partner and I frequently argue with each other" and, "When my partner and I argue, the arguments or problems we have are quite serious." Finally, participants rated their relationship satisfaction using four straightforward items (e.g., "I am extremely happy with my current romantic relationship").

As predicted, results showed that couples that reported similar goals reported less conflict in the relationship and more relationship satisfaction. Because we measured both partners' goals, instead of one partner's perceptions, we can rule out the role of perceptual illusions and biases in producing the link between goal similarity and conflict.

IS THERE ANYTHING UNIQUE ABOUT GOALS? GOAL SIMILARITY VERSUS OTHER TYPES OF COMPATIBILITY

We next returned to examine another component from the larger longitudinal study of dating and married couples described earlier, which included measures of personality and attitudes and allowed us to compare the effects of goal similarity with other kinds of similarity. Two weeks after completing the online premeasure, couples attended a laboratory session in which they individually reported on the frequency of disagreements in their relationships and provided ratings of their commitment to and identification with academic achievement goals and health and fitness goals, goals that undergraduate students commonly pursue. The goal measure was an average of four items assessing the commitment to and importance of the goal. For example, participants indicated their agreement with statements like, "This goal is very important to me." To construct a measure of goal similarity, we calculated an absolute difference score to represent the magnitude of the difference between both partners' ratings of their commitment to academic achievement and to fitness and health goals and averaged those two measures. Participants also provided measures of other kinds of personal variables, such as in personality, religious beliefs, and attitudes. It is very likely that partners with different types of personalities would have greater conflict (imagine an extravert and an introvert making social plans) and that partners with different social attitudes would also have more disagreements (imagine a socialist and a libertarian discussing current events over dinner). Indeed, as briefly discussed in the introduction, there is evidence for the effects of similarity in personality and attitudes on relationship satisfaction (Gaunt, 2006). Including these measures in our analyses allowed us to determine whether similarities in personal goal pursuits have any remaining predictive power when accounting for these other important factors.

Overall, our results supported the importance of goal similarity in conflict. As predicted, and replicating the effect from the last described study, using this new (more objective) measure of goal similarity did not change the results. When partners reported similar levels of commitment to and identification with their important personal goals, they also reported lower incidence of conflict with their partner. This relation held when we controlled for relationship satisfaction and, most importantly, when we controlled for the absolute levels of goal commitment of both partners. Because the effect holds even when controlling for individual reports of goal commitment, we can be more confident that it is indeed the discrepancy between the partners' goals, rather than something about one of the partners' goal pursuits itself, that predicts conflict (see Kenny & Acitelli, 1994).

Next, we were interested in examining whether there is a unique role for goal similarity or compatibility in particular or whether what we are capturing with our goal similarity measures is another type of similarity, such as similar attitudes, values, or personality types. To examine this idea, we analyzed the link between our difference score measure of goal similarity and conflict while controlling for a number of other potentially useful predictors. Goal similarity turned out to be a strong and robust predictor of conflict, even when compared with consequential variables such as similarity in political and social attitudes, religious beliefs, values, and Big Five personality traits. That is, it continued to be a significant negative predictor of conflict.

HOW DOES MANIPULATING GOAL INCOMPATIBILITY AFFECT CONFLICT?

In the final study that we describe, we aimed to find experimental evidence to support the idea that dissimilar personal goals could affect interpersonal conflicts. We activated the mental representation of a health and fitness goal and examined its influence on participants' responses to hypothetical relationship scenarios in which there was potential for conflict. To activate the goal, we relied on advances in the understanding of nonconscious goal pursuit (Chapter 6 in this volume), using a subtle priming technique. We were interested in whether participants would indicate that they would be more or less accommodating and cooperative in these hypothetical scenarios depending on (1) whether they were primed with the health and fitness goal and (2) whether they had indicated (earlier in the session) that they and their partner were similar or dissimilar in this goal domain. We predicted that participants who reported dissimilarities with their partner in the importance of health and fitness goals would respond to the primed goal by being less cooperative and accommodating in the hypothetical scenarios.

Participants were adult U.S. women who were currently in a romantic relationship. They began by answering questions about their personal goal pursuits. One such question asked participants to indicate whether they and their partner valued several goals equally, including career goals, family goals, and health and fitness goals. This item read, "When it comes to health and fitness goals…," and participants could choose one of three items: "My partner cares much less than I do"; "My partner and I care equally"; and "My partner cares much more than I do." Approximately 40% of participants indicated that they cared more about the goal than their partner; another 40% indicated they and their partner valued the goal equally; and the final 20% indicated that their partner cared more about the goal. We combined participants who said their partner cared either more or less about the goal into one group we term the "dissimilar" group. Participants who reported equal goal importance were termed the "similar" group. (Results for the two different "dissimilar" groups did not differ.)

Participants also completed a short scrambled sentence task (Srull & Wyer, 1979), in which they were randomly assigned to be exposed to words related to either health and fitness goal-relevant words (e.g., *fit, healthy*) or control words matched for valence (e.g., *book, artistic*) embedded in larger strings of neutral words. They also completed a scale designed to assess their desire to be cooperative and accommodating to their partners' preferences. The items were modeled after prior research on accommodative behaviors in relationships (Arriaga & Rusbult, 1998; Rusbult, Verette, Whitney, Slovik, & Lipkus, 1991) but were shortened to meet the requirements for online data collection. Participants read a scenario that presented them with a decision to either cooperate with their partners' interests or to refuse to do so (i.e., to be other- versus self-interested) and then chose one of four response options that varied in the extent to which they were positive and constructive. For example, one scenario read, "Imagine that your partner insisted on inviting a friend over to dinner, even though you don't like this friend. How likely would you be to engage in each of the following actions?" Participants chose from the following options: "I would refuse"; "I would protest but give in"; "I would grudgingly agree"; and "I would cheerfully agree." The other scenarios asked about participants' responses when their partners rented a movie they didn't want to see, forgot to run an important errand, and made a big mess at home. The scenarios were designed to be mundane examples of decisions members of couples make each day about how to respond when their interests do not coincide with their partners' interests.

As predicted, we found that for participants who reported that they and they partner held dissimilar values toward health and fitness goals, the goal prime led to less accommodating responses to the hypothetical scenarios. For participants who reported similar levels of caring about health and fitness goals, the goal prime did not affect their responses. Stated another way, within the control condition, there was no effect of similarity on accommodating responses; within the health goal prime condition, there was an effect of similarity, such that participants who perceived goal similarity with their partners reported more accommodating responses than did partners who perceived goal dissimilarity.

This study provides experimental support for the role of personal goal similarity in everyday relationship interactions and suggests one possible explanation of the link between similarity and conflict in the first four studies. When participants were reminded of a personal goal—in this case, health and fitness—they were less accommodating to the preferences of dissimilar (vs. similar) partners, in decisions completely unrelated to the health and fitness domain. They were less likely to agree to decisions that were in their partners' but not in their own interests, and they were more likely to say they would feel angry and get in a fight with their partners when those partners engaged in mundane negative acts. By demonstrating that the effect of similar goals is stronger when the personal goal itself is activated, and, relying on prior reports of the goal similarity, this study provides evidence for the causal role of personal goals in these effects—when the goal was not currently active, participants were equally accommodating to partners who shared and didn't share the goal.

FUTURE DIRECTIONS AND CONCLUSIONS

Thus, the current research provides support for the interdependence theory notion that dissimilar goal pursuits can predict daily conflict within interpersonal relationships. Five studies using varied measures and methodologies demonstrated that when partners do not value personal goals to the same degree they tend to report more occurrences of conflict within the relationship and more negative responses to potential conflicts and disagreements. Although these findings demonstrate that goal similarity, a previously neglected topic within research on relationship conflicts, is related to the occurrence of conflict, they leave many questions unanswered. Most importantly, the findings presented here offer intriguing evidence of some of the potential mechanisms underlying this link, like the depleting nature of interacting with someone who pursues different goals, but it is clear that there may be many other processes at work. Future research that experimentally manipulates some of the posited mechanisms would be particularly valuable.

One interesting extension of the current findings would be to examine how goal similarity and conflict relate across the duration of close relationships. Because personal goals are likely to change over the lifespan of an average relationship, it may particularly enlightening to examine the links between goals and relationships as goals change (Fitzsimons & Fishbach, 2010). For example, it is likely that some couples who once shared similar goals will encounter conflicts that have arisen due to changes in one or both partners' goals across time. As Holmes and Murray (1996) note, "The compatibility of important goals is best thought of as a moving window rather than a fixed quality of a relationship." As another example, couples that start out their relationship with dissimilar goals may well grow to possess more similar goals over time, either because both partners' goals grow together or because one partner adopts the other's goals.

Another important direction for future research is to examine the role of dissimilar relationship goals, like goals for increased intimacy versus independence, and dissimilar joint goals, like goals to buy a bigger house versus save money. Because outcomes are likely to be even more interdependent for such goals and because relationship-level factors have been shown to have an important effect on conflict behaviors (Simpson, Rholes, & Phillips, 1996) the effects of dissimilar relationship goals may be both pervasive and powerful.

Finally, although we presented the hypothesis that similar personal goals will reduce conflict, it is also quite conceivable that shared goals could promote conflict under some circumstances. If two partners share the same goal, there is an increased opportunity for social comparison and competition. Imagine that two partners both volunteer for the same charity and that both have goals to become leaders within the charity. Help, understanding, and support may increase, but so too might competition, resentment, and strife. One moderating variable that would determine the presence of these negative outcomes for similarity in personal goals would be the link between the partners' personal goals—whether success by one partner would imply failure by another. Such a link could be the result of objective characteristics of the situation (e.g., there can be only one charity president) or subjective characteristics brought by the partners (e.g., competitive or insecure partners may be likelier to feel negatively about their partner's successes). Future research examining these potential moderators would be particularly valuable.

These are only a few of the many avenues available for future research in this area. The effects of personal goal pursuits on interpersonal relationships, and, in turn, the effects of relationships on personal goal pursuits, are only beginning to be understood (Finkel & Fitzsimons, forthcoming; Fitzsimons & Finkel, in press; see also Chapters 2 and 6 in this volume). However, the current research presents an important step forward in our research on this interplay of self-regulatory and relational processes. In all of our prior work (e.g., Fitzsimons & Bargh, 2003; Fitzsimons & Shah, 2008), we have focused on only one partner's goal pursuits and feelings about the relationship while acknowledging that such an approach is seriously limited, as real interactions involve two individuals' goal pursuits (see Rusbult, Finkel, & Kumashiro, 2009). In the current research, we try for the first time in our lab to examine the dyadic links between both partners' goals, a first step toward building a rich understanding of how these effects play out in real relationships.

REFERENCES

Arriaga, X. B., & Rusbult, C. E. (1998). Standing in my partner's shoes: Partner perspective-taking and reactions to accommodative dilemmas. *Personality and Social Psychology Bulletin, 24*, 927–948.

Baumeister, R. F. (1998). The self. In D. T. Gilbert, S. T. Fiske, & G. Lindzey (Eds.), *Handbook of social psychology* (4th ed., pp. 680–740). New York: McGraw-Hill.

Berscheid, E. (1983). Emotion. In H. H. Kelley, E. Berscheid, A. Christensen, J. H. Harvey, T. L. Huston, G. Levinger, et al. (Eds.), *Close relationships* (pp. 110–168). New York: Freeman.

Berscheid, E. (1991). The emotion-in-relationships model: Reflections and update. In W. Kessen, A. Ortony, & F.I.M. Craik (Eds.), *Memories, thoughts, and emotions: Essays in honor of George Mandler* (pp. 323–335). Hillsdale, NJ: Erlbaum.

Berscheid, E., & Ammazzalorso, H. (2001). Emotional experience in close relationships. In G. Fletcher & M. Clark (Eds.), *Blackwell handbook of social psychology* (Vol. 2: Interpersonal Processes, pp. 308–330). Oxford, United Kingdom: Blackwell.

Berscheid, E., & Walster, E. (1978). Issues in studying close relationships: Conceptualizing and measuring closeness. In C. Hendrick (Ed.), *Close relationships: Review of personality and social psychology* (Vol. 10, pp. 63–91). Newbury Park, CA: Sage.

Bohns, V. K., Lucas, G. M., Molden, D. C., Finkel, E. J., Coolsen, M. K., Kumashiro, M., et al. (2010). *When opposites fit: Increased relationship well-being from partner complementarity in regulatory focus.* Unpublished manuscript, University of Toronto.

Braiker, H. B., & Kelley, H. H. (1979). Conflict in the development of close relationships. In R. L. Burgess & T. L. Huston (Eds.), *Social exchange in developing relationships* (pp. 135–168). New York: Academic Press.

Brunstein, J. C., Dangelmayer, G., & Schultheiss, O. C. (1996). Personal goals and social support in close relationships: Effects on relationship mood and marital satisfaction. *Journal of Personality and Social Psychology, 71*, 1006–1019.

Buunk, B., & Bosman, J. (1986). Attitude similarity and attraction in marital relationships. *Journal of Social Psychology, 126*, 133–134.

Byrne, D. (1961). Interpersonal attraction and attitude similarity. *Journal of Abnormal and Social Psychology, 62*, 713–715.

Byrne, D. (1971). *The attraction paradigm.* New York: Academic Press.

Byrne, D., Clore, G. L., & Worchel, P. (1966). The effect of economic similarity-dissimilarity on interpersonal attraction. *Journal of Personality and Social Psychology, 4*, 220–224.

Dal Cin, S., Anderson, J. E., Holmes, J. G., & Young, S. B. (2010). *Accordance in personal goals and relationship outcomes.* Unpublished data, University of Waterloo.

Dalton, A., Chartrand, T. L., & Finkel, E. (2010). The depleted chameleon: Self-regulatory consequences of social asynchrony. *Journal of Personality and Social Psychology, 98,* 605–617.

Esterberg, K., Moen, P., & Dempster-McCain, D. (1994). Transition to divorce: A life-course approach to women's marital duration and dissolution. *Sociological Quarterly, 35,* 289–307.

Fehr, B., & Harasymchuk, C. (2005). The experience of emotion in close relationships: Toward an integration of the emotion-in-relationships and interpersonal script models. *Personal Relationships, 12,* 181–196.

Finkel, E. J., Campbell, W. K., Brunell, A. B., Dalton, A. N., Scarbeck, S. J., & Chartrand, T. L. (2006). High-maintenance interaction: Inefficient social coordination impairs self-regulation. *Journal of Personality and Social Psychology, 91,* 456–475.

Finkel, E. J., & Fitzsimons, G. M. (forthcoming). Effects of self-regulation on interpersonal relationships. In K. D. Vohs & R. F. Baumeister (Eds.), *Handbook of self-regulation* (2nd ed.).

Fishbach, A., Friedman, R. S., & Kruglanski, A. W. (2003). Leading us not into temptation: Momentary allurements elicit overriding goal activation. *Journal of Personality and Social Psychology, 84,* 296–309.

Fitzsimons, G. M., & Bargh, J. A. (2003). Thinking of you: Nonconscious pursuit of interpersonal goals associated with relationship partners. *Journal of Personality and Social Psychology, 84,* 148–163.

Fitzsimons, G. M., & Finkel, E. J. (forthcoming). Effects of interpersonal relationships on self-regulation. In K. D. Vohs & R. F. Baumeister (Eds.), *Handbook of self-regulation,* 2nd edition.

Fitzsimons, G. M., & Finkel, E. J. (in press). Interpersonal influences on self-regulation. *Current Directions in Psychological Science.*

Fitzsimons, G. M., & Fishbach, A. (2010). Shifting closeness: Interpersonal effects of personal goal progress. *Journal of Personality and Social Psychology, 98,* 535–549.

Fitzsimons, G. M., & Shah, J. Y. (2008). How goal instrumentality shapes relationship evaluations. *Journal of Personality and Social Psychology, 95,* 319–337.

Fitzsimons, G. M., & Shah, J. Y. (2009). Confusing one instrumental other for another: Goal effects on social categorization. *Psychological Science, 20,* 1468–1472.

Gaunt, R. (2006). Couple similarity and marital satisfaction: Are similar spouses happier? *Journal of Personality, 74,* 1401–1420.

Griffin, D., Murray, S., & Gonzalez, R. (1999). Difference score correlations in relationship research: A conceptual primer. *Personal Relationships, 6,* 505–518.

Holmes, J. G., & Murray, S. L. (1996). Conflict in close relationships. In E. T. Higgins & A. W. Kruglanski (Eds.), *Social psychology: Handbook of basic principles* (pp. 622–654). New York: Guilford.

Karney, B. R., & Bradbury, T. N. (1995). The longitudinal course of marital quality and stability: A review of theory, method, and research. *Psychological Bulletin, 118,* 3–34.

Kelley, H. H. (1979). *Personal relationships: Their structure and processes.* Hillsdale, NJ: Erlbaum.

Kelley, H. H., & Thibaut, J. (1978). *Interpersonal relations: A theory of interdependence.* New York: Wiley.

Kenny, D. A. (1994). *Interpersonal perception: A social relations analysis.* New York: Guilford.

Kenny, D. A., & Acitelli, L. K. (1994). Measuring similarity in couples. *Journal of Family Psychology, 8,* 417–431.

Luo, S., & Klohnen, E. C. (2005). Assortative mating and marital quality in newlyweds: A couple-centered approach. *Journal of Personality and Social Psychology, 88,* 304–326.

Messick, D. M., & Brewer, M. B. (1983). Solving social dilemmas. In L. Wheeler & P.R. Shaver (Eds.), *Review of Personality and Social Psychology* (Vol. 4, pp. 11–44). Beverly Hills, CA: Sage.

Meyer, J. P., & Pepper, S. (1977). Need compatibility and marital adjustment in young married couples. *Journal of Personality and Social Psychology, 35*, 331–342.

Montoya, R. M., Horton, R., & Kirchner, J. (2008). Is actual similarity necessary for attraction? A meta-analysis of actual and perceived similarity. *Journal of Social and Personal Relationships, 25*, 889–922.

Morry, M. M. (2005). Relationship satisfaction as a predictor of similarity ratings: A test of the attraction–similarity hypothesis. *Journal of Social and Personal Relationships, 22*, 561–584.

Morry, M. M. (2007). The attraction–similarity hypothesis among cross-sex friends: Relationship satisfaction, perceived similarities, and self-serving perceptions. *Journal of Social and Personal Relationships, 24*, 117–138.

Reis, H. T., Clark, M. S., & Holmes, J. G. (2004). Perceived partner responsiveness as an organizing construct in the study of intimacy and closeness. In D. Mashek & A. Aron (Eds.), *The handbook of closeness and intimacy* (pp. 201–225). Mahwah, NJ: Lawrence Erlbaum Associates.

Rosenbaum, M. E. (1986). The repulsion hypothesis: On the nondevelopment of relationships. *Journal of Personality and Social Psychology, 51*, 1156–1166.

Rusbult, C. E., Finkel, E. J., & Kumashiro, M. (2009). The Michelangelo Phenomenon. *Current Directions in Psychological Science, 18*, 305–309.

Rusbult, C. E., Martz, J. M., & Agnew, C. R. (1998). The investment model scale: Measuring commitment level, satisfaction level, quality of alternatives, and investment size. *Personal Relationships, 5*, 357–391.

Rusbult, C. E., Verette, J., Whitney, G. A., Slovik, L. F., & Lipkus, I. (1991). Accommodation processes in close relationships: Theory and preliminary empirical evidence. *Journal of Personality and Social Psychology, 60*, 53–78.

Simpson, J. A., Rholes, W. S., & Phillips, D. (1996). Conflict in close relationships: An attachment perspective. *Journal of Personality and Social Psychology, 71*, 899–914.

Srull, T. K., & Wyer, R. S. (1979). The role of category accessibility in the interpretation of information about persons: Some determinants and implications. *Journal of Personality and Social Psychology, 37*, 1660–1672.

Surra, C. A., & Longstreth, M. (1990). Similarity of outcomes, interdependence, and conflict in dating relationships. *Journal of Personality and Social Psychology, 59*, 501–516.

Wiltermuth, S. S., & Heath, C. (2009). Synchrony and cooperation. *Psychological Science, 20*, 1–5.

13

Silent Rage
When Being Ostracized Leads to Aggression

LISA ZADRO
University of Sydney

Pain can be alleviated by morphine but the pain of social ostracism cannot be taken away.

Derek Jarman (1994, p. 113)

INTRODUCTION

Over the past decade, there has been considerable debate as to whether being ostracized (being excluded and ignored; Williams, 2007) leads targets to behave in either a prosocial or antisocial manner toward others. Whereas some researchers have found that being explicitly rejected leads targets to behave in an aggressive manner toward either the source of ostracism or innocent bystanders (e.g., Twenge, Baumeister, DeWall, Ciarocco, & Bartels, 2007), others have found evidence suggesting that being excluded prompts targets to respond in ways that increase their opportunities for reinclusion (e.g., conforming; see Williams, Cheung, & Choi, 2000). Unraveling these contradictory findings has been the focus of recent research.

This chapter examines the possible psychological (i.e., primary need threat), contextual (i.e., relationship type and status), and emotional (i.e., negative affect and feelings of anger) factors that may motivate targets to enact punitive and vengeful behaviors as a consequence of being excluded and ignored. Factors that potentially moderate the consequences of exclusion are discussed in terms of whether they ameliorate or exacerbate aggressive reactions. Finally, the chapter introduces new experimental research using a novel ostracism paradigm, "O-Cam," a simulated Web conference that specifically investigates the forms of vengeance that targets of ostracism are willing to impose on sources.

THE FUNCTIONS OF OSTRACISM

Ostracism is often described as one of the most innocuous forms of interpersonal conflict and a preferable alternative to verbal or physical abuse (Williams, 2007; see also Chapters 4 and 6 in this volume). The virtues of silence are preached in proverbs, informing us that "silence is golden" and that "if you have nothing nice to say, say nothing at all." The very act of ostracizing another individual (i.e., the target of ostracism) simply involves not speaking to them or acknowledging their presence—there are no raised voices or physical blows. In fact, ostracism can be used in the presence of others with onlookers being none the wiser. The "benign" appearance of this tactic is why many institutions use forms of ostracism as punishment in preference to other methods of interpersonal conflict. For instance, schools typically advocate using time-out (i.e., physically removing the student from their peers) to discipline students as opposed to corporal punishment. Similarly, solitary confinement—a form of physical ostracism—is used as a means of punishing prisoners for infractions committed behind bars.

If we examine the ways that ostracism is used across different age groups, cultures, and species, it is apparent that all forms of ostracism have two broad goals. The first goal is to remove undesirable members from the group, particularly those who may harm or jeopardize the safety and well-being of the rest of the group. The very term *ostracism* comes from the ancient Athenian (488–487 B.C.) practice of exiling citizens whose dictatorial ambitions posed a threat to the democratic nature of the state (Zippelius, 1986). In modern times, we still remove members of society who harm others through imprisonment, which is an institutionalized form of exile. A beneficial consequence of removing undesirables is that the remaining members of the group often become more cohesive—they function as a stronger unit that benefits the group as a whole (Gruter & Masters, 1986; Williams, 2001). Thus, removing undesirable members ensures that the group (and indeed its values) remains safe and intact.

The second potential goal of ostracism is corrective, seeking to ensure that the target of ostracism changes their thoughts, feelings, or behaviors to become aligned with those of the rest of the group. In this regard, ostracism is used as a form of discipline or punishment; it gives recalcitrant members a glimpse of what it would be like without the support of the sources and hence what is in store for them if they do not comply with the group. There are many examples of ostracism being used as means of disciplining wayward group members. For instance, within romantic (or indeed other close interpersonal) relationships, individuals may use "the silent treatment" on their partner to punish them for actual or perceived wrongdoing, thereby discouraging the partner from behaving in the same way in future.

However, regardless of the reason, ostracism can have devastating consequences for the target. For animals, being ostracized by the group—and thus being removed from the protection of other members—will often lead to starvation and death (Goodall, 1986). For humans, the results of being ostracized by a source (individual or group) may not have such grave consequences on survival but may still have other devastating effects. For instance, there is considerable evidence to suggest that a loss of social support can have an adverse impact on health and well-being comparable to damaging health factors such as obesity, smoking, and high blood pressure (Kiecolt-Glaser, Cacioppo, Malarkey, & Glaser, 1992). A lack of social support can also delay recovery from illnesses and surgery and even hinder compliance with prescribed medical regimens (see Cobb, 1976).

Given the negative ramifications of losing group membership or social support—particularly if the source of ostracism is a partner or loved one—it is not surprising that targets tend to respond by changing their behavior to regain favor with the sources. In a series of interviews with targets and sources of long-term ostracism, Zadro (2004, 2009) found that targets often behaved in a prosocial and conciliatory fashion toward the sources of ostracism. Prosocial and conciliatory responses are designed to rectify or relieve the ostracism situation. Such responses include forgiveness seeking (i.e., apologizing to the source for any action that may have warranted the ostracism; for a discussion on why such tactics may have negative effects on targets, see Chapter 14 in this volume), discussion (i.e., trying to elicit a response from sources by speaking to them in a nonconfrontational manner), and ingratiation (i.e., attempts to elicit a conversation through flattery, pandering to the source's needs or wants, or purchasing items such as flowers or gifts). By carrying out prosocial and conciliatory strategies, the target aims to repair the relationship with the sources and thereby to put an end to any emotional or physiological pain they may have experienced during the ostracism episode.

Yet, despite the potentially adverse consequences to the target's health and well-being that may result from being ostracized, Zadro (2004, 2009) found that several targets of long-term ostracism responded in an antisocial and reactionary manner to being excluded and ignored. Specifically, these targets reported acting in a vengeful manner toward the sources of ostracism and even recounted instances where they had responded in an antisocial manner toward innocent bystanders.

Thus, there is anecdotal evidence that ostracism can lead to prosocial or antisocial responses in different situations. Yet why does ostracism lead to such diverse behavioral responses? Why do some targets try to appease the source whereas others retaliate and even attack innocent others? To answer these questions, it is first necessary to examine the potential psychological and emotional responses to ostracism; after all, it is these responses that provide an invaluable piece of the puzzle when trying to determine whether targets will respond in a pro- or antisocial manner when they are rejected and ignored (see also Chapter 3 in this volume).

PSYCHOLOGICAL EFFECTS OF BEING OSTRACIZED: THE EFFECTS OF OSTRACISM ON PRIMARY NEEDS

Williams's (1997, 2001) model of ostracism predicts that ostracism (compared with other forms of interpersonal conflict) has the potential to threaten four fundamental human needs: belonging, control, self-esteem, and meaningful existence—an assertion that has been supported by over a decade of empirical investigation (see Williams, 2007 for review). Targets are motivated (behaviorally, emotionally, and cognitively) to refortify these lost or threatened needs. However, if the ostracism episode is prolonged or if the target is repeatedly excluded and ignored by the sources, the threatened needs become internalized leading to detrimental psychological and health-related consequences (see Zadro, 2004).

The desire to regain the primary needs threatened during ostracism plays an important motivating force in determining whether targets respond in a prosocial /conciliatory or an antisocial/reactionary manner. Regaining a sense of belongingness, for instance, would first entail trying to regain one's membership in the group (or, if the target is being ostracized by a partner or loved one, to regain one's place in the partnership). To best pursue this goal, targets may first try to behave in an affiliative manner toward sources (i.e., by enacting tactics such as ingratiation, discussion, and forgiveness seeking). If these attempts to repair the relationship are unsuccessful, the target could also try to affiliate with new individuals or groups to regain a sense of belongingness. In contrast, attempts to regain the remaining needs (i.e., control, self-esteem, and meaningful existence) could easily lend themselves to more antisocial and reactionary actions. For instance, targets may lash out verbally or physically to regain control over others or their environment; targets whose self-esteem has been adversely affected by being ignored may try to bolster their own feelings of self-worth by denigrating others; if a target feels invisible, as is often the case when one's sense of meaningful existence is threatened, acting in an aggressive fashion—picking a fight, yelling an insult— will ensure that the person will receive attention, even though this attention is essentially negative.

Several factors may determine whether targets regain their needs using antisocial methods. Although all four primary needs are threatened, there may be individual differences in the way that targets prioritize the reestablishment of these needs. For instance, picture an ostracism situation whereby a target is being excluded and ignored at their workplace by a fellow employee. Although the ostracism episode may threaten all four of the target's primary needs, the target's desire to regain control of the situation—and hence regain social standing among others in the office—may actually be a greater priority to the target than regaining a sense of belonging (i.e., by repairing the relationship with the source), particularly if the relationship with the source is fairly superficial and the target has a strong support network outside of the office. This desire to regain control may possibly lend itself to behaving antisocially toward the source.

The prioritization of needs may also be a product of preexisting trait differences among targets. For instance, those with preexisting low levels of one or more of the primary needs (e.g., low self-esteem) may try harder to regain that need once it has been further threatened by ostracism. Other individual differences, such as attachment style, may also cause some targets to prioritize the regaining of certain needs after being ostracized; this may be particularly the case with anxiously attached individuals who have a particular fear of rejection (see Chapter 2 in this volume).

Gender may also play a role in the extent to whether targets regain their needs in an antisocial fashion. For instance, Williams and Sommer (1997) found that ostracized females worked comparatively harder on a collective task postostracism rather than a coactive task whereas ostracized males tended to socially loaf more during the collective task than during the coactive task. Williams and Sommer concluded that being ostracized motivated targets to try and regain their threatened needs; however, ostracized females attempted to regain a sense of belonging whereas males instead gave priority to regaining self-esteem or possibly a sense of control over their environment. In doing so, males responded in a less than prosocial fashion toward the group (i.e., social loafing).

Given the gender differences, and possibly also trait differences, that influence the ways in which targets prioritize regaining their threatened primary needs, it is not surprising that there are a range of possible anti- and prosocial reactions to ostracism.

THE ROLE OF EMOTIONS IN DETERMINING PROSOCIAL OR ANTISOCIAL RESPONSES TO OSTRACISM

Jean Jacques Rousseau (1712–1778) was once quoted as saying, "Absolute silence leads to sadness. It is the image of death." This sentiment is echoed by targets of long-term ostracism who report powerful emotional responses to being ostracized (Zadro, 2004, 2009). In addition to feeling sadness while being socially excluded, targets of long-term ostracism reported feeling a range of negative emotions including despair, loneliness, horror, anguish, helplessness, pain, shame, and anxiety. Almost all targets reported feeling angry after ostracism. For instance, one target who was repeatedly ignored by her daughter almost resorted to violence during a family holiday during which the daughter refused to speak or participate in any activities. She stated:

> I'm not violent. Well, I avoid violence like the plague. I grabbed her by the waist, and I thought, "Gee what am I doing?" I was actually going to throw her across the restaurant—I was that angry. That's how I was the whole time—I was angry the whole time.

The anecdotal findings suggesting a link between ostracism and negative affect have received some empirical support, including evidence that social exclusion leads to feelings of sadness and hurt feelings (e.g., Buckley, Winkel, & Leary, 2004; Chow, Tiedens, & Govan, 2008; however, for an exception, see Twenge, Cantanese, & Baumeister, 2002).

There is growing evidence that negative affective states often trigger adaptive cognitive, motivational, and behavioral reactions (see Chapter 8 in this volume). Yet how does negative affect fuel antisocial behaviors postostracism? According to Berkowitz (1990), negative affect has a primary role in the activation of thoughts and memories associated with anger as well as "rudimentary" feelings of anger. Indeed, targets in experimental studies of ostracism often reported feeling significantly angrier than those who were included in the ostracism paradigm (e.g.,

Chow et al., 2008; Zadro, Williams, & Richardson, 2004). Recently, researchers have begun to examine the link between anger and aggression postostracism. For instance, Chow et al. found that participants who reported feeling angrier after being ostracized during an Internet ball-tossing game (Cyberball; see Williams et al., 2000) were more likely to behave in an antisocial manner toward the sources of ostracism than those who reported feeling sad. Thus it seems that anger may promote antisocial reactions whereas sadness seems to produce more vigilant, attentive, and adaptive styles of responding.

Given the psychological and emotional trauma that targets suffer while being ostracized, it is not surprising that they may express their frustration, anger, and pain by behaving in an antisocial fashion. The question then becomes—whom do targets choose to be the focus of their antisocial actions?

"ALL ARE PUNISHED"?: WHO IS THE FOCUS OF POSTOSTRACISM AGGRESSION?

When targets respond to ostracism in an antisocial and reactionary fashion, they can potentially direct their actions toward three parties: (1) the source of ostracism (i.e., revenge or retaliation); (2) innocent bystanders (i.e., physical or verbal aggression); or (3) themselves (i.e., self-harm or self-defeating behaviors).

Aggressing Against Sources of Ostracism

Antisocial and reactionary acts that targets commit against sources of ostracism could be construed as acts of revenge or retaliation for being ostracized. There are several reasons targets may be motivated to seek out vengeance against those who have ostracized them. Walster, Walster, and Berscheid (1978) state that acts of revenge within interpersonal relationships may be motivated by the desire to restore equity in the relationship. In an ostracism situation, the target is at the complete mercy of the source; the source chooses when to ostracize the target and if or when he or she will stop the episode. By choosing to ostracize the target, the source has achieved complete power over the target and the relationship. Acts of vengeance may be one of the only ways the target could topple the source from his or her position of power, thereby redressing the equity imbalance in the relationship.

Revenge may also assist targets to regain lost or threatened primary needs. Specifically, revenge may allow targets to regain their sense of control by throwing off their role of "passive victim" (see Frijda, 2007) and instrumentally engaging in behaviors that increase control over the situation and over other people. Retaliatory action may also give the target some level of control over the future of their relationship with the sources, in the sense that acting in a retaliatory fashion may help to discourage sources from ostracizing the target in subsequent conflict situations (see Pinker, 1997). Vengeful acts are designed to attract the attention of the source, which in turn will make the target feel less invisible and hence help restore a sense of meaningful existence (see Yoshimura, 2007). Revenge researchers have also found that vengeance is often motivated by a desire to regain self-worth, which would be attractive to targets of ostracism whose self-esteem has been thwarted by being socially excluded (e.g., McCullough, Bellah, Kilpatrick, & Johnson, 2001). However, while revenge may allow the target to regain a sense of control, self-esteem, and meaningful existence, depending on the nature of the vengeful act, it may further erode the target's relationship with the source—thereby further thwarting the target's sense of belonging—and may even lead to further retaliation on behalf of the source.

Interviews with targets of long-term ostracism revealed that targets often engaged in antisocial or vengeful acts, usually as a means of eliciting a response from the source or as a way of venting their frustrations (Zadro, 2004, 2009). Although several targets reported using verbal abuse on sources, acts of physical abuse were (thankfully) rare; however, targets may have been reluctant to admit being violent even if it had occurred. Targets who did admit to using physical abuse resorted to this tactic after other tactics (such as forgiveness seeking or discussion) had failed.

The interviews provided a few, mild examples of physical aggression toward sources, but the media often highlights episodes of ostracism that have serious, and even lethal, consequences. Schoolyard shootings, such as that conducted at Columbine High School, are often retaliatory strikes by students who have been widely rejected by their peers. In a case study of school shootings in the United States between 1995 and 2001, Leary, Kowalski, Smith, and Phillips (2003) found that individuals who had rejected the shooter were typically targeted and were often among the victims.

Although few targets of long-term ostracism admitted to responding in a physically aggressive manner, it became apparent that targets rarely just sat back and allowed themselves to be repeatedly rejected and ignored without retaliating in some fashion. Some targets actively spoke about "getting revenge" for being subjected to lengthy episodes of silence, particularly when they perceived the episodes to be unwarranted. For some, getting revenge amounted to simple acts of reputation defamation (i.e., they spoke badly about the source to others). In contrast, other targets detailed elaborate and potentially harmful, revenge scenarios. Zadro (2009) conducted a focus group with four generations of Sicilian women to discuss their experiences as targets of relational ostracism (i.e., ostracism by their relationship partner). There were clear differences between the ways younger and older Sicilian women coped with the silent treatment. Younger Sicilian women tended to quickly curtail any ostracism attempts on the part of their spouse, usually through strong language and an explicit threat to leave the relationship if the silent treatment continued. However, for two reasons, these tactics were not available to most of the older women. First, they were in patriarchal relationships where their husbands held all power; in many cases, these women experienced physical abuse from their spouse and hence did not want to act in a way that would incite further abuse. Second, leaving the relationship was not an option; there were strong social sanctions against divorce, and the "shame" of such an act would then lead the women to be additionally ostracized by their friends and family.

Instead, older Sicilian women pursued active and very creative campaigns of revenge that operated under the sources' radar (which could be construed as campaigns of passive aggression; see Chapter 4 in this volume). In many instances, these campaigns continued for years—well after the ostracism episode. For instance, one target—an Italian woman in her late 50s—said that her husband had rejected her sexually 20 years earlier and had instigated a brief affair with a woman in his workplace. In return, the target punished her husband by adding more and more butter to his meals in the hopes of slowly elevating his cholesterol to painful (and possibly lethal?) levels. Another woman reported moving her husband's possessions around the home—keys, watch, tools—to the point where he started to wonder about his sanity. Older Sicilian women also spoke of acting "less positively" (rather than negatively) as a means of acting out against ostracism. Such acts included giving their husband a smaller piece of dessert than those received by the rest of the family rather than simply depriving him of dessert entirely or failing to invite his family around to visit as often as expected—a cardinal sin in an Italian household where family means everything. These acts were not conducted to gain the notice of the source; rather, they were performed so that the target would have the satisfaction of regaining their sense of control, and possibly even their self-esteem, after multiple acts of ongoing neglect and exclusion.

For some targets, "fighting fire with fire" becomes the best type of defense. These targets choose to simply ostracize the sources: either to give the source a taste of the emotional pain that the target has experienced ("[the silent treatment] is not something that I would usually do, but if [the source] is going to act like that toward you, well I can give as good as a I get") or to simply get the source's attention. Other targets resorted to retaliatory ostracism when they no longer cared to pursue a relationship with the source.

There has been considerable experimental research examining the ways that targets perceive sources of ostracism. Typically, sources of ostracism were viewed as less likeable (Pepitone & Wilpizeski, 1960) and generally rated unfavorably (Geller, Goodstein, Silver, & Sternberg, 1974) and were rarely rewarded by the target in subsequent tasks (Geller et al.).

Recent studies have focused on examining whether being ostracized leads to antisocial responses toward ostracizers. For instance, Bourgeois and Leary (2001) found that participants who were rejected tended to derogate their ostracizers, which supports anecdotal evidence of reputation defamation postostracism. According to Bourgeois and Leary, derogation of ostracizers can serve an adaptive function because it diminishes the desire to be accepted by the source and hence reduces the potential impact of ostracism on the target's psychological well-being.

Aggressing Against Bystanders and Observers

Targets of ostracism do not always take out their anger and frustration on the source of ostracism. Instead, there is anecdotal evidence suggesting that targets will often lash out at innocent bystanders. This may seem counterproductive; after all, affiliating with a new person provides targets with the opportunity to regain primary needs, particularly their sense of belonging. However, according to the interviews with long-term targets and sources of ostracism (Zadro, 2004), targets often direct their ire toward nonsources. Behaving in an antisocial manner toward others rather than the source may occur for a variety of reasons. For instance, if targets do not want to further jeopardize their relationship with the source, then they may take out their frustration on others. Similarly, targets may abuse innocent third parties if there is a power disparity between the target and the source and the cost of direct retaliation is far too high. For instance, one long-term target reported that his employer had ignored him for several weeks, refusing to speak to him directly and excluding him from memos and interoffice emails. Although the target was angry and frustrated by his employer's behavior, he could not act on his feelings because he was terrified that he would lose his job. Instead, his family bore the brunt of his anger; he was verbally abusive and short-tempered to his wife and children (Zadro, 2009).

Behaving in an antisocial and reactionary manner toward third parties may allow a target not only to vent negative emotions such as anger but also to regain thwarted primary needs. For instance, targets may regain a sense of control over others and their environment by taking out their anger on those around them. They may also increase their feelings of self-worth by focusing on the shortcomings of others. As well as being cathartic, such behavior toward others will also get them attention, which will help them to regain their sense of meaningful existence.

Despite the possibility of regaining primary needs, there are evidently drawbacks to lashing out against a third party. If we return to the example of the businessman who took out his frustration and helplessness over being ostracized on his wife and family, it is clear that the target is jeopardizing his relationship with his wife and children by mistreating them. He is also further weakening his sense of belonging and his social support network in general by eroding his ties to his loved ones.

Several experimental studies have examined the ways that targets respond to strangers postostracism. For the most part, these studies indicate that targets of ostracism tend to exhibit prosocial or cooperative behaviors toward neutral or novel individuals (e.g., conforming to incorrect group judgments to better fit with the group; Williams & Sommer, 1997; Williams et al., 2000), suggesting that they are behaving in a manner that will promote inclusion and subsequent social connection (see Maner, DeWall, Baumeister, & Schaller, 2006). However, in these studies, targets were not given the opportunity to act in an aggressive fashion.

Much recent ostracism research examines whether targets will act in an antisocial and reactionary manner toward innocent bystanders (e.g., Twenge et al., 2001; Warburton, Williams, & Cairns, 2006. Typically, these studies have revealed that the link between ostracism and aggression is not clear-cut. For instance, Warburton et al. (2006) found that targets of ostracism only aggressed toward an innocent third party when the targets' sense of control had been further thwarted in a previous task. Targets whose sense of control had been restored were not more likely to aggress. These findings suggest that ostracism per se may not be sufficient to cause targets to aggress, particularly against someone who is not the source of ostracism. Instead, a trigger is needed—in this instance, a further loss of control—to elicit an antisocial and reactionary response.

In other studies assessing antisocial behavior postostracism, the "innocent bystander" is not all that innocent—that is, the bystander often provokes the target in some way that in turn elicits an antisocial and reactionary response. In a series of studies, Twenge, Baumeister, Tice, and Stucke (2001) examined whether social exclusion leads to forms of aggressive behavior. They found that participants who had been rejected acted aggressively toward another participant who had insulted or provoked them. In only one study did the researchers find that the targets also acted aggressively toward an innocent bystander. Yet, tellingly, targets of social exclusion were not more aggressive to a bystander who praised them.

When examining real-life instances of violence precipitated by rejection, both bystanders and sources may be subjected to antisocial acts. For instance, the journal entries of the Columbine High School massacre gunmen Eric Harris and Dylan Klebold revealed that being continually ostracized and rejected by fellow classmates was a key causal factor in their decision to open fire on students and staff. Although sources would have been involved in the ostracism, some of the people shot were probably innocent of any wrongdoing (see Leary et al., 2003).

Recent studies have aimed to compare the response of targets toward both sources and innocent bystanders. For instance, in a study by Zadro et al. (2010), participants were ostracized, included, or ostracized then reincluded during a game of Cyberball. They then participated in a Resource Dilemma task (see Hardy & van Vugt, 2006; see also Chapter 15 in this volume), whereby participants were asked to indicate how much of a 100-cent resource they would allocate to the other players and to themselves. This task allowed participants to behave ingratiatingly, cooperatively, or antisocially toward either the individuals they had just played Cyberball with or two new players. When compared with included participants in the Cyberball task, ostracized participants behaved more antisocially when playing with the sources of ostracism (i.e., they allocated almost two-thirds of the resource to themselves, leaving little in the resource to split among the sources) but in an ingratiating manner when playing with new players (i.e., they took less than a third of the resource for themselves, leaving a lot more of the resource to split among the new players). Neither of these behaviors was observed in reincluded targets, as their thwarted needs were somewhat refortified when sources reaccepted them into the game.

Aggression Against the Target: Self-Harm Postostracism

The literature often fails to acknowledge that targets of ostracism can turn their negative feelings, their frustrations, and their thwarted needs inward, internalizing the cause of ostracism and effectively punishing themselves for the ostracism incident. This reaction is common among targets who have experienced prolonged periods of ostracism or who have been repeatedly ignored by multiple sources (Zadro, 2004, 2009). These threatened needs often manifest in self-destructive thoughts ("I often think to myself, 'When is this going to end?'"; "I've thought of suicide"). Unfortunately, many targets often act on these self-destructive thoughts, leading to a host of self-harm behaviors including promiscuity, alcoholism and drug addiction, self-mutilation, and even suicide attempts (Zadro, 2004).

The negative, self-defeating behaviors demonstrated by long-term targets of ostracism are also evident—in lesser form—in laboratory manipulations of ostracism and rejection. For instance, in a series of studies, Twenge et al. (2002) found that participants who were told that they would have a future devoid of social bonds were more likely to engage in various forms of self-defeating behavior including increased risk taking (e.g., betting on a long shot rather than a safer option) and engaging in fewer health-enhancing behaviors (e.g., choosing to eat a candy bar rather than a muesli bar). Thus, the threat of social exclusion led to the pursuit of activities that have pleasurable short-term effects but, ultimately, aversive long-term consequences.

THE MODERATORS OF OSTRACISM: FACTORS THAT MAY PRECIPITATE OR CURTAIL THE DESIRE TO ACT AGGRESSIVELY

There is considerable evidence suggesting that being ostracized has an adverse effect on primary needs and affect. According to Berkowitz (1990), once negative affect has activated the cognitive constructs associated with anger and aggression, individuals begin to think about possible "attributions, appraisals, and schematic conceptions that can then intensify, suppress, enrich, or differentiate the initial reaction" (p. 494). This second phase—whereby targets go through the "suppression" or "enrichment" of the negative or aggressive affect that has arisen from the ostracism incident—is essential for understanding why some targets choose to act in an antisocial and reactionary manner postostracism; specifically, it is at this stage that various moderating factors come into play, whether singularly or in combination.

Numerous factors may, either singularly or in combination, moderate the effects of ostracism. First, specific aspects of the ostracism episode may determine whether a target responds in an antisocial and reactionary fashion. For instance, the physical location of the episode may facilitate or inhibit antisocial responses. Unlike physical or verbal abuse, ostracism can be used by sources in public, often without observers even noticing that it is occurring. If an ostracism episode occurs in public, however, it would be difficult for a target to respond in an antisocial fashion (particularly in a physically aggressive fashion) without attracting the attention of onlookers—unless the target is so desperate for attention that even negative attention is considered preferable to being ignored.

Second, the identity of the source may also be an important moderating variable. Many targets stated that it was "easier," and far less aversive, to be ignored by a stranger than a loved one (Zadro, 2004). When ostracized by a loved one, targets typically expressed a desire to preserve their relationship with the source. Hence, they typically tried to act in an affiliative manner to ensure that the episode ended as quickly as possible and the relationship remained intact. Targets were typically less mindful of their relationship with an ostracizing stranger or acquaintance; thus, if given a sufficient trigger, targets may be more likely to act in an antisocial fashion when ostracized by strangers rather than by loved ones. Laboratory studies have found that the identity of the source typically does not moderate the immediate consequences of ostracism; that is, being ignored by a computer versus a human (Zadro, Williams, & Richardson, 2004) or by a despised out-group (i.e., the KKK; Gonsalkorale & Williams, 2007) does not moderate the deleterious effects of ostracism on the four primary needs.

There is, however, some evidence that the identity of the source may moderate affective responses. For instance, Zadro et al. (2004) found that targets who were ostracized during Cyberball by a computer-generated player reported feeling significantly angrier than those who had been ostracized by a human player. If targets feel angrier when ostracized by specific sources, then it is possible that this anger may manifest in antisocial reactions, particularly if there are further environmental triggers.

Third, the number of sources may also be a moderating factor. When ostracized by a single source, targets have the opportunity to regain threatened needs by affiliating with others in their social support network. When ostracized by multiple sources, or sources in different environments (e.g., if targets are given the silent treatment by their partner at home as well as by their colleagues at work), there may be fewer opportunities to regain thwarted needs and, hence, a greater risk that lost needs will be internalized. Long-term targets who were ostracized by multiple targets were more likely to make internal attributions for the ostracism episodes ("It's all my fault!"; Zadro, 2004). This prompted some targets to respond in an antisocial and destructive fashion; that is, they attempted to restore lost social bonds by aligning themselves with unsavory or unscrupulous others (e.g., joining gangs). In some instances, targets of multiple sources feel sufficiently angry and disenfranchised to retaliate aggressively against their ostracizers (e.g., in the case of the various U.S. schoolyard shootings where shooters felt rejected and excluded by their peers; see Leary et al., 2003). Targets may also turn their aggression inward and commit acts of self-harm—for instance, engaging in promiscuous behavior as a means of feeling wanted and loved or indulging in alcohol and recreational drugs as a means of escaping the problem. The devastation of being ignored by so many is clearly evident in the following letter sent by a young woman in her 20s who was ignored by her school peers (Zadro, 2004):

> In high school, the other students thought me weird and never spoke to me. I tell you in all honesty that at one stage they refused to speak to me for 153 days, not one word at all.... That was a very low point for me in my life and on the 153rd day, I swallowed 29 Valium pills. (p. 61)

Fourth, the causal clarity of the ostracism episode may also fuel antisocial responses. For instance, if targets know why they are being ignored, they can focus their attention on pursuing tactics that rectify the situation and that are more likely to lead to reacceptance (e.g., ingratiation or discussion that focuses on apologizing). However, if targets are unaware of why they are being ignored, then the helplessness and frustration felt in such a situation may fuel an aggressive response, particularly if there is a further trigger to elicit aggressive behavior toward the sources or innocent bystanders (e.g., they experience a further loss of control).

Finally, the length of the ostracism episode may also contribute to antisocial responses postostracism. According to the social reconnection hypothesis, exclusion motivates targets to forge social bonds with others only to the extent that they can realistically provide social reconnection (Maner et al., 2006). At the onset of ostracism, targets typically use strategies that they believe will appease the source (i.e., discussion or ingratiation). If these are unsuccessful and the ostracism episode stretches indefinitely, targets may view the prospect of future interaction as increasingly hopeless and may thus act in a vengeful fashion in a desperate attempt to have their existence acknowledged.

Just as a host of situational factors may moderate antisocial and reactionary responses to ostracism, individual differences are sure to play a role in postostracism responses. Although little research to date has specifically examined the role of individual differences in moderating antisocial responses to ostracism (for an exception, see Buckley et al., 2004), researchers have found that individual differences such as social anxiety (e.g., Oaten, Jones, Williams, & Zadro, 2008; Zadro, Boland, & Richardson, 2006), and self-esteem (e.g., Nezlek, Kowalski, Leary, Blevins, & Holgate, 1997), do moderate targets' responses to being socially excluded and rejected. Future research needs to explore the extent and ways individual differences, coupled with situational changes, moderate responses to ostracism. By understanding the role of moderating factors (singularly and in combination) in determining postostracism aggression, we can begin to develop strategies that will not only curtail the effects of ostracism but potentially will veer targets away from responding antisocially.

OSTRACISM AND REVENGE: A NEW PROGRAM OF RESEARCH

Recently, we have begun to conduct a series of studies that examine the range of vengeful and retaliatory behaviors that targets are willing to conduct against sources of ostracism (see Goodacre, 2007; Goodacre & Zadro, 2010). Unlike previous studies, we do not focus solely on physical aggression but rather see it as only one aspect of the possible arsenal of antisocial and retaliatory behaviors at the target's disposal.

To assess the effects of ostracism on revenge and retaliation, we created a new paradigm—O-Cam—a simulated Webcam conference that takes place between the target and two students from a local university. During this Web conference, the target is informed that each student will give a brief, prewritten speech about university life. Although the paradigm has the appearance of a real Web-based interaction, the "students" are actually actors whose actions have been prerecorded. Two O-Cam conditions are prerecorded: one where the students appear to listen to the target as the target makes a speech (the inclusion condition); and another where the students appear to listen to the target's speech for 30 seconds and then turn to each other and begin having a conversation, completely ignoring the target (the ostracism condition). A demonstration of the paradigm can be seen at http://www.psych.usyd. edu.au/research/ostracism/ (Username: guest; Password: Bach). Unlike other social exclusion and ostracism paradigms, O-Cam allows participants to be ostracized in the physical presence of the sources of ostracism yet requires no confederates to participate during the task. We hypothesized that being able to watch the sources of ostracism as they interact together during the ostracism episode (all the while ignoring the target) would elicit strong, emotional responses in the target.

Unlike previous studies, which typically use a single indicator of antisocial behavior (e.g., the "hot sauce allocation" measure of physical aggression used by Warburton et al., 2006), the current study examined several aspects of revenge and retaliation. The construct of revenge and retaliation was assessed using a new measure based on research by Yoshimura (2007) on the different categories of vengeance behaviors. Specifically, the questionnaire examined participants' desire to engage in four common revenge and retaliation type behaviors: (1) active distancing (i.e., removing oneself from the physical presence of the sources); (2) reputation defamation (i.e., attempts to reduce the target's positive public image); (3) physical aggressiveness (i.e., attempts to cause the target physical discomfort, emotional distress or pain); and (4) resource removal (i.e., withholding rewards from the sources; for psychometric properties of the questionnaire, see Goodacre, 2007).

Overall, the findings suggest that ostracized participants endorsed acts of active distancing, reputation defamation, and resource removal significantly more than their included counterparts. Yet they did not wish to behave in a more physically aggressive manner toward those who excluded them. This supports previous research that has found that ostracism alone is not sufficient to elicit physical aggression; rather, it requires a further trigger, such as a further loss of control, to elicit responses that induce a desire to cause bodily harm (e.g., Warburton et al., 2006).

Overall, these findings indicated that even a single brief exposure to ostracism, instigated by previously unknown peers across an electronic medium, is powerful enough to elicit antisocial behavior without provocation. It should be noted, however, that although ostracized targets sought to distance themselves from the sources of their rejection they also expressed an interest in connecting with a new group of people, indicating that ostracized targets are responding in a more complex fashion than previously expected, simultaneously acting in a pro- and antisocial manner as a means of attaining short-term benefits (i.e., vengeful acts that may give them a sense of temporary satisfaction) and long-term gains (i.e., seeking out new affiliative ties).

Our future studies will continue the search for triggers and moderators of aggression postostracism. Moreover, we hope to refine our behavioral measures; often the aggression measures used in social exclusion studies could be viewed as measures of condoned aggression—that is, participants are given permission to aggress by being told that they can give as much hot sauce or as many noise blasts (at whatever volume) that they wish. The target can rationalize that if the experimenter is allowing them to perform these actions then no real harm can come to the target. The aim is to find new ways of assessing antisocial and aggressive responses that are less contrived and parallel real-world to attain a richer understanding of the motivations behind postostracism aggression.

REFERENCES

Berkowitz, L. (1990). On the formation and regulation of anger and aggression: A cognitive–neoassociationistic analysis. *American Psychologist, 45,* 494–503.

Bourgeois, K. S., & Leary, M. R. (2001). Coping with rejection: Derogating those who choose us last. *Motivation and Emotion, 25*, 101–111.

Buckley, K. E., Winkel, R. E., & Leary M. R. (2004). Reactions to acceptance and rejection: Effects of level and sequence of relational evaluation. *Journal of Experimental Social Psychology, 40*, 14–28.

Chow, R. M., Tiedens, L. Z., & Govan, C. (2008). Excluded emotions: The role of anger in antisocial responses to ostracism. *Journal of Experimental Social Psychology, 44*, 896–903.

Cobb, S. (1976). Social support as a moderator of life stress. *Psychosomatic Medicine, 38*, 300–314.

Frijda, N. (2007). *The laws of emotion.* Cambridge, UK: Cambridge University Press.

Geller, D. M., Goodstein, L., Silver, M., & Sternberg, W. C. (1974). On being ignored: The effects of the violation of implicit rules of social interaction. *Sociometry, 37*, 541–556.

Goodacre, R. (2007). *O-Cam: A new social ostracism paradigm.* Unpublished honor's thesis, University of Sydney.

Goodacre, R., & Zadro, L. (2010). "O-Cam": A new paradigm for investigating the effects of ostracism. *Behavior Research Methods, 42*, 768–774.

Gonsalkorale, K., & Williams, K. D. (2007). The KKK won't let me play: Ostracism even by a despised outgroup hurts. *European Journal of Social Psychology, 37*, 1176–1186.

Goodall, J. (1986). Social rejection, exclusion, and shunning among the Gombe chimpanzees. *Ethology and Sociobiology, 7*, 227–236.

Gruter, M., & Masters, R. D. (1986). Ostracism as a social and biological phenomenon: An introduction. *Ethology and Sociobiology, 7*, 149–158.

Hardy, C., & Van Vugt, M. (2006). Giving for glory in social dilemmas: The competitive altruism hypothesis. *Personality and Social Psychology Bulletin, 32*, 1402–1413.

Jarman, D. (1994). *At your own risk: A saint's testament.* Minneapolis: University of Minnesota Press.

Kiecolt-Glaser, J. K., Cacioppo, J. T., Malarkey, W. B., & Glaser, R. (1992). Acute psychological stressors and short-term immune changes: What, why, for whom, and to what extent? *Psychosomatic Medicine, 54*, 680–685.

Leary, M. R., Kowalski, R. M., Smith, L., & Phillips, S. (2003). Teasing, rejection, and violence: Case studies of the school shootings. *Aggressive Behavior, 29*, 202–214.

Maner, J. K., DeWall, C. N., Baumeister, R. F., & Schaller, M. (2006). Does social exclusion motivate interpersonal reconnection? Resolving the "porcupine problem." *Journal of Personality & Social Psychology, 92*, 42–55.

McCullough, M. E., Bellah, C. G., Kilpatrick, S. D., & Johnson, J. L. (2001). Vengefulness: Relationships with forgiveness, rumination, well-being, and the Big Five. *Personality and Social Psychology Bulletin, 27*, 601–610.

Nezlek, J. B., Kowalski, R. M., Leary, M. R., Blevins, T., & Holgate, S. (1997). Personality moderators of reactions to interpersonal rejection: Depression and trait self-esteem. *Personality and Social Psychology Bulletin, 23*, 1235–1244.

Oaten, M., Jones, A., Williams, K. D., & Zadro, L. (2008). The effects of ostracism on self-regulation in the socially anxious. *Journal of Social and Clinical Psychology, 27*, 471–504.

Pepitone, A., & Wilpizeski, C. (1960). Some consequences of experimental rejection. *Journal of Abnormal and Social Psychology, 60*, 359–364.

Pinker, S. (1997). *How the mind works.* New York: W. W. Norton.

Twenge, J. M., Baumeister, R. F., DeWall, C. N., Ciarocco, N. J., & Bartels, J. M. (2007). Social exclusion decreases prosocial behavior. *Journal of Personality and Social Psychology, 92*, 56–66.

Twenge, J. M., Baumeister, R. F., Tice, D. M., & Stucke, T. S. (2001). If you can't join them beat them: Effects of social exclusion on aggressive behavior. *Journal of Personality and Social Psychology, 81*, 1058–1069.

Twenge, J. M., Catanese, K. R., & Baumeister, R. F. (2002). Social exclusion causes self-defeating behavior. *Journal of Personality and Social Psychology, 83*, 606–615.

Walster, E., Walster, G. W., & Berscheid, E. (1978). *Equity: Theory and research.* Boston: Allyn and Bacon.

Warburton, W. A., Williams, K. D., & Cairns, D. R. (2006). When ostracism leads to aggression: The moderating effects of control deprivation. *Journal of Experimental Social Psychology, 42*, 213–220.

Williams, K. D. (1997). Social ostracism. In R. M. Kowalski (Ed.), *Aversive interpersonal behaviors* (pp. 133–170). New York: Plenum.

Williams, K. D. (2001). *Ostracism: The power of silence.* New York: Guilford Press.

Williams, K. D. (2007). Ostracism. *Annual Review of Psychology, 58*, 425–452.

Williams, K. D., Cheung, K. T., & Choi, W. (2000). Cyberostracism: Effects of being ignored over the Internet. *Journal of Personality and Social Psychology, 79*, 748–762.

Williams, K. D., & Sommer, K. L. (1997). Social ostracism by coworkers: Does rejection lead to loafing or compensation? *Personality & Social Psychology Bulletin, 23*, 693–706.

Yoshimura, S. (2007). Goals and emotional outcomes of revenge activities in interpersonal relationships. *Journal of Social and Personal Relationships, 24*, 87–98.

Zadro, L. (2004). *Ostracism: Empirical studies inspired by real-world experiences of silence and exclusion.* Unpublished doctoral dissertation, University of New South Wales, Sydney.

Zadro, L. (2009). *Further interviews with targets and sources of long-term ostracism.* Unpublished manuscript, University of Sydney.

Zadro, L., Boland, C., & Richardson, R. (2006). How long does it last? The persistence of the effects of ostracism in the socially anxious. *Journal of Experimental Social Psychology, 42*, 692–697.

Zadro, L., Dale, E., Van Vugt, M., Griffiths, B., Richardson, R., Williams, K. D., et al. (2010). *To ingratiate or retaliate? An empirical investigation of the conditions that promote prosocial versus antisocial behaviours in ostracised targets.* Unpublished manuscript, University of Sydney.

Zadro, L., Williams, K. D., & Richardson, R. (2004). How low can you go? Ostracism by a computer is sufficient to lower self-reported levels of belonging, control, self-esteem, and meaningful existence. *Journal of Experimental Social Psychology, 40*, 560–567.

Zippelius, R. (1986). Exclusion and shunning as legal and social sanctions. *Ethology and Sociobiology, 7*, 159–166.

14

The Doormat Effect
On the Dangers of Resolving
Conflict via Unilateral Forgiveness

LAURA B. LUCHIES
Northwestern University

ELI J. FINKEL
Northwestern University

G iven enough time, close relationship partners are bound to experience conflicts in which one person hurts, angers, or upsets the other. How can they resolve such conflicts? Scholars and clinicians have designed and implemented several interventions to bolster victims' forgiveness of interpersonal transgressions (e.g., Hebl & Enright, 1993; Rye & Pargament, 2002; Worthington, Kurusu, Collins, Berry, Ripley, & Baier, 2000; for a review, see Wade & Worthington, 2005). These interventions share the assumption that bolstering victims' forgiveness will benefit the victims. In other words, forgiveness interventions assume that victims have control over their own outcomes: if they forgive, they will experience better outcomes than if they do not forgive.

Past research shows some support for this assumption. Forgiveness has been linked to improved psychological health, physical health, and relational well-being. For example, those who forgive tend to experience psychological health benefits such as greater life satisfaction and fewer psychological distress symptoms (Bono, McCullough, & Root, 2008; Orcutt, 2006). They also tend to experience physical health benefits such as better cardiac functioning and less physiological stress (McCullough, Orsulak, Brandon, & Akers, 2007; Waltman, Russell, Coyle, Enright, Holter, & Swoboda, 2009). Finally, they tend to experience relational benefits such as greater closeness and commitment to their perpetrators as well as enhanced conflict resolution, which predicts subsequent relationship quality (Hannon, Rusbult, Finkel, & Kumashiro, 2010; Tsang, McCullough, & Fincham, 2006).

However, might perpetrators also have control over victims' outcomes? That is, might perpetrators' behavior, in tandem with victims' behavior, affect the quality of victims' outcomes following betrayals such as ostracism (see Chapters 3 and 13 in this volume), harm toward a loved one (see Chapter 10 in this volume), or nasty feedback (see Chapter 10 in this volume)? McCullough (2008) recently argued that forgiveness evolved to help people preserve their valuable relationships. We posit that, when forgiveness helps victims preserve a relationship that is likely to be valuable to them in the future, it leads to positive outcomes for the victim, but when it preserves a relationship that is unlikely to be valuable it leads to negative outcomes.

What determines whether a continued relationship between the victim and the perpetrator is likely to be valuable? The perpetrator's behavior. At a dispositional level, perpetrators can indicate that a continued relationship is likely to be valuable for their victims by behaving in an agreeable manner. At a conflict-specific level, one way perpetrators can indicate that a continued relationship is likely to be valuable for their victims is by "making up for" their offenses. Indeed, past research has shown that agreeableness predicts perpetrators' amend-making behavior: highly agreeable individuals act in a prosocial, constructive manner during interpersonal conflicts (Jensen-Campbell & Graziano, 2001) and are more likely than their less agreeable counterparts to accept responsibility and make reparation after committing a betrayal (Chiaramello, Sastre, & Mullet, 2008). According to this analysis, scholars and practitioners who have, explicitly or implicitly, suggested that forgiveness is uniformly good for victims might have oversimplified the story because victims do not have complete control over their own outcomes. Rather, the consequences of victims' forgiveness hinge on their perpetrators' behavior.

INTERDEPENDENCE THEORY: THREE TYPES OF CONTROL OVER OUTCOMES

Interdependence Theory (Kelley & Thibaut, 1978; Kelley et al., 2003; Thibaut & Kelley, 1959) provides a framework for understanding the control two individuals have over their own and each others' outcomes, and this framework can be applied to the control victims and perpetrators have over victims' outcomes. Following a betrayal, perpetrators may or may not make amends and victims may or may not forgive. Victims' outcomes for each combination of their own and their perpetrators' behavior can be plotted in a 2 × 2 table, as illustrated in Figure 14.1. (Perpetrators' outcomes can be included in the table as well, although we focus only on victims' outcomes because we seek to address the extant literature's focus on victims' outcomes.)

In interdependence terminology (Kelley et al., 2003), *actor control* (formerly called "reflexive control") is the amount of control one has over one's own outcomes. The amount of actor control victims have over their own outcomes can be derived by calculating the average difference between the victims' outcomes in the "Forgive" column and the victims' outcomes in the "Do Not Forgive" column—that is, ((A +

Victim

		Forgive	Do Not Forgive
Perpetrator	Make Amends	**A**	**B**
	Do Not Make Amends	**C**	**D**

Actor Control =   ((A + C) – (B + D)) / 2
Partner Control =   ((A + B) – (C + D)) / 2
Joint Control =   ((A + D) – (B + C)) / 2

Figure 14.1   How to calculate actor control, partner control, and joint control over victims' postconflict outcomes.

C) – (B + D)) / 2. Actor control is analogous to the main effect victim forgiveness has on victims' outcomes. *Partner control* (formerly called "fate control") is the amount of control one's partner has over one's outcomes. The amount of partner control perpetrators have over victims' outcomes can be derived by calculating the average difference between the victims' outcomes in the "Make Amends" row and the victims' outcomes in the "Do Not Make Amends" row—that is, ((A + B) – (C + D)) / 2. Partner control is analogous to the main effect perpetrator amends has on victims' outcomes. *Joint control* (formerly called "behavior control") is the amount of control one's self and one's partner jointly have over one's outcomes. The amount of joint control victims and perpetrators have over victims' outcomes can be derived by calculating the average difference between the victims' outcomes in the upper-left and lower-right cells and the victims' outcomes in the upper-right and lower-left cells—that is, ((A + D) – (B + C)) / 2. Joint control is analogous to the interaction effect between victim forgiveness and perpetrator amends on victims' outcomes. This framework can be used to determine the amount of actor, partner, and joint control victims and perpetrators have over victims' outcomes and can thereby shed light on the potential dangers of unilateral forgiveness interventions, which frequently assume that victims' outcomes are determined primarily by actor control.

A REVIEW OF RECENT EVIDENCE OF JOINT CONTROL OVER VICTIMS' POSTCONFLICT OUTCOMES

A series of four recent studies investigated the interactive effects of victims' and perpetrators' behavior on victims' outcomes (Luchies, Finkel, McNulty, & Kumashiro, 2010); all four studies examined these conflict dynamics between partners in close, attachment-bonded relationships (see Chapters 2, 6, and 12 in this volume) rather than in negotiations between nonclose interactants (see Chapters 5 and 7 in this volume). We review this program of research, which includes two longitudinal studies (the first and fourth studies) and two experimental studies (the second and third studies) that examine the effects of victim forgiveness and perpetrator amends on victims' postconflict self-respect and self-concept clarity. As explained already, forgiveness interventions assume that victims' outcomes are primarily subject to actor control. In contrast, we expect that victims and perpetrators share joint control over victims' outcomes. That is, we hypothesize that the effect of forgiving on one's self-respect and self-concept clarity depends on the perpetrator's behavior: when the perpetrator has made amends, we expect that forgiveness will bolster one's self-respect and self-concept clarity. But when the perpetrator has not made amends, we expect that forgiveness will diminish one's self-respect and self-concept clarity.

FORGIVENESS TENDENCIES AND PARTNER AGREEABLENESS JOINTLY PREDICT TRAJECTORIES OF SELF-RESPECT

The first study was a longitudinal investigation in which both members of 72 recently married couples completed up to nine questionnaires over the first 5 years of marriage. At the beginning of the study, participants reported (1) their tendency to forgive their spouse by imagining themselves in five situations that described their spouse transgressing against them (e.g., snapping at and insulting the self, lying about inappropriate behaviors with someone of the opposite sex) and indicated the extent to which they would feel and express forgiveness in each situation; (2) their agreeableness (e.g., "I take time out for others," "I feel little concern for others" [reversed]); and (3) their self-respect ("I wish I could have more respect for myself" [reversed]). Every 6–8 months following the initial assessment, participants completed additional reports of their self-respect. Although the extent to which perpetrators act in an agreeable manner is not our focal measure of perpetrator behavior, agreeableness has been linked with acting in a prosocial, constructive manner during interpersonal conflicts (Jensen-Campbell & Graziano, 2001) and with seeking forgiveness (Chiaramello et al., 2008), which includes accepting responsibility and making reparation after committing a betrayal (Sandage, Worthington, Hight, & Berry, 2000). Because agreeable individuals tend to make amends, we use agreeableness as a proxy for amends in this study.

We conducted growth curve analyses (cf. Singer & Willett, 2003) to assess the associations of forgiveness and partner agreeableness with linear self-respect trajectories. Specifically, we predicted changes in participants' self-respect over time from their tendency to forgive their spouse, their spouse's agreeableness, time, and the interaction terms among these variables. Looking first at the main effects of victims' and perpetrators' behavior, in turn, on victims' outcomes, there were no significant main effects of forgiveness or spouse agreeableness on trajectories of victims' self-respect. Thus, there was no evidence that victims have actor control or that perpetrators have partner control over changes in victims' self-respect over time.

Turning to the interaction effect of victims' behavior and perpetrators' behavior on victims' outcomes, the trajectory of self-respect for participants who reported a strong tendency to forgive their spouse depended on their spouse's agreeableness. Highly forgiving participants whose spouse reported high levels of agreeableness experienced increases in self-respect over time. In contrast, highly forgiving participants whose spouse reported low levels of agreeableness experienced decreases in self-respect over time. Thus, victims and perpetrators shared joint control over changes in victims' self-respect over time.

Although these findings are consistent with the idea that victims and perpetrators share joint control over victims' self-respect, this study did not provide the experimental evidence necessary to conclude that forgiveness and perpetrator behavior caused the observed changes in self-respect over time. In addition, it did not examine whether victims' self-concept clarity follows the same pattern as their self-respect. Finally, it used an indirect measure of amends. We designed the next study to address these limitations.

EXPERIMENTALLY MANIPULATED PERCEPTIONS OF FORGIVENESS AND AMENDS JOINTLY AFFECT SELF-RESPECT AND SELF-CONCEPT CLARITY

The second study was an experiment in which 49 undergraduates received false feedback (using a procedure we adapted from Karremans, Van Lange, Ouwerkerk, & Kluwer, 2003) regarding the extent to which they have forgiven and the extent to which their perpetrator has made amends for a specific, real-life betrayal. Participants were asked to recall a recent incident in which a close other hurt, angered, or upset them. After providing a description of the incident, participants typed in the first name of the perpetrator and answered questions about the extent to which the perpetrator had made amends.

Then, participants read about the bogus "forgiveness test," which they were told would assess the extent to which they had forgiven their perpetrator. The forgiveness test capitalized on the experiential validity of the Implicit Association Test (IAT; Greenwald, McGhee, & Schwartz, 1998), which was originally developed to assess people's implicit associations between categories by comparing their reaction times when categorizing words or images from target categories in different blocks of trials. The categories used in the forgiveness test were (1) the perpetrator's first name and other first names and (2) words with positive valence (e.g., *love, acceptance*) and words with negative valence (e.g., *hate, rejection*). In one block of trials, participants were instructed to press the same key when presented with positive words and the perpetrator's name. In another block, they were instructed to press the same key when presented with negative words and the perpetrator's name.

After completing this bogus forgiveness test, participants read that, when a person has forgiven a perpetrator, associations between positive words and the name of the perpetrator are stronger than associations between negative words and the name of the perpetrator. But when a person has not completely forgiven the perpetrator, associations between negative words and the name of the perpetrator are stronger. Then, they read that these associations can be measured through reaction times. Next, rather than scoring participants' actual performance on the forgiveness test, we instead gave them false feedback regarding their reaction times. Participants in the low forgiveness condition were told that they responded faster in the block of trials in which they responded with the same key to negative words and the name of the perpetrator than in the block of trials in which they responded with the same key to positive words and the name of the perpetrator, which indicates that they have not completely forgiven the perpetrator. Participants in the high forgiveness condition were told that they responded faster in the block of trials in which they responded with the same key to positive words and the name of the perpetrator than in the block of trials in which they responded with the same key to negative words and the name of the perpetrator, which indicates that they have largely forgiven the perpetrator.

Next, participants received false feedback regarding their responses to the questions they had answered earlier in the study about the extent to which their perpetrator had made amends. Participants in the weak amends condition were told that, compared with others who had previously participated in the study, their responses indicated that the extent to which their perpetrator had made amends was in the 17th percentile, which means that their perpetrator has made only weak amends. Participants in the strong amends condition were told that their responses indicated that the extent to which their perpetrator had made amends was in the 83rd percentile, which means that their perpetrator has made strong amends.

Following these manipulations, participants completed measures of self-respect and self-concept clarity ("I have a lot of respect for myself" and "I have a clear sense of who I am and what I am," respectively). Next, participants completed manipulation checks assessing the extent to which (1) they had forgiven the perpetrator and (2) the perpetrator had made amends. Finally, they were probed for suspicion and debriefed. The manipulation checks indicated that the manipulations were successful: participants in the high forgiveness condition reported having offered greater forgiveness than those in the low forgiveness condition, and participants in the strong amends condition reported having received greater amends than those in the weak amends condition.

We conducted two analyses of variance (ANOVAs) with forgiveness and amends feedback conditions as the between-subjects factors and with self-respect and self-concept clarity, in turn, as the dependent variable. Looking first at the main effects of victims' and perpetrators' behavior, in turn, on victims' outcomes, there were no significant main effects of forgiveness or amends on self-respect or self-concept clarity. Thus, there was no evidence that victims have actor control or that perpetrators have partner control over victims' postconflict self-respect or self-concept clarity.

Turning to the interaction effect of victims' behavior and perpetrators' behavior on victims' outcomes, although the descriptive patterns of self-respect were in the predicted directions, the forgiveness × amends interaction effect on self-respect did not reach conventional levels of significance. However, the effect of forgiveness on self-concept clarity did depend on whether the perpetrator made amends. Descriptively speaking, participants who were led to believe they had forgiven a perpetrator who made strong amends reported higher self-concept clarity than those who were led to believe they had not forgiven a perpetrator who made strong amends. In contrast, participants who were led to believe they had forgiven a perpetrator who made weak amends reported lower self-concept clarity than those who were led to believe they had not forgiven a perpetrator who made weak amends. Thus, to the extent that the effect of participants' experimentally manipulated perceptions of forgiveness and amends on their self-respect and self-concept clarity parallels the effect of actual levels of forgiveness and amends, victims and perpetrators shared joint control over victims' postconflict self-concept clarity.

This study extended the first study by examining the effects of experimentally manipulating participants' perceptions of their own forgiveness of and perpetrator amends made for actual betrayals on both self-respect and self-concept clarity. We designed the following study to provide an additional test of the causal effects of forgiveness and amends on self-respect and self-concept clarity.

WELL-CONTROLLED LEVELS OF FORGIVENESS AND AMENDS JOINTLY AFFECT ANTICIPATED SELF-RESPECT AND SELF-CONCEPT CLARITY

The third study was an experiment in which 247 undergraduates imagined themselves as the victim of a partner betrayal. Specifically, participants were asked to imagine themselves in a scenario (which we adapted from Boon & Sulsky, 1997) in which their romantic partner betrayed their trust by telling a mutual friend very private details about the participant's past. Participants in the strong amends condition read that their partner admitted his or her mistake, apologized, and tried very hard to make up for it, whereas those in the weak amends condition read that their partner did not admit his or her mistake, did not apologize, and did not try at all to make up for it. Next, participants in the high forgiveness condition read that they decided to forgive their partner, whereas those in the low forgiveness condition read that they decided not to forgive their partner. After imagining themselves in the scenario, participants completed measures assessing the levels of self-respect and self-concept clarity they anticipated they would have if they had just gone through the described situation ("I would have a lot of respect for myself" and "I would have a clear sense of who I am and what I am," respectively).

We conducted two ANOVAs with forgiveness and amends conditions as the between-subjects factors and with self-respect and self-concept clarity, in turn, as the dependent variable. Looking first at the main effects of victims' and perpetrators' behavior, in turn, on victims' outcomes, there were marginally significant main effects of forgiveness, such that greater forgiveness caused lower anticipated self-respect and self-concept clarity. There were also significant main effects of amends, such that greater amends caused higher anticipated self-respect and self-concept clarity. Thus, there was some evidence that victims have actor control over their anticipated postconflict self-respect and self-concept clarity but that forgiving may have a negative effect on victims' outcomes. And there was evidence that perpetrators have partner control over victims' anticipated postconflict self-respect and self-concept clarity.

Turning to the interaction effect of victims' behavior and perpetrators' behavior on victims' outcomes, the effect of forgiveness on both self-respect and self-concept clarity depended on whether the perpetrator made amends. Descriptively speaking, participants who imagined offering forgiveness when their partner made amends reported they would experience higher self-respect and self-concept clarity than those who imagined withholding forgiveness when their partner made amends. In contrast, participants who imagined offering forgiveness when their partner did not make amends reported they would experience lower self-respect and self-concept clarity than those who imagined withholding forgiveness when their partner did not make amends. Thus, victims and perpetrators shared joint control over victims' anticipated postconflict self-respect and self-concept clarity.

Although these results established that forgiveness and amends caused the observed differences in anticipated levels of self-respect and self-concept clarity, hypothetical scenarios may seem artificial, and participants' anticipated self-respect and self-concept clarity scores may reflect their theories of how they should view themselves in the described situation rather than how they actually would view themselves. Therefore, it remains important to examine associations among forgiveness, amends, self-respect, and self-concept clarity as they naturally occur following actual betrayals. We designed the final study to examine these associations.

ACTUAL LEVELS OF FORGIVENESS AND AMENDS JOINTLY PREDICT SELF-RESPECT AND SELF-CONCEPT CLARITY

The fourth study was a longitudinal investigation in which 69 undergraduates involved in dating relationships completed 14 biweekly online questionnaires over 6 months. On each questionnaire, participants reported their self-respect and self-concept clarity ("I respect myself" and "In general, I have a clear sense of who I am and what I am," respectively). Later in the questionnaire, participants answered yes or no to the following question: "Has your partner done anything over the past 2 weeks that was upsetting to you?" Participants who answered no moved on to an unrelated set of questions. Those who answered yes completed measures assessing forgiveness ("I have forgiven my partner for this behavior"), amends ("My partner tried to make amends to me for this upsetting behavior"), and betrayal severity ("This behavior was highly distressing to me").

We conducted two sets of multilevel regression analyses predicting self-respect and self-concept clarity, in turn, from forgiveness, amends, and betrayal severity. Looking first at the main effects of victims' and perpetrators' behavior, in turn, on victims' outcomes after severe betrayals, there were no significant main effects of forgiveness. But there were marginally significant main effects of amends, such that greater amends predicted higher self-respect and self-concept clarity. Thus, there was no evidence that victims have actor control over their postconflict self-respect or self-concept clarity. However, there was some evidence that perpetrators have partner control over victims' postconflict self-respect and self-concept clarity.

Turning to the interaction effect of victims' behavior and perpetrators' behavior on victims' outcomes after severe betrayals, the association of forgiveness with both self-respect and self-concept clarity depended on the extent to which the perpetrator made amends. Increasing levels of forgiveness predicted more self-respect and self-concept clarity when the partner made strong amends for highly distressing betrayals. In contrast, descriptively speaking, increasing levels of forgiveness predicted less self-respect and self-concept clarity when the partner made weak amends for severe betrayals. Thus, victims and perpetrators shared joint control over victims' postconflict self-respect and self-concept clarity.

This study complemented the previous studies by examining prospective reports of forgiveness, amends, self-respect, and self-concept clarity following actual betrayals in ongoing relationships, and these results showed that the associations of forgiveness with self-respect and self-concept clarity depend on the extent to which the perpetrator has made amends. Across the four studies, our hypothesis that victim's behavior and perpetrators' behavior wield joint control over victims' self-respect and self-concept clarity was supported strongly and consistently. The first study demonstrated that the association of marital forgiveness with trajectories of self-respect depends on spouse agreeableness, which is associated with making amends. The three subsequent studies demonstrated that the effect of forgiveness on self-respect and self-concept clarity depends on perpetrator amends. In addition, our two subhypotheses were supported: forgiving bolsters one's self-respect and self-concept clarity if the perpetrator tends to act in a generally agreeable manner or makes amends, but diminishes one's self-respect and self-concept clarity if the perpetrator tends to act in a generally disagreeable manner or does not make amends. All 14 simple effects were in the predicted directions, but not all of them achieved statistical significance. We conducted a meta-analysis to formally test whether the simple effects garnered reliable support across studies in this research program. (The first study was not included in the meta-analysis because change in self-respect over time, rather than absolute levels of self-respect, was the primary unit of analysis.)

META-ANALYSIS

We calculated meta-analytic (1) main effects of forgiveness on self-respect and self-concept clarity, (2) main effects of amends on self-respect and self-concept clarity, (3) interaction effects of forgiveness and amends on self-respect and self-concept clarity, (4) simple effects of forgiveness on self-respect and self-concept clarity when the perpetrator made strong amends, and (5) simple effects of forgiveness on self-respect and self-concept clarity when the perpetrator made weak amends. Because the meta-analytic effects combine the results of studies using experimentally manipulated perceptions of, hypothetical levels of, and actual levels of forgiveness and amends, and because these effects may differ from one another, they should be interpreted with caution. But because the pattern of results was similar for all three studies, the meta-analytic results likely reflect the effects of actual levels of forgiveness and amends on self-respect and self-concept clarity. Looking first at the main effects of victims' and perpetrators' behavior, in turn, on victims' outcomes, the meta-analysis revealed that, across studies, there were no significant main effects of forgiveness on self-respect or self-concept clarity. Thus, across studies, there was no evidence that victims have actor control over their postconflict self-respect or self-concept clarity. This null result contrasts with the literature linking forgiveness to a variety of positive outcomes and fails to support the notion that forgiveness is a panacea. But there were significant main effects of amends, such that greater amends caused higher self-respect and self-concept clarity. Thus, across studies, there was evidence that perpetrators have partner control over victims' postconflict self-respect and self-concept clarity.

Turning to the interaction effect of victims' behavior and perpetrators' behavior on victims' outcomes, the meta-analysis revealed that there were significant forgiveness × amends interaction effects for both self-respect and self-concept clarity. The meta-analysis also provided strong support for both simple effects. Across Studies 2–4, forgiveness significantly bolstered self-respect and self-concept clarity when the perpetrator made strong amends, but forgiveness significantly diminished self-respect and self-concept clarity when the perpetrator made only weak amends. Thus, victims and perpetrators shared joint control over victims' postconflict outcomes, such that if the perpetrator has made amends then forgiving increases one's self-respect and self-concept clarity, but if the perpetrator has not made amends then forgiving decreases one's self-respect and self-concept clarity.

The predicted means from the meta-analysis for victims' self-respect and self-concept clarity are presented in Figures 14.2 and 14.3, respectively. Calculating the amount of actor control, partner control, and joint control using the formulas presented in the Introduction confirms that victims do not have complete control over their own outcomes. Rather, victims have a small and nonsignificant amount of actor control (−.21 and −.20 for self-respect and self-concept clarity, respectively); collapsing across levels of perpetrator amends, victims who forgive report

		Victim	
		Forgive	Do Not Forgive
Perpetrator	Make Amends	**4.63** (0.25)	**4.23** (0.03)
	Do Not Make Amends	**3.53** (-0.37)	**4.34** (0.09)

Actor Control =   ((4.63 + 3.53) − (4.23 + 4.34)) / 2 = -.21
Partner Control = ((4.63 + 4.23) − (3.53 + 4.34)) / 2 = .49
Joint Control =   ((4.63 + 4.34) − (4.23 + 3.53)) / 2 = .60

Figure 14.2   Actor control, partner control, and joint control over victims' meta-analyzed postconflict self-respect. Table values in bold are raw scores on a 1–7 scale. Table values in parenthesis are standardized scores.

		Victim	
		Forgive	Do Not Forgive
Perpetrator	Make Amends	**4.86** (0.29)	**4.40** (0.00)
	Do Not Make Amends	**3.74** (-0.42)	**4.59** (0.12)

Actor Control = ((4.86 + 3.74) − (4.40 + 4.59)) / 2 = -.20
Partner Control = ((4.86 + 4.40) − (3.74 + 4.59)) / 2 = .46
Joint Control = ((4.86 + 4.59) − (4.40 + 3.74)) / 2 = .65

Figure 14.3   Actor control, partner control, and joint control over victims' meta-analyzed postconflict self-concept clarity. Table values in bold are raw scores on a 1–7 scale. Table values in parenthesis are standardized scores.

an average of two-tenths of a scale point less self-respect and self-concept clarity than those who do not forgive. In contrast, perpetrators have a significant amount of partner control (.49 and .46 for self-respect and self-concept clarity, respectively); collapsing across levels of victim forgiveness, victims who receive strong amends report an average of four- to five-tenths of a scale point more self-respect and self-concept clarity than those who receive only weak amends. Importantly, victims and perpetrators also share a significant amount of joint control (.60 and .65 for self-respect and self-concept clarity, respectively); victims who either forgive a perpetrator who made strong amends or do not forgive a perpetrator who made only weak amends report an average of six- to seven-tenths of a scale point more self-respect and self-concept clarity than those who either forgive a perpetrator who made only weak amends or do not forgive a perpetrator who made strong amends.

ADDITIONAL EVIDENCE OF JOINT CONTROL OVER VICTIMS' POSTCONFLICT OUTCOMES

Two experiments and two longitudinal studies provided consistent evidence that victims and perpetrators share joint control over victims' postconflict self-respect and self-concept clarity. Is there evidence that victims and perpetrators share joint control not only over victims' psychological health outcomes, such as self-respect and self-concept clarity, but also over victims' relational well-being and physical health outcomes? The answer appears to be yes. In a longitudinal study of married couples, McNulty (2008) found that, although individuals whose spouses rarely behaved negatively experienced more stable marital satisfaction over the first 2 years of marriage to the extent they were more forgiving, individuals whose spouses frequently behaved negatively experienced steeper declines in marital satisfaction to the extent they were more forgiving. That is, whether greater marital forgiveness predicted greater stability or steeper declines in marital satisfaction depended on how frequently one's spouse behaved badly, indicating that perpetrators and victims share joint control over victims' relational well-being.

Another study indicated that perpetrators and victims also may share joint control over victims' physical health outcomes. In a study of women at a domestic violence shelter, Gordon, Burton, and Porter (2004) found that those who reported the greatest forgiveness of their abusive partner were the most likely to report they intended to return to their partner. Returning to an abusive partner may well heighten the risk of being abused again, but whether or not returning to a previously abusive partner leads to further abuse depends on the perpetrator's behavior.

The findings of the previously reviewed studies, together with the findings of McNulty (2008) and Gordon et al. (2004), suggest that victims and perpetrators share joint control over an array of victims' outcomes, including their self-respect, self-concept clarity, marital satisfaction, and risk of being physically abused. Yet another body of research suggests that victims have actor control over other outcomes, including their life satisfaction (Bono et al., 2008), commitment to their perpetrators (Tsang et al., 2006) and physiological stress (McCullough et al., 2007). It may be that some outcomes are subject primarily to joint control whereas other outcomes are subject primarily to actor control. For instance, a victim who forgives a perpetrator who has not made amends might experience decreased self-respect and self-concept clarity at the same time as increased commitment to the perpetrator. By examining multiple outcomes of forgiveness in the same study, future work could explore whether the costs of forgiving in the absence of amends outweigh the benefits of doing so.

CONCLUDING REMARKS

Given that victims and perpetrators share joint control over victims' postconflict outcomes, our data suggest that conflict resolution strategies designed to promote victims' forgiveness should aim to heighten victims' sensitivity to whether forgiveness is likely to be beneficial in their particular situation. Furthermore, forgiveness interventions should be supplemented with strategies designed to promote perpetrators' amend making (e.g., the Victim Offender Reconciliation Program; see, e.g., Green, 1984; Ristovski & Wertheim, 2005). Such "amends interventions" could adapt many of the methods used in forgiveness interventions, including helping perpetrators develop empathy for their victims, having perpetrators recall times they were hurt by others, and encouraging perpetrators to make a commitment to make amends for their misdeeds.

Moreover, because receiving amends facilitates forgiveness (e.g., McCullough, Worthington, & Rachal, 1997), interventions that successfully increase the extent to which perpetrators make amends may also increase the extent to which victims forgive. Past research has shown that, when perpetrators not only apologize but also offer to compensate their victims for their offenses, victims are especially likely to forgive (Bottom, Gibson, Daniels, & Murnighan, 2002; Darby & Schlenker, 1982). Moreover, in an analysis of videotaped conflict discussions, perpetrator amends expressed during one 2-minute segment were positively associated with victim forgiveness expressed during the following segment, controlling for forgiveness expressed in the initial segment (Hannon et al., 2010).

Conflict resolution strategies that successfully promote both perpetrator amends and victim forgiveness are optimal because they are likely to yield the most favorable outcomes. In all four studies examining victims' postconflict self-respect and self-concept clarity, victims' self-views were the most positive when they forgave perpetrators who had made amends. By recognizing that, just as two people are involved when a relationship ruptures, so, too, are two people involved in mending those ruptures, individuals who seek to heal their own or others' broken relationships might do so more successfully.

REFERENCES

Bono, G., McCullough, M. E., & Root, L. M. (2008). Forgiveness, feeling connected to others, and well-being: Two longitudinal studies. *Personality and Social Psychology Bulletin, 34,* 182–195.

Boon, S. D., & Sulsky, L. M. (1997). Attributions of blame and forgiveness in romantic relationships: A policy-capturing study. *Journal of Social Behavior and Personality, 12,* 19–44.

Bottom, W. P., Gibson, K., Daniels, S. E., & Murnighan, J. K. (2002). When talk is not cheap: Substantive penance and expressions of intent in rebuilding cooperation. *Organization Science, 13*(5), 497–513.

Chiaramello, S., Sastre, M. T. M., & Mullet, E. (2008). Seeking forgiveness: Factor structure, and relationships with personality and forgivingness. *Personality and Individual Differences, 45,* 383–388.

Darby, B. W., & Schlenker, B. R. (1982). Children's reactions to apologies. *Journal of Personality and Social Psychology, 43*(4), 742–753.

Gordon, K. C., Burton, S., & Porter, L. (2004). Predicting the intentions of women in domestic violence shelters to return to partners: Does forgiveness play a role? *Journal of Family Psychology, 18,* 331–338.

Green, S. (1984). Victim-offender reconciliation program: A review of the concept. *Social Action & the Law, 10,* 43–52.

Greenwald, A. G., McGhee, D. E., & Schwartz, J. L. K. (1998). Measuring individual differences in implicit cognition: The Implicit Association Test. *Journal of Personality and Social Psychology, 74,* 1464–1480.

Hannon, P. A., Rusbult, C. E., Finkel, E. J., & Kumashiro, M. (2010). In the wake of betrayal: Amends, forgiveness, and the resolution of betrayal. *Personal Relationships, 17,* 253–278.

Hebl, J. H., & Enright, R. D. (1993). Forgiveness as a psychotherapeutic goal with elderly females. *Psychotherapy, 30,* 658–667.

Jensen-Campbell, L. A., & Graziano, W. G. (2001). Agreeableness as a moderator of interpersonal conflict. *Journal of Personality, 69,* 323–362.

Karremans, J. C., Van Lange, P. A. M., Ouwerkerk, J. W., & Kluwer, E. S. (2003). When forgiving enhances psychological well-being: The roles of interpersonal commitment. *Journal of Personality and Social Psychology, 84,* 1011–1026.

Kelley, H. H., Holmes, J. G., Kerr, N. L., Reis, H. T., Rusbult, C. E., & Van Lange, P. A. M. (2003). *An atlas of interpersonal situations.* New York: Cambridge University Press.

Kelley, H. H., & Thibaut, J. W. (1978). *Interpersonal relations: A theory of interdependence*. New York: Wiley.

Luchies, L. B., Finkel, E. J., McNulty, J. K., & Kumashiro, M. (2010). The doormat effect: When forgiving erodes self-respect and self-concept clarity. *Journal of Personality and Social Psychology, 98*, 734–749.

McCullough, M. E. (2008). *Beyond revenge: The evolution of the forgiveness instinct*. San Francisco: Jossey-Bass.

McCullough, M. E., Orsulak, P., Brandon, A., & Akers, L. (2007). Rumination, fear, and cortisol: An in vivo study of interpersonal transgressions. *Health Psychology, 26*(1), 126–132.

McCullough, M. E., Worthington, E. L., & Rachal, K. C. (1997). Interpersonal forgiving in close relationships. *Journal of Personality and Social Psychology, 73*, 321–336.

McNulty, J. K. (2008). Forgiveness in marriage: Putting the benefits into context. *Journal of Family Psychology, 22*, 171–175.

Orcutt, H. K. (2006). The prospective relationship of interpersonal forgiveness and psychological distress symptoms among college women. *Journal of Counseling Psychology, 53*, 350–361.

Ristovski, A., & Wertheim, E. H. (2005). Investigation of compensation source, trait empathy, satisfaction with outcome and forgiveness in the criminal context. *Australian Psychologist, 40*, 63–69.

Rye, M. S., & Pargament, K. I. (2002). Forgiveness and romantic relationships in college: Can it heal the wounded heart? *Journal of Clinical Psychology, 58*, 419–441.

Sandage, S. J., Worthington, E. L., Hight, T. L., & Berry, J. W. (2000). Seeking forgiveness: Theoretical context and an initial empirical study. *Journal of Psychology and Theology, 28*, 21–35.

Singer, J.D., & Willett, J.B. (2003). *Applied longitudinal data analysis*. New York: Oxford University Press.

Thibaut, J. W., & Kelley, H. H. (1959). *The social psychology of groups*. New York: Wiley.

Tsang, J., McCullough, M. E., & Fincham, F. D. (2006). The longitudinal association between forgiveness and relationship closeness and commitment. *Journal of Social and Clinical Psychology, 25*(4), 448–472.

Wade, N. G., & Worthington, E. L. (2005). In search of a common core: A content analysis of interventions to promote forgiveness. *Psychotherapy: Theory, Research, Practice, Training, 42*, 160–177.

Waltman, M. A., Russell, D. C., Coyle, C. T., Enright, R. D., Holter, A. C., & Swoboda, C. M. (2009). The effects of a forgiveness intervention on patients with coronary artery disease. *Psychology and Health, 24*, 11–27.

Worthington, E. L., Kurusu, T. A., Collins, W., Berry, J. W., Ripley, J. S., & Baier, S. B. (2000). Forgiving usually takes time: A lesson learned by studying interventions to promote forgiveness. *Journal of Psychology and Theology, 28*, 3–20.

Section IV

Social, Cultural, and Evolutionary Factors in Social Conflict and Aggression

15

The Male Warrior Hypothesis

MARK VAN VUGT

VU University Amsterdam, The Netherlands

*A*lien biologists collecting data about different life forms on Planet Earth would no doubt come up with contradictory claims about human nature. They would witness the human capacity to help complete strangers in sometimes large groups, yet they would also observe many incidents of extreme violence, especially between groups of males. To make sense of the data, the alien researchers would probably conclude that humans are a fiercely tribal social species. Some time ago, Charles Darwin speculated about the origins of human tribal nature: "A tribe including many members who, from possessing in a high degree the spirit of patriotism, fidelity, obedience, courage, and sympathy, were always ready to aid one another, and to sacrifice themselves for the common good, would be victorious over most other tribes; and this would be natural selection" (1871, p. 132). Unfortunately Darwin's brilliant insight was ignored for more than a century by fellow scientists, yet it is now gaining impact. Here I offer an evolutionary perspective on the social psychology of intergroup conflict, offering new insights and evidence about the origins and manifestation of coalitional and intergroup aggression.[1]

Social scientists are increasingly adopting an evolutionary approach to develop novel hypotheses and to integrate data on various aspects of human social behavior (Buss, 2005; Van Vugt & Schaller, 2008). The evolutionary approach is based on the premise that the human brain is a product of evolution through natural selection in the same way our bodies are the products of natural selection. Evolutionary-minded psychologists further propose that the human brain is essentially social, comprising many functionalized mechanisms—or adaptations—to cope with the

---

[1] I will use the terms *coalitional* and *intergroup aggression* interchangeably throughout this chapter. Although there is a difference in scale, both types of aggression involve individuals who as members of groups commit acts of aggression against members of other groups (Brewer & Brown, 1998).

various challenges of group living (Van Vugt & Schaller, 2008). One such specialized mechanism is coalition formation. Forming alliances with other individuals
confers considerable advantages in procuring and protecting reproductively relevant resources (e.g., food, territories, mates, offspring) especially in large and
diverse social groups. Coalitional pressures may have led in human evolution to the
emergence of some rather unique human traits such as language, theory of mind,
culture, and warfare. It has been argued that ultimately the need to form ever
larger coalitions spurred the increase in human social network size and led to a
concomitant brain size to hold these networks together and to deal effectively with
an intensified competition for resources—this has been dubbed the Machiavellian
Intelligence hypothesis, the Social Brain hypothesis, or the Social Glue hypothesis
(Byrne & Whiten, 1988; Dunbar; Van Vugt & Hart, 2004). According to these
hypotheses, our social brain is therefore essentially a tribal brain.

In searching for the origins of the human tribal brain it is useful to make a distinction between *proximate* and *ultimate* causes. An act of intergroup aggression
such as war, terrorism, gang-related violence or hooliganism could be explained at
two different levels at least. First, why did this particular group decide to attack the
other? This proximate question interests most sociologists, political scientists, his-
torians, and social psychologists studying social conflict. Second, one could ask why
humans have evolved the capacity to engage in intergroup aggression—this ultimate question interests mostly evolutionary-minded psychologists and anthropolo-
gists. Addressing questions at different levels produces a more complete picture, but
these levels should not be confused (Buss, 2005; Van Vugt & Van Lange, 2006).

In terms of ultimate causes of intergroup aggression, three classes of explanations
are generally invoked (Kurzban & Neuberg, 2005; Van Vugt, 2009; see also Chapters
10 and 18 in this volume). The first treats it as a by-product of an adaptive in-group
psychology. Being a highly social and cooperative species, humans likely possess tendencies to favor helping members of in-groups (Brewer, 1979; Brewer & Caporael,
2006; Tajfel & Turner, 1986). As a result of this in-group favoritism, people show
either indifference or (perhaps worse) a dislike for members of out-groups. An alternative by-product hypothesis views intergroup aggression as an extension of interpersonal aggression. The argument is that humans have evolved specialized mechanisms
to engage in aggression against conspecifics and that these mechanisms have been
co-opted to cope with a relatively novel evolutionary threat, namely, aggression
between groups (Buss, 2005). The third class focuses explicitly on an adaptive intergroup psychology. The argument is that humans likely evolved specific psychological
mechanisms to interact with members of out-groups because such situations posed
a significant reproductive challenge for ancestral humans. This latter hypothesis
accounts for the highly textured social psychology of intergroup relations and is therefore more persuasive. For instance, people do not have some hazy negative feeling
toward an out-group; in some instances out-groups motivate a desire to approach or
avoid and in other instances to fight, dominate, exploit, or exterminate.

Recent work on prejudice and intergroup relations recognizes this textured
nature of intergroup psychology and has generated many new insights and empirical findings consistent with this view (Cottrell & Neuberg, 2005; Kurzban & Leary,
2001; Schaller, Park, & Faulkner, 2003; Sidanius & Pratto, 1999; Van Vugt, De

Cremer, & Janssen, 2007; Van Vugt, 2009). Given the complexity of intergroup relations, there are probably many different adaptive responses pertaining to the nature and type of intergroup challenge. From an evolutionary perspective, it becomes clear that not all intergroup situations are equal because not all out-groups are equal. For instance, not all out-groups consist of coalitions of individuals who engage in coordinated action—think of the homeless, the elderly, or people with blue eyes. Humans are likely to have evolved coalition-detection mechanisms that are responsive to various indicators of tribal alliances (Kurzban, Tooby, and Cosmides, 2001). As Kurzban and Leary note, "Membership in a potentially cooperative group should activate a psychology of conflict and exploitation of out-group members—a feature that distinguishes adaptations for coalitional psychology from other cognitive systems" (p. 195). In modern environments, heuristic cues such as skin color, speech patterns, and linguistic labels—regardless of whether they actually signal tribal alliances—may engage these mechanisms (Kurzban et al.; Schaller et al.). Perhaps equally important, many other salient cues such as gender, age, or eye color may be far less likely to engage this tribal psychology. We should note that although this tribal psychology likely evolved in the evolutionary context of competition for resources (e.g., territories, food, and mates), this does not imply that it is contemporarily activated only within contexts involving actual intergroup conflict as proposed, for instance, by realistic conflict theory (Campbell, 1999).

The specific psychological reactions of individuals in intergroup contexts should further depend on whether one's group is the aggressor. For the aggressors, desires to dominate and exploit—and the associated psychological tendencies— would be functional. For the defending party, desires to yield, to avoid, or to make peace, along with the associated psychological tendencies, would be functional. Of course, in many situations, a group's position as being the dominant or subordinate party is transient or ambiguous so it is likely that the two psychological tendencies are activated in similar situations by similar cues and moderated by similar variables (social dominance theory; Sidanius & Pratto, 1999).

THE MALE WARRIOR HYPOTHESIS

An important implication of this evolutionary tribal brain hypothesis is that intergroup conflict may have affected the psychologies of men and women differently. Intergroup conflict has historically involved rival coalitions of males fighting over scarce reproductive resources, and this is true for early humans as well as chimpanzees, our closest genetic relative (Chagnon, 1988; De Waal, 2006; Goodall, 1986). Men are by far the most likely perpetrators and victims of intergroup aggression, now and in the past. As a consequence, this aspect of coalitional psychology is likely to be more pronounced among men, which we dubbed the *male warrior hypothesis* (MWH, see Table 15.1; Van Vugt et al., 2007; Van Vugt, 2009). This hypothesis posits that due to a long history of male-to-male coalitional conflict men have evolved specialized cognitive mechanisms that enable them to form alliances with other men to plan, to initiate, to execute, and to emerge victorious in intergroup conflicts with the aim of acquiring or protecting reproductively relevant resources.

TABLE 15.1   The Male Warrior Hypothesis: Domains of Evidence,
Hypothesized Mechanisms, Predictions, and Support for Gender Differences

Domain of Evidence	Hypothesized Mechanism	Prediction About Gender Difference	Supported
1. Intergroup aggression	Propensity to engage in intergroup aggression	Men are more likely to make unprovoked out-group attacks	Yes
		Men report having more (competitive) intergroup experiences	Yes
2. Intergroup prejudice	Infrahumanization or dehumanization of members of antagonistic out-groups	Men are more likely to infrahumanize members of out-groups	Yes
3. Intragroup dynamics	In-group cooperation in response to outgroup threat	Men contribute more to group during intergroup competition	Yes
	In-group loyalty during intergroup conflict	Men show more in-group loyalty during intergroup conflict	
	Male leadership bias in intergroup conflict	Groups show stronger preference for male leaders during intergroup competition	
4. Tribal politics	Political support for intergroup aggression	Men show stronger political support for warfare in opinion polls	Yes
	Preferences for social dominance hierarchies	Men score higher on social dominance orientation scale	Yes
5. Tribal social identity	Affiliation to tribal groups	Men are more likely to make spontaneous tribal associations when defining themselves	Yes

Evolutionary Models

The MWH fits into a tradition of evolutionary hypotheses about gender differences in social behavior. There is already considerable evidence for gender differences in morphology, psychology, and behavior that are functionally related to different selection pressures operating on men and women throughout human, primate, and mammal evolution (Campbell, 1999; Eagly & Wood, 1999; Geary, 1998; Taylor et al., 2000). Due to a combination of differences in parental investment and parental certainty men and women pursue somewhat different mating strategies (Buss & Schmitt, 1993; Trivers, 1972). In humans—as in most other mammals—mothers invest more heavily in their offspring; consequently, it will be physiologically and genetically costlier for women to be openly aggressive (Archer, 2000; Campbell, 1999; Taylor et al., 2000). Yet, as the less investing sex and under the right conditions, it can be attractive for men to form aggressive coalitions with the aim of acquiring and protecting valuable reproductive resources.

Tooby and Cosmides's (1988) risk contract hypothesis specifies four conditions for the evolution of coalitional aggression, which underscores the evolutionary logic of the hypothesized gender differences in warrior psychology. First, the average long-term gains in reproductive success (i.e., mating opportunities) must be sufficiently large to outweigh the average costs (i.e., injury or death). Second, members of warfare coalitions must believe that their group is likely to emerge victorious in battle. Third, the risk that each member takes and the importance of each member's contribution to victory must translate into a corresponding share of benefits (cf. the free-rider problem). Fourth, when individuals go into battle they must be cloaked in a "veil of ignorance" about who will live or die. Thus, if an intergroup victory produces, on average, a 20% increase in reproductive success, then as long as the risk of death for any individual coalition member is less than 20% (e.g., 1 in 10 die) such warrior traits could be selected for. This model assumes that the spoils of an intergroup victory are paid out in extra mating opportunities for the individual males involved, and thus it is essentially an individual selection model based on sexual selection.

Alternatively, a specific male warrior psychology could have evolved via group-level selection. Multilevel selection theory holds that if there is substantial variance in the reproductive success among groups then group selection becomes a genuine possibility (Wilson, Van Vugt, & O'Gorman, 2008). As Darwin (1871) noted, groups of selfless individuals do better than groups of selfish individuals. Although participating in intergroup conflict is personally costly—because of the risk of death or injury—genes underlying propensity to serve the group can be propagated if group-serving acts contribute to group survival. In a recent empirical test of this model, Choi and Bowles (2007) showed via computer simulations that altruistic traits can spread in populations as long as there is competition between groups and altruistic acts benefit in-group members and harm out-group members (parochial altruism).

One condition conducive to group-level selection occurs when the genetic interests of group members are aligned, such as in kin groups. In kin-bonded groups, individuals benefit not just from their own reproductive success but also from the success of their family members (inclusive fitness; Hamilton, 1964). Ancestral human groups are likely to have been based around male kin members, with females moving between groups to avoid inbreeding (so-called patrilocal groups). This offers a complementary reason for the evolution of male coalitional aggression: because the men are more heavily invested in their group, they have more to lose when the group ceases to exist. In addition, the collective action problem underlying coalitional aggression is less pronounced when group members' genetic interests are aligned. Incidentally (but perhaps not coincidentally), the same patrilocal structure is found in chimpanzees: male chimpanzees also engage in coalitional aggression (Goodall, 1986; Wrangham & Peterson, 1996).

These evolutionary models do not preclude the possibility of cultural processes at work that could exacerbate or undermine male warrior instincts (Richerson & Boyd, 2005). In fact, many of the evolved propensities for coalitional aggression are likely to be translated into actual psychological and behavioral tendencies by socialization practices and cultural norms. Thus, it is entirely possible that in certain environments it could be advantageous for societies to suppress male warrior tendencies (so-called peaceful societies) or to turn females into dedicated warriors.

A modern-day example of the latter is the state of Israel, which is involved in a continuous war with its Arab neighbors. To increase its military strength, Israel has a conscription army of both men and women and currently has the most liberal rules regarding the participation of females in actual warfare (Goldstein, 2003). We would expect the socialization practices among Israeli girls to match those of boys, potentially attenuating any innate psychological differences.

Evidence for the MWH From Across the Behavioral Sciences

Evidence for various aspects of this male warrior phenomenon can be found throughout the behavioral science literature, for instance, in anthropology, history, sociology, political science, biology, psychology, and primatology. As stated, across all cultures, almost any act of intergroup aggression is perpetrated by coalitions of males, for instance, in situations of warfare, genocide, rebellion, terrorism, street gangs, and hooligan violence (Goldstein, 2003; Livingstone Smith, 2007). Evidence of male-to-male coalitional aggression goes back as far as 200,000 years (e.g., mass graves containing mostly male skeletons with evidence of force; Keeley, 1996). Men are also the most likely victims of intergroup aggression. On average, male death rates due to warfare among hunter-gatherers are 13% (according to archaeological data) and 15% (according to ethnographic data; Bowles, 2006), suggesting a relatively strong selection pressure on male warrior traits. The figure is sometimes even higher. Among the Yanomamö in the Amazon Basin, an estimated 20–30% of adult males die through tribal violence (Chagnon, 1988), compared with less than 1% of the U.S. and European populations in the twentieth century. Finally, the primate literature reveals that, among chimpanzees, adult males form coalitions to engage in violence against members of neighboring troops. This suggests that there is phylogenetic consistency between humans and one of our most closely related species (Wilson & Wrangham, 2003).

Male warriors in traditional societies have higher status, more sexual partners, and more children (Chagnon, 1988), suggesting a direct reproductive benefit; Richard Dawkins (1976) labeled this the "Duke of Marlborough" effect. The sexual attractiveness of the male warrior might still be operative in modern society. A U.S. study revealed that male youth street gang members have more sexual partners than ordinary young males (Palmer & Tilley, 1995). We recently found that military men have greater sex appeal, especially if they have shown bravery in combat (Leunissen & Van Vugt, 2010). Thus, there may be reputational benefits associated with "warrior" behaviors in men (cf. competitive altruism; Hardy & Van Vugt, 2006).

In light of the support for the MWH, it is noteworthy that many published intergroup studies in social psychology do not report the results for men and women separately and that some use only male samples. One of the classic social psychological studies, the Stanford prison experiment (Zimbardo, 1971), which highlighted some disturbing aspects of human coalitional aggression, used an all-male sample. Team game experiments also often use all male groups (e.g., Bornstein, 2003). In a personal communication, one of the authors of this study (Bornstein, 2006) suggested that pilot research showed that female groups were less competitive.

PSYCHOLOGICAL MECHANISMS UNDERLYING MALE WARRIOR PHENOMENON

The MWH offers an integrative, conceptual framework in which findings from diverse literatures can be woven into a coherent story. However, this approach runs the risk of being a "just so" story about the role of coalitional aggression in human evolution. It would be much better if we could make specific predictions about gender differences in the psychological mechanisms underlying this warrior psychology and could test these predictions in carefully controlled studies. If men have a more pronounced warrior psychology, we should expect them to think and feel differently about intergroup conflict and to be more likely to plan, support, and commit acts of intergroup aggression (Van Vugt, 2009). In addition, men in groups should make adaptive intergroup choices depending on information about the sex, size, and formidability of the out-group. For instance, they should respond with anger and aggression toward a numerically weaker out-group and with fear and avoidance to a stronger out-group (especially an all-male group). Finally, these reactions are likely to be produced automatically and spontaneously.

To test various aspects of the male warrior hypothesis and to find evidence for gender differences in evolved psychological mechanisms, I will present some research findings pertaining to various domains such as (1) frequency and likelihood of aggression toward out-groups; (2) protection of in-groups against external threats; (3) likelihood of political support for intergroup aggression; and (4) tribal social identifications. By and large, these studies provide preliminary support for the male warrior hypothesis, yet much work still remains to be done.

Propensity for Intergroup Aggression

A first prediction from the MWH is that men should, on average, have a lower threshold to engage in acts of intergroup aggression when given the opportunity. We tested this in various ways. First, we examine how men and women make decisions in war games simulated in the laboratory. A study by Johnson et al. (2006) found that, on being told that they are the leader of a fictitious country interacting with leaders of other countries, men are significantly more likely to attack another country without provocation (i.e., "preemptive strike"). Moreover, warfare is most intense when men are playing against other men despite not knowing the sex of their rivals. The lower threshold for intergroup aggression may be due to expectations of success. Indeed, men held more positive illusions about winning these simulated intergroup conflicts, a belief that increased the probability that they would attack their opponent (Johnson et al.). Another study analyzing the same dataset found that more male-typical 2D:4D digit ratios, which are thought to index prenatal testosterone exposure, predicted aggression in the war-game experiments over and above sex. These gender differences also emerge when individuals play economic games between groups: all-male groups tend to be more competitive than all-female groups or mixed-sex groups (Wildschut, Pinter, Vevea, Insko, & Schopler, 2003).

Second, there is ample evidence that men and women differ in their involvement in acts of intergroup aggression outside the laboratory (Pemberton, Insko, & Schopler, 1996). When asked to indicate the frequency of various categories of social interactions over the past month, men reported more group-to-group interactions (mean [M] = 18.47, standard deviation [SD] = 73.48) than women (M = 12.77, SD = 59.68). Furthermore, men rated these interactions as more competitive (M for male vs. female = 3.17 vs. 2.31, SD = 2.50 for male vs. 2.22 for female; scale is 1 = very cooperative, 5 = very competitive).

Thus, consistent with the MWH, men experience intergroup competition more often, have a lower threshold to start an intergroup conflict, and are more optimistic about winning such conflicts.

Intergroup Prejudice and Stereotyping

The MWH further predicts that men are more likely to be prejudiced and to openly discriminate against members of out-groups, especially those that can be viewed as coalitional threats. One manifestation of out-group prejudice is infrahumanization, the tendency to consider members of out-groups subhuman or animal like, which is often a precursor of intergroup violence (Haslam, 2006; Leyens et al., 2001). The evolutionary logic is that by considering out-groups as psychologically inferior it will be psychologically easier to treat them badly. In a recent study (Van Vugt, 2009), men and women—all Christians—were asked to describe a Christian or Muslim target using either human-typical (e.g., *civil*) or animal-typical (e.g., *feral*) words. Christian men were more likely to describe the Muslim target in animal-typical ways, thus showing evidence of infrahumanization. The MWH also predicts that infrahumanization strategies are most likely in male-to-male intergroup contests, but this remains to be tested.

Men also show other intergroup biases such as racism and xenophobia more readily and especially in threatening situations Several experiments yield a greater sensitivity of out-group stereotypes for in-group men, especially under conditions of intergroup conflict (Gerard & Hoyt, 1974; Sidanius, Cling, & Pratto, 1991). Schaller, Park, and Mueller (2003) showed that men use danger-relevant stereotypes toward out-group members more when influenced by cues of ambient darkness. Finally, the notorious out-group homogeneity effect disappears when in-group members are shown angry faces of out-group males but not females (Ackerman et al., 2006), which is consistent with the idea that out-group males pose a heightened threat.

These findings support the MWH in that men are more likely to be prejudiced against members of out-groups, especially when these constitute a coalitional threat; in addition, out-group men are more likely to be discriminated against.

Protecting the Group Against External Threats

The MWH also expects the presence of psychological mechanisms that enable men to protect their in-group against external threats. To defend the group requires people to bond together and to help the in-group (Brewer & Brown, 1998; Van Vugt et al., 2007). Based on the MWH, we hypothesize that during intergroup conflict particularly men will step up their efforts to help the in-group. Consistent with this prediction, in public-good games we found that men raised their group contributions but only when we activated competition between groups (Van Vugt et al.). In Experiment 1, Van Vugt et al. found that during intergroup competition 92% of men (but only 53% of women) contributed to the public good. In addition, men showed greater in-group loyalty by sticking with the group even if it was more (financially) attractive to leave (Van Vugt et al., 2007). As a proxy for in-group cohesion, men were also more likely to increase their identification with the group under conditions of intergroup conflict. It remains to be seen whether men are also more likely altruistic punishers of free-riding group members during intergroup conflict, as the MWH would predict.

Males are also more likely to be chosen as group leaders during intergroup conflict. Van Vugt and Spisak (2008) found that when two equally suitable candidates of different sexes, Sarah and John, vied for the position of group leader in an intergroup conflict groups preferred the male leader (78%). The male leader was also more effective in eliciting followers' group contributions during intergroup threat. (Interestingly, when the problem shifted toward conflict within the in-group virtually all groups preferred the female leader.)

Preference for Hierarchies

There is some evidence that male groups have different group dynamics that make them more suitable to engage in coalitional aggression. Whereas female groups are more egalitarian, groups of males form more hierarchical groups, and these hierarchies tend to be more stable over time. The difference in group structure corresponds with gender differences in leadership style (Eagly & Johnson, 1990; Van Vugt, 2006). Military specialists assume that hierarchy formation is an effective response in dealing with intergroup conflict that requires an urgent, coordinated response.

Research on developmental differences in social play reflects the male warrior tendencies. Boys play in larger groups than girls and more often play complex competitive team games, which sometimes involve the use of weapons such as toy guns and swords (Geary, 1998). Boys also put greater social pressure on team members to conform to group norms during play activities (Sherif et al., 1961), and they have more transient friendships with a larger number of peers than girls (Geary). Thus, consistent with the MWH, men have psychological mechanisms that enable them to work in and function better in larger and more hierarchically structured groups and the primary function of such group structures is to compete with other groups.

Support for Tribal Politics

The MWH further predicts gender differences in political attitudes toward intergroup conflict. We hypothesize that men would show relatively stronger political support for warfare as a solution to international conflict because they have more to gain potentially (at least in ancestral times) from intergroup conflict. We tested this prediction using data from a random selection of 10 recent national and international opinion polls that we were able to find on the Internet and found consistent gender differences (sometimes large, other times small, but always in the same direction). For instance, a *Washington Post* poll in 2003 (*N* = 1,030) asked the question, "Do you support the US having gone to war in Iraq?", to which 82% of men agreed versus 72% of women. As another example, a recent poll by *Gallup News* (*N* = 7,074) found that 46% of men (vs. 37% of women) disagreed with the statement, "Do you think the Iraq war was a mistake?"

The MWH also expects men to have a stronger preference for between-group dominance hierarchies, the inevitable outcome of intergroup conflict. To test this prediction, we asked an international survey of people to complete the short 10-item social dominance orientation scale (Pratto, Sidanius, Stallworth, & Malle, 1994). This seven-point scale contains items such as, "Some groups of people are simply inferior to others"; "We should do what we can to equalize conditions for different groups"; and "To get ahead in life, it is sometimes necessary to step on other groups." Consistent with other data (Pratto et al.) we found that men were significantly more socially dominant (M = 2.56, SD = 1.13) than women (M = 2.28, SD = 1.0).

Thus, in agreement with the MWH, men are generally more belligerent in their tribal politics.

Tribal Social identity

A final prediction from the MWH is that men's personal self-concept should be affected more strongly by their affiliations to tribal groups. In contrast, women's self-concept should be influenced primarily by having meaningful connections with close others. Men have indeed a more collective sense of self that is more strongly derived from their group memberships and affiliations (Baumeister & Sommer, 1997). Gabriel and Gardner (1999) asked students to describe themselves by completing the statement, "I am...." They found that male students were twice as likely to make statements referring to a tribal association (e.g., "I am a member of a fraternity").

In a recent study (Van Vugt et al., 2007) we asked 100 people around the University of Kent campus to indicate their favorite color and to explain why they picked this particular color. Among men, almost 30% mentioned a tribal association (e.g., their favorite football team, the colors of the flag of their country of origin); none of the women did so.

Thus, men's social identity seems to be more strongly based on their tribal affiliations than women's, which is consistent with the MWH.

IMPLICATIONS FOR INTERGROUP RELATIONS

This chapter presented a framework for studying the psychology of intergroup aggression from an evolutionary perspective. This analysis suggests that not all intergroup relations are alike because not all out-groups are alike. How groups interact with each other is determined by the specific contextual threats and opportunities. When such challenges correspond to evolutionarily relevant threats—threats that were significant enough in ancestral social environments that humans have evolved to deal with them—they activate a specific tribal psychology. Here I have argued that a history of coalitional aggression has produced a distinct human tribal brain including an interrelated set of functional cognitive and behavioral reactions to attack and defend against members of out-groups. Furthermore, as the most likely perpetrators and victims, I have hypothesized that the male psychology has been particularly affected by intergroup conflict episodes and have dubbed this the male warrior hypothesis. I reviewed the literature on gender differences in intergroup psychology in light of predictions from the male warrior hypothesis and found them to be generally supportive. Further tests are needed.

In addition to intergroup conflict there might be a host of other significant ancestral challenges involving other groups, which are not discussed here. Disease avoidance is one such threat, and we would expect a different set of functional responses to a contagion threat rather than a physical threat from an out-group; for instance, behavioral avoidance rather than aggression. When a disease threat is salient, perhaps women respond more strongly. There is some evidence that women are more prejudiced toward strangers when in their most fertile menstrual phase (Navarette, Fessler, & Eng, 2007). In general, we know very little about the intergroup psychology of females. In addition, the neuroscience underpinning gender differences in intergroup psychology ought to be examined—for instance, which hormonal differences drive these gender differences in tribal psychology?

The evolutionary framework makes various suggestions for interventions to improve intergroup relations. When out-groups pose a coalitional threat, interventions might be targeted specifically at male-to-male interactions because they are the most likely perpetrators and victims of intergroup aggression. In terms of their objectives, interventions will be particularly successful when they eliminate the sense of threat associated with a particular out-group altogether. Attempts must be made to individuate members of such out-groups, for instance, by accentuating their personal achievements rather than the achievements of their group. A second aim of interventions is to alter the perceptual cues that elicit threat responses toward particular out-groups such as new immigrant groups. For instance, language, dress code, and particular rituals or customs serve as tribal markers, and the less noticeable they are the more these out-groups will receive positive treatment. Thus, for the sake of attenuating the effects of coalitional psychology, it is important for societies to make it easier for new immigrant groups to adopt the language and customs of the in-group. Third, interventions might be focused on changing the specific cognitive and affective responses toward out-groups. However, if it is true that these responses are evolved, then the link between threat and response might be difficult to inhibit or extinguish (cf. fear of snakes and spiders; Ohman & Mineka, 2001). Nevertheless, we suspect that frequent positive interactions with members of out-groups will, over time, reduce initial aversion or hostility. For instance, the Jigsaw classroom experiments (Aronson & Bridgeman, 1979) demonstrate that cooperative relations between members of different ethnic groups are a good means of reducing prejudice.

REFERENCES

Abrams, D., Ando, K., & Hinkle, S. (1998). Psychological attachment to the group: Cross-cultural differences in organizational identification and subjective norms as predictors of workers' turnover intentions. *Personality and Social Psychology Bulletin, 24,* 1027–1039.

Ackerman, J. M., Shapiro, J. R., Neuberg, S. L., Kenrick, D. T., Becker, D. V., & Griskevicius, V. (2006). They all look the same to me (unless they're angry), *Psychological Science, 17,* 836–840.

Archer, J. (2000). Sex differences in aggression between heterosexual partners: A meta-analytic review. *Psychological Bulletin, 126,* 651–680.

Aronson, E., Blaney, N., Stephan, C., Sikes, J., & Snapp, M. (1978). *The jigsaw classroom.* Beverly Hills, CA: Sage.

Aronson, E., & Bridgeman, D. (1979). Jigsaw groups and the desegregated classroom: In pursuit of common goals. *Personality and Social Psychology Bulletin, 5,* 438–446.

Batson, C. D., Sager, K., Garst, E., Kang, M., Rubchinsky, K., & Dawson, K. (1997). Is empathy-induced helping due to self–other merging? *Journal of Personality and Social Psychology, 73,* 495–509.

Baumeister, R. F., & Sommer, K. L. (1997). What do men want? Gender differences and two spheres of belongingness: Comment on Cross and Madson (1997). *Psychological Bulletin, 122,* 38–44.

Becker, S. W., & Eagly, A. H. (2004). The heroism of women and men. *American Psychologist, 59,* 163–178.

Bornstein, G. (2003). Individual, group, and collective interests. *Personality and Social Psychology Review, 7,* 129-145. doi: 10.1207/S15327957PSPR0702_129-145

Bornstein, G. (2006). Personal communication.

Bowles, S. (2006). Group competition, reproductive levelling, and the evolution of human altruism. *Science, 314,* 1569–1572.

Branscombe, N. R., & Wann, D. L. (1991). The positive social and self-concept consequences of sports team identification. *Journal of Sport & Social Issues, 15,* 115–127.

Brewer, M. B. (1979). In-group bias in the minimal intergroup situation: A cognitive–motivational analysis. *Psychological Bulletin, 86,* 307–324.

Brewer, M. B., & Brown, R. J. (1998). Intergroup relations. In D. T. Gilbert, S. T. Fiske, & G. Lindzey (Eds.), *The handbook of social psychology* (4th ed., pp. 554–594). New York: McGraw-Hill.

Brewer, M. B., & Campbell, D. T. (1976). *Ethnocentrism and intergroup attitudes: East African evidence.* New York: Sage.

Brewer, M. B., & Caporael, L. (2006). An evolutionary perspective on social identity: Revisiting groups. In M. Schaller, J. A. Simpson, & D. T. Kenrick (Eds.), *Evolution and social psychology* (pp. 143–161). New York: Psychology Press.

Burnstein, E., Crandall, C., & Kitayama, S. (1994). Some neo-Darwinian decision rules for altruism: Weighing cues for inclusive fitness as a function of the biological importance of the decision. *Journal of Personality and Social Psychology, 67,* 773–789.

Buss, D. M. (2005). *Handbook of evolutionary psychology.* Hoboken, NJ: Wiley.

Buss, D. M., & Schmitt, D. P. (1993). Sexual strategies theory: An evolutionary perspective on human mating. *Psychological Review, 100,* 204–232.

Byrne, D., & Whiten, A. (1988). *Machiavellian intelligence: Social expertise and the evolution of intellect in monkeys, apes, and humans.* New York: Oxford University Press.

Campbell A. (1999). Staying alive: Evolution, culture, and intra-female aggression. *Behavioural and Brain Sciences, 22,* 203–252.

Campbell, D.T. (1965). Ethnocentric and other altruistic motives. In D. Levine, (Ed.), *Nebraska symposium on motivation.* Lincoln: University of Nebraska Press.

Chagnon, N. A. (1988). Life histories, blood revenge, and warfare in a tribal population. *Science, 239*, 985–992.

Choi, J.-K., & Bowles, S. (2007). The coevolution of parochial altruism and war. *Science, 318*(5850), 636–640.

Cialdini, R. B., Brown, S. L., Lewis, B. P., Luce, C., & Neuberg, S. L. (1997). Reinterpreting the empathy-altruism relationship: When one into one equals oneness. *Journal of Personality and Social Psychology, 73*, 481–494.

Cosmides, L., & Tooby, J. (1992). Cognitive adaptations for social exchange. In J. Barkow et al. (Eds.), *The adapted mind: Evolutionary psychology and the generation of culture* (pp. 163–228). New York: Oxford University Press.

Cottrell, C. A., & Neuberg, S. L. (2005). Different emotional reactions to different groups: A sociofunctional threat-based approach to "prejudice." *Journal of Personality and Social Psychology, 88*, 770–789.

Daly, M., & Wilson, M. (1988). *Homicide*. Hawthorne, NY: de Gruyter.

Darwin, C. (1871). *The descent of man, and selection in relation to sex*. London: Murray.

Dawkins, R. (1976). *The selfish gene*. Oxford: Oxford University Press.

De Cremer, D., & Van Vugt, M. (1999). Social identification effects in social dilemmas: A transformation of motives. *European Journal of Social Psychology, 29*, 871–893.

De Waal, F. (2006). *Our inner ape*. London: Granta Books.

Dovidio, J. F., Piliavin, J. A., Schroeder, D. A., & Penner, L. A. (2006). *The social psychology of prosocial behavior*. London: Lawrence Erlbaum.

Dunbar, R. (2004). *The human story: A new history of mankind's evolution*. London: Faber and Faber.

Eagly, A. H., & Johnson, B. T. (1990). Gender and leadership style: A meta-analysis. *Psychological Bulletin, 108*, 233–256.

Eagly, A. H., & Wood, W. (1999). The origins of sex differences in human behavior: Evolved dispositions versus social roles. *American Psychologist, 54*, 408–423.

Faulkner, J., Schaller, M., Park, J. H., & Duncan, L. A. (2004). Evolved disease-avoidance mechanisms and contemporary xenophobic attitudes. *Group Processes and Intergroup Relations, 7*, 333–353.

Fehr, E., & Gächter, S. (2002). Altruistic punishment in humans. *Nature, 415*, 137–140.

Fiske, S. T. (2002). What we know now about bias and intergroup conflict, the problem of the century. *Current Directions in Psychological Science, 11*, 123–128.

Gabriel, S., & Gardner, W. L. (1999). Are there his and hers types of interdependence? The implications of gender differences in collective versus relational interdependence for affect, behavior and cognition. *Journal of Personality and Social Psychology, 77*, 642–655.

Gaertner, S. L., & Dovidio, J. F. (2000). *Reducing intergroup bias: The common ingroup identity model*. Philadelphia: Psychology Press.

Geary, D. C. (1998). *Male, female: The evolution of human sex differences*. Washington, DC: American Psychological Association.

Gerard, H. B., & Hoyt, M. F. (1974). Distinctiveness of social categorization and attitude toward ingroup members. *Journal of Personality and Social Psychology, 29*, 836–842

Goldstein, J. (2003). *War and gender*. Cambridge, UK: Cambridge University Press.

Goodall, J. (1986). *The chimpanzees of Gombe: Patterns of behavior*. Cambridge, MA: Harvard University Press.

Hamilton, W. D. (1964). The genetical evolution of social behaviour. *Journal of Theoretical Biology, 7*, 1–52.

Hardy, C. L., & Van Vugt, M. (2006). Nice guys finish first: The competitive altruism hypothesis. *Personality and Social Psychology Bulletin, 32*, 1402–1413.

Haslam, N. (2006). Dehumanization: An integrative review. *Personality and Social Psychology Review, 10*, 252–264

Hewstone, M., Rubin, M., & Willis, H. (2002). Intergroup bias. *Annual Review of Psychology*, 53, 575–604.

Insko, C. A., Schopler, J., Graetz, K. A., Drigotas, S. M., Currey, D. P., Smith, S. L., et al. (1994). Interindividual–intergroup discontinuity in the prisoner's dilemma game. *Journal of Conflict Resolution, 38,* 87–116.

Insko, C. A., Schopler, J., Hoyle, R. H., Dardis, G. J., & Graetz, K. A. (1990). Individual–group discontinuity as a function of fear and greed. *Journal of Personality and Social Psychology, 58,* 68–79.

Johnson, D. D. P., McDermott, R., Barrett, E. S., Crowden, J., Wrangham, R., McIntyre, M. H., et al. (2006). Overconfidence in war ames: Experimental evidence on expectations, aggression, gender and testosterone. *Proceedings of the Royal Society B, 273,* 2513–2520.

Judd, C. M., & Park, B. (1988). Out-group homogeneity: Judgments of variability at the individual and group levels. *Journal of Personality and Social Psychology, 54,* 778–788.

Keeley, L. (1996). *War before civilization.* New York: Oxford University Press.

Kenrick, D. T., Li, N. P., & Butner, J. (2003). Dynamical evolutionary psychology: Individual decision rules and emergent social norms. *Psychological Review, 110,* 3–28.

Kurzban, R., & Leary, M. R. (2001). Evolutionary origins of stigmatization: The functions of social exclusion. *Psychological Bulletin, 127,* 187–208.

Kurzban, R., & Neuberg, S. (2005). Managing ingroup and outgroup relationships. In D. M. Buss (Ed.), *The handbook of evolutionary psychology* (pp. 653–675). Hoboken, NJ: Wiley.

Kurzban, R., Tooby, J., & Cosmides, L. (2001). Can race be erased? Coalitional computation and social categorization. *Proceedings of the National Academy of Sciences, 98,* 15387–15392.

Leach, C. W., Spears, R., Branscombe, N. R., & Doosje, B. (2003). Malicious pleasure: Schadenfreude at the suffering of another group. *Journal of Personality and Social Psychology, 84,* 932–943.

Leunissen, J., & Van Vugt, M. (2010). *I love the man in the uniform: Why women prefer male warriors.* Unpublished manuscript, University of Kent.

Leyens, J. P., Rodriquez-Perez, A., Rodriguez-Torres, R., Gaunt, R., Paladino, M., Vaes, J., et al. (2001). Psychological essentialism and the differential attribution of uniquely human emotions to ingroups and outgroups. *European Journal of Social Psychology, 31,* 395–411.

Livingstone Smith, D. (2007). *The most dangerous animal in the world: Human nature and the origins of war.* New York: St. Martins Press.

Maner, J. K., Kenrick, D. T., Becker, D. V., Robertson, T. E., Hofer, B., Neuberg, S. L., et al. (2005). Functional projection: How fundamental social motives can bias interpersonal perception. *Journal of Personality and Social Psychology, 88,* 63–78.

Marques, J. M., Yzerbyt, V. Y., & Leyens, J. P. (1988). The "black sheep effect": Extremity of judgments towards ingroup members as a function of group identification. *European Journal of Social Psychology, 18,* 1–16.

Navarrete, C., Fessler, D., & Eng, S. (2007). Elevated ethnocentrism in the first trimester of pregnancy. *Evolution and Human Behavior, 28,* 60–65.

Neuberg, S. L., & Cottrell, C. A. (2006). Evolutionary bases of prejudice. In M. Schaller, J. A. Simpson, & D. T. Kenrick (Eds.), *Evolution and social psychology* (pp. 163–187). New York: Psychology Press.

Öhman, A., & Mineka, S. (2001). Fear, phobia, and preparedness: Toward an evolved module of fear and fear learning. *Psychological Review, 108,* 483–522.

Palmer, C. T., & Tilley, C. F. (1995). Sexual access to females as a motivation for joining gangs: An evolutionary approach. *Journal of Sex Research, 32,* 213–217.

Pemberton, M. B., Insko, C. A., & Schopler, J. (1996). Memory for and experience of differential competitive behavior of individuals and groups. *Journal of Personality and Social Psychology, 71,* 953–966.

Pratto, F., Sidanius, J., Stallworth, L. M., & Malle, B. F. (1994). Social dominance orientation: A personality variable predicting social and political attitudes. *Journal of Personality and Social Psychology, 67,* 741–763.

Richerson, P., & Boyd, R. (2005). *Not by genes alone: How culture transformed human evolution.* Chicago: University of Chicago Press.

Schaller, M. (2003). Ancestral environments and motivated social perception: Goal-like blasts from the evolutionary past. In S. J. Spencer, S. Fein, M. P. Zanna, & J. M. Olson (Eds.), *Motivated social perception: The Ontario Symposium* (pp. 215–231). Mahwah, NJ: Erlbaum.

Schaller, M., & Abeysinghe, A. M. N. D. (2006). Geographical frame of reference and dangerous intergroup attitudes: A double-minority study in Sri Lanka. *Political Psychology, 27,* 615–631.

Schaller, M., & Neuberg, S. L. (in press). Intergroup prejudices and intergroup conflicts. In C. Crawford & D. L. Krebs (Eds.), *Foundations of evolutionary psychology: Ideas, issues, and applications.* Mahwah, NJ: Erlbaum.

Schaller, M., Park, J. H., & Faulkner, J. (2003). Prehistoric dangers and contemporary prejudices. *European Review of Social Psychology, 14,* 105–137.

Schaller, M., Park, J. H., & Kenrick, D. T. (2007). Human evolution and social cognition. In R. I. M. Dunbar & L. Barrett (Eds.), *Oxford handbook of evolutionary psychology* (pp. 491–504). Oxford, UK: Oxford University Press.

Schaller, M., Park, J. H., & Mueller, A. (2003). Fear of the dark: Interactive effects of beliefs about danger and ambient darkness on ethnic stereotypes. *Personality and Social Psychology Bulletin, 29,* 637–649.

Sherif, M., Harvey, O. J., White, B. J., Hood, W. R., & Sherif, C. W. (1961). Intergroup conflict and cooperation: *The Robbers Cave experiment.* Norman, Oklahoma: University Book Exchange.

Sidanius, J., Cling, B. J., & Pratto, F. (1991). Ranking and linking as a function of sex and gender role attitudes. *Journal of Social Issues, 47,* 131–149.

Sidanius, J., & Pratto, F. (1999). *Social dominance: An intergroup theory of social hierarchy and oppression.* New York: Cambridge University Press.

Tajfel, H., & Turner, J. C. (1979). An integrative theory of intergroup conflict. In W. G. Austin & S. Worchel (Eds.), *The social psychology of intergroup relations* (pp. 33–47). Monterey, CA: Brooks/Cole.

Tajfel, H., & Turner, J. C. (1986). The social identity theory of intergroup behavior. In S. Worchel & W. G. Austin (Eds.), *Psychology of intergroup relations* (pp. 7–24). Chicago: Nelson-Hall.

Taylor, S. E., Klein, L. C., Lewis, B. P., Gruenewald, R.A.R., Gurung, R. A., & Updegraff, J. A. (2000). Biobehavioral responses to stress in females: Tend-and-befriend not fight-or-flight. *Psychological Review, 107,* 411–429.

Tooby, J., & Cosmides, L. (1988). *The evolution of war and its cognitive foundations* (Institute for Evolutionary Studies Tech. Rep. No. 88-1). Palo Alto, CA: Institute for Evolutionary Studies.

Trivers, R. L. (1971). The evolution of reciprocal altruism. *Quarterly Review of Biology, 46,* 35–57.

Trivers, R. L. (1972). Parental investment and sexual selection. In B. Campbell (Ed.), *Sexual selection and the descent of man* (pp. 136–179). Chicago: Aldine.

Turner, J. C., Hogg, M. A., Oakes, P., Reicher, S., & Wetherell, M. (1987). *Rediscovering the social group: A self-categorization theory.* Oxford, UK: Blackwell.

Van Vugt, M. (2006). The evolutionary origins of leadership and followership. *Personality and Social Psychology Review, 10*, 354–372.

Van Vugt, M. (2009). Sex differences in intergroup competition, agreesion, and warfare. Annals of the New York Academy of Sciences, 1167, 124–134. DOI: 10.1111/j.1749-6632.2009.04539.x

Van Vugt, M., & Chang, K. (2008). *Group reactions to loyal and disloyal members: The moderating role of member criticality.* Unpublished manuscript, University of Kent.

Van Vugt, M., De Cremer, D., & Janssen, D. P. (2007). Gender differences in cooperation and competition: The male-warrior hypothesis. *Psychological Science, 18*, 19–23.

Van Vugt, M., & Hart, C. M. (2004). Social identity as social glue: The origins of group loyalty. *Journal of Personality and Social Psychology, 86*, 585–598.

Van Vugt, M., & Schaller, M. (2008). Evolutionary perspectives on group dynamics: An introduction. *Group Dynamics, 12*, 1–6.

Van Vugt, M., Snyder, M., Tyler, T. R., & Biel, A. (Eds.). (2000). *Cooperation in modern society: Promoting the welfare of communities, states and organizations.* New York: Routledge.

Van Vugt, M., & Spisak, B. (2008). Sex differences in leadership emergence during competitions within and between groups. Psychological Science, 19, 854–858. doi: 10.1111/j.1467-9280.2008.02168.x

Van Vugt, M., & Van Lange, P.A.M. (2006). The altruism puzzle: Psychological adaptations for prosocial behavior: In M. Schaller, J. A. Simpson, & D. T. Kenrick (Eds.), *Evolution and social psychology* (pp. 237–261). New York: Psychology Press.

Wildschut, T., Pinter, B., Vevea, J. L., Insko, C. A., & Schopler, J. (2003). Beyond the group mind: A quantitative review of the interindividual–intergroup discontinuity effect. *Psychological Bulletin, 129*, 698–722.

Wilson, E. O. (1975). *Sociobiology: The new synthesis.* Cambridge, MA: Harvard University Press.

Wilson, D. S., Van Vugt, M., & O'Gorman, R. (2008). Multilevel selection theory and major evolutionary transistions: Implications for psychological science. *Current Directions in Psychological Science, 17*, 6–9.

Wilson, M., & Wrangham, R. (2003). Intergroup relations in chimpanzees. *Annual Review of Anthropology, 32*, 363–392.

Wrangham, R. W., & Peterson, D. (1996). *Demonic males: Apes and the origins of human violence.* Boston, MA: Houghton Mifflin Co.

Zdaniuk, B., & Levine, J. M. (2001). Group loyalty: Impact of members' identification and contributions. *Journal of Experimental Social Psychology, 37*, 502–509.

Zimbardo, P. (1971). The power and pathology of imprisonment. *Congressional Records, 15*, 10–25.

16

Implications of Global Climate Change for Violence in Developed and Developing Countries

CRAIG A. ANDERSON and MATT DELISI

Iowa State University

R apid global climate change, taking place over decades rather than millennia, is a fact of twenty-first-century life. Human activity, especially the release of greenhouse gases, has initiated a general warming trend. The 10 warmest years on record between 1880 and 2008 were the last 10. This trend is expected to continue until the atmospheric composition returns to a preindustrial-era norm.

Climate change effects on specific regions are expected to vary considerably. Though most parts of the globe are warming, a few places may experience cooler climates as ocean and wind currents shift. Some regions are experiencing increased rainfall, whereas many others are having prolonged droughts. In 2007, the Intergovernmental Panel on Climate Change (IPCC) released a report that included numerous projections of likely effects by the end of this century, under varying assumptions of how world governments, industries, and people respond. The best-case scenario assumes huge reductions in net greenhouse gas production, beginning almost immediately. In this scenario, climate models predict an average global temperature increase of 1.8°C (3.24°F) and an average sea-level increase of 28 cm (11 inches). The worst-case scenario, which assumes a business-as-usual approach, predicts increases of 4.0°C (7.2°F) and 43 cm (17 inches). Other projections, some of which have already become apparent, include increases in heat waves and heavy precipitation; decreases in precipitation in subtropical areas; and increases in tropical cyclones. More specific projections include (1) 5–8% increase in the proportion of Africa that is arid and semiarid; (2) major flooding of heavily populated areas of Asia from rising sea levels and storms; (3) inundation of low-lying islands; (4) severe water shortages in Australia and New Zealand; (5) drought in southern Europe; (6) decreased soil moisture and food crops in Latin America; and (7) increased winter flooding and summer heat waves in North America. More recent research being prepared for the next IPCC report suggests that the new best-case scenario will be worse than the old worst-case scenario, with sea levels rising a least 1 meter (Vermeer & Rahmstorf, 2009). Because 13% of the world's population—hundreds of millions of people—live in low-lying coastal areas (Engelman, 2009, p. 41), this latter projection is particularly disturbing. Indonesia may lose as many as 2,000 small islands in the next 20 years to rising sea levels (Engelman, p. 3).

In addition to the changes in average temperature and rainfall, climate models also predict an increase in extreme weather events. Recent data suggest that this increase has already begun, with dramatic increases in floods, wind storms, and drought disasters in the last 20 years (Engelman, 2009, pp. 16, 30). Hurricanes, cyclones, and other tropical storms also are increasing in intensity. The problem with rising sea levels concerns not just the height of high tides but also storm surge. A once-a-century storm in New York City, for example, will occur about once every 3 years (Rahmstorf, 2009) if average sea level increases by 1 meter.

Research from psychology, sociology, political science, economics, history, and geography suggest that rapid global warming can increase the incidence of violent behavior in at least three ways. One involves direct effects of uncomfortably warm temperatures on irritability, aggression, and violence. A second involves indirect effects of global warming on factors that put children and adolescents at risk for developing into violence-prone adults. The third involves indirect effects of rapid climate change on populations whose livelihoods and survival are suddenly at risk, effects that influence economic and political stability, migration, and violent intergroup conflict. For example, various governmental and scientific reports have noted that climate change has exacerbated existing tensions and conflicts centered in the Darfur region of Sudan and in Bangladesh.

Heat and Aggression

Much research has established that uncomfortably warm temperatures can increase the likelihood of physical aggression and violence (Anderson & Anderson, 1998; Anderson, Anderson, Dorr, DeNeve, & Flanagan, 2000; for a concise review see Anderson, 2001). Three types of studies have tested and found considerable support for this heat hypothesis: experimental studies, geographic region studies, and time period studies.

Experimental Studies of the Heat Effect   Early experimental studies of heat effects yielded considerable inconsistency in outcomes, perhaps because of participant suspicion and measurement issues. Later studies provided better tests and cleaner results. For example, Vrij, van der Steen, and Koppelaar (1994) conducted a field experiment in which Dutch police officers were randomly assigned to perform a training session involving a simulated burglary under hot or comfortable

conditions. Officers in the hot condition reported more aggressive and threatening impressions of the suspect and were more likely to draw their weapon and to shoot the simulated suspect.

Anderson et al. (2000) reported a series of laboratory experiments on both hot and cold temperature effects. In separate experiments, uncomfortably warm temperatures (relative to comfortable temperature) increased participants' feelings of anger and hostility, their perceptions of hostility in observed dyadic interactions, and their initial retaliatory aggressive behavior against a person whose prior harmful behavior was of an ambiguous nature. Recent experiments by Wilkowski, Meier, Robinson, Carter, & Feltman (2009) linked heat-related imagery to a host of anger and aggression-related perceptions and judgments.

Geographic Region Studies of the Heat Effect

Studies dating back to the nineteenth century suggest that hotter regions have higher violent crime rates than cooler regions (Anderson, 1989). However, even within the same country regions differ in many ways other than climate. Some of these other differences (e.g., poverty, unemployment, age distribution, culture) are risk factors for violence. The best geographic region studies include statistical controls for such factors. Even when such factors are controlled, temperature predicts violent crime rates. For example, hotter U.S. cities have higher violence rates than cooler cities, even after statistically controlling for 14 risk factors including age, education, race, economic, and culture of violence factors (Anderson & Anderson, 1996). Recent work by Van de Vliert (2009; in press; under review) further suggests that climate and economic conditions jointly influence culture in ways that encourage or discourage aggression and violence. Particularly vulnerable are populations that live in regions that are both climatically challenging (hot, cold, or both) and impoverished.

Time Period Studies of the Heat Effect   "Time period" studies compare aggression rates within the same region but across time periods that differ in temperature. Studies vary considerably in terms of the time periods for which violence and temperature are assessed. Overall, results are remarkably consistent. Hotter time periods (e.g., days, seasons, years) are associated with higher levels of violence. For example, riots in the United States are relatively more likely on hotter than cooler days (Carlsmith & Anderson, 1979). Similarly, violent crimes across a wide range of countries and measures occur more frequently during hotter seasons than cooler ones (Anderson, 1989).

Of course, other violence-related factors may differ between hotter versus cooler time periods, even within the same region. For example, in the United States large numbers of youth are out of school during the summer months, so one could argue that the routine activities of the population might account for seasonal differences in violence. Several studies have addressed this and other alternative explanations of heat-related time period effects. Although it is clear that routine activities do influence aggressive behavior, it is also clear that such alternative explanations do not parsimoniously account for many observed effects. For example, in two studies Anderson and Anderson (1984) found significant day-of-week effects on daily violent crime rates, in addition to heat effects. Other time-related routine activities, such as youth being out of school in the summer, cannot account for the heat effect found in Study 1 (Chicago), because that study included only the summer months. Similarly, routine activity theory cannot account for the finding that Major League Baseball pitchers are more likely to hit batters with a pitched ball on hot days than on cool days, even after statistically controlling for the possibility of sweat influencing the pitcher's control (Reifman, Larrick, & Fein, 1991).

Differences in violent crime rates for hotter versus cooler days have been found within cities as varied as Houston, Chicago, and Minneapolis (Anderson & Anderson, 1984, 1998). Even after controlling for routine activity effects of time of day and day of week, violent crimes are relatively more frequent in hotter weather (e.g., Anderson & Anderson, 1998; Bushman, Wang, & Anderson, 2005a, 2005b). Interestingly, nonviolent crime (burglary, motor vehicle theft) rates are largely unrelated to heat.

When the time period is years (instead of days or seasons), the kinds of potentially confounded variables change. For example, U.S. youth are out of school in the summer regardless of whether the year is slightly warmer or cooler. When considering year-based studies and global warming effects, one might be concerned about whether aggression-related factors such as age distribution (e.g., proportion of the population that is in the high-crime age range) and income inequality (e.g., LaFree & Drass, 1996) might be confounded with time or systematic temperature changes. We conducted two new studies to examine the effects of yearly changes in temperature on violent and nonviolent crime in the United States, beginning with 1950.

Study 1: Hot Years and Violent Crime

Method

Data   This study extends Anderson, Bushman, and Groom's (1997) Study 1. Major additions are 13 years of new data and several aggression-related control variables. Data for the years 1950–2008 were obtained from U.S. government sources. From the FBI's Uniform Crime Reports we created two crime measures. *Violent crime* was defined as the sum of the homicide and assault rates per 100,000 population. *Nonviolent crime* was defined as the sum of the burglary and motor vehicle theft rates per 100,000 population.[1]

The primary predictor variable, annual average temperature, was computed from data from the National Oceanic and Atmospheric Administration. Control variables were year, age (proportion of the population in the 15–29 high-crime age range), prison (number of incarcerated state and federal inmates per 100,000 population), poverty (percent of families living below the poverty line), and the Gini index of income distribution inequality (perfectly equal distribution yields a

---

[1] As in prior studies, robbery and rape were excluded for theoretical reasons. Both appear to have a greater mixture of aggressive motives (intent to harm) and nonaggressive motives. See Anderson et al., 1997.

Gini index of 0, perfect inequality = 1.0). Year effects might reflect a host of cultural and population changes, such as increased reporting of assaults and improvements in trauma care. The other control variables have obvious theoretical links to violence.

Correlated Residuals   Time-series data often have a problem in which the residuals are correlated with time. The most common version is when the residuals at any given time period (T) are correlated with the residuals at the subsequent time period ($T + 1$). Such "autocorrelations" make ordinary least squares (OLS) procedures inappropriate for estimating regression parameters. With a sufficiently large sample of time periods, autoregression (AR) techniques can be used to reduce or eliminate autocorrelations among residuals and can thus yield more accurate results. In all regression analyses, chi-square tests (Ljung & Box, 1978) were used to assess goodness of model fit regarding the presence of correlated residuals. When the chi-square statistic suggested that the model provided a poor fit to the data, autoregressive parameters were added. This process was iteratively repeated until the chi-square test statistic indicated nonsignificant autocorrelations in the new residuals.

The present study addresses five alternative explanations for heat-related time period effects on violent behavior: (1) seasonal fluctuations; (2) correlated residuals; (3) coincidental crime, year, and global warming trends; (4) coincidental age distribution shifts; and (5) coincidental income and poverty shifts. The first alternative explanation is dealt with by using the year as the unit of analysis. The remaining alternatives are handled by statistical controls. Nonviolent crime analyses are included as a point of comparison.

Results   Table 16.1 presents descriptive statistics and zero-order correlations among the variables. Average annual temperature has increased during this 59-year period ($r = .54$). Note the substantial zero-order correlations among violent crime, temperature, and year. This suggests that in addition to checking for autocorrelated residuals a conservative statistical procedure would also control for year effects. Finally, note that nonviolent crime was not strongly correlated with temperature.

Table 16.2 presents the results of OLS and AR analyses on violent crime (top section) and nonviolent crime (bottom section). OLS regression revealed a large effect of temperature on violent crime; each 1°F increase in average annual temperature was associated with 79 more serious and deadly assaults per 100,000 people. However, the AR test revealed significant autocorrelations among the residuals (χ^2 (6) = 196, $p < .05$). We added AR parameters to the model until the autocorrelation test became nonsignificant (three parameters were needed). This greatly reduced the slope relating temperature to violent crime, but this heat effect remained statistically and practically significant. In the next step we controlled for year. The temperature effect on violent crime remained essentially unchanged. The year effect also was significant; each year added 4.90 violent crimes per 100,000 people. We examined a host of models with the other control variables (age, prison rate, poverty, Gini). Only prison rate yielded a significant effect. With three autoregressive parameters—temperature, year, and prison—in the model the temperature

TABLE 16.1   Correlations Among the Predictor and Outcome Variables, Study 1, 1950–2008

	Year	Temp	Age	Prison	Pov	Gini	Vio	NVio
Year	1.00	0.54	0.04	0.90	-0.75	0.88	0.87	0.52
Temp	0.54	1.00	-0.19	0.61	-0.18	0.61	0.48	0.11
Age	0.04	-0.19	1.00	-0.36	-0.44	-0.30	0.25	0.78
Prison	0.90	0.61	-0.36	1.00	-0.43	0.97	0.69	0.13
Pov	-0.75	-0.18	-0.44	-0.43	1.00	-0.36	-0.71	-0.79
Gini	0.88	0.61	-0.30	0.97	-0.36	1.00	0.72	0.16
Vio	0.87	0.48	0.25	0.69	-0.71	0.72	1.00	0.75
Nvio	0.52	0.11	0.78	0.13	-0.79	0.16	0.75	1.00

Descriptive Statistics

	Year	Temp	Age	Prison	Pov	Gini	Vio	NVio
Mean	1979	57.85	0.227	231	16.1	0.382	239.1	1300
St.Dev.	17.2	0.78	0.025	153	5.6	0.027	127.7	544
Min.	1950	56.60	0.195	93	11.1	0.348	55.7	385
Max.	2008	59.70	0.272	512	32.5	0.432	451.3	2163

Notes: N = 59. If $r > .25$ then $p < .05$. Temp, annual average temperature. Age, proportion of U.S. population in the 15–29 age range. Prison, number of incarcerated state and federal inmates per 100,000 population. Pov, percent of families living below the poverty line. Gini, index of income distribution equality (perfectly equal distribution yields a Gini index of 0; perfect inequality = 1.0). Vi, serious and deadly assaults per 100,000 population. Nvio, burglaries and motor vehicle thefts per 100,000 population.

TABLE 16.2   Destructive Testing Results Using Auto-Regressive Parameters and Competitor Variables, Study 1, 1950–2008

Violent[a]	AR Test	Temperature Effect				Year Effect			Prison Effect		
Model	χ^2	df	b	SE	t						
OLS	196°	6	79	19.1	4.15°						
AR-3	3.80	3	4.11	1.25	3.30°	b	SE	t			
AR-3	4.07	3	4.16	1.25	3.33°	4.90	1.68	2.91°	b	SE	t
AR-3	3.27	3	4.19	1.21	3.47°	8.34	1.88	4.43°	-.42	.203	-2.07°

NonVio[b]	AR Test		Age Effect		
Model	χ^2	df	b	SE	t
OLS	186°	6	16,646	1778	9.37°
AR-3	4.85	3	9645	3321	2.90°

Temp, annual average temperature. Age, proportion of U.S. population in the 15–29 age range. AR, autoregression. OLS, ordinary least squares.
[a] Serious and deadly assault: Assault + homicide.
[b] Nonviolent crime: Burglary + motor vehicle theft.
° $p < .05$. + $p < .10$ if $t > 1.67$.

effect remained significant (b = 4.19). Finally, the greater the proportion of the U.S. population that was imprisoned, the smaller the violent crime rate.

A host of OLS and AR models on nonviolent crime did not yield a single significant temperature effect. Indeed, after appropriate AR parameters were in the model, only age was a significant predictor of nonviolent crime rates. For every 1% increase in the proportion of high-crime age individuals in the population, there was an increase of 96 nonviolent crimes per 100,000 people.

Study 2: Hot Summers and Violent Crime

Method

Data   This study extends Anderson et al.'s (1997) Study 2. It examines violent crime in the summer months in the United States relative to nonsummer months. Major additions are 9 years of new data and several aggression-related control variables. Data for the years 1950–2004 were collected from numerous governmental sources. Seasonal data were unavailable after 2004.

Basically, the dataset is the same as for the prior study, with two major exceptions. First, the outcome variable is the difference between the percent of the year's crimes that were committed during the summer months (June, July, August) and the average of the other three seasons, adjusted for number of days in each season. If violent crimes were equally likely to occur regardless of season, then the summer months would account for exactly 25% of them, and the summer effect score used in this study would be zero. If violent crimes were relatively more (less) likely in the summer months, the summer effect would be greater (less) than zero. A similar summer effect was computed for nonviolent crimes.

The second major difference from Study 1 was the temperature measure. Across a sample of cities, we recorded the number of hot days (maximum temperature was $\geq$ 90°F) per year. The vast majority of hot days in the continental United States occur during the summer months, so this measure is a good indicator of the hotness of each of the 55 summers.

Predictions   We expected the summer effect on violent crime to be significantly greater than zero, when averaged across years. Furthermore, we expected years with more hot days to yield larger summer effects on violent crime than years with fewer hot days.

Results   As expected, the average summer effect on violent crime was significantly greater than zero (M = 2.57, $t(54)$ = 18.52, p < .05). Violent crimes are overrepresented in the summer months. In fact, in only 2 of the 55 years was the summer effect negative.

Concerning the second hypothesis, there was no evidence of autocorrelations among the residuals in any of the analyses of violent crime, so OLS analyses were appropriate. The only variable that significantly predicted the size of the summer effect on violent crime was the number of hot days (b = .068, $t(53)$ = 3.07, p < .05). None of the control variables (including year) had a significant effect, nor did they

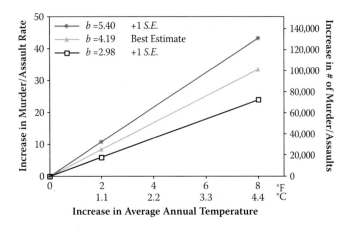

Figure 16.1   Heat effect on violent crime in the United States, 1950–2008.

substantially reduce the size of the hot days effect. Nonviolent crime was unaffected by number of hot days.

General Discussion of the Heat Effect on Aggression

In sum, the heat hypothesis has been repeatedly confirmed. Laboratory studies suggest that this is largely the result of heat-induced increases in irritability and in hostile interpersonal perception biases. There is additional evidence that these effects can be further traced to thermoregulation and emotion regulation areas of the brain (Anderson, 1989; Boyanowsky, 1999, 2008; Boyanowsky, Calvert-Boyanowsky, Young, & Brideau, 1981). The implication for global warming is that at the level of the individual person increased exposure to uncomfortably hot temperatures will increase the likelihood of interpersonal conflict and violence. It is difficult to estimate with confidence how big an impact global warming will have on violent crime in modern societies, but Figure 16.1 provides some rough estimates based on the results of Study 1. If average annual temperature in the United States increases by 8°F (4.4°C), the best estimate of the effect on the total murder and assault rate is an increase of about 34 per 100,000 people, or over 100,000 more such serious and deadly assaults per year in a population of 305 million.

One response to high heat in industrialized countries is increased use of air conditioning in buildings, cars, buses, and trains. Although such actions might mitigate heat-induced increases in aggression, they increase the production of greenhouse gases.

There are no comparable daily, seasonal, or annual data on the heat effect on violent crime in less developed countries. However, the findings summarized in previous sections suggest that uncomfortably hot temperatures can have a fairly direct effect on aggressive and violent tendencies, perhaps through neuro and hormonal pathways that are common to thermoregulation and emotion (see Chapter 9 in this volume).

DEVELOPMENT OF VIOLENCE-PRONE INDIVIDUALS

Global climate change will likely increase the proportion of children and youth exposed to risk factors known to increase the likelihood of becoming a violence-prone individual—someone who frequently uses physical aggression or violence to deal with conflict, to get desired resources, and to impulsively and shortsightedly satisfy one's wants (Gottfredson & Hirschi, 1990; Moffitt, 1993). Studies of violent youth and criminals reveal a host of psychological, neuropsychological, genetic, and environmental risk factors that play a major role in determining who becomes a violence-prone person. These interrelated risk factors include male gender; strongly heritable antisocial traits including impulsivity, sensation seeking, low intelligence, and poor self-regulation; poverty; poor prenatal and childhood nutrition; familial dysfunction; growing up in violent neighborhoods; psychopathy; low education; and disorganized and unstable neighborhoods (DeLisi, 2005).

Food, Violence, and Antisocial Behavior

Potentially one of the most catastrophic effects of rapid climate change centers on food availability. Today, one in eight U.S. households with infants is food insecure—the family has limited or uncertain availability of nutritionally adequate and safe foods. In many parts of the world, food insecurity is a much larger problem. This means that a robust proportion of impoverished children (notwithstanding the multifaceted independent effects of poverty on antisocial behavior) face the specter of poor nutrition or malnutrition—conditions with severe long-term consequences for crime and violence. A recent study is illustrative. Jianghong Liu and colleagues examined the longitudinal relationship between malnutrition and subsequent externalizing and antisocial behaviors using a birth cohort of children from the island of Mauritius, off the coast of Africa. Children who were malnourished at age 3 were significantly more aggressive and hyperactive at age 8, more aggressive and prone to externalizing (acting out) behaviors at age 11, and more hyperactive and more likely to exhibit symptoms of conduct disorder at age 17 (Liu, Raine, Venables, & Mednick, 2004).

It is not merely armchair conjecture to assert that food scarcity will result in increased violence-prone individuals; history has already told such a story. From October 1944 to May 1945, residents of the western Netherlands experienced moderate to severe food scarcity caused by a German army blockade. Over 100,000 Dutch men born between 1944 and 1946 were studied to examine the effects of gestational nutritional deficiency on subsequent proneness to violence (Neugebauer, Hoek, & Susser, 1999). Men exposed to severe maternal nutritional deficiency during the first and second trimesters were 2.5 times more likely than men not exposed to severe maternal nutritional deficiency to develop antisocial personality disorder, a psychiatric diagnosis characterized by recurrent use of violence and other antisocial behaviors. Other studies linking poverty to poor developmental outcomes are reviewed by Huston and Bentley (2010). Similarly, recent work by Chen, Cohen, and Miller (2010) reveals that poverty effects on children's stress levels (assessed by cortisol) is exacerbated by perceived threat and by chaos in their daily living conditions.

Environmental–Genetic Interplay

Children in regions of famine, prolonged droughts, civil unrest, and wars (see next section) are exposed to many known risk factors for the development of violence-prone adolescents and adults. Longitudinal studies have shown that even fairly brief exposures (e.g., a few months) to some of these risk factors can put the individual child (or fetus) on a high-risk developmental trajectory.

Caspi and colleagues (2002) examined the interaction between monoamine oxidase A (MAOA)—an enzymatic degrader that modulates neurotransmitters—and childhood maltreatment on later antisocial outcomes. For all antisocial outcomes, the association between maltreatment and antisocial behavior was conditional on the MAOA genotype. Just 12% of the sample had both the genetic risk (low-activity MAOA levels) and maltreatment; they accounted for 44% of the total convictions for violent crime. Moreover, 85% of those who had both risk factors developed some form of antisocial behavior. In the absence of maltreatment, the genotypic risk factor did not manifest itself behaviorally. Similar gene–environment interactions have been found for early life, environmental adversity, and psychiatric outcomes (Caspi et al., 2003; Uher & McGuffin, 2010).

If global warming brings about a world of dramatically increased environmental risk and an unknown number of environmental pathogens, then it is likely that a proportional proliferation of behavioral risks will result as these pathogenic environments moderate genetic and neuropsychological risks within individuals. Recall the pernicious and long-term effects of malnutrition and violent and antisocial behavior. Malnutrition, particularly when it is endured during gestation, causes a host of neuropsychological deficits relating to neuronal reduction, brain toxicity, altered neurotransmission, and other physiological effects. These neuropsychological deficits also interact with genes to predict antisocial behavior. For example, Beaver, DeLisi, Vaughn, and Wright (2010) found that neuropsychological deficits (such as those implicated by prenatal nutritional deficiency) interacted with the low-activity polymorphism in the MAOA gene to predict violent behavior, delinquency, and low self-control across two time periods.

Terrorism Susceptibility

Recent research into terrorism and suicide bombers has led to a better understanding of the social and environmental conditions that are conducive to the development of individuals willing to use such extreme tactics (Kruglanski, Chen, Dechesne, Fishman, & Orehek, 2009; see also Chapter 10 in this volume). Briefly, these researchers have shown that such extremely violent tactics can emerge from a "quest for personal significance," triggered by failure to satisfy basic human motives to belong to a significant group and to contribute to its welfare. A variety of events can lead to feelings of failure and exclusion, events such as personal trauma, loss of family through violence, and social humiliation. Under the right (or wrong) circumstances, including (1) an available ideology to justify violence against the perceived perpetrators of trauma, humiliation, and violent loss; and (2) social pressures to engage in violence against the perpetrators as a means of gaining or restoring one's own signifi-cance to one's group, even suicidal terrorism becomes a viable option to the individual (see Chapter 3 in this volume for a related discussion of aggression and ostracism).

CIVIL UNREST, ECOMIGRATION, GENOCIDE, AND WAR

Both the heat effect and the development of violence-prone individuals focus on violence at the individual level. This third link between climate change and vio-lence focuses on larger groups of people—communities, tribes or clans, societies, and countries. This is a particularly complex set of phenomena. Emerging research from several fields suggests that rapid climate change (heating or cooling) often leads to increases in violence. There are several ways this can happen. For example, in subsistence economies rapid changes in climate lead to a decreased availability of food, water, and shelter. Depending on the level of social–political organiza-tion, such shortages can lead to civil unrest and civil war, to migration to adjacent regions and conflict with the people who already live in that region, and even to genocide and war. Although it would be overly simplistic to blame the bloody conflicts in Africa and Asia during the latter twentieth and this first decade of the twenty-first century on climate change and environmental disasters, it also would be incorrect to ignore the role played by the economic hardships (including starva-tion) wrought by the prolonged droughts and resulting resource shortages. Civil unrest, revolutions, and wars require recruits and leaders who are willing to risk much to gain valuable resources.

Case Studies

Historical research shows that environmental disasters, many linked to relatively rapid climate changes, can lead to increases in group-level violence. Of course, not all environmental disasters are caused by climate change. For example, earthquakes, tsunamis, and volcanoes can and do cause environmental disasters but are not directly related to climate change. However, floods due to exces-sive rainfall or melting glaciers, droughts, hurricanes, and cyclones are climate-change related.

This section concerns whether environmental disasters increase violence rates and severity, regardless of whether the environmental disaster was the direct result of climate change.

In the recent past, evidence of such effects comes from the U.S. Dust Bowl of the 1930s, clashes in Bangladesh and India since the 1950s, and Hurricane Katrina in the United States in 2005 (Reuveny, 2008). The cases differ in many ways, includ-ing political organization and strength. But in each case, there is evidence that envi-ronmental disaster led to increased interpersonal violence, a result of *ecomigration* (migration of a large number of people as a result of ecological disaster).

Hurricane Katrina   When Katrina hit Louisiana and Mississippi in fall 2005, it flooded about 80% of New Orleans and destroyed much of the Biloxi–Gulfport area. More than a million people left the area. This ecomigration was to at least 30 different states, with Texas (especially Houston) absorbing the most, at least initially. Texas officials ran 20,000 criminal checks and found minimal criminal data on their Katrina immigrants. Nonetheless, Houston recorded huge increases in homicides in the following months, relative to the same months in the year prior to Katrina (Reuveny, 2008). There were other indicators (e.g., polls) of tension between the long-time residents and the newcomers. However, there was no outbreak of civil war and no evidence of armed intergroup conflict. This seems to be generally true of ecomigrations in well-organized highly industrialized countries.

U.S. Dust Bowl   In the 1930s, poor farming practices combined with a prolonged drought and strong winds to produce an environmental disaster in the Great Plains, particularly Oklahoma. About 2.5 million people left the area, primarily for adjacent states, but about 300,000 went to California. There are numerous reports of hostility and violence between the residents and the ecomigrants, including police efforts to block the migrants or to scatter them from their settlements, beatings, and shack burnings (Reuveny, 2008).

Bangladesh   Population pressures from a very high fertility rate combined with unsustainable farming practices and environmental disasters (possibly related to climate change) led to large-scale migrations to adjacent regions in Bangladesh and across the border to India. From 1976 to 2000 about 25 million people were affected by droughts, 270 million by floods, and another 41 million by rain and wind storms. Making matters worse, in 1975 the Indian Farakka Barrage began diverting water from the Ganges River to other parts of India, decreasing the amount flowing into its historic tributaries in Bangladesh. The resulting salt-water intrusion from the Indian Ocean and increased silting of the riverbed resulted in additional floods, erosion, and environmental degradation.

An estimated 12 to 17 million Bangladeshis have migrated to adjacent states in India since the 1950s. Clashes between the residents and the migrants have occurred along socioeconomic, religious, ethnic, and national lines, resulting in thousands of deaths, especially after the 1983 elections. Indeed, 1,700 Bengalis were killed in a 5-hour rampage in 1983.

1967 Arab–Israeli War   There is historical evidence of water issues contributing to conflict in the Middle East at least as early as the seventh century B.C. (Gleick, 1993). Since the establishment of Israel in 1948 the region has periodically been at war, for a variety of political and religious reasons. But water issues also play an important role in the conflicts, especially issues concerning the Jordan River basin. This basin is shared by Israel, Jordan, Lebanon, and Syria. According to Gleick (p. 85), "one of the factors directly contributing to the 1967 War was the attempt by members of the Arab League in the early 1960s to divert the headwaters of the Jordan River away from Israel." (For additional examples of important water conflicts, historical as well as contemporary, see Gleick, 1993; Postel & Wolf, 2001).

Time-Period Studies

Little Ice Age Effects   Following the Medieval Warm Period, the Little Ice Age (roughly 1300–1850) ushered in cooler temperatures, shorter growing seasons, and a host of other climate-related changes. Scholars from a variety of disciplines have begun examining the relationships among relatively rapid shifts in climate and a host of human population events, including war. Fagan (2000) weaves a careful story of climate shifts and their impact on Europeans, linking farming practices and outcomes, social and cultural changes, civil unrest, and war. Though careful to avoid extreme claims of environmental determinism, he makes a strong case for viewing rapid climate change (in this case, cooling) as contributing to war and other forms of violence. Briefly, rapid climate change disrupted food production, leading to food shortages, famines, civil unrest, and war. This process seems particularly important in agrarian societies that do not have the political and economic resources to effectively deal with food shortages and famine. Indeed, according to Fagan the French Revolution was fueled in part by food shortages that were largely the result of the failure of farming practices to adapt to the changed climate.

Zhang and colleagues (Zhang, Brecke, Lee, He, & Zhang, 2007; Zhang, Zhang, Lee, & He, 2007) took a more statistical approach to examining the question of whether rapid shifts in climate from 1000 to 1900 were linked to wars. Using data from the Northern Hemisphere and from China, they found statistical support for their model, which is very similar to Fagan's (2000).

It might seem strange to include studies of rapid cooling in a work that is focused on global warming and violence. However, the basic model is the same regardless of whether a rapid shift in climate is warming or cooling, flooding or drought. A systematic change in climate that threatens basic human resources puts stress on economic and social systems. That stress can lead to ecomigration and conflict or directly to war over resources.

Civil War in Africa   Burke, Miguel, Satyanath, Dykema, and Lobell (2009) recently analyzed civil wars in Africa from 1981 to 2002. Some models included per capita income and form of government as well as temperature and precipitation. Overall, the results showed a strong positive relation between temperature increases and civil war. For a 1°C increase in temperature, there was a 5.9% increase in civil war. Given the base rate of civil war in this dataset (11%), this represents a 54% relative increase in the likelihood of civil war for each 1°C increase in temperature. The authors noted that a 1°C increase is projected by 2030 and that if future wars are as deadly as past ones an additional 393,000 battle deaths can be expected in this region.

Additional Ecomigration and War-Related Forms of Violence

A recent report by the United Nations (Engelman, 2009) highlighted a number of additional ways global climate change can lead to increased violence. Perhaps the most notable is the likely increase in violent crimes committed against women and children as a consequence of their increased vulnerability in subsistence economies that suffer an ecological disaster. With the breakdown of societal norms and increased economic stress come increases in rape, assault, and homicide. As far as we know, there are no studies directly linking global warming to such effects, but such outcomes have been documented in the aftermath of severe floods, food shortages, and war ("civil" or otherwise).

IMPLICATIONS

Collectively, these three ways global climate change increases human violence suggest a rather dire future. We prefer to end on a more positive note. Action can be taken, by individuals, groups, and governments. One obvious action is to reduce greenhouse gas emissions, thereby reducing the magnitude and speed of climate change. Many individuals, groups, and governments are taking actions, albeit somewhat belatedly.

In addition to the technological and lifestyle changes being actively developed, discussed, and implemented, it also seems worthwhile to consider an infrequently discussed option, the potential benefits of better population control. One thousand years ago the world population was about 300 million. Currently it is about 7 billion. Some have estimated that the world population will peak at around 10 billion. Most of that increase will take place in developing countries, with huge increases in greenhouse gas emissions as a result of carbon-intensive industrialization and increasing consumption. Generally speaking, as a country becomes more industrialized and wealthy, the carbon footprint per person increases dramatically, and population growth eventually slows. The conundrum we face is how to reduce total greenhouse gas emissions while improving the quality of life of the large proportion of people currently living in poverty. One recent study found that, "dollar-for-dollar, investments in voluntary family planning and girls' education would also in the long run reduce greenhouse-gas emissions at least as much as the same investments in nuclear or wind energy" (Engelman, 2009, p. 26).

Developed and developing countries will be affected differently by global warming. In some ways, developed countries will be less affected, in part because of their locations but more importantly because they have more resources per capita to deal with the changes. It is unlikely that famines will strike the richest countries, for example. However, no country will be immune to the violence consequences of global climate change. The heat effect on individual levels of aggression and violence applies to all countries. Similarly, it seems obvious that even wealthy countries are likely to see increases in the proportion of children exposed to known risk factors for the development of violence-prone youth and adults. It is less obvious how wealthy countries will be affected by the third process, which leads to increases in civil unrest, ecomigration, genocide, and war. But even if developed countries do not experience sufficient economic and social stress to induce war (civil or international), civil unrest and ecomigration within them will likely lead to increases in violent crime, especially after ecological disasters such as floods. Furthermore, increased poverty, civil dissolution, and wars in developing countries have an impact on developed countries. In some cases, the impact derives from the global economy and the need for resources. Also, differences between the have and have-not countries create breeding grounds for international terrorist groups.

What actions could reduce the likelihood of climate change–induced violence? There is some limited evidence that the heat–aggression effect on individuals can be reduced by simply making people aware that when they are uncomfortably hot they tend to react to minor provocations in inappropriately hostile ways. However, given the immediacy and subtlety of the heat effect on irritability, hostile perception biases, and aggression, it is doubtful that such an educational intervention will have a large impact.

On the other hand, the other two ways global warming increases human violence appear to be good candidates for intervention. If governments began preparing now to feed, shelter, educate, and move at-risk populations to regions in which they can maintain their livelihoods and their cultures, we could dramatically reduce both the development of violence-prone individuals and the civil unrest, ecomigration, and war problems. This will cost huge amounts of money and will require more international cooperation than our planet has ever seen. Failure to do so will result in additional disasters for millions of people.

REFERENCES

Anderson, C. A. (1989). Temperature and aggression: Ubiquitous effects of heat on occurrence of human violence. *Psychological Bulletin, 106,* 74–96.

Anderson, C. A. (2001). Heat and violence. *Current Directions in Psychological Science, 10,* 33–38.

Anderson, C. A., & Anderson, D. C. (1984). Ambient temperature and violent crime: Tests of the linear and curvilinear hypotheses. *Journal of Personality and Social Psychology, 46,* 91–97.

Anderson, C. A., & Anderson, K. B. (1996). Violent crime rate studies in philosophical context: A destructive testing approach to heat and southern culture of violence effects. *Journal of Personality and Social Psychology, 70,* 740–756.

Anderson, C. A., & Anderson, K. B. (1998). Temperature and aggression: Paradox, controversy, and a (fairly) clear picture. In R. Geen & E. Donnerstein (Eds.), *Human aggression: Theories, research, and implications for social policy.* (pp. 247–298). San Diego, CA: Academic Press.

Anderson, C. A., Anderson, K. B., Dorr, N., DeNeve, K. M., & Flanagan, M. (2000). Temperature and aggression. *Advances in Experimental Social Psychology, 32,* 63–133.

Anderson, C. A., Bushman, B. J., & Groom, R. W. (1997). Hot years and serious and deadly assault: Empirical tests of the heat hypothesis. *Journal of Personality and Social Psychology, 73,* 1213–1223.

Beaver, K. M., DeLisi, M., Vaughn, M. G., & Wright, J. P. (2010). The intersection of genes and neuropsychological deficits in the prediction of adolescent delinquency and low self-control. *International Journal of Offender Therapy and Comparative Criminology, 54,* 22–42.

Boyanowsky, E. O. (1999). Violence and aggression in the heat of passion and in cold blood. *International Journal of Law and Psychiatry, 22,* 257–271.

Boyanowsky, E. O. (2008). *Explaining the relationship among environmental temperatures, aggression and violent crime: Emotional-cognitive stress under thermoregulatory conflict (The ECS-TC Syndrome).* Presented at the Biannual World Meeting of the International Society for Research on Aggression, Budapest, Hungary, July 8–13.

Boyanowsky. E. O., Calvert-Boyanowsky, J., Young, J., & Brideau, L. (1981). Toward a thermoregulatory model of violence. *Journal of Environmental Systems, 11,* 81–87.

Burke, M. B., Miguel, E., Satyanath, S., Dykema, J. A., & Lobell, D. B. (2009). Warming increases the risk of civil war in Africa. *Proceedings of the National Academy of Sciences, 106*(49), 20670–20674.

Bushman, B. J., Wang, M. C., & Anderson, C.A. (2005a). Is the curve relating temperature to aggression linear or curvilinear? Assaults and temperature in Minneapolis reexamined. *Journal of Personality and Social Psychology, 89,* 62–66.

Bushman, B. J., Wang, M. C., & Anderson, C.A. (2005b). Is the curve relating temperature to aggression linear or curvilinear? A response to Bell (2005) and to Cohn and Rotton (2005). *Journal of Personality and Social Psychology, 89,* 74–77.

Carlsmith, J. M., & Anderson, C. A. (1979). Ambient temperature and the occurrence of collective violence: A new analysis. *Journal of Personality and Social Psychology, 37,* 337–344.

Caspi, A., McClay, J, Moffitt, T. E., Mill, J., Martin, J., Craig, I. W., et al. (2002). Role of genotype in the cycle of violence in maltreated children. *Science, 297,* 851–854.

Caspi, A., Sugden, K., Moffitt, T. E., Taylor, A., Craig, I. W., Harrington, H., et al. (2003). Influence of life stress on depression: Moderation by a polymorphism in the 5-HTT gene. *Science, 301,* 386–389.

Chen, E., Cohen, S., & Miller, G. E. (2010). How low socioeconomic status affects 2-year hormonal trajectories in children. *Psychological Science, 21,* 31–37.

DeLisi, M. (2005). *Career criminals in society.* Thousand Oaks, CA: Sage.

Engelman, R. (Ed.). (2009). *The state of world population 2009.* New York: United Nations Population Fund.

Fagan, B. (2000). *The Little Ice Age: How climate made history 1300–1850.* New York: Basic Books.

Gleick, P. H. (1993). Water and conflict. *International Security, 18*(1), 79–112.

Gottfredson, M. R., & Hirschi, T. (1990). *A general theory of crime.* Stanford, CA: Stanford University Press.

Huston, A. C., & Bentley, A. (2010). Human development in societal context. *Annual Review of Psychology, 61,* 411–437.

Intergovernmental Panel on Climate Change. (IPCC). (2007). Parry, M.L., Canziani, O.F., Palutikof, J.P., van der Linden, P.J. & Hanson, C.E. (Eds.). *Intergovernmental Panel on Climate Change.* Cambridge, UK: Cambridge University Press.

Kruglanski, A. W., Chen, X., Dechesne, M., Fishman, S., & Orehek, E. (2009). Fully committed: Suicide bombers' motivation and the quest for personal significance. *Political Psychology, 30,* 331–357.

LaFree, G., & Drass, K.A. (1996). The effects of changes in intraracial income inequality and educational attainment on changes in arrest rates for African Americans and Whites, 1957–1990. *American Sociological Review, 61,* 614–634.

Ljung, G. M., & Box, G. E. P. (1978). On a measure of lack of fit in time series models. *Biometrika, 65,* 297–303.

Liu, J., Raine, A., Venables, P. H., & Mednick, S. A. (2004). Malnutrition at age 3 years and externalizing behavior problems at ages 8, 11, and 17 years. *American Journal of Psychiatry, 161,* 2005–2013.

Moffitt, T. E. (1993). Adolescence-limited and life-course-persistent antisocial behavior: A developmental taxonomy. *Psychological Review, 100,* 674–701.

Neugebauer, R., Hoek, H. W., & Susser, E. (1999). Prenatal exposure to wartime famine and development of antisocial personality disorder in early adulthood. *Journal of the American Medical Association, 282*, 455–462.

Postel, S. L., & Wolf, A. T. (2001). Dehydrating conflict. *Foreign Policy, 126*, 60–67.

Rahmstorf, S. (2009). *Climate seminar.* Presented at the COWI conference, May 11, Kongens, Lyngby, Denmark. Downloaded January 4, 2010 from http://www.youtube.com/v/9bILFEdLy28

Reifman, A. S., Larrick, R. P., & Fein, S. (1991). Temper and temperature on the diamond: The heat-aggression relationship in Major League Baseball. *Personality and Social Psychology Bulletin, 17*, 580–585.

Reuveny, R. (2008). Ecomigration and violent conflict: Case studies and public policy implications. *Human Ecology. 36*, 1–13.

Uher, R., & McGuffin, P. (2010). The moderation by the serotonin transporter gene of environmental adversity in the etiology of depression: 2009 update. *Molecular Psychiatry, 15*, 18–22.

Van de Vliert, E. (2009). *Climate, affluence, and culture.* New York: Cambridge University Press.

Van de Vliert, E. (in press). Climato-economic origins of variation in ingroup favoritism. *Journal of Cross-Cultural Psychology.*

Van de Vliert, E. (under review). Bullying the media: Cultural and climato-economic readings of press repression versus press freedom.

Vermeer, M., & Rahmstorf, S. (2009). Global sea level linked to global temperature. *Proceedings of the National Academy of Science, 106*, 21527–21532, downloaded January 4, 2010 from http://www.pnas.org

Vrij, A., van der Steen, J., & Koppelaar, L. (1994). Aggression of police officers as a function of temperature: An experiment with the Fire Arms Training System. *Journal of Community and Applied Social Psychology, 4*, 365–370.

Wilkowski, B. M., Meier, B. P., Robinson, M. D., Carter, M. S., & Feltman, R. (2009). "Hot-headed" is more than an expression: The embodied representation of anger in terms of heat. *Emotion, 9*, 464–477.

Zhang, D. D., Brecke, P., Lee, H. F., He, Y. Q., & Zhang, J. (2007). Global climate change, war, and population decline in recent human history. *Proceedings of the National Academy of Science, 104*, 19214–19219.

Zhang, D. D., Zhang, J., Lee, H. F., & He, Y. Q. (2007). Climate change and war frequency in Eastern China over the last millennium. *Human Ecology, 35*, 403–414.

17

The Media and Aggression
From TV to the Internet

ED DONNERSTEIN
University of Arizona

R ecently the American Academy of Pediatrics (AAP) issued a policy statement on media violence (American Academy of Pediatrics, 2009a). The
statement was clear in terms of its findings, position, and recommendations. In rather straightforward terms the AAP noted:

> Exposure to violence in media, including television, movies, music, and video
> games, represents a significant risk to the health of children and adolescents.
> Extensive research evidence indicates that media violence can contribute to
> aggressive behavior, desensitization to violence, nightmares, and fear of being
> harmed. Pediatricians should assess their patients' level of media exposure
> and intervene on media-related health risks. (p. 1495)

The recommendations for parents, practitioners, and the industry were equally
frank and suggested some of the following:

- Remove televisions, Internet connections, and video games from chil-
  dren's bedrooms.
- Avoid screen media for infants or toddlers younger than 2 years.
- Avoid the glamorization of weapon-carrying and the normalization of vio-
  lence as an acceptable means of resolving conflict.
- Eliminate the use of violence in a comic or sexual context or in any other
  situation in which the violence is amusing, titillating, or trivialized.
- Eliminate gratuitous portrayals of interpersonal violence.
- If violence is used, it should be used thoughtfully as serious drama, always
  showing the pain and loss suffered by victims and perpetrators.

- Video games should not use human or other living targets or award points for killing, because this teaches children to associate pleasure and success with their ability to cause pain and suffering to others.

I would expect that the AAP's statement and recommendations would probably be accepted by a substantial majority of researchers in the area of media violence, and aggression in general, including those participating in this Symposium (Anderson, Gentile, & Buckley, 2007; Huesmann, 2007; Strasburger, Jordan, & Donnerstein, 2010). And as a public health organization the AAP is not alone in its recommendation; groups like the American Medical Association, the American Academy of Child and Adolescent Psychiatry, and the American Psychological Association have all issued statements over the years pertaining to the "harmful" impact of media violence on children.

In this chapter we will provide an overview for this and other research related to these harmful effects but with an additional focus on how violence is disseminated through the lens of newer media technology. Much of the research on media violence has traditionally been on the media of television and of course on video games. This media form is not obsolete; rather, for many children and adolescents the medium for this viewing might not be the time-honored television screen but instead the Internet, which offers an array of new issues to consider. The following section examines the role of the Internet as it relates to the concerns we have about the influence of media violence.

THE INTERNET AS A MEDIUM FOR MEDIA VIOLENCE

Unlike traditional media such as TV, there are relatively few studies on the impact of Internet violence. These are reviewed later in the chapter, but it is interesting to note at the outset the recent commentary of researchers about the potential and far-reaching influences of this "newer" technology:

> The Internet is fast becoming the telephone of the 21st century, with an estimated 97% of young people between the ages of 12 and 18 years using online communication. Almost all youths now have online access, and this access may increase opportunities for children and youths to be exposed to violence. (Ybarra, West, Markow, Leaf, Hamburger, & Boxer, 2008, p. 930)
>
> For many youth it has become the major source of information and entertainment. It is perhaps the one medium where children may come across non-intentionally content that is less available in traditional media such as severe violence, violent pornography, child pornography, hate groups. (Feilitzen, 2009)

The Internet becomes the medium in which traditional media like TV, film, and video games can be downloaded, viewed, and processed cognitively. The most recent survey of children and adolescent media use by the Kaiser Foundation (2010) indicated that the amount of time viewing TV content had increased over the last decade but that this increase is accounted for primarily by the viewing of such programming over the Internet and mobile devices. The Internet is also

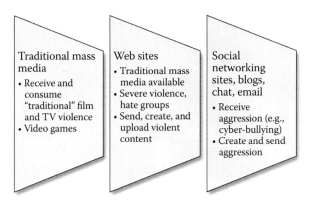

Figure 17.1   The Internet, new technology, and mass media violence.

a vehicle, however, for the creation of aggressive images and the acting out of aggressive behavior. It is both passive and active. It incorporates our conception of how children and adolescents cognitively process conventional media violence, but it adds a new dimension—actually being aggressive. We can see in Figure 17.1 (adapted from comments by Feilitzen, 2009) how this might be conceptualized, both in terms of the Internet generally and in the use of new technologies as mobile phones.

The Internet allows the individual to view traditional TV and film and video games through live streaming or downloads. For the child or adolescent, access to what might be considered restricted materials (adult rated) is much easier via both legal and "illegal" outlets. Web sites offer another dimension to the viewing of violence: the creation and uploading of violent materials. Web sites offer not only the prospect of viewing more severe violence (e.g., real decapitations and executions) but also access to hate and terrorist groups. The viewer, however, can now become the creator of violent images in an almost formulaic manner and can place that material across the globe instantaneously. Finally, Web sites and in particular social networking sites, blogs, chat rooms, and email not only allow for the creation of aggression but also provide the ability to actually persistently aggress against another (i.e., cyberbullying). One phenomenon, which brings this to a "strange" confluence, is "happy slapping," where a victim is assaulted and the depiction is uploaded to the Internet. As Calvete et al. (2008) noted, adolescents who use their mobile phones with this aim are characterized by several types of aggressiveness, by justification of violence beliefs, and by high exposure to violence in the family and media.

Consequently, unlike traditional media such as TV, the Internet and these new technologies give children and adolescents access to just about any form of content they can find (e.g., Livingstone & Haddon, 2009). For the first time, these individuals will be able (often with little effort) to have the ability to view almost any form of sexual behavior, violent content, or other risk-related content (Donnerstein, 2009; Strasburger et al., 2010). Unlike years past, this can be done in the privacy of their own room with little knowledge or supervision of their parents. The interactive nature of the Internet, which can lead to more arousal and more cognitive activity, would suggest that influences such as those found from media violence would be facilitated (see Huesman, 2007).

MEDIA USE AND THE CHILD AUDIENCE

American children and adolescents spend significant time in front of a screen (Strasburger et al., 2010). In their national survey of media use in the United States, the Kaiser Family Foundation (2006, 2010) found that children and adolescents were spending on average more time in front of a screen than reading or being active outdoors. More interesting was the finding that of all those under the age of 3, an age many would suggest is more vulnerable to effects, over two-thirds use some screen media a day, and a third are already using a computer. A child's bedroom is no longer a place of isolation in that media technology is part of the furniture. Two-thirds had a television set, one-half had a VCR or DVD player or video game console, and nearly one-third had Internet access or a computer. More importantly, the use of the Internet and mobile devices for media consumption has increased significantly, particularly with the rapid expansion of broadband availability.

While it took decades for TV to become part of the family household, Internet use has achieved this in a short time frame. Recent research by the Pew Internet and American Life Project (Pew Foundation, 2009) revealed that 93% of youth aged 12 to 17 are online sometime during the day, and 71% have a cell phone. Whether it is watching videos (57%), using social networking sites (65%), or playing video games (97%), children and adolescents have incorporated new technology into their daily lives. These frequencies are also observed across 21 different countries within Europe. The EU Kids Online Project found that in 2005 on average 70% of 6–17-year-olds used the Internet. By 2008, it was at 75% with the largest increase occurring among younger children (6–10) in which 60% were now online (Livingstone & Haddon, 2009).

In thinking about this use of the mass media, we need to remember that very often those who are the most vulnerable to negative impacts (e.g., aggression, deceptive advertising) are children, and their processing of the media is different from adults. In the first place, younger children interpret media messages differently. They pay more attention to perceptual features and more salient contextual features rather than to plot. They are less cognizant of consequences and motives. Children also have difficulty distinguishing between fantasy and reality. This plays an extremely important role in children's media viewing in that when we examine the effects from exposure to media violence one critical contextual variable is the perceived reality of the aggression. Finally, children have difficulties and are less capable of linking scenes together. Adults recognize that the perpetrator of aggression was caught, punished, or reprimanded for his or her behavior in the final scene. A young child does not always perceive this relationship.

We need to realize that not all violent portrayals pose the same risk of harm to viewers. Research indicates that certain depictions of violence increase the risk of antisocial effects more than others (see Strasburger, Wilson, & Jordan, 2009). Simply put, the context or way violence is presented influences its impact on the audience. Based on an extensive review of studies in this area, researchers (Smith & Donnerstein, 2003; Wilson et al., 2002) have identified a range of contextual features that influence how audiences will respond to televised violence (e.g., advertisements; Tajima et al., 2008) and also to video game violence (Horiuchi et. al., 2008). The most important contextual factors are attractive perpetrators, the presence of weapons, graphic and extensive violence, consequences for aggression such as punishments or pain, and realism.

Much of the violence presented in the media is often sanitized and glamorized, and in children's programming it often is presented as humorous (Strasburger et al., 2009). These contextual factors are important in determining the "risk" of exposure primarily to young children. Portrayals with an attractive perpetrator and that are realistic, justified, go unpunished, and show no harm are the most problematic for young children. These types of media depictions occur most often in the types of shows viewed by children (e.g., Wilson et al., 2002).

Interactive media seems to be no different from traditional television when it comes to depictions of concern for children and adolescents. A recent analysis of video games revealed that more than half of all games—including 90% rated as appropriate for children aged 10 years and older (Anderson et al., 2007)— contain violence. Contextual characteristics that are considered more of a risk for subsequent aggressive behavior have also been found in video games. In a recent analysis justified violence was found in 60% of the games, violence with weapons was found in 65%, and reward for violence in 89%. Factors we might consider as inhibiting aggression such as punishments for violence were found in only 26% of the games (Horiuchi et al., 2008).

By definition, the Internet encompasses all the types of violence depicted in traditional media and video games. While there is no major content analysis for video games like there is for traditional media, researchers acknowledge that more real-world violence, hate groups, violent pornography, and other forms of violence are more prevalent (Ybarra et al., 2008). There is currently a lack of data on how many children or adolescents are intentionally viewing these sites and whether the Internet's increased ease of access to these types of depictions has resulted in high rates of exposure among young viewers (Hamburger, Ybarra, Leaf, & West, 2009).

MEDIA VIOLENCE EFFECTS: TELEVISION, VIDEO GAMES, AND THE INTERNET

In this section we will briefly examine the known effects of media violence on aggressive behavior. Even though the review is separated into three categories (TV, video games, Internet), the interrelationships are evident. Since one major goal of this chapter was to examine the unique aspects of newer technologies, in particular the Internet, this classification seems more functional.

Television

In a report on youth violence, the surgeon general of the United States (2001) identified a series of risk factors that were considered to (1) increase the probability that a young person will become violent, and (2) predict the onset, continuity, or escalation of violence. In considering these varying factors, the surgeon general's report noted that more important than any individual risk factor is the accumulation of factors. When considering the most important factors in youth violence, being a male had the highest effect size. Among other major factors and their effect sizes were the following:

Substance abuse = .30
Antisocial parents = .23
Weak social ties = .15
Media violence = .13
Low IQ = .12
Broken home = .09
Abusive parents = .07
Antisocial peers = .04

Though it is not the major contributor, media violence is considered, especially when other factors are present, a significant force in the development and onset of aggressive behavior in youth. As researchers have strongly suggested, exposure to violent media needs to be part of the measures taken when risk factors for aggressive behavior are considered (Boxer, Huesmann, Bushman, O'Brien, & Moceri, 2009; Bushman, Huesmann, & Whitaker, 2009).

Any critical examination of the literature would indicate that exposure to media violence can contribute to a range of antisocial effects on viewers (Huesmann & Kirwil, 2007). The conclusion that violence on television contributes to negative effects on viewers is hardly novel. The effects that seem to be most pronounced are the learning of aggressive attitudes and behaviors, desensitization to violence, and increased fear of being victimized by violence (see Huesmann, 2007; Huesmann & Taylor, 2006).

Over the last 40 years, several governmental and professional organizations have conducted exhaustive reviews of the scientific literature to ascertain the relationship between exposure to media violence and aggression. These investigations have documented consistently that exposure to media violence contributes to aggressive behaviors in viewers and may influence their perceptions and attitudes about violence in the real world. Heavy viewing of media violence is correlated with aggressive behavior and increased aggressive attitudes (see Anderson et al., 2003 for an extensive review). The correlation between viewing violence in the media and exhibiting aggressive behavior is fairly stable over time, place, and demographics (e.g., Huesmann, Moise, Podolski, & Eron, 2003). Experimental and longitudinal studies also support the position that viewing televised violence is related causally to aggressive behavior (Anderson et al.). Even more important, naturalistic field studies and cross-national investigations reveal that viewing televised aggression leads to increases in subsequent real-life aggression and that such behavior can become part of a lasting behavioral pattern (Bushman et al., 2008; Huesmann, Boxer, & Bushman, 2009). These studies have been consistent in research conducted in a number of different countries (see Bushman & Huesmann, 2006; Huesmann, 2007).

From a theoretical perspective, Huesmann (2007; see also Chapters 16 and 19 in this volume) and others (e.g., Anderson & Bushman, 2002) would agree that the short-term effects of exposure to media violence are mostly due to (1) priming processes, (2) arousal processes, and (3) immediate modeling of specific behaviors (observational learning). Long-term effects seem to be due to (1) longer-term learning of cognitions and behavioral scripts and (2) the activation and desensitization of emotional processes.

Video Games

In terms of demonstrating increased aggressive behavior from exposure, the research on video games is as consistent as that with television violence (see Anderson et al., 2007, 2010 for an extensive review). Meta-analyses (Anderson, 2004; Anderson & Bushman, 2001; Anderson et al., 2010) have been consistent in their findings. While some have disagreed with these studies (Ferguson, 2010), the consensus of researchers is that effects from playing violent video games have been shown for the following:

1. Increased aggressive behavior (Anderson et al., 2008)
2. Hostile affect (Carnagey & Anderson, 2005)
3. Physiological arousal (Anderson & Bushman, 2001)
4. Aggressive cognitions (Anderson & Huesmann, 2003; Bluemke, Friedrich, & Zumbach, 2010)
5. Reductions in prosocial behavior from desensitization (e.g., Bushman & Anderson, 2009)

These results have been observed both in short-term and longitudinal studies as well as cross-culturally (e.g., Anderson et Al., 2008, 2010).

Anderson (2000, 2007) noted that there are strong compelling reasons to expect that violent video games, due to their interactive nature, would have stronger effects on aggression than more traditional forms of media violence such as TV. In video games the process of identification with the aggressor, active participation, repetitive actions, a hostile virtual reality, and reinforcement for aggressive actions are all strong mechanisms for the learning and retention of aggressive behaviors and attitudes (Gentile & Anderson, 2003).

The Internet

A number of areas deserve consideration when discussing the effects of the Internet as a potentially unique contributor to aggressive behavior. As we noted earlier, the Internet not only acts as a platform for the viewing of media but also is a vehicle for acting out aggression. It is this later function that for many health professionals has been of importance. For that reason we will examine first the concerns about cyberbullying and sexual exploitation. Following this discussion we will look at the content of violent media that might be considered unique, or certainly more accessible, on the Internet.

Cyberbullying   The one area that seems to be of prime importance is cyberbullying. It has become a significant social issue primarily among health-care and other professionals (AAP, 2009b). Olweus (1993) defined bullying as follows:

> A person is bullied when he or she is exposed, repeatedly and over time, to negative actions on the part of one or more other persons, and he or she has difficulty defending himself or herself. (p. 14)

This definition includes three important components in that it is (1) aggressive behavior that involves unwanted, negative actions, (2) involves a pattern of behavior repeated over time, and (3) involves an imbalance of power or strength. Cyberbulling, often referred to as Internet harassment or Internet aggression, incorporates these components and in many ways is similar to other forms of bullying (e.g., Heirman & Walrave, 2008; Williams & Guerra, 2007) but takes place over the Internet to repeatedly harass, threaten, or maliciously embarrass. Research also suggests that Internet bullying shares common predictors with verbal and, to some extent, physical bullying (see Williams & Guerra). While there are certainly debates about the usage of the term, both policy makers and the public across many countries have incorporated the term cyberbullying into their lexicon, and it will be used in this chapter. It involves the following behaviors (NCPC, 2009):

- Sending unsolicited or threatening email
- Encouraging others to send the victim unsolicited or threatening email
- Sending viruses by email (electronic sabotage)
- Spreading rumors
- Making defamatory comments about the victim in public discussion areas
- Sending negative messages directly to the victim
- Impersonating the victim online by sending an inflammatory message that causes others to respond negatively to the victim
- Harassing the victim during a live chat
- Leaving abusive messages on Web site guest books
- Sending the victim pornography or other knowingly offensive graphic material
- Creating a Web page that depicts the victim in negative ways

Those conducting research in this area would acknowledge that victims of cyberbullying as well as children who are bullied in person may experience many of the same effects, such as a drop in grades, lowered self-esteem, a change in interests, or depression (see *Journal of Adolescent Health*, 2007; NCPC, 2009). Chapter 3 in this volume discusses cyberostracism—the effects of being ignored and excluded over the Internet, which can lead to similar effects (e.g., anger, aggression) as "face-to-face" ostracism. However, cyberbullying can seem more extreme to its victims because of several factors:

- It occurs in the child's home. The place the child or adolescent often sees as secure now represents being a victim.
- It can be harsher because of the anonymity of the aggressor and inability to see the victim's reactions. The ability to empathize with the victim is much more difficult in these situations (see Chapter 7 in this volume).
- It can be far-reaching in that once posted on a Web site it is "forever" in cyberspace.
- It may seem inescapable since not going online takes away one of the major places children and adolescents socialize.

The recent U.S. Department of Justice (2009) National Survey of Children's Exposure to Violence found that Internet harassment was less common than other forms of bullying. It was found that 6% reported Internet harassment within the past year and 8% during their lifetimes. While this may appear at first glance a small percentage, we need to remember that this was a national survey within the United States and that these percentages certainly represented a significant number of youth who are impacted.

Surveys reported by the Pew Foundation (2007) and Hinduja and Patchin (2009) indicate that, although cyberbullying is less common than school bullying, anywhere between 15 and 35% of youth report having experienced it. The data also indicate that 10–20% of students admit to cyberbullying others, and girls are just as likely, if not more so, to be involved in this type of behavior as boys (e.g., Kowalski & Limber, 2007). These effects seem to be consistent in the United States, Australia, and Europe (e.g., Brandtzæg, Staksrud, Hagen, & Wold, 2009). Most of these surveys indicate that involvement in cyberbullying seems to peak in the middle school years (grades 6–8). There is also recent research to suggest overlap among victims of school bullying and online harassment both within the United States and Germany (e.g., Wolak, Mitchell, & Finkelhor, 2007; Katzer, Fetchenhauer, & Belschak, 2009).

A number of researchers are beginning to examine the platform for cyberbullying. Although this research is just emerging, there is some evidence to suggest that at least within the United States chat rooms and instant messaging (IM) are more frequently employed whereas email is the preferred technology in Europe (Brandzæg et al., 2009).

Sexual Exploitation   Another major concern with the Internet is the sexual exploitation of children and adolescents. Sending sexual information over email or postings on bulletin boards has been a long-term issue. One of the most comprehensive series studies on these issues has come from the Crimes Against Children Research Center at the University of New Hampshire (http://www.unh.edu/ccrc). This excellent series of studies (Wolak, Finkelhor, Mitchell, & Ybarra, 2008) involved a random national sample of 1,500 children ages 10–17 interviewed in 2000 and then an additional sample of 1,500 interviewed in 2005. This procedure allowed the researches to look at the changes in youths' experiences with the Internet. The major findings from this study can be summarized as follows:

1. There was an increase over the 5-year period from 25% to 34% of the youth who indicated that they were exposed to unwanted sexual materials. It is interesting to note that this increase occurred in spite of the fact that more families were using Internet filtering software (over 50%) during this period. A European study of 21 countries (Livingstone & Haddon, 2009) indicates that about 40% of youth report exposure to pornography.

2. A total of 15% of all of the youth reported an unwanted sexual solicitation online in the previous year, with 4% reporting an incident on a social networking site specifically. Perhaps more importantly, about 4% of these were considered "aggressive" in that the solicitor attempted to contact the user offline. These are the episodes most likely to result in actual victimizations.

3. Additionally, in this study 4% of those surveyed were asked for nude or sexually explicit pictures of themselves. Of more concern may be the finding that less than 5% of these were reported to law enforcement officials or the Internet provider. In many jurisdictions, these constitute criminal requests to produce child pornography (Wolak et al., 2008).

4. In the study, 4% said they were upset or distressed as a result of these online solicitations. These are the youth most immediately harmed by the solicitations themselves.

5. These researchers also reported an increase in online harassment and bullying. Many of these episodes occur from confrontations in school from individuals who know each other. Most of those who were harassed were females.

Two interesting questions have been raised about the Internet and sexual exploitation (Wolak et al., 2008; Ybarra & Mitchell, 2008). First, does the Internet make children more accessible to offenders? And if offenders participate in sex sites and have easier access to child pornography, does this "trigger" the offense, or would it have occurred anyway? Both answers are speculative, and additional research is imperative to more fully understand the complexities of the Internet and child exploitation.

With respect to the first question, the Internet can make children more accessible to offenders through social networking sites, email, and texting in a manner that is more anonymous and outside the supervision of parents. Children may also find the "privacy" and anonymity of electronic communication more conducive to discussions of intimate relationships than in a face-to-face situation.

With respect to the second question, there are suggestions that the Internet can facilitate sexual offending such as pedophilia via the rapid exchange of images, the locating of victims, and development of networks (e.g, Beech, Elliott, Birgden, & Findlater, 2008; McDonald, Horstmann, Strom, & Pope, 2009). The rationale suggested is as follows (see Wolak et al., 2008):

- There is easier access to child pornography, which can evoke or promote interests in children.
- There are Web sites and Internet groups that explicitly encourage and legitimize sexual behaviors with youth.

- There is the initial anonymity for contact and solicitation of a child. Social networking sites and chat rooms make access easier.

As Wolak et al. (2008) noted, alternative hypotheses should be considered. In the end, much more in-depth research is needed, particularly in an area that is both new and often times more difficult to investigate.

Exposure to Violence on the Internet

Concerns about children and adolescents' use of the Internet are not limited to sexual content. Exposure to violent or hateful content has also been among the types of materials considered risky. Among these types of content are Web sites for terrorism and other radical violent organizations. Some online archives provide instructions for making bombs or other weapons. Since the events of September 11, terrorist groups make extensive use of the Internet to recruit and spread propaganda. Chapter 10 in this volume offers an excellent insight into this type of terrorist activity. The proliferation of hate speech and hate groups has also become easily accessible on the Web. A report by the Simon Wiesenthal Center (2009) indicates that in the past decade there has been a tenfold increase of Internet-based hate groups that make extensive use of social networking sites for recruitment.

In an extensive survey of European countries, the EU Kids Online project (Livingstone & Haddon, 2009) found that seeing violent or hateful content was experienced by approximately one-third of teenagers, making it one of the higher risk concerns. One problem, however, was that the severity and nature of the violent content encountered was not well researched, mainly for ethical reasons.

This is one of the major research problems in this area. It is difficult in these studies to separate out the content one could see offline anyway and simply use the Internet as a medium for viewing. It is true that the Internet allows children and adolescents easier access to materials we already consider risk related (violence on TV and film, video game violence), but a more important question is the role that material "unique" to the Internet might play in aggressive behaviors. The research in this area is limited, and as some have suggested we do not really yet know how many youth are "intentionally" viewing violent Web sites or are being exposed to graphic realistic violence (Hamburger et al., 2009). As we already noted regarding child predators, we are still in need of further research on the unique role of the Internet content in these areas.

However, some recent research does suggest that the types of materials found exclusively on the Internet may have a relationship to aggressive behavior. In a national survey of youth, Ybarra et al. (2008) found an association between the viewing of Internet violence and self-reported seriously aggressive behavior. While exposure to violence in the media overall was related to aggressive behavior, youth who reported that many or all of the Web sites they visited depicted real people fighting, shooting, or killing were five times more likely to report engaging in seriously violent behavior. These types of sites seemed to be unique to the Internet and included (1) hate sites, (2) Web sites showing pictures of dead people or people dying, or a "snuff" site, (3) Web sites showing satanic rituals, (4) Web sites showing pictures of war, death, or "terrorism," or (5) Web sites showing cartoons, such as stick people or animals, being beaten up, hurt, or killed. The authors speculated that the interactive environment of the Internet and the depiction of real people engaged in violence may explain the stronger association with reported seriously violent behavior. We need to keep in mind that this is a cross-sectional design study and does not establish causality.

Another national survey conducted in Taiwan also suggests some unique contribution of the Internet to youth aggression. In a survey of over 9,000 adolescents, Ko, Yen, Liua, Huang, and Yen (2009) found that heavy users of the Internet were more likely to self-report aggressive behavior during the past year. This was the case after controlling for the viewing of violent television programs. This reported aggression also occurred more often in students who were involved in online chatting, adult sex Web sites, online gaming, online gambling, and bulletin board systems. The authors suggest that these later activities offer both anonymity and group identification.

Another concern, suggested earlier, is the proliferation and access to hate groups and other potentially violent organizations through Web sites, chat rooms, and other Internet platforms that have the potential to recruit, organize, and reinforce individuals for aggressive-related behaviors. In his book on democracy and the Internet, *Republic.com*, Sunstein (2001) acknowledges the risks we encounter with an open and uncensored Internet. Using one example for the group Unorganized Militias, he noted:

> A crucial factor behind the growth of the Unorganized Militia has been the use of computer networks, allowing members to make contact quickly and easily with like-minded individuals to trade information, discuss current conspiracy theories, and organize events. (p. 22)

A number of excellent discussions in this volume on in-group attachments (see Chapters 2 and 10) speak to Sunstein's (2001) assertion. The question considered earlier, however, about the uniqueness of the Internet from offline exposure to violent materials can also be raised with regard to hate or radical groups. While there is an increase in the proliferation of these groups as well as (1) examinations of their content (e.g., Douglas, McGarty, Bliuc, & Lala, 2005) and (2) speculation of their influences, there is little systematic research on the specific influences of these online sites and discussion groups for subsequent offline behaviors. In a recent review of this literature, McDonald, Horstmann, Strom, and Pope (2009) noted that the efficacy of Web-based hate groups is still unclear.

A recent study by Wojcieszak (2009) does suggest that participation in radical online groups, such as neo-Nazis, increases offline actions that support neo-Nazi movements as well as in actions that promote these movements. This study certainly has a number of limitations such as causality, self-selection, and validity of behavioral outcomes. Nevertheless, it examines the role of the Internet as an alternative to traditional face-to-face socialization in underanalyzed communities.

Sexual Violence   While it is important to examine the unique characteristics of Internet content, we should not summarily dismiss the inadvertent (or perhaps intentional) exposure to materials children or adolescents would have difficulty viewing offline. One concern raised about children and adolescents' interaction with the Web is the inadvertent exposure not only to extreme forms of violence but also to sexual violence (e.g., Donnerstein, 2009; Feilitzen, 2009; Strasburger et al., 2010). To date, there has been virtually no research on the effects of exposure to sexual violence on adolescent viewers, although researchers have speculated on its impact (e.g., Malamuth & Impett, 2001; Donnerstein & Smith 2001; Wright, Malamuth, & Donnerstein, 2010). For ethical reasons these studies are nearly impossible to undertake. However, numerous studies involving college-age students have revealed that depictions of sexual violence in the media can promote antisocial attitudes and behavior. Given that some of this research has involved R-rated films, there is every expectation that adolescents and children would be exposed to these types of materials via the Internet. Particularly detrimental are violent images in pornography and elsewhere that portray the myth that women enjoy or in some way benefit from rape, torture, or other forms of sexual violence (e.g., Donnerstein, 2000, 2008; Harris, 2009). If anything, we might expect even stronger effects of such content on younger viewers who may lack the necessary critical viewing skills and the experience to discount these portrayals. To an adolescent who is searching the Web for information about relationships, the inadvertent exposure to sexual violence may be a potent source of influence on initial attitudes toward sexuality.

Summary   In many ways the issue of Internet violence is perhaps at a place that video game violence was a decade ago. There is a good deal of speculation and theoretical assumptions to assume that the Internet will be a substantial factor in the development of aggression. What brought video game violence to the forefront was solid empirical and theory-driven research (e.g., Anderson et al., 2007, 2010). We are beginning to see this within the realm of research on the Internet and violence. In considering the future of this research, a number of individuals reviewing this research across various countries have pointed to areas that need specific consideration (e.g., Livingstone & Haddon, 2009; McDonald et al., 2009). Some of these recommendations are as follows:

1. Longitudinal research to examine the causal relationships between online participation and engaging in criminal acts
2. The major risk factors (i.e., individual, environmental, social) that are related to someone "acting" on this Internet exposure
3. Given the increasing use of the Internet by younger children (under the age of 12), there is a need for specific research on this population. In particular are studies on those in the under-6-year-old range who will have less capacity to "cope" with riskier online content.
4. Research on expanding platforms like mobile phones and virtual game environments as well as peer-to-peer exchanges
5. Increased research on public health issues like self-harm, suicide, drugs, and addiction

CONCLUSION

In this chapter we set out to address the issues surrounding the effects of exposure to media violence on primarily children and adolescents. This is not a new endeavor, as many in the psychological community have written about these varying effects for decades (e.g., Anderson et al., 2010; Huessman, 2007). For many, there has been the overall assumption that exposure to mass media violence can be influential in the behavior and attitudes of children, adolescents, and even adults. My intent in this review was not to reiterate what has been focused on in the past but rather to expand the discussion to newer technologies, in particular the Internet. In this manner the focus becomes one on mediated violence and examines the varying mediums youth have at their disposal for being exposed to what we would consider risk-related content.

In reflecting on this brief review, it would be safe to conclude that the mass media, in all its domains, is a contributor to a number of antisocial behaviors and health-related problems in children and adolescents. We must keep in mind, however, that the mass media is but one of a multitude of factors that contribute and, in many cases, is not always the most significant. Nevertheless, it is one of the factors in which proper interventions can mitigate its impact and, furthermore, can be controlled with reasonable insight (Strasburger et al., 2010).

Unlike the more traditional mediums for exposure to media violence, there is general agreement that considerably more research is needed with regard to the Internet in its role as a technology for the learning, social, and cognitive development of children and adolescents. There is no question that we need to enrich our understanding of these new technologies as more and more children come online and the technology itself changes and expands.

When thinking about these newer technologies we should keep in mind what Huesmann (2007) noted about the decades of research and theory on traditional media. This extensive research and theory development has provided us with significant insights into the role new technology will play in the development and mitigation of aggressive behavior. As some have said, "The technology conduit may be changing, but the influential processes (e.g., priming, activation and desensitization) may be the same" (Ferdon & Hertz, 2007, p. 55).

REFERENCES

American Academy of Pediatrics (AAP). (2009a). *Policy statement—media violence.* Council on Communications and Media. http://www.pediatrics.org/cgi/doi/10.1542/peds.2009-2146 doi:10.1542/peds.2009-2146

American Academy of Pediatrics. (AAP). (2009b). *Policy statement—role of the pediatrician in youth violence.* Committee on Injury, Violence, and Poison Prevention. http://www.pediatrics.org/cgi/doi/10.1542/peds.2009-0943 doi:10-1542/peds.2009-0943

Anderson, C. A. (2000). *Violent video games increase aggression and violence.* U.S. Senate Committee on Commerce, Science, and Transportation hearing on the impact of interactive violence on children, March 21.

Anderson, C. A. (2004). An update on the effects of playing violent video games. *Journal of Adolescence, 27,* 113–122.

Anderson, C. A. (2007). *The bottom line on violent video games: What we know and what we don't know.* Paper presented at the meeting of the American Academy of Pediatrics.

Anderson, C., Berkowitz, L., Donnerstein, E., Huesmann, R., Johnson, J., Linz, D., et al. (2003). The influence of media violence on youth. *Psychological Science in the Public Interest, 4,* 81–110.

Anderson, C. A., & Bushman, B. J. (2001). Effects of violent video games on aggressive behavior, aggressive cognition, aggressive affect, physiological arousal, and prosocial behavior: A meta-analytic review of the scientific literature. *Psychological Science, 12,* 353–359.

Anderson, C. A., & Bushman, B. J. (2002). Human aggression. *Annual Review of Psychology, 53,* 27–51.

Anderson, C. A., & Huesmann, L. R. (2003). Human aggression: A social–cognitive view. In M. A. Hogg & J. Cooper (Eds.), *The Sage handbook of social psychology* (pp. 296–323). London, England: Sage.

Anderson, C. A., Gentile, D. A., & Buckley, K. E. (2007). *Violent video game effects on children and adolescents.* Oxford, UK: Oxford University Press.

Anderson, C. A., Sakamoto, A., Gentile, D. A., Ihori, N., Shibuya, A., Yukawa, S., et al. (2008). Longitudinal effects of violent video games on aggression in Japan and the United States. *Pediatrics, 122,* 1067–1072.

Anderson, C. A., Shibuya, A., Ihori, N., Swing, E. L., Bushman, B. J., Sakamoto, A., et al. (2010). Violent video game effects on aggression, empathy, and prosocial behavior in eastern and western countries: A meta-analytic review. *Psychological Bulletin, 136*(2), 151–73.

Beech, A. R., Elliott, I. A., Birgden, A., & Findlater, D. (2008). The Internet and child sexual offending: A criminological review. *Aggression and Violent Behavior, 13,* 216–228.

Bluemke, M., Friedrich, M., & Zumbach, J. (2010). The influence of violent and nonviolent computer games on implicit measures of aggressiveness. *Aggressive Behavior, 36,* 1–13.

Boxer, P., Huesmann, L. R., Bushman, B. J., O'Brien, M., & Moceri, D. (2009). The role of violent media preferences in cumulative developmental risk for violence and general aggression. *Journal of Youth and Adolescence, 38,* 417–428.

Brandtzæg, P. B., Staksrud, E., Hagen, I., & Wold, W. (2009). Norwegian children's experiences of Cyberbullying when using different technological platforms. *Journal of Children and Media, 3,* 349–365.

Bushman, B. J., & Anderson, C. A. (2009). Comfortably numb: Desensitizing effects of violent media on helping others. *Psychological Science, 20,* 273–277.

Bushman, B. J., Boxer, P., Johnson, T., Huesmann, R., O'Brien, M., & Moceri, D. (2008). *Relation of young adult violent and criminal behavior to habitual exposure to violent media during childhood and adolescence.* Presented at the meeting of the International Society for Research on Aggression. Budapest, Hungary.

Bushman, B. J., & Huesmann, L. R. (2006). Short-term and long-term effects of violent media on aggression in children and adults. *Archives of Pediatrics & Adolescent Medicine, 160,* 348–352.

Bushman, B. J., Huesmann, L. R., & Whitaker, J. (2009). Violent media effect. In M. B. Oliver & R. Nabi (Eds.), *The Sage handbook of media processes and effects* (pp. 361–376). Thousand Oaks, CA: Sage.

Calvete, E., Orue, I., Estevez, L. V., Garcia, A., Mendiola, J., Garramiola, J., et al. (2008). *Violence through mobile phones in adolescents.* Presented at the meeting of the International Society for Research on Aggression. Budapest, Hungary.

Carnagey, N. L., & Anderson, C. A. (2005). The effects of reward and punishment in violent video games on aggressive affect, cognition, and behavior. *Psychological Science, 16*, 882–889.

Crimes Against Children Research Center. (CCRC). (2006). *Second youth Internet safety survey* (YISS-2). Available from http://www.unh.edu/ccrc

Donnerstein, E. (2000). Pornography: research, theory, implications. In A.E. Kazdin (Ed.), *Encyclopedia of Psychology* (pp. 788–795). New York: Oxford University Press.

Donnerstein, E. (2008). Mass media: A general view. In L. Kurtz (Ed.), *Encyclopedia of violence, peace, and conflict* (2nd ed., pp.1184–1192). Oxford: Elsevier.

Donnerstein E. (2009). The Internet. In V. Strasburger, B.Wilson, & A. Jordan, *Children, adolescents and the media* (2nd ed., pp. 471–498). Thousand Oaks, CA: Sage.

Donnerstein, E., & Smith, S. (2001). Sex in the media: Theory, influences and solutions. In D. Singer & J. Singer (Eds.), *Handbook of children and the media* (pp. 289–308). Thousand Oaks, CA: Sage.

Douglas, K. M., McGarty, C., Bliuc, A., & Lala, G. (2005). Understanding cyberhate: Social competition and social creativity in online white supremacists groups. *Social Science Computer Review, 23*, 68–76.

Feilitzen, C. (2009). *Influences of mediated violence: A brief research summary.* Guthenberg, Sweden: International Clearinghouse on Children, Youth and Media, NORDICOM, University of Gothenburg.

Ferdon, C. D., & Hertz, M. F. (2007). Electronic media, violence, and adolescents: An emerging public health problem. *Journal of Adolescent Health 41*, S1–S5.

Ferguson, C. J. (2010). A meta-analysis of normal and disordered personality across the lifespan. *Journal of Personality and Social Psychology, 98*(4), 659–667.

Gentile, D. A., & Anderson, C. A. (2003). Violent video games: The newest media violence hazard. In D. Gentile (Ed.), *Media violence and children* (pp. 131–152), Westport, CT: Praeger.

Hamburger, M., Ybarra, M., Leaf, P., & West, M. (2009). *Violence on the Internet: How many youth are really looking?* Presented at the annual meeting of the American Society of Criminology.

Harris, R. J. (2009). *A cognitive psychology of mass communication* (Routledge Communication Series). London: Taylor & Francis.

Heirman, W., & Walrave, M. (2008). Assessing concerns and issues about the mediation of technology in cyberbullying. *Cyberpsychology: Journal of Psychosocial Research on Cyberspace, 2*. Available from http://www.cyberpsychology.eu/index.php

Hinduja, S., & Patchin, J. W. (2009). *Bullying beyond the schoolyard: Preventing, and responding to cyberbullying.* Thousand Oaks, CA: Sage Publications (Corwin Press).

Horiuchi, Y., Minamisawa, U., Shibuya, A., Suzuki, K., Sakamoto, A., Linz, D., et al. (2008). *Analysis of violent content in Japanese video games.* Presented at the meeting of the International Society for Research on Aggression. Budapest, Hungary.

Huesmann, L. R. (2007). The impact of electronic media violence: Scientific theory and research. *Journal of Adolescent Health, 41*, S6–S13.

Huesmann, L. R., Boxer, P., & Bushman, B. (2009). *The relation between exposure to video violence in childhood and serious youth violence and delinquency.* Presented at the annual meeting of the American Society of Criminology. Atlanta, Georgia.

Huesmann, L. R., & Kirwil, L. (2007). Why observing violence increases the risk of violent behavior by the observer. In D. J. Flannery, A. T. Vazsonyi, & I. D. Waldman (Eds.), *The Cambridge handbook of violent behavior and aggression* (pp. 545–570). Cambridge, England: Cambridge University Press.

Huesmann, L. R., Moise, J., Podolski, C. P., & Eron, L. D. (2003). Longitudinal relations between children's exposure to TV violence and their aggressive and violent behavior in young adulthood: 1977–1992. *Developmental Psychology, 39*, 201–221.

Huesmann, L. R., & Taylor, L. D. (2006). Media effects in middle childhood. In A. C. Huston & M. N. Ripke (Eds.), *Developmental contexts in middle childhood: Bridges to adolescence and adulthood* (pp. 303–326). Cambridge, England: Cambridge University Press.

Journal of Adolescent Health (2007). Volume 41, Supplement: Youth Violence and Electronic Media: Similar Behaviors, Different Venues?

Kaiser Family Foundation. (2006). *The media family: Electronic media in the lives of infants, toddlers, preschoolers, and their parents.* Menlo Park, CA: Author.

Kaiser Family Foundation. (2010). *Generation M2: Media in the lives of 8- to 18-year-olds.* Menlo Park, CA: Author.

Katzer, C., Fetchenhauer, D., & Belschak, F. (2009). Cyberbullying—who are the victims? A comparison of victimization in Internet chatrooms and victimization in school. *Journal of Media Psychology, 21,* 25–36.

Ko, C. H., Yen, J. Y., Liua, S. C., Huang, C. F., & Yen, C. F. (2009). The associations between aggressive behaviors and Internet addiction and online activities in adolescents. *Journal of Adolescent Health, 44,* 598–605.

Kowalski, R. M., & Limber, S. P. (2007). Electronic bullying among middle school students. *Journal of Adolescent Health, 41,* S22–S30.

Livingstone, S., & Haddon, L. (2009). *EU Kids Online: Final report.* London: EU Kids Online.

Malamuth, N., & Impett, E. A. (2001). Research on sex in the media. In D. Singer & J. Singer (Eds.), *Handbook of children and the media* (pp. 269–288). Thousand Oaks, CA: Sage.

McDonald, H. S., Horstmann, N., Strom, K. J., & Pope, M. W. (2009). *The impact of the Internet on deviant behavior and deviant communities.* The Institute for Homeland Security Solutions. Available from http://www.ihssnc.org

National Crime Prevention Council (NCPC). (2009). *Homepage.* Available from http://www.ncpc.org/

Olweus, D. (1993). *Bullying at school: What we know and what we can do.* Malden, MA: Blackwell.

Pew Foundation. (2007). *The Pew Internet Project: Teens online.* Philadelphia, PA: The Pew Charitable Trusts.

Pew Foundation. (2009). *The Pew Internet & American Life Project.* Philadelphia, PA: The Pew Charitable Trusts.

Simon Wiesenthal Center. (2009). Homepage. Available from http://www.wiesenthal.com

Smith, S., & Donnerstein, E. (2003). The problem of exposure: Violence, sex, drugs, and alcohol. In D. Ravitch & J. Viteritti (Eds.), *Kid stuff: Marketing sex and violence to America's children* (pp. 65–95). Baltimore: Johns Hopkins University Press.

Strasburger, V. C., Jordan, A. B., & Donnerstein, E. (2010). Health effects of media on children and adolescents. *Pediatrics, 125,* 756–767.

Strasburger, V. C., Wilson, B., & Jordan, A. (2009). *Children, adolescents and the media* (2nd ed.). Thousand Oaks, CA: Sage.

Sunstein, C. R. (2001). *Republic.com.* Princeton, NJ: Princeton University Press.

Surgeon General of the United States. (2001). *Youth violence: A report of the surgeon general.* Washington, DC: Department of Health and Human Services, U.S. Government Printing Office.

Tajima, S., Suzuki, K., Sado, M., Hasegawa, Y., Horiuchi, Y., Linz, D., et al. (2008). *Contextual features of violence depiction in television advertisings.* Presented at the meeting of the International Society for Research on Aggression. Budapest, Hungary.

U.S. Department of Justice. (2009). *National Survey of Children's Exposure to Violence.* Office of Juvenile Justice and Delinquency Prevention, Washington, DC.

Williams, K. R., & Guerra, N. G. (2007). Prevalence and predictors of Internet bullying. *Journal of Adolescent Health, 41,* S14–S21.

Wilson, B., Smith, S., Potter, J. Kunkel, D., Linz, D., Colvin, C., & Donnerstein, E. (2002). Violence in children's television programming: Assessing the risks. *Journal of Communication, 52,* 5–35.

Wojcieszak, M. (2009). "Carrying online participation offline"—mobilization by radical online groups and politically dissimilar offline ties. *Journal of Communication, 59,* 564–586.

Wolak, J., Finkelhor, D., Mitchell, K. J., & Ybarra, M. L. (2008). Online "predators" and their victims: Myths, realities, and implications for prevention and treatment. *American Psychologist, 63,* 111–128.

Wolak, J., Mitchell, K. J., & Finkelhor, D. (2007). Does online harassment constitute bullying? An exploration of online harassment by known peers and online-only contacts. *Journal of Adolescent Health, 41,* S51–8.

Wright, P., Malamuth, N., & Donnerstein, E. (2010). Research on sex in the media: What do we know about effects on children and adolescents? In D. Singer & J. Singer (Eds.), *Handbook of children and the media* (2nd ed.). Thousand Oaks, CA: Sage.

Ybarra, M. L., & Mitchell, K. J. (2008). How risky are social networking sites? A comparison of places online where youth sexual solicitation and harassment occurs. *Pediatrics, 121,* 350–357.

Ybarra, M. L., West, M. D., Markow, D., Leaf, P. J., Hamburger, M., & Boxer, P. (2008). Linkages between Internet and other media violence with seriously violent behavior by youth. *Pediatrics, 122,* 929–937.

18

Are Supernatural Beliefs Commitment Devices for Intergroup Conflict?

ROBERT KURZBAN and JOHN CHRISTNER

University of Pennsylvania

A rguably the most important political event of the albeit still young twenty-first century was a case of intergroup conflict in which supernatural beliefs played a pivotal role. The attack on the World Trade Center in New York City, the Pentagon in Washington, D.C., and the foiled attack by the hijackers of United Airlines Flight 93 on September 11, 2001, was motivated by intergroup conflict but was made possible in no small part because the perpetrators had beliefs about the afterlife. While we do not attempt here to sort out the many causal antecedents of this attack, which are undoubtedly complex (see also Chapters 2, 10, and 16 in this volume), we do propose an explanation for the broader phenomenon: why people entertain supernatural beliefs and their relationship to intergroup conflict.

INTRODUCTION

True beliefs are useful, so much so that philosophers have argued that the only thing minds are good for is "the fixation of true beliefs" (Fodor, 2000, p. 68), sentiments that have been echoed by others (e.g., Dennett, 1987; Millikan, 1984; for a recent discussion, see McKay & Dennett, 2009). The general idea is intuitive and compelling: true beliefs aid in accomplishing goals and, with appropriate inference machines, in generating additional true beliefs.

Symmetrically, false beliefs are, in general, less useful. Acting on the basis of beliefs that do not capture something true about the world can lead to any number of bad outcomes. False beliefs about what is edible can lead to poisoning, false beliefs about what is sharp can lead to cuts, and so on. False supernatural beliefs, as Wright (2009) recently documented, cause their bearers to engage in an array of costly behaviors, including enduring—even self-inflicting—severe harm and, from an evolutionary standpoint, the most costly choice of all, electing to forgo reproduction (see also Iannaccone, 1992).

In light of these arguments, one would expect minds—absent some selective force—to be designed to resist adopting false beliefs. There are, however, important exceptions. Consider binary decisions such as fleeing or not fleeing from a potential predator in which the costs of errors (misses, false alarms) and the benefits of being correct (hits, correct rejections) are asymmetrical. In such cases, if the system is forced to adopt one belief or other and to act on the basis of the belief, selection will not favor maximizing the probability of true belief; it will rather maximize expected value (Cosmides & Tooby, 1987; Green & Swets, 1966). That is, if we assume that there must be a belief either that the predator is present or that it is absent (as opposed to some probabilistic representation), then even weak evidence should give rise to the (likely false) belief that the predator is present so that the appropriate action (i.e., fleeing) can be taken.

This principle is reflected in the design of both human artifacts, such as the smoke detector, and human physiology (Nesse, 2001, 2005; Nesse & Williams, 1994). A smoke detector cannot signal that there might be a fire, so it signals that it "believes" there is one even on scant evidence. In humans, all-or-none defenses such as the immune system (Nesse, 2001) reflect the same idea.

This principle governs the design of evolved mechanisms for inferences about the state of the world across any number of domains. As Wiley (1994) put it, rather than maximize percent correct, "basic decision theory suggests that a criterion should maximize the expected utility for the receiver…" (p. 172). Wiley shows, using a standard signal detection analysis, that selection can favor "adaptive gullibility" (i.e., erring on the side of false positives in the context of mating) and "adaptive fastidiousness" (i.e., erring on the side of misses in the context of detecting prey). The propensity for error—false "beliefs" about what is and is not a mate or prey—is built into these mechanisms because selection will sift in design space for designs that maximize fitness rather than accuracy. This is as true for evolved human systems as it is for other organisms' systems (Haselton & Buss, 2000; Nesse & Williams, 1994; Tooby & Cosmides, 1987).

There is a second important selection pressure that can counteract the tendency for evolution to favor truth-preserving belief systems. This pressure arises in the context of strategic interactions, in which individuals' payoffs are affected by others' actions (von Neumann & Morgenstern, 1944; Smith, 1982). To see the potential advantages of false beliefs, denote p as the true state of the world and p° as a false belief (p ≠ p°). Suppose ego is better off in terms of social advantages if everyone believed p° rather than p. (Suppose p° is that ego is highly intelligent, for example.) Suppose further that ego, by herself believing p°, increases the chances that others will adopt p°. (We assume that "genuine" belief can have advantages over simply dissembling, perhaps by virtue of the probability of persuasion; Trivers, 2000.) In such a case, by virtue of the effects p° has on others' behavior, it can be advantageous for ego to believe p° (Nesse & Lloyd, 1992; Trivers, 2000). So-called positive illusions (Taylor & Brown, 1988) might be such cases, in which false positive beliefs about oneself can aid in persuading others to adopt this strategically advantageous belief p° (Kurzban & Aktipis, 2006, 2007). Systems can come to be designed to generate and adopt p°'s as long as the costs of the false belief do not outweigh the strategic benefits (Kurzban, in press).

It is important to bear in mind both the power and the limits of this type of argument. Putative cases of design to bring about false beliefs must respect the distinction between, on one hand, when the decision one makes in and of itself determines one's payoff and, on the other hand, when the decision one makes and what one communicates to other agents affects one's payoff.

The distinction is important because the relentless calculus of decision theory and natural selection punishes mechanisms that do not maximize expected value. Holding aside what is communicated to another individual—and thereby potentially changing his or her behavior and, in consequence, the decision maker's downstream payoff—a mechanism that maximizes expected value cannot be beaten. (Maximizing expected value is, of course, not the same as maximizing percent correct, as indicated already.)

Substantial confusion surrounds this point. For example, consider the putative benefits of being "too" optimistic. Systems that generate errors that cause one to try more than one "should"—given the expected value of trying or not trying—will lose the evolutionary game to systems that maximize expected value. There is no way around this. The contemporary emphasis on "positive thinking" may also involve a variety of significant costs for similar reasons (see also Chapter 8 in this volume).

Some models also purport to show that error can be advantageous even without consideration of the strategic advantages of influencing others' behavior. However, these models succeed only because they artificially penalize strategies that maximize expected value. Nettle (2004), for example, models a decision in which communication plays no role, so an algorithm that maximizes expected value cannot be beaten by any other strategy without giving nonmaximizers help. In the model, "optimists"—who overestimate the chance of success—are given exactly such help: the model's "rational" (nonoptimistic) agents rely on and use completely inaccurate estimates of the chance of success. When (rational) agents have no information at all about the chance of success, they should use the decision-theoretic correct estimate of .5 in making their decision. It is true that when the expected payoff of trying is higher than the expected cost of failing, then "optimists" are better off than the "rational" agents (and symmetrically for pessimists; see also Haselton & Nettle, 2006), but the model's "optimists" and "pessimists" win only because they throw out the misleading information that the "rational" agents do not. As we explore subsequently, one prominent model of supernatural punishment runs into this problem as well.

Outside of cases such as these, as far as we know (McKay & Dennett, 2009), in which there is an advantage to error because of considerations of decision theory or the value of the communicative effect of one's decisions, one would not expect to find mechanisms designed to adopt false beliefs. Further, one would expect human computational architecture to be designed to reject false beliefs, given their potential costs.

From this perspective, the fact that humans seem to have mechanisms that endorse supernatural beliefs—which are (by assumption) guaranteed to be false—is puzzling. First is the bare fact that humans seem not just disposed but also positively eager to endorse supernatural beliefs (Dawkins, 2006; Dennett, 2006). Second, these beliefs seem to have high costs. Even holding aside the relationship between supernatural beliefs and intergroup conflict—the subject here—supernatural beliefs seem to play a large role in any number of costly behaviors. This would include things like time-consuming (but useless) prayer, building monuments to nonexistent gods, sacrificing goats or other animals without consuming them, doing rain dances, and taking risks because of predictions of divine intervention.

So, holding aside the two previous arguments, selection should, everything else equal, have eliminated belief-generation mechanisms that had the property of generating and acquiring supernatural beliefs. Why, then, are supernatural beliefs so pervasive in our species?

THEORIES OF SUPERNATURAL BELIEF

Many scholars have addressed the issue of the origin of supernatural belief. Here we discuss only a few prominent models, which, broadly, fall into two classes. The first class is by-product explanations. On this view, humans have mechanisms designed to construct, transmit, and acquire representations for one function, and supernatural beliefs emerge as a side effect of the way these systems operate. We review these first and then turn to the second possibility: that the mechanisms that generate supernatural beliefs are designed for precisely this function.

By-product Views

One of the most prominent by-product models of supernatural beliefs begins with the broad idea that people transmit information socially. People learn from one another in part because there are tremendous cost savings in socially rather than individually learning information (Boyd & Richerson, 1985). Further, given social learning, it follows that, by virtue of the way that learning mechanisms operate, some kinds of ideas, beliefs, and practices will be more likely to be generated, recalled, and transmitted than others (e.g., Sperber, 1985). This is a natural consequence of any social learning system, and this idea is easily seen in the domain of language, in which various rules constrain the grammar entertained by language learners (Pinker, 1994).

From this, it follows that, by an evolutionary process, certain ideas will tend to persist and be observed over time more than others. Ideas that are "sticky," having properties that make them memorable and transmitted (Bartlett, 1932), will be observed more than those that do not "fit" with human cognition.

One of the major models surrounding supernatural beliefs—the "ontological heresy" (OH) model—begins with this idea and turns on one important element of learning systems: that there seem to be categories of entities that the mind is prepared to learn about. Each of these categories comes with a set of defining characteristics that apply to all entries within it, so when a new entry is added many of its features are "automatically" assigned, eliminating the need to relearn them. For example, categories like PERSON, ANIMAL, TOOL, PLANT, or OBJECT each provide a scaffolding of inferences on which to build new concepts. When learning about a new animal, people do not need to relearn that the animal's innards resemble those of conspecifics, that it has offspring that grow into adults, that it moves of its own accord and pursues goals, and so on. These inferences are automatically provided by the ANIMAL category.

The OH model highlights that supernatural beliefs tend to be representations that conform to ontological templates but, crucially, depart from them in a particular way and that this combination—conformity plus exception—gives rise to their "stickiness."

Consider a ghost, which is a PERSON but violates the usual template in that it passes through objects and, most importantly, is not alive, a critical feature of a PERSON. A ghost, then, can be understood as a PERSON—preserving most PERSON-related properties (e.g., has a mind, moves around) plus violations—a ghost can pass through solid matter whereas people cannot.

Boyer and Bergstrom (2008) recently wrote about ideas such as ghosts:

> Such notions are salient and inferentially productive because they combine specific features that violate some default expectations for the domain with nonviolated expectations held by default as true of the entire domain (Boyer, 1994). These combinations of explicit violation and tacit inference are culturally widespread and constitute a memory optimum (Barrett & Nyhof, 2001; Boyer & Ramble, 2001). This may be because explicit violations of expectations are attention-grabbing, whereas preserved nonviolated expectations allow one to reason about the postulated agents or objects (Boyer, 1994). (p. 119)

The key point is the notion of a "memory optimum." On this view, supernatural beliefs persist as a by-product of the fact that human computational systems "like" representations that allow one to reason about them (the PERSON part of a ghost or spirit) combined with the fact that we also attend more to ideas that violate our expectations (the nonliving component of being a ghost). Supernatural beliefs, on this view, persist as a by-product of mechanisms designed for inferences and attention.

A related by-product view is that some beliefs, by virtue of their content and their tendency to move from one head to another, replicate themselves not because the beliefs are useful to the people who have them but simply because they are the sorts of beliefs that lead to their own propagation. Dennett (2006) argues that religious systems of belief seem to have properties that make them good at replicating themselves, including the injunction to transmit information to children, to reproduce, and to conquer and convert others. These features of a belief system, he argues, contribute to the spread of the beliefs themselves.

There are three primary difficulties of these models. First, as the costs of supernatural beliefs increase, so does the strength of selection to "clean up" the system, making by-product claims less plausible. That is, by-product explanations are unlikely to the extent that costs are high and selection could have selected out these supernatural-belief-generation systems without compromising the system that these belief-generation systems are a by-product of. We believe that these costs are, indeed, high and that there is no reason to think selection could not have modified learning systems to resist, rather than endorse, supernatural beliefs. Second, by-product hypotheses explain why supernatural beliefs are memorable but not why supernatural beliefs are endorsed (Dennett, 2006). These are two importantly distinct claims. Finally, models such as Dennett's rest on largely domain-general and content-free learning systems, which, from an evolutionary view, are unlikely to characterize human psychology (Tooby & Cosmides, 1992).

Adaptationist Views

The second class of arguments suggests that the mechanisms underlying supernatural belief acquisition are designed to adopt them. On this view, there is some advantage to having supernatural beliefs, and this advantage explains the existence of the mechanisms designed to generate and adopt them.

One prominent account is that supernatural beliefs "steered individuals away from costly social transgressions resulting from unrestrained, evolutionarily ancestral, selfish interest (acts which would rapidly become known to others, and thereby incur an increased probability and severity of punishment by group members)" (Johnson & Bering, 2006, p. 219). That is, those with supernatural beliefs—particularly false beliefs about punishment and the afterlife—would have avoided actions that would have led to costs in the real world, thus making them better off.

This argument is a game theoretical argument that agents with these supernatural beliefs could invade a population of agents without them. In evaluating this argument, the key is to consider a population at equilibrium. This would be a population of agents who maximize expected value. In a world in which some acts are punished, maximizing expected value entails taking into account the probability of detection and the costs of punishment. Maximizing individuals do not take advantage of all opportunities for selfish, norm-violating gain; they take advantage of opportunities with positive expected value. Johnson and Bering (2006) assume this issue away: "As long as the net costs of selfish actions from real-world punishment by group members exceeded the net costs of lost opportunities from self-imposed norm abiding, then god-fearing individuals would outcompete non-believers" (p. 219). However, there is no reason to think that the default state is a design that favors engaging in (selfish) actions with negative expected value. Indeed, the reverse is the case. Selection should continuously push computational mechanisms toward such optima, subject to all the usual constraints (see, e.g., Dawkins, 1982). In the absence of an argument about a constraint that is pushing the design off this optimum, game theoretic models must assume expected value maximization as the default.

Further, even if one were to assume that at some point a population were out of equilibrium in this way, such a population is always invadable—again, by agents who do not adopt outcome-reducing supernatural beliefs. If the social world were like poker, consider the cost of having the view that those who bluff will endure endless punishment in the afterlife (and, therefore, never bluff). Such people are at a disadvantage and will lose, eventually, to those who use bluffing as a tactic, unhindered by false beliefs about the costs.

A second adaptationist argument for supernatural beliefs turns on the value of such beliefs in the context of signaling to others (see Chapter 9 in this volume on the value of signaling in the context of anger). Arguments of this nature draw on the behavioral ecology literature, especially models that show that some signals evolve because of, rather than in spite of, their cost (Grafen, 1990; Zahavi, 1975). The typical example is the peacock's tail. Because the large tail has great energetic costs and makes one vulnerable to predation, only very healthy and high-quality organisms can afford to support them. For this reason, peahens that select peacocks with such tails as mates are at an advantage.

In the context of religion, it has been argued that enduring the high costs imposed by religions (e.g., physical harm, deprivation of food and water, labor requirements) send signals to others (Irons, 2001; Sosis & Alcorta, 2003). In particular, it has been argued that these costs commit those who endure the costs to the group. (See Henrich, 2009 for a recent related but distinct idea.)

However, care must be exercised in the relationship between cost and signal. In the case of the peacock's tail, the cost conveys something about quality as an intrinsic feature of the cost. Poor-quality peacocks simply cannot endure the cost. The same argument does not apply to costs and commitment. Enduring a cost to enter a group does not, as an inherent consequence of the cost, prevent someone from defecting or leaving the group. All costs in this sense are sunk, as are costs that are imposed while one is in the group (such as a tithe).

Performing rituals can indeed be costly, and such rituals often include supernatural beliefs as justification. Enduring such costs might be signaling something. However, it is not clear that these costs honestly signal commitment, given that it is possible to endure costs and then leave the group. Having said that, some kinds of signals might, in fact, make leaving more difficult. We now turn to this issue and our own view of the function of supernatural beliefs.

SUPERNATURAL BELIEFS AS COMMITMENT DEVICES

The Value of Commitment

Difficulties with existing explanations for supernatural beliefs suggest that it might be worthwhile to look for alternatives. The idea sketched here requires several inferential steps and is therefore perhaps not the most elegant model, but it arguably solves the problems with previous models.

We begin with the premise that human evolutionary history was characterized by shifting coalitions and alliances (DeScioli & Kurzban, 2009; Kurzban & Neuberg, 2005; Cosmides, Tooby, & Kurzban, 2001; Sidanius & Kurzban, 2003; Tiger, 1969; Tooby, Cosmides, & Kurzban, 2003). This is not to say that some alliances weren't relatively stable, such as those arranged along kin lines, as observed in other species, such as baboons (Cheney & Seyfarth, 2007). The argument turns only on the notion that there was some volatility in alliances.

We further assume that, in a world of alliances, being a member of an alliance is a benefit, and, symmetrically, not being a member of an alliance is a cost. Once people can form alliances, individuals left out of the protection of a group are subject to easy exploitation. Evidence that people derive pleasure from membership in groups (Baumeister & Leary, 1995) and experience pain when excluded from them (Chapters 3 and 13 in this volume) is indicative of motivational systems executing this function.

In this hypothetical world of shifting group memberships, there would, of course, be many dimensions along which people are evaluated for possible membership in a group. These would presumably have to do with properties of the individual, such as skills, intelligence, physical condition, and social connections.

While these properties are all no doubt important, one key parameter might be the extent to which an individual is viewed as likely to change sides as the fault lines of conflict shift. When alliances are dynamic, a member who can, when opportunity arises, shift to the competing group is extremely dangerous. This suggests that the ability to signal that one will not—or, even better, cannot—switch alliances can be a benefit, rather than a cost, because committing can make one a more valuable group member (Frank, 1988). This idea is a specific case of the general notion that removing one's own options can be strategically advantageous if it is signaled to others (Schelling, 1960).

This idea might help to explain various practices surrounding group membership. Scarification—the practice of making permanent marks on one's skin with colors or shallow cuts—might be designed to help persuade others that one is committed to one's group (e.g., Rush, 2005). To the extent that rivals would not accept an individual with these permanent marks into their group, these signals are honest in the technical sense of the term.

Scarification and tattoos (like false beliefs) can be dangerous, leading to the possibility of damage or infection. Despite this, it is still practiced widely, pointing to the possibility of an evolved appetite for visible signals of commitment, whether to groups or romantic partners.

Supernatural Beliefs as Loyalty Signals

Beliefs, unlike scars and tattoos, are invisible and easily revised. Spoken statements are themselves ephemeral, limiting their effectiveness as commitment devices. Having said that, giving rise to a belief in another person's head can, under certain circumstances, recruit the power of commitment. For example, as Frank (1988) discusses, information that makes one vulnerable can be useful in this context. If Alfred tells Bob information that would be disastrous for Alfred should it get out, Alfred has, effectively, assured Bob that he won't act in such a way that would make Bob unfavorably disposed toward him. When Bob knows information that would compromise Alfred—perhaps where to find evidence of a crime that Alfred has committed—Bob can be assured of Alfred's loyalty. So, transmitting certain kinds of information to others can increase the extent to which they are likely to believe you will remain a loyal ally, which can yield important benefits.

Broadcasting beliefs might allow commitment. For example, public statements of loyalty to a particular group—or antipathy for other local groups—might help assure potential allies of one's commitment. However, talk is cheap, and such pronouncements do not bind one's actions in the same way that tattoos, scars, or disclosing incrimination information does. Opinions can change; apologies and restitution can be made.

Some statements, however, might make one what Boyer (personal communication, October 20, 2007) has called "unclubbable," meaning undesirable as a member of a group or community. Such statements, according to the logic of commitment above, are, to be clear, potentially good things: from the standpoint of commitment to a group, ways to disqualify oneself from alternative group memberships are the goal.

Consider the following statements:

1. °Christopher Columbus discovered America in 1215.
2. °The earth is flat.
3. °I enjoy eating my own feces.

Statements 1 and 2, in modern times, would, it seems reasonable to say, invite relatively negative evaluations. Everything else equal, people prefer group members who do not have beliefs that are thought to be obviously false. However, even if it were known that someone had such false beliefs, he or she would not necessarily be subject to social exclusion.

Statement 3, in contrast, as long as it is not said in obvious jest, would be particularly likely to elicit negative evaluations. As the literature on social stigma suggests, such deviations from normal human behavior elicit very strong negative evaluations (Kurzban & Leary, 2001).

The problem with 1 and 2, then, is that they are not strong enough—they don't make you unclubbable in any group. Statement 3, in contrast, is too strong; it makes you unclubbable in every group.

So, to solve the commitment problem, what is required is the sincere endorsement of a belief that makes one unclubbable in every group except the group to which one is trying to signal loyalty. What sort of belief will make one a poor candidate for group membership in nearly every group except the one that one is currently in or wishes to commit to?

To return to Statement 3, what makes someone unclubbable about this is the departure from canonical human nature. Human social cognitive systems appear designed to sift through the social world, evaluating others as potential mates, allies, and group members. Departures from the skeletal structure of basic features of human nature act as cues that count heavily against candidates for social interaction (Kurzban & Leary, 2001).

Recall our discussion of Boyer's (1994) ideas surrounding intuitive ontology. To a first approximation, by virtue of shared human computational architecture, people share intuitive ontological commitments. Supernatural beliefs violate these commitments. In this sense, supernatural beliefs are singularly good at making one appear to have beliefs that violate fundamental causal intuitive principles. In this, they are very different from garden-variety false beliefs. Beliefs 1 and 2 are false, but their falseness does not come by virtue of a conflict with intuitive ontology.

In this sense, supernatural beliefs might be well suited to making one unclubbable because they connote deviation from the species-typical design. Individuals who do not respect the basic principles that govern causal reasoning about fundamental categories in the world—ARTIFACTS, ANIMALS, and PEOPLE—are by and large seen (with a key exception) as mentally ill.

The *Diagnostic and Statistical Manual (DSM)* reflects this idea. In the *DSM*, fourth edition, text revised (*DSM-IV-TR*), a delusion is defined this way: "A false belief based on incorrect inference about external reality that is firmly sustained despite what almost everybody else believes and despite what constitutes incontrovertible and obvious proof or evidence to the contrary" (APA, 2000). Harris (2005, p. 821) points out the similarity between a supernatural belief and a delusion: "We have names for people who have many beliefs for which there is no rational justification. When their beliefs are extremely common we call them 'religious'; otherwise, they are likely to be called 'mad,' 'psychotic,' or 'delusional'" (p. 72).

The key point is that supernatural beliefs will be easily identified by people as false because of people's intuitive ontological commitments. This will lead people to infer that the person who endorses such beliefs—and "firmly sustains" them—is, to a first approximation, insane. The mentally ill are one of the most heavily stigmatized groups (Corrigan, 2005).

This has one very large exception, as indicated by the definition in the *DSM-IV-TR*. False beliefs that that are shared by "almost everybody else" are not considered delusions. Consider the following:

4. °Eating another person gives you access to his or her soul.
5. °If a special person says special magic words in a special building, certain crackers turn into the body of a person who was alive but is now dead.
6. °A certain kind of tree can be made to fruit if a pretty woman kicks it.
7. °Keeping your dead grandmother's hair in a jar keeps her spirit around.

First, it is worth asking if one can intuit which of these beliefs are supernatural beliefs culled from the world's cultures and which are delusional beliefs culled from the clinical literature. (Note that 4 and 7 are drawn from clinical accounts, whereas 5 and 6 are religious beliefs.)

People who endorse such beliefs might be taken for either mentally ill or not, depending on the social context in which such beliefs are uttered, specifically whether the supernatural belief is commonly held by the other people in a social group. Among those who believe in transubstantiation, 5 will not make one appear mentally ill. Indeed, endorsing this belief not only does not elicit exclusion but, in fact, in some communities is also essentially a requirement for inclusion. Wright (2009) quotes an interesting observation of this general phenomenon suggested by the Apostle Paul, who asks, if "the whole church comes together and speaks in tongues, and outsiders or unbelievers enter, will they not say that you are out of your mind?" (p. 270).

The very first commandment, of course, echoes this idea. The call to monotheism, and the harsh punishments in the Old Testament for polytheism, is consistent with the idea that supernatural beliefs are for preventing membership in other groups. The first commandment essentially prevented switching in a world in which other groups were worshiping multiple deities. In this sense, the modern practice of religious tolerance can be seen as evidence for, rather than against, our position. The massive efforts that must be made to try to get people to be tolerant of others' religious views suggests that this is not the default state.

Relatedly, Iannaccone (1994), drawing on earlier arguments by Kelley (1986), suggests that religious groups are successful because the things that make them distinctive "invite ridicule, isolation, and persecution" (p. 1182) and that such groups "demand of members some distinctive, stigmatizing behavior that inhibits participation or reduces productivity in alternative contexts…" (p. 1188). These are ideas that resonate closely with the notion that supernatural beliefs are effective ways to commit to one group over others. Note that Iannacone, however, suggests that the benefit of such costs has to do with public goods rather than the present argument. He quotes Singh (1953): "The Guru wanted to raise a body of men who would not be able to deny their faith when questioned, but whose external appearance would invite persecution and breed the courage to resist it" (p. 31; see also Iannaccone, 1992). Though the present argument focuses on supernatural beliefs, certainly it is plausible that there are other ways to make oneself unclubbable, through, for instance, physical appearance or one's choice of foods. As long as one's behavior reduces the (perception of) the chance of switching groups, the present argument holds.

Summary

To summarize, our argument begins with the notion that supernatural beliefs that preclude membership in other groups are valuable because they represent commitment. Supernatural beliefs, which violate the basic ontological commitments of evolved intuitive theories, make one appear mentally ill to those who do not share such beliefs, an idea reflected in modern psychiatric classification. If supernatural beliefs do have this property, then there could have been selection for mechanisms designed to generate and endorse locally distinctive supernatural beliefs. Such a mechanism potentially solves the commitment problem by allowing one to preclude membership in any groups other than the local one.

Supernatural beliefs have advantages over other potentially distinctive local beliefs. For example, false beliefs about history, although they might be locally distinctive, do not preclude membership in other groups. Supernatural beliefs, unlike other beliefs that might be locally shared, have the particular property of committing one to the local group that shares the supernatural belief, making them functional in a way that essentially any nonsupernatural belief could not. This gives a functional explanation for Boyer's (1994) finding regarding supernatural beliefs and might help to explain how the costs of false beliefs might be offset.

It seems plausible—though this is not central to the present argument—that rituals might be ways to signal one's endorsement of the false belief that goes beyond simple statements to that effect. Taking communion, for example, might help to persuade others that one endorses Belief 5. Other rituals, instead of being costly signals, might be means of persuading others that one really endorses particular supernatural beliefs. This changes the value of ritual from signaling cost per se to signaling belief.

IMPLICATIONS FOR INTERGROUP CONFLICT

One puzzling feature of religious conflict is the degree of antipathy between groups that share nearly all of their supernatural beliefs, with only a handful of such beliefs distinguishing them. The various antipathies of the world's major monotheistic religions are well known, as is the blood spilled over details of supernatural beliefs among the divisions of Christianity. One might have predicted that similarity reduced hostility, with, say, monotheistic Catholics most fiercely antagonistic toward polytheistic Hindu but less toward Mormons. This does not, however, seem to be the case. Despite massive overlap in large numbers of false beliefs, a tiny number of such beliefs that differ seem to be sufficient for striking negative emotion and hostility, as one sees in fights among sects. (For some data on the relationship between organized religion and aggression, see Chapter 19 in this volume.)

There are, of course, many possible explanations for this phenomenon, including the fact that groups with similar beliefs might be engaged in conflict for the same resources (Wright, 2009) because of their proximity, but it sits well with the present view. If supernatural beliefs are designed specifically for the purpose of committing people to particular groups because of the potential for conflict, then it is not surprising that differences in supernatural beliefs between groups should breed fear and hostility.

Along similar lines, the present view resonates well with the fact that organized religions are the locus of trust and cooperation (Wilson, 2002). If shared supernatural beliefs are a good cue to group commitment, then they ought to bring about emotions of trust and support. In the context of intergroup competition, mutually beneficial within-group transactions are very valuable. It is worth noting that there is nothing in and of itself that suggests that false beliefs held in common would lead to trust and strong community ties.

The foregoing suggests that supernatural beliefs should play a special role in both within- and between-group social relationships (see also Chapter 10 in this volume). Within groups, shared supernatural beliefs and any acts that are indicative of such shared beliefs (e.g., particular rituals) should make others feel that the person in question is trustworthy and a loyal member of the group. This should be particularly the case for public activities, which would serve the function of disqualifying one from membership in other groups. This is distinct from other kinds of beliefs. For example, false shared historical beliefs should not lead to inferences of trustworthiness in the same way that supernatural beliefs might.

In short, we argue that supernatural beliefs are not, in themselves, accidental consequences of design; neither is the fact that they are at the center of intergroup conflict an accidental consequence of design. On the present view, then, mechanisms that give rise to supernatural beliefs that cause their bearer to be feared and hated by others who do share the belief are functioning precisely as they were designed.

REFERENCES

American Psychiatric Association. (APA). (2000). *Diagnostic and statistical manual of mental disorders* (4th ed., text revision). Washington, DC: Author.

Barrett, J., & Nyhof, M. (2001). Spreading nonnatural concepts. *Journal of Cognition and Culture, 1,* 69–100.

Bartlett, F. C. (1932). *Remembering: A study in experimental and social psychology.* Cambridge, UK: Cambridge University Press.

Baumeister, R. F., & Leary, M. R. (1995). The need to belong: Desire for interpersonal attachments as a fundamental human motivation. *Psychological Bulletin, 117,* 497–529.

Boyd, R., & Richerson, P. J. (1985). *Culture and the evolutionary process.* Chicago: University of Chicago Press.

Boyer, P. (1994). *The naturalness of religious ideas: A cognitive theory of religion.* Berkeley: University of California Press.

Boyer, P., & Bergstrom, B. (2008). Evolutionary perspectives on religion. *Annual Review of Anthropology, 37,* 111–130.

Boyer, P., & Ramble, C. (2001). Cognitive templates for religious concepts: Cross-cultural evidence for recall of counter-intuitive representations. *Cognitive Science, 25,* 535–564.

Cheney, D. L., & Seyfarth, R. M. (2007). *Baboon metaphysics: The evolution of a social mind.* Chicago: University of Chicago Press.

Corrigan, J. (2005). Is the experimental auction a dynamic market? *Environmental & Resource Economics, 31,* 35–45.

Cosmides, L., & Tooby, J. (1987). From evolution to behavior: Evolutionary psychology as the missing link. In J. Dupré (Ed.), *The latest on the best: Essays on evolution and optimality* (pp. 277–306). Cambridge, MA: MIT Press.

Cosmides, L., Tooby, J., & Kurzban, R. (2003). Perceptions of race. *Trends in Cognitive Sciences, 7,* 173–179.

Dawkins, R. (1982). *The extended phenotype: The gene as the unit of selection.* Oxford, UK: W.H. Freeman & Co.

Dawkins, R. (2006). *The God delusion.* New York: Bantam Books.

Dennett, D. C. (1987). *The intentional stance.* Cambridge, MA: MIT Press.

Dennett, D. C. (2006). *Breaking the spell: Religion as a natural phenomenon.* New York: Penguin Books.

DeScioli, P., & Kurzban, R. (2009). Mysteries of morality. *Cognition, 112,* 281–299.

Fodor, J. (2000). *The mind doesn't work that way.* Cambridge, MA: MIT Press.

Frank, R. (1988). *Passions within reason: The strategic role of the emotions.* New York: W.W. Norton & Co.

Grafen, A. (1990). Biological signals as handicaps. *Journal of Theoretical Biology, 144,* 517–546.

Green, D. M., & Swets, J. A. (1966). *Signal detection theory and psychophysics.* New York: John Wiley and Sons.

Harris, S. (2005). *The end of faith: Religion, terror, and the future of reason.* New York: W. W. Norton & Co.

Haselton, M. G., & Buss, D. M. (2000). Error management theory: A new perspective on biases in cross-sex mind reading. *Journal of Personality and Social Psychology, 78,* 81–91.

Haselton, M. G., & Nettle, D. (2006). The paranoid optimist: An integrative evolutionary model of cognitive biases. *Personality and Social Psychology Review, 10,* 47–66.

Henrich, J. (2009). The evolution of costly displays, cooperation, and religion: Credibility enhancing displays and their implications for cultural evolution. *Evolution and Human Behavior, 30,* 244–260.

Iannaccone, L. R. (1992). Sacrifice and stigma: Reducing free-riding in cults, communes, and other collectives. *Journal of Political Economy, 100,* 271–291.

Iannaccone, L. R. (1994). Why strict churches are strong. *American Journal of Sociology* 99, 1180–1211.

Irons, W. (2001). Religion as a hard-to-fake sign of commitment. In R. Nesse (Ed.), *Evolution and the capacity for commitment* (pp. 292–309). New York: Russell Sage Foundation.

Johnson, D. D. P., & Bering, J. M. (2006). Hand of God, mind of man: Punishment and cognition in the evolution of cooperation. *Evolutionary Psychology, 4,* 219–233.

Kelley, D. M. (1986). *Why conservative churches are growing: A study in sociology of religion with a new preface for the ROSE edition.* Macon, GA: Mercer University Press.

Kurzban, R. (in press). *Why everyone (else) is a hypocrite: Evolution and the modular mind.* Princeton, NJ: Princeton University Press.

Kurzban, R., & Aktipis, C. A. (2006). Modular minds, multiple motives. In M. Shaller, J. Simpson, & D. Kenrick (Eds.), *Evolution and social psychology* (pp. 39–53). New York: Psychology Press.

Kurzban, R., & Aktipis, C. A. (2007). Modularity and the social mind: Are psychologists too self-ish? *Personality and Social Psychology Review, 11,* 131–149.

Kurzban, R., & Leary, M. R. (2001). Evolutionary origins of stigmatization: The functions of social exclusion. *Psychological Bulletin, 127,* 187–208.

Kurzban, R., & Neuberg, S. (2005). Managing ingroup and outgroup relationships. In D. Buss (Ed.), *The handbook of evolutionary psychology* (pp. 653–675). Hoboken, NJ: Wiley.

Kurzban, R., Tooby, J., & Cosmides, L. (2001). *Can race be erased? Coalitional computation and social categorization.* Proceedings of the National Academy of Sciences, 98, 15387–15392.

McKay, R. T., & Dennett, D. C. (2009). The evolution of misbelief. *Behavioral and Brain Sciences, 32,* 493–561.

Millikan, R. (1984). *Language, thought, and other biological categories.* Cambridge, MA: MIT Press.

Nesse, R. M. (2005). Natural selection and the regulation of defenses: A signal detection analysis of the smoke detector principle. *Evolution and Human Behavior, 26,* 88–105.

Nesse, R. M. (2001). *Evolution and the capacity for commitment.* New York: Russell Sage Foundation.

Nesse, R. M., & Lloyd, A. T. (1992). The evolution of psychodynamic mechanisms. In J. Barkow, L. Cosmides, & J. Tooby (Eds.), *The adapted mind: Evolutionary psychology and the generation of culture* (pp. 601–624). New York: Oxford University Press.

Nesse, R. M., & Williams, G. C. (1994). *Why we get sick: The new science of Darwinian medicine.* New York: Vintage Books.

Nettle, D. (2004). Adaptive illusions: Optimism, control and human rationality. In D. Evans & P. Cruse (Eds.), *Emotion, evolution and rationality* (pp. 193–208). Oxford, UK: Oxford University Press.

Pinker, S. (1994). *The language instinct: How the mind creates language.* New York: HarperCollins.

Rush, J. A. (2005). *Spiritual tattoo: A cultural history of tattooing, piercing, scarification, branding, and implants.* Berkeley, CA: Frog, Ltd.

Schelling, T. (1960). *The strategy of conflict.* Cambridge, MA: Harvard University Press.

Sidanius, J., & Kurzban, R. (2003). Evolutionary approaches to political psychology. In D. O. Sears, L. Huddy, & R. Jervis (Eds.), *Oxford handbook of political psychology* (pp. 146–181). Oxford, UK: Oxford University Press.

Singh, K. (1953). *The Sikhs.* London: Allen & Unwin.

Smith, J. M. (1982). *Evolution and the theory of games.* Cambridge, UK: Cambridge University Press.

Sosis, R., & Alcorta, C. (2003). Signaling, solidarity, and the sacred: The evolution of religious behavior. *Evolutionary Anthropology, 12,* 264–274.

Sperber, D. (1985). *On anthropological knowledge*. Cambridge, UK: Cambridge University Press.

Taylor, S. E., & Brown, J. D. (1988). Illusion and well-being: A social psychological perspective on mental health. *Psychological Bulletin, 103*, 193–210.

Tiger, L. (1969). *Men in groups*. New York: Random House.

Tooby, J., & Cosmides, L. (1992). The psychological foundations of culture. In J. Barkow, L. Cosmides, & J. Tooby (Eds.), *The adapted mind* (pp. 19–136). New York: Oxford University Press.

Trivers, R. (2000). The elements of a scientific theory of self-deception. *Annals of the New York Academy of Sciences, 907*, 114–131.

Von Neumann, J., & Morgenstern, O. (1944). *Theory of games and economic behavior*. Princeton, NJ: Princeton University Press.

Wiley, R. H. (1994). Errors, exaggeration, and deception in animal communication. In L. Real (Ed.), *Behavioral mechanisms in evolutionary ecology* (pp. 157–189). Chicago: University of Chicago Press.

Wilson, D. S. (2002). *Darwin's cathedral: Evolution, religion, and the nature of society*. Chicago: University of Chicago Press.

Wright, R. (2009). *The evolution of God*. New York: Little, Brown and Company Hachette Book Group.

Zahavi, A. (1975). Mate selection: A selection for a handicap. *Journal of Theoretical Biology, 53*, 205–214.

19

The Effect of Religious Participation on Aggression Over One's Lifetime and Across Generations

L. ROWELL HUESMANN

University of Michigan

ERIC F. DUBOW

University of Michigan and Bowling Green State University

PAUL BOXER

Rutgers University and University of Michigan

*D*uring the past decade, there has been a burgeoning interest in the role of religiosity in family functioning and child and adolescent adjustment (e.g., Bridges & Moore, 2002; Mahoney, Pargament, Swank, & Tarakeshwar, 2001) and as a resource for adults coping with stress (Pargament, 1997, 2007). The focus of this chapter is on the role of religiosity across the life span in predicting adulthood aggressiveness. We use data from a 40-year prospective longitudinal study to examine (1) the extent to which parental religiosity when a child is 8 years old is related to the child's religiosity at ages 19, 30, and 48, and the grandchild's religiosity; and (2) the extent to which grandparental, parental, and child religiosity act as long-term protective factors against aggressive behavior in childhood, youth, and adulthood.

THE IMPORTANCE OF RELIGIOSITY

According to the Gallup Consulting Organization (2008), 93% of Americans 18 years of age and older reported that they believe in God or a universal spirit; 54% reported that religion is "very important" in their lives, and another 26% reported that religion is "fairly important" in their lives; 61% said that they are a member of a church or synagogue, and 38% said that they had attended religious services in the past 7 days; and 57% agreed that religion can answer all or most of today's problems. In a nationally representative sample of eighth through twelfth graders, Wallace, Forman, Caldwell, and Willis (2003) found that 60% of adolescents reported that religion is an important part of their lives, and 50% said they attend religious services regularly. While comparable statistics are difficult to obtain for other countries, the available statistics for other Western countries are not that different. For example, 88% of Italians say they belong to a church, and about 30% say they attend regularly. According to the 1996 World Values Survey (1996), only about 36% of Europeans said they never (or practically never) attended church. Thus, while the current study focuses entirely on the United States, where most of the data relating religiosity to behavior have been obtained, cautious generalizations to the rest of the world are possible.

In extensive reviews of the literature on the role of religion in child and adolescent adjustment, Bridges and Moore (2002) and Mahoney et al. (2001) reported that high levels of parent and child religiosity (most often measured by parental or self-reports of frequency of church attendance, frequency of prayer, and importance of religion to one's life) were linked to lower levels of delinquency, behavior problems, and substance use and to higher levels of adolescent responsibility. Relatedly, Chapter 14 in this volume shows that forgiving is related to religion. While history has shown that religious devotion can promote terrorism and aggression in some cases (e.g., Chapter 10 in this volume), the majority of empirical research to date seems to indicate that religious participation is related to more positive outcomes in youth.

EMPIRICAL STUDIES OF THE RELATION BETWEEN RELIGIOSITY AND AGGRESSION AND DELINQUENCY

Johnson, De Li, Larson, and McCullough (2000) reviewed 40 studies published from 1985 to 1997 on the relation between religiosity and delinquency. A total of 30 of the 40 studies showed a negative relation between religiosity and delinquency. Only five studies had a longitudinal design.

Several studies have assessed the relation between parental religiosity and child aggression and delinquency, and most have shown negative correlations between parental church attendance and risk for aggression, delinquency, or criminality of their children (Ellis & Pettersson, 1996; Pettersson, 1991). Bartkowski, Xu, and Levin (2008) used data from the nationally representative Early Childhood Longitudinal Study-K sample (over 20,000 kindergarten and first graders in 1998–1999). Parental religiosity was measured by frequency of church attendance, religious homogamy (similarity between parents in terms of frequency of church attendance), and frequency of discussions of religion with the child. Higher levels of each parent's frequency of attendance and religious homogamy were related to most parent- and teacher-rated measures of child development, including higher levels of self-control and lower levels of impulsiveness and externalizing behavior problems. Kim, McCullough, and Cicchetti (2009) examined a sample of maltreated and nonmaltreated children. Among nonmaltreated children, parents' importance of faith was related to lower levels of internalizing and externalizing behaviors in middle childhood, and parental religious influence seemed to be stronger when the child reported lower levels of importance of religion. These effects were not observed for maltreated children; however, in a separate study Kim (2008) found protective effects of religiosity on internalizing symptoms for maltreated females. Finally, using data from our Columbia County Longitudinal Study (CCLS), we found that boys whose parents attended church more frequently when the boys were 8 years old were less at risk for criminality by age 30 than were equally aggressive 8-year-old boys whose parents attended church less frequently (Huesmann, Eron, & Dubow, 2002). This finding held even after controlling for family interaction variables and the child's IQ.

Several recent studies assessed adolescents' self-reports of their own religiosity. Herrenkohl et al. (2003) used data from the Seattle Social Development Study. The participants were children who were high in teacher ratings of aggression at age 10. Lower probability of violence at age 18 was associated with several age-15 variables: attendance at religious services, good family management by parents, and school bonding. Pearce, Jones, Schwab-Stone, and Ruchkin (2003), in a sample of high-risk urban adolescents, found that religiousness assessed by church attendance and self-rated religiousness was associated negatively with conduct disorder and that "private religiousness" (e.g., prayer, reading religious literature) was associated with decreases over 1 year in conduct disorder. Regnerus and Elder (2003) used data from the National Longitudinal Study of Adolescent Health to examine whether religiosity would be most important for high-risk youth because religious support "provides functional communities amid dysfunction" (p. 635). The children were in grades 7–12 at time 1 and were assessed 1 year later as well. Under conditions of higher poverty, there was indeed a stronger relation between frequency of church attendance and "staying on track academically," which included a composite of grade point average, getting homework completed, getting along with teachers, not being suspended or expelled, and not skipping school. Fowler, Ahmed, Tompsett, Jozefowicz-Simbeni, and Toro (2008) examined a sample of over 300 low-income African American and Caucasian emerging adults (average age 20 years old). Public religious affiliation (i.e., the value the participants held in their church membership) buffered the relation between exposure to community violence and substance use. Private religiousness (i.e., the extent to which participants indicated that their religious beliefs provided them with personal meaning) buffered the relation between exposure to community violence and deviant behavior and conduct problems, but this finding was limited to African American participants.

THEORETICAL EXPLANATIONS FOR WHY PARENTAL AND CHILD RELIGIOSITY SHOULD PROTECT AGAINST AGGRESSION AND DELINQUENCY

Researchers have reviewed theoretical explanations for potentially positive effects of parental and child religiosity on family functioning and child and adolescent outcomes (e.g., Bridges & Moore, 2002; Mahoney et al., 2001; McCullough & Willoughby, 2009; Smith, 2003). We organize these explanations into three categories. The first explanation is that religion is a marker for other structural characteristics in the home, such as good parenting. Bridges and Moore and Mahoney et al. noted that religion may directly affect parenting by imbuing child rearing with a moral and spiritual significance leading the parent to see the child as a "holy gift from God" who requires special attention and care or by offering specific child-rearing guidance. The authors also noted indirect effects of religion on parenting; that is, religiosity may enhance the stability and quality of, and satisfaction with, the marital relationship, as well as parental mental health, which in turn can promote positive parenting. Mahoney et al. reviewed 94 studies on the effects of religion on marital and family functioning and found broad support for these direct and indirect effects of parents' religiosity. For example, Gunnoe, Hetherington, and Reiss (1999) found that parents' religiosity (how religion is manifested in their interactions with others) predicted higher levels of observed authoritative parenting (a warm, supportive environment coupled with high age-appropriate demands), which in turn predicted adolescents' and parents' reports of the adolescents' social responsibility (perseverance, self-control, obedience to parents and teachers). Across several studies, the correlations between parental religiosity and child outcomes persist even after controlling for variables thought to influence both parent religiosity and child outcomes (e.g., socioeconomic status, the child's cognitive ability).

Parents also impart their religious beliefs and behaviors to their children; in turn, as reviewed earlier, the child's religiosity is related to lower levels of aggression and delinquency. Kirkpatrick and Shaver (1990) suggested that the child's developing religious beliefs and practices are influenced by those of their parents, and this transmission is affected by the quality of the parent–child relationship. If the child is securely attached to the parent, the child is more likely to adopt the parent's beliefs (see Chapter 2 in this volume). Gunnoe and Moore (2002), using data from the National Longitudinal Survey of Youth, found that for late adolescents and early adults (ages 17–22), frequency of their church attendance and importance of religion were predicted by earlier parental religious influences such as attending church as a child, maternal importance of religion, and attending religious school. These findings held even after controlling for family socioeconomic status and the child's cognitive ability. Across studies, Flor and Knapp (2001) reported correlations in the .50 range between parent and offspring religiosity.

A second theoretical explanation for religion's potentially positive effects on child development is that the religious establishment provides support to help parents with problem children successfully deal with the problems. This explanation stems from social control theory (Hirschi & Stark, 1969) and also is consistent with research and theory on social capital (e.g., Coleman, 1988) and social support (e.g., Dubow & Ullman, 1989). Smith (2003) suggested that the religious community is a form of social capital that can support parental values and can provide cross-generational relationships for the child and "network closure" (dense networks of individuals who know the child and the child's parents, so they can provide information to the parents about any negative child behaviors). Similarly, religious communities of peers and religious leaders also can provide formal as well as informal social support to parents and children; for example, parents might seek guidance from clergy on handling child problems, whereas children might rely on peer networks through their religious institutions for advice or more nondirective forms of support.

A third theoretical explanation of religion's positive effects on child development is that religious exposure builds strong internal self-regulating standards in a child, such as normative beliefs opposing aggression or faith that this is God's plan and "things will get better" (e.g., Smith, 2003). McCullough and Willoughby (2009) reviewed studies published through July 2008 to test key propositions relevant to the relation between religion and self-control. Across studies, there were small but significant correlations between religiosity and personality traits indicative of self-control (e.g., agreeableness, conscientiousness) and self-control mediated the relation between religiosity and substance use in one study (Desmond et al., 2008, cited in McCullough & Willoughby, 2009). In a series of five experiments, Koole (2007) showed that prayer had a salutary effect on affect regulation: praying for a person in need was shown to promote a more positive mood. The promotion of positive affect is hypothesized to be protective against aggression and antisocial behavior. Still, despite the important experimental evidence that has been obtained, examining the development through childhood of internalized standards that promote prosocial behavior and reduce the likelihood of antisocial behavior as the function of exposure to religious practices and institutions requires a longitudinal design.

THE COLUMBIA COUNTY LONGITUDINAL STUDY

In the remainder of this chapter we examine the relation between religiosity and aggression with data from the 40-year Columbia County Longitudinal Study. The CCLS is a prospective study of 856 8-year-olds who were in the third grade in Columbia County, New York, in 1960, when they and their parents were first interviewed. The children were subsequently reinterviewed at ages 19, 30, and 48. We examine the continuity of religiosity from youth to adulthood and across three generations, how this religiosity relates to concurrent and future aggression within and across generations, and how religiosity modifies the expected trajectory of aggression from childhood to adulthood and across generations.

Methods

The Columbia County Longitudinal Study was initiated in 1960 (Eron, Walder, & Lefkowitz, 1971) when the original sample of 856 children, all of the third graders in Columbia County, New York, were first assessed at Wave 1 of what has now became a 40-year, four-wave longitudinal study. Subsets of the sample were reassessed 10 years later in 1970 when the participants were 19; 11 years after that in 1981 when the participants were 30; and 19 years after that in 2000 when the participants were 48 on average. This project has generated a large amount of data concerning how aggression develops from childhood into adulthood (see Eron, Huesmann, & Zelli, 1991; Eron et al., 1971; Huesmann, Dubow, & Boxer, 2009; Huesmann, Eron, Lefkowitz, & Walder, 1984) as well as how childhood and adolescent aggression negatively affect adulthood success (e.g., Dubow, Boxer, & Huesmann, 2008; Dubow, Huesmann, Boxer, Pulkkinen, & Kokko, 2006).

Participants and Procedures   When the study began in 1960, the sample of 856 children was drawn from all of the public and private schools in Columbia County, New York. Over 90% of the original sample was Caucasian; 51% were male, and 49% were female. In this first wave, 85% of the participants' mothers and 71% of their fathers also were interviewed. The participants came from a broad range of socioeconomic backgrounds (mean [M] = 5.01, standard deviation [SD] = 2.23 on a 10-point scale of father's occupational status derived by Eron et al., 1971, based on seven-point scale from Warner, Meeker, & Eells, 1960; this mean reflects jobs such as craftsmen, foremen, and skilled tradesmen) and displayed a wide range of intelligence (mean IQ of 104, SD = 14).

In 1970, 427 participants (211 boys, 216 girls) were reinterviewed for Wave 2. They had a modal age of 19 years and had completed 12.6 years of education on average. In 1981, there was a third wave of interviews, but we will not be using data from that wave in this chapter as religiosity was not assessed.

In 1999–2002, 523 of the participants (268 males, 255 females; 61% of the original sample) were reinterviewed for Wave 4. Their mean age was 48.46 years old (SD = .77); their average education level was between some college and a college degree; their average occupational attainment was middle-class status (the average occupational prestige code using Stevens & Hoisington's [1987] prestige scores reflected jobs such as sales, bookkeepers, secretaries); and 69% of the original participants were living with their spouses. Their average verbal achievement score on the WRAT was 99.15 (SD = 13.72). During this same wave, we interviewed 536 offspring of our original subjects. They were the offspring of 325 different subjects. To keep the sample independent for this study we selected the oldest offspring when more than one was interviewed. This gave us a sample of 349 independent children, youth, and young adults who were children of our original subjects and grandchildren of the parents we interviewed in 1960. This sample was 51% female and 49% male. The ages of the offspring ranged from 8 to 33 with a mean age of 21.75.

Interviews   Data collection procedures for the first three waves of the study have been reported elsewhere (e.g., Eron et al., 1971; Huesmann et al., 1984, 2002; Lefkowitz, Eron, Walder, & Huesmann, 1977). At age 8, two main sources of data were used: classroom-based peer nominations and extensive individual parent interviews. At age 19, participants were administered a variety of self-report measures, as well as peer nominations, in individual interviews at a field office.

At age 48, interviews were conducted by computer in a field office and by mail or telephone for participants who could not come to the office. The offspring of the subjects were interviewed using the same procedures as for the subjects in Wave 4 except that phone and mail interviews were not conducted with any who were younger than 13.

Attrition Information   Of the 39% who were not interviewed at age 48, 37 were confirmed dead, 112 had disappeared and could not be found despite intense efforts, 40 could not be interviewed because of distance and scheduling difficulties, and 144 refused. A comparison of means on age-8 scores revealed that, compared with participants who were reinterviewed at age 48, participants who were not reinterviewed had higher levels of aggression, t (854) = 4.06, p < .001 ($M_{\text{difference}}$ = .13, $SE_{\text{difference}}$ = .03), lower levels of popularity, t (854) = 4.19, p < .001 ($M_{\text{difference}}$ = 4.45, $SE_{\text{difference}}$ = 1.06), lower peer compliance, t (854) = 3.86, p < .001 ($M_{\text{difference}}$ = 3.40, $SE_{\text{difference}}$ = .88), and lower IQ at age 8, t (852) = 5.69, p < .001 ($M_{\text{difference}}$ = 5.70, $SE_{\text{difference}}$ = 1.00). However, analyses of the 1960 data from the 39% who dropped out also revealed that there was no substantial restriction of range on any 1960 variable due to the attrition.

Measures

Specific Aggression Measures for All Waves   *Peer-nominated aggression* was assessed at ages 8 and 19 using a peer-nomination procedure developed by Eron et al. (1971), who defined aggression as "an act whose goal response is injury to another object" (p. 30). Their 10 peer-nominated aggression items cover physical (e.g., "Who pushes and shoves other children?"), verbal (e.g., "Who says mean things?"), acquisitive (e.g., "Who takes other children's things without asking?"), and indirect (e.g., "Who makes up stories and lies to get other children into trouble?") aggressive acts. The score (α = .90) represents the proportion of times the child was nominated by classmates on the 10 items out of the times the child could have been nominated. At age 8 this was the number of children in the classroom. At age 19, because participants already had left high school, the proportion for a participant was computed based on the number of other participants who said they know that participant "well enough to answer some questions about them."

Self-reports on peer-nomination questions were obtained for the children who were interviewed in Wave 4 as their wide geographic distribution make obtaining peer nominations impossible. For the younger offspring the same questions were used as had been used for the subjects when they were 8 years old; for the older offspring we used the questions that had been used with the 19-year-olds.

Severe physical aggression was assessed for the subject at ages 19, 30, and 48 and for the child of the subject in Wave 4 through self-reports of how often in the last year they engaged in each of four behaviors: (1) choked someone; (2) slapped or kicked someone; (3) punched or beaten someone; (4) knifed or shot at someone or threatened to do it (1 = never to 4 = a lot). Scores were log-transformed for analysis due to skewness (α = .66).

Aggressive personality was measured at ages 19, 30, and 48 and among children of the subjects who were 13 or older in Wave 4 by taking the sum of scales 4, 9, and F from the Minnesota Multiphasic Personality Inventory (MMPI; Hathaway & McKinley, 1940). In earlier studies by our group (e.g., Huesmann et al., 1984; Huesmann, Lefkowitz, & Eron, 1978), the summed T-scores of these three scales reflected a reliable and valid measure of antisocial–aggressive behavior ($\alpha = .78$).

For the analyses, we first converted the aggression measures obtained in each wave (peer nomination, self-report of peer-nomination questions, self-report of serious physical aggression, MMPI F + 4 + 9) to standardized z-scores. At each age, where more than one aggression measure exists (i.e., ages 19 and 30), we computed a measurement model for combining the measures. Then a composite measure of aggression was computed as the weighted mean of the one to three aggression scores available for the subject during that wave or for the subject's child during Wave 4. Because these composite scores are standardized within each wave of data, they provide a standard scale on which individuals' locations can be compared across waves independently of total sample shifts in aggressiveness or differences in measures obtained.

Religiosity   In Wave 4, the subjects and their offspring both indicated *their frequency of religious service attendance* on a nine-point scale ("How often do you attend religious services?", rated as 1 = never, 2 = less than once a year, 3 = 1–2 times a year, 4 = several times a year, 5 = about once a month, 6 = 2–3 times a month, 7 = nearly every week, 8 = every week, and 9 = several times a week). Additionally, both the subjects and their offspring reported on their religious preference; their spirituality ("To what extent do you consider yourself a spiritual or religious person?", rated as 1 = not spiritual or religious at all, 2 = slightly spiritual or religious, 3 = moderately spiritual or religious, 4 = very spiritual or religious); and their frequency of praying ("How often do you pray privately in places other than a church, mosque, or synagogue?", rated as 1 = never, 2 = less than once a month, 3 = once a month, 4 = a few times a month, 5 = once a week, 6 = a few times a week, 7 = once a day, 8 = more than once a day).

In Wave 1, the parents of the subjects were also asked their *frequency of religious service attendance* (response scale: 0 = never, 1 = a few times a year, 2 = about once a month, 3 = a few times a month, 4 = once a week, 5 = more than once a week). They were also asked their religion preference, but they were not asked any questions about spirituality or praying.

Similarly in Wave 2, the 19-year-old subjects themselves were asked to report on their *frequency of religious service attendance* using the same procedure and scale as used with the parents in Wave 1.

Other Outcomes and Covariates   In Wave 4, we also assessed the *normative beliefs about aggression* of both the subjects and their offspring (Huesmann & Guerra, 1997). The normative belief scale is a 20-item scale that asks the respondent about his or her approval of aggression, such as, "Suppose a man says something bad to another man, John. Do you think it is OK for John to hit him? (4 =

perfectly OK, 3 = sort of OK, 2 = sort of wrong, 1 = really wrong). The normative beliefs scale score is the mean of all the responses and has been shown to be a highly reliable assessment of approval of aggression by the respondent (Huesmann & Guerra, 1997).

In Wave 1, *parents' educational level* (Eron et al., 1971) reflects the parents' self-reported levels of educational attainment (1 = under 7 years to 7 = graduate or professional training). The family score was computed as the mean of the mother's and father's educational level.

Finally, in Wave 1 we also obtained the subject's *IQ score*. The child's IQ was assessed with the California Short-Form Test of Mental Maturity (Sullivan, Clark, & Tiegs, 1957). Kuder–Richardson reliability coefficients range from .87 to .89 across grades; the total score correlates approximately .75 with other IQ measures.

Results

Religions of Participants   In Figure 19.1, the distribution of self-reported religious affiliations is shown for the participants in the study when they were 8 years old (as reported by their parents) and when they were 48 years old (as self-reported). In Figure 19.2, their church (or synagogue or mosque) attendance is graphed for the same two times. The sample was predominately Christian–Protestant and Christian–Catholic in 1960 with a small sample of Jewish and other (including "no") affiliations. By 2000, the sample was still predominately Protestant or Catholic, but a much larger proportion reported "other" or "no" affiliation. Also, as shown in Figure 19.2, by 2000 when the subjects were 48 years old, on average they attended religious services much less than their parents had attended them 40 years earlier.

Religiosity   The three measures of religiosity that were assessed in Wave 4 among the 48-year-old subjects and among their offspring (average age = 21.75) were highly correlated as shown in Table 19.1. A factor analysis of the three measures showed that one factor could explain 69 to 71% of the variance in the scales

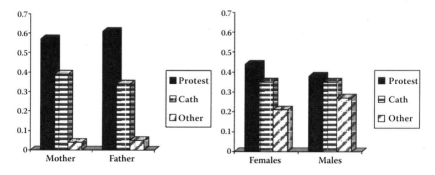

Figure 19.1   The religions of the parents of the subjects when the subjects were age 8 (left panel) and the religions of the subjects themselves 40 years later at age 48 (right panel).

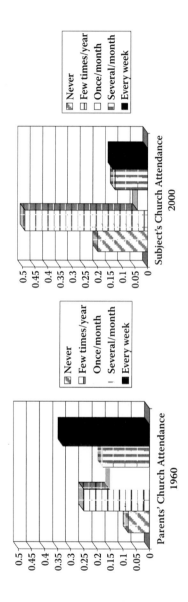

Figure 19.2 The church attendance of the parents of the subjects when the subjects were age 8 and the church attendance of the subjects themselves 40 years later at age 48.

TABLE 19.1   Correlations Between Different Components of Religiosity in 2000 at Age 48 (Below Diagonal) and at Age 12 to 30 (Average Age 21.75; Above the Diagonal)

	Subject's Self-Reported Religious Participation	Subject's Self-Reported Frequency of Prayer	Subject's Self-Reported Spirituality
Subject's self-reported religious participation		.48° (N = 303)	.56° (N = 204)
Subject's self-reported frequency of prayer	.52° (N = 481)		.67° (N = 204)
Subject's self-reported spirituality	.46° (N = 479)	.65° (N = 480)	

° $p < .001$.

in both cases. Furthermore, all three scales had loadings of .77 to .88 in both cases. Consequently, any one of the measures could be used to represent religiosity adequately. As only the measure of religious participation was collected in Waves 1 and 2 as well as in Wave 4 on the subjects and on their children, we decided to use that measure for all analyses.

Continuity of Religious Participation   The correlations over 40 years between the subject's parent's religious participation when the subject was 8 years old, the subject's own religious participation at age 19 and at age 48, and the subject's child's religious participation when the subject was 48 are shown in Table 19.2. Religious participation clearly displays continuity within and across generations. Most notably, perhaps, the subject's child's religious participation correlates .52 ($p < .001$) with the subject's concurrent religious participation at age 48, correlates .28 ($p < .001$) with the subject's religious participation 30 years earlier, and correlates .21 ($p < .001$) with the grandparent's religious participation 40 years earlier. Of course, these later correlations represent only modest effect sizes, and there is substantial variability in the trajectories of religious participation over the life course and across generations. When we partitioned religious participation into upper, middle, and lower tertiles (called High, Medium, and Low Participation), we found that in only about 44% of the cases was the level of participation the same within the subject at ages 19 and 48; in only about 20% of the cases was the level of religious participation the same for the family when the subject was 8, 19, and 48; and in only about 10% of the cases was the level of participation exactly the same for the grandparent, the subject at age 8 and 48, and for the subject's child when the subject was 48. Additionally, in general the participation rates declined over the 40 years from 1960 to 2000, as was shown in Figure 19.2.

The Relation of Religious Participation to Aggression Over Time and Generations   In Table 19.3, the correlations are shown between the religious participation of the subject's parents, the subject, and the subject's child and the concurrent and subsequent aggressive behavior and beliefs of the subject and

TABLE 19.2   Correlations of Religiosity Over Three Generations and 48 Years

	Subject's Parents' Religious Participation When Subject Is Age 8	Subject's Religious Participation at Age 19	Subject's Religious Participation at Age 48	Subject's Child's Religious Participation When Subject Is Age 48
Subject's parents' religious participation when subject is age 8				
Subject's religious participation at age 19	.36°° (N = 374)			
Subject's religious participation at age 48	.17° (N = 401)	.31°° (N = 305)		
Subject's child's religious participation when subject is age 48	.21°° (N = 274)	.28°° (N = 196)	.52°° (N = 294)	

° $p < .01$.
°° $p < .001$.

the subject's child. The correlations at each age between a person's own religious participation and his or her own aggressive behavior are negative and significant. Higher religious participation is related to lower concurrent aggression. The effect sizes are not large but are significant: –.20 at age 19 and –.13 at age 48. Additionally, the grandparents' religious participation assessed in 1960 not only correlates significantly negatively (–.09, $p < .05$) with their child's concurrent aggression at age 8 but also correlates significantly negatively with their grandchild's aggression and aggressive beliefs 40 years later (–.15, $p < .01$; –.13, $p < .05$). This is true even though the grandparent's religious participation does not correlate significantly with the subject's (their own child's) aggression at age 19 or 48, and the subject's religious participation at age 48 does not correlate significantly with the grandchild's concurrent aggressiveness. All in all, this table of negative correlations provides evidence that not only is a person's aggressiveness negatively related to their concurrent religious participation, but it is also related negatively to higher levels of religious participation within the family system.

It is illustrative to examine these relations over time in terms of how predictive very frequent religious participation is of lower aggression compared with very infrequent religious participation. We partitioned religious participation into approximate thirds where high participation means attending services once a week or more, low participation means attending church never or no more than once a year, and medium participation is everything in between. We then analyzed the mean differences for the high and low groups on the aggression measures at each point in time. The results are shown in Figure 19.3. In every single case, those high in religious participation score lower on aggression and aggressive beliefs than those low in religious participation. However, not all of the relations are significant. Mostly

TABLE 19.3   Correlations of Religious Participation With Aggression Over Three Generations

	Subject's Parents' Religious Participation When Subject Is Age 8	Subject's Religious Participation at Age 19	Subject's Religious Participation at Age 48	Subject's Child's Religious Participation When Subject Is Age 48
Subject's aggression at age 8	−.09°° (N = 706)	−.04 (N = 427)	−.04 (N = 481)	−.05 (N = 325)
Subject's aggression at age 19	−.04 (N = 373)	−.20°°°° (N = 426)	−.21°°°° (N = 305)	−.14°° (N = 196)
Subject's aggression at age 48	−.05 (N = 399)	−.09 (N = 303)	−.13°°° (N = 476)	−.16°°° (N = 293)
Subject's beliefs approving of aggression at age 48	−.02 (N = 398)	−.11°° (N = 304)	−.22°°°° (N = 476)	−.12°° (N = 293)
Subject's child's aggression when subject is age 48	−.15°°° (N = 292)	−.17°° (N = 215)	−.07 (N = 316)	−.13°° (N = 325)
Subject's child's beliefs approving of aggression when subject is age 48	−.13°° (N = 275)	−.07 (N = 208)	−.11° (N = 304)	−.19°°°° (N = 307)

° $p < .10$.
°° $p < .05$.
°°° $p < .01$.
°°°° $p < .001$.

the results are consistent with the correlations in Table 19.3 but show that the correlations reflect large differences between fairly high and fairly low levels of participation rather than small differences across the continuum of participation scores.

Predicting Adult Aggression from Youth Aggression and Religious Participation   In a number of prior publications, the continuity of aggression within and across generations in the Columbia County Longitudinal Study has been shown to be substantial (Huesmann et al., 1984, 2009). The analyses so far have shown both that there is continuity of religious participation across time and generations and that religious participation is inversely related to aggressiveness concurrently and over time and generations. Given these results, it makes sense to examine whether religious participation in youth predicts adult aggressiveness when one controls for youth aggression. We created a composite religious participation score for Waves 1 and 2 by taking the mean of the standardized participation scores for each wave (Wave 1 religious participation reported by subject's parent and Wave 2 religious participation reported by subject). We also created a comparable composite aggression score for Waves 1 and 2 in the same way. We conducted a regression analysis predicting the subject's Wave 4 aggression from these two variables and their interaction (product of their standardized scores). The results are shown in Table 19.4.

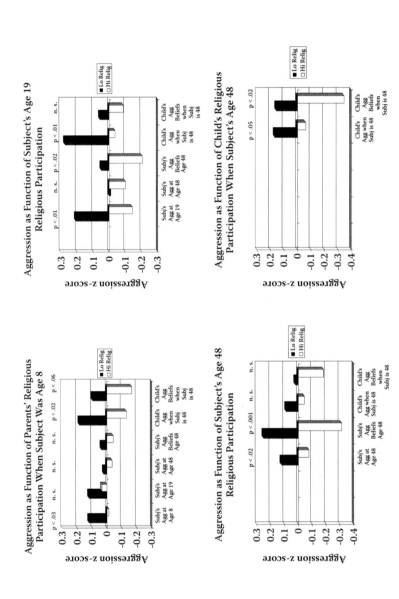

Figure 19.3   Mean aggressive behavior and mean aggressive beliefs for the subject at age 8, 19, and 48 and for the subject's child when the subject is 48 as a function of the frequency of religious participation of the subject, the subject's parents, and the subject's child over the 40 years of the study.

TABLE 19.4   Multiple Regression Predicting Subjects' Aggressive Behavior at Age 48 From Their Aggressive Behavior at Age 8 and 19 and Their Participation in Religious Services at Age 8 and 19 Controlling for Their Gender, Intelligence, and Parents' Educational Level

	Step 1 Standardized Regression Coefficients	Step 2 Standardized Regression Coefficients	Step 3 Standardized Regression Coefficients
Subject's aggression as youth (mean of ages 8 & 19)	.35°°	.38°°	.38°°
Subject's religious participation as youth (mean of ages 8 & 19)	−.04	−.04	−.02
Interaction of subject's youth aggression and youth participation in religious activities		.15°	.15°
Subject's gender			−.01
Subject's IQ at age 8			.04
Subject's parent's level of education			−.17°°
R^2	.123°°	.143°°	.169°°

° $p < .01$.
°° $p < .001$.

As expected, youth aggressiveness is revealed to be a highly significant predictor of adult aggressiveness 30 to 40 years later ($\beta = .38$, $p < .001$). The regression also reveals that a youth's level of religious participation 30 to 40 years earlier does not add at all significantly to this prediction even though their religious participation at age 8 and 19 correlated negatively with their concurrent aggression at that time. However, while that early religious participation does not have a direct effect on adult aggression, it does significantly moderate the trajectory of aggression from youth to adulthood as indicated by the highly significant interaction effect of youth participation and youth aggression on adult aggression ($\beta = .15$, $p < .002$). To understand the meaning of this interaction, we plotted it in Figure 19.4 in two ways—first as a three-dimensional plot showing the surface defined by the complete regression equation and second as a limit plot showing how high and low youth aggression and high and low religious participation in youth (as defined by plus and minus one SD) combine to predict adult aggression.

The results are striking. If one accepts that the direction of effects must be from religious participation to aggression, the results indicate that high religious participation exacerbates the effects of youth aggression on adult aggression. For those lower on youth aggression, high religious participation is predictive of even lower adult aggression and lower participation of higher aggression. For those higher on youth aggression, the effect is reversed. High religious participation is predictive of even higher adult aggression and lower participation of lower aggression.

One may wonder if these effects are independent of other participant characteristics. The third column of Table 19.4 shows that they are. The participant's

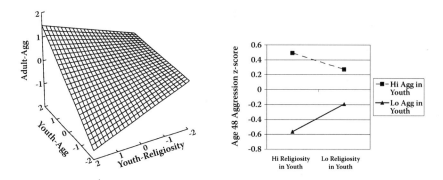

Figure 19.4   The moderating effect of youth religious participation on the relation between youth aggression (mean of ages 8 and 19) and adult aggression at age 48.

gender and IQ at age 8 do not change the results at all, and, while the parent's education level is a significant predictor of the subject's aggression 40 years later, its inclusion in the model does not change the moderating effect of religious participation in youth.

A similar regression analysis was conducted to predict the subject's child's aggression when the subject was 48 (mean age of child = 21.75). While the subject's lifelong aggression was a highly significant predictor of the subject's child's aggression when the subject was 48 (β = .25, p < .001), the analysis revealed no similar interactive effect of the subject's lifelong religious participation on cross-generational transmission of aggression and no main effect of the subject's religious participation on the offspring's aggression.

Finally, we constructed a longitudinal structural model to represent both the effects of religious participation on aggression and the continuity of aggression and religious participation within and across generations. The final model that best fit the data is shown in Figure 19.5.

Again, we make the assumption in this model that the relation between religious participation and aggression (to the extent any relation exists) is in the causal direction of participation affecting aggression. The model fits quite well (full information maximum likelihood [FIML] solution, N = 856, chi-square = 27.8, df = 23, p > .22, comparative fit index [CFI] = .99, root mean square error of approximation [RMSEA] = .016). The model shows the expected strong continuity of both aggression and religiosity over the life course and across generations with stronger continuity within generations for aggression and across generations for religiosity. The model also shows significant concurrent direct negative effects of the subject's religiosity at age 19 to his or her aggression at age 19 and from the parent's religiosity in 1960 to the child's concurrent aggression at age 8. The effects from subjects' age-48 religiosity to their age-48 aggression were only marginally significant as were the effects of children's religiosity on their own aggression in 2000. However, taken together, the four concurrent paths certainly indicate that religiosity has a dampening main effect on concurrent aggression. Furthermore, the interactive effect of subjects' religiosity and aggression in their youth on their adult aggression

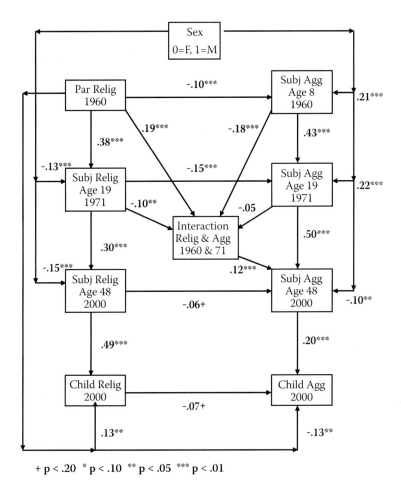

+ p < .20   * p < .10   ** p < .05   *** p < .01

Figure 19.5 Structural model showing direct and indirect effects of religious participation throughout the life course on subsequent aggression in the self and in one's offspring (full information maximum likelihood [FIML] solution, N = 856, chi-square = 27.8, df = 23, p > .22, comparative fit index [CFI] = .99, root mean square error of approximation [RMSEA] = .016).

that we had discovered with the regression analysis remained significant and substantial in this model (β = .12, p < .008). Being high on religiosity in youth seems to exacerbate the tendency of low aggressive youth toward low aggression in the future and high aggressive youth toward high aggression in the future. The model explains 24% of the variation in the subject's age-48 aggression, 12% of the variation in the subject's age-48 religiosity, 7% of the variation in the subject's child's aggression, and 27% of the variation in the child's religiosity. The standardized total effect sizes of prior family religiosity combined with concurrent self-religiosity on aggression were .078 for age-48 subject aggression and .146 for the subject's children in Wave 4. Though these are not large effect sizes, they are significant and large enough to be important.

Discussion

Our analysis of these four waves of data spanning three generations and 40 years showed first that religious participation, prayer, and spirituality are highly intercorrelated and can be represented substantially by a single construct. Because of this result and because participation in religious services is the only measure we had in all four waves, we based all our analyses on this measure. Obviously, this is a potential weakness, and our results must be considered in the context that spiritual individuals who never participate in religious services are misclassified in these analyses. Of course, the most likely effect of this omission would be to weaken our effect sizes for religiosity.

We found clear evidence both that participation in religious activities has a main effect on reducing concurrent aggression at any age and in youth has an additional effect of exacerbating the tendencies of low aggressive youth to grow up to be low aggressive adults and of high aggressive youth to grow up to be high aggressive adults. These effects were not due to relations between religiosity and gender, IQ, or the educational level of the family. These effects remained in the context of a longitudinal model that accounted for the substantial continuity of religiosity and aggression both over the life span and across generations.

Although this study demonstrates these effects fairly conclusively, it does not explain why they occur. As we discussed in the introduction, religiosity, and particularly participation in religious activities, has a number of benefits that could explain the main effects of religiosity in reducing aggression in addition to affecting normative beliefs about aggression. The three main theoretical ideas we reviewed were as follows:

1. Parents' religiosity is a marker of more proximal factors that influence child outcomes (e.g., good parenting, the child's developing religiosity).
2. Religious organizations provide social support when problems occur.
3. Religious exposure builds strong internal self-regulating standards in a child, such as normative beliefs opposing aggression.

Relevant to the third explanation, we did show that an adult's and youth's normative beliefs about the appropriateness of aggression were significantly related to their religiosity in the direction that more religiosity predicted lower approval of aggression. However, the direct relation between religiosity and concurrent normative beliefs was modest (−.19 to −.22 in Table 19.3). Consequently, while we could not directly test mediation models because scores on normative beliefs were available only in Wave 4 of the study, it is unlikely that the effect sizes of religiosity on normative beliefs are large enough to completely explain the total effects of religiosity on aggression. Similarly, the fact that the relations between religiosity and aggression were not diminished much when we controlled for gender, child IQ, and parental level of education suggests that no association between religiosity and any of these other variables related to aggression can account for the effect by itself as the first explanation might suggest.

Undoubtedly, our most notable result was the finding that high religiosity exacerbates the tendency of high-aggressive youth to grow up to be high-aggressive adults and low-aggressive youth to grow up to be low-aggressive youth. This result was not expected and is contrary to our original hypothesis that the social support provided through participating in religious activities might ameliorate the tendency of youth to respond to stressors and social problems with aggression.

We propose that this interactive exacerbating effect most likely reflects a "self-justification" process. Most religious texts can be read in different ways and can equally well provide justification for behaving aggressively or prosocially (see also Chapter 18 in this volume for the possible divisive effects of supernatural beliefs). Christians can focus on "turning the other cheek" when provoked or on obtaining "an eye for an eye." If one has already been behaving aggressively in one's youth, participating in religious activities and focusing on texts supporting aggression may make it easier to self-justify one's aggressiveness by providing consensual validation for the behavior. On the other hand, if one is already behaving less aggressively, one can find consensual validation for those behaviors in religion as well. Thus, while religious participation can promote peaceful behavior among already peaceful youth, it can also increase the risk for violence (and fundamentalist terrorism; see Chapter 10 in this volume) among those youth leaning toward aggression.

Certain cognitive characteristics associated with high religious participation may also contribute to the exacerbating effect of religiosity on early behavioral trends. Research on "cognitive closure" (Kruglanski et al., 1996) suggests that high need for closure individuals "freeze" more strongly on early ideas and norms. If, as seems plausible, families who participate regularly in religious activities have a higher need for cognitive closure, then it would not be surprising that their children tend to continue down the behavioral paths of aggressiveness or nonaggressiveness that are established early in life.

Final determination of the processes through which religious participation influences aggression must await more developmental studies assessing the hypothesized factors involved in the processes. Nevertheless, it seems fair to conclude from this study that the view that religiosity has a straightforward protective effect in reducing the development of aggression is too simplistic. It is true that participating in religious activities has a general protective main effect on concurrent aggression and promotes religious participation later in life and in subsequent generations and that these effects are relatively independent of IQ, educational level, and gender. However, these main effects are limited by the significant tendency of participation in religious activities to turn the developmental trajectory of aggression upward for youth high in aggression and downward for youth low in aggression. Intense religious participation may promote nonaggressive peaceful behavior among youth already tending in that direction, but it also seems to exacerbate the tendencies of aggressive youth to develop into more aggressive young adults. Whether this exacerbating effect is more due to the self-affirming support for behavior that religion can provide or due to the tendency of those needing cognitive closure to participate in religion remains to be investigated.

REFERENCES

Bartkowski, J. P., Xu, X., & Levin, M. L. (2008). Religion and child development: Evidence from the Early Childhood Longitudinal Study. *Social Science Research, 37*, 18–36.

Bridges, L., & Moore, K. A. (2002). *Religion and spirituality in childhood and adolescence.* Washington, DC: Child Trends.

Coleman, J. S. (1988). Social capital in the creation of human capital. *American Journal of Sociology, 94*, S95–S120.

Dubow, E. F., Boxer, P., & Huesmann, L. R. (2008). Childhood and adolescent predictors of early and middle adulthood alcohol use and problem drinking: The Columbia County Longitudinal Study. *Addiction, 103*, 36–47.

Dubow, E. F., Huesmann, L. R., Boxer, P., Pulkkinen, L., & Kokko, K. (2006). Middle childhood and adolescent contextual and personal predictors of adult educational and occupational outcomes: A mediational model in two countries. *Developmental Psychology, 42*(5), 937–949.

Dubow, E. F., & Ullman, D. G. (1989). Assessing social support in elementary school children: The survey of children's social support. *Journal of Clinical Child Psychology, 18*, 52–64.

Ellis, L., & Pettersson, J. (1996). Crime and religion: An international comparison among thirteen industrial nations. *Personality and Individual Differences, 20*, 761–768.

Eron, L. D., Huesmann, L. R., & Zelli, A. (1991). The role of parental variables in the learning of aggression. In D. Pepler & K. Rubin (Eds.), *The development and treatment of childhood aggression* (pp. 169–188). Hillsdale, NJ: Lawrence Erlbaum Associates.

Eron, L. D., Walder, L. O., & Lefkowitz, M. M. (1971). *Learning of aggression in children.* Boston: Little, Brown.

Flor, D. L., & Knapp, N. F. (2001). Transmission and transaction: Predicting adolescents' internalization of parental religious values. *Journal of Family Psychology, 15*, 627–645.

Fowler, P. J., Ahmed, S. R., Tompsett, C. J., Jozefowicz-Simbeni, D. M. H., & Toro, P. A. (2008). Community violence and externalizing problems: Moderating effects of race and religiosity in emerging adulthood. *Journal of Community Psychology, 36*, 835–850.

Gallup Consulting Organization. (2008). Available from http://www.gallup.com/poll/1690/religion.aspx.

Gunnoe, M., Hetherington, M., & Reiss, D. (1999). Parental religiosity, parenting style, and adolescent social responsibility. *Journal of Early Adolescence, 19*, 199–225.

Gunnoe, M. L., & Moore, K. A. (2002). Predictors of religiosity among youth aged 17–22: A longitudinal study of the National Survey of Children. *Journal for the Scientific Study of Religion, 41*, 613–622.

Hathaway, S. R., & McKinley, J. C. (1940). *The MMPI manual.* New York: Psychological Corporation.

Herrenkohl, T. I., Hill, K. G., Chung, I. J., Guo, J., Abbott, R.D., & Hawkins, J.D. (2003). Protective factors against serious violent behavior in adolescence: A prospective study of aggressive children. *Social Work Research, 27*, 179–191.

Hirschi, T., & Stark, R. (1969). Hellfire and delinquency. *Social Problems, 17*, 202–213.

Huesmann, L. R., Dubow, E. F., & Boxer, P. (2009). Continuity of aggression from childhood to early adulthood as a predictor of life outcomes: Implications for the adolescent-limited and life-course-persistent models. *Aggressive Behavior, 35*, 136–149.

Huesmann, L. R., Eron, L. D., & Dubow, E. F. (2002). Childhood predictors of adult criminality: Are all risk factors reflected in childhood aggressiveness? *Criminal Behavior and Mental Health, 12,*185–208.

Huesmann, L. R., Eron, L. D., Lefkowitz, M. M., & Walder, L. O. (1984). Stability of aggression over time and generations. *Developmental Psychology, 20,* 1120–1134.

Huesmann, L. R., & Guerra, N. G. (1997). Children's normative beliefs about aggression and aggressive behavior. *Journal of Personality and Social Psychology, 72*(2), 408–419.

Huesmann, L. R., Lefkowitz, M. M., & Eron, L. D. (1978). The sum of MMPI scales F, 4, and 9 as a measure of aggression. *Journal of Consulting and Clinical Psychology, 46*(5), 1071–1078.

Johnson, B. R., De Li, S., Larson, D. B., & McCullough, M. (2000). A systematic review of the religiosity and delinquency literature: A research note. *Journal of Contemporary Criminal Justice, 16,* 32–52.

Kim, J. (2008). The protective effects of religiosity on maladjustment among maltreated and non-maltreated children. *Child Abuse & Neglect, 32,* 711–720.

Kim, J., McCullough, M. E., & Cicchetti, D. (2009). Parents' and children's religiosity and child behavioral adjustment among maltreated and non-maltreated children. *Journal of Child and Family Studies, 18,* 594–605.

Kirkpatrick, L. A., & Shaver, P. R. (1990). Attachment theory and religion: Childhood attachments, religious beliefs, and conversion. *Journal for the Scientific Study of Religion, 29,* 315–334.

Koole, S. L. (2007). *Raising spirits: An experimental analysis of the affect regulation functions of prayer.* Unpublished manuscript, Vrije Universiteit, Amsterdam.

Kruglanski, A. W., & Webster, D. M. (1996). Motivated closing of the mind: "Seizing" and "freezing." *Psychological Review, 103,* 263–283.

Lefkowitz, M. M., Eron, L. D., Walder, L. O., & Huesmann, L. R. (1977). *Growing up to be violent: A longitudinal study of the development of aggression.* New York: Pergamon.

Mahoney, A., Pargament, K., Swank, A., & Tarakeshwar, N. (2001). Religion in the home in the 1980s and 1990s: A meta-analytic review and conceptual analysis of links between religion, marriage, and parenting. *Journal of Family Psychology, 15,* 559–596.

McCullough, M. E., & Willoughby, B. L. B. (2009). Religion, self-regulation, and self-control: Associations, explanations, and implications. *Psychological Bulletin, 135,* 69–93.

Pargament, K. I. (1997). *The psychology of religion and coping: Theory, research, practice.* New York: Guilford.

Pargament, K. I. (2007). *Spiritually integrated psychotherapy: Understanding and addressing the sacred.* New York: Guilford.

Pearce, M. J., Jones, S. M., Schwab-Stone, M. E., & Ruchkin, V. (2003). The protective effects of religiousness and parent involvement on the development of conduct problems among youth exposed to violence. *Child Development, 74,* 1682–1696.

Pettersson, T. (1991). Religion and criminality: Structural relationships between church involvement and crime rates in contemporary Sweden. *Journal for the Scientific Study of Religion, 30,* 279–291.

Regnerus, M. D., & Elder, G.H. (2003). Staying on track in school: Religious influences in high- and low-risk settings. *Journal for the Scientific Study of Religion, 42,* 633–649.

Smith, C. (2003). Theorizing religious effects among American adolescents. *Journal for the Scientific Study of Religion, 42,* 17–30.

Stevens, G., & Hoisington, E. (1987). Occupational prestige and the 1980 U. S. labor force. *Social Science Research, 6,* 74–105.

Sullivan, E. T., Clark, W. W., & Tiegs, E. W. (1957). *California short-form test of mental maturity.* Los Angeles: California Test Bureau.

Wallace Jr., J. M., Forman, T. A., Caldwell, C. H., & Willis, D. S. (2003). Religion and U.S. secondary school students: Current patterns, recent trends, and sociodemographic correlates. *Youth & Society, 35*, 98–125.

Warner, W. L., Meeker, M., & Eells, K. (1960). *Social class in America*. New York: Harcourt.

Werner, E. E., & Smith, R. S. (1982). *Vulnerable but invincible: A longitudinal and youth study of resilient children*. New York: McGraw-Hill.

World Values Survey. (1996). Available from http://www.worldvaluessurvey.org/

Index